H

BERLITZ

·B·L·U·E·P·R·I·N·T·

GREECE

Editor
BARBARA ENDER

Photography
LUC CHESSEX

Layout and Site Maps
MAX THOMMEN

Cartography
HALLWAG AG, BERN

*Although we make every effort to ensure the accu-
racy of all the information in this book, changes
occur incessantly. We cannot therefore take responsibility for facts, addresses and circumstances
in general that are constantly subject to alteration.*

**2nd Printing
1990/1991 Edition**

Cover photo (Lindos, entrance gate to Temple of
Athena), pp. 10, 33, 161, 191, 204, 260 and 263
DOMINIQUE MICHELLOD; pp. 30, 89, 92,
139, 141 and 185 DANIEL VITTET; pp. 78 and
79 (right) ANDRÉ HELD; pp. 79 (left) and 216
PRISMA INTERFOTO; p. 52 JACK ALT-
MAN; p. 59 MAX THOMMEN; p. 209
FRANCE VAUTHEY.

Acknowledgements
We would like to thank Anna Iliokratidou and
Alexandra Vergopoulos, and their colleagues of
the Greek National Tourist Office, for their coop-
eration. We are also very grateful to Miki Benaki,
Aleko Mamiatis, Nicholas Campbell, Dimitra
Fotopoulou, Eileen Harr-Kyburz and Alice
Taucher for their help in preparing this book.

*Further information on the major cities and islands
of Greece can be found in the pocket-size Berlitz
Travel Guide series.*

BERLITZ®

·B·L·U·E·P·R·I·N·T·

GREECE

By JACK ALTMAN
and the Staff of Berlitz Guides

BLACK
SEA

BULGARIA

YUGOSLAVIA

TURKEY

ADRIATIC SEA

ALBANIA

Thessaloniki   Kavala

Kastoria   Chalkidiki   Thasos   Samothrace

Mt. Olympus △   Mt. Athos

Meteora   Limnos

Corfu   Ioannina   Volos   AEGEAN SEA

Paxi   Arta   Sporades

Lefkas   Skyros   Lesbos

Ithaca   Delphi   Thebes   Euboea   Chios

Cephalonia   Patras   ATHENS   N

Zakynthos   Corinth   Andros   Samos
          Mycenae   Tinos

          Nafplio   Cyclades   Mykonos   Icaria

Mistra Sparta   Saronic   Paros   Naxos   Kos

          Islands   Dodecanese

IONIAN SEA   Monemvasia   Santorini

          Kythira   Rhodes

MEDITERRANEAN   SEA   Karpathos

0   50   100 km   Iraklion
                                   Crete
0   50   100 miles

TURKEY

Contents

*Map coordinates next to the subheadings refer to
the Road Atlas section.*

An Invitation to Coffee with Socrates or a Siesta with Aphrodite

Apollo's sun bears down on the market place and, over a coffee or ouzo in the shade, the village sages continue to debate the state of the republic. A shepherd snoozes in a silent olive grove, far from the great city where Athenian drivers wage boisterous battle amid the pestilential fumes of Hades. Out in the islands, fair Aphrodite rises from the waves after a long charter flight from Stockholm. Poseidon ducks the ferryboat and cruise traffic, but Zeus can smile down on it all, now that he has got used to the Greek army skiing on the slopes of his Mount Olympus.

The philosophic tools with which the ancient Greeks founded a splendid but fragile edifice called Western civilization also come in handy for a successful stay in their country 2,500 years later: stoicism at the airport; hedonism at the beach; a Platonic sense of beauty in the temples and museums; cynicism when buying a genuine antique; democracy in line for a restaurant table; Socratic wisdom in a political quarrel. After centuries of tumultuous conquest and civil war, Greece is still a privileged domain of rugged joys and tranquil contemplation.

A Land of Mountains

Like many another historically vital nation, Greece stands at a crossroads, with the Slavonic Balkans beyond its northern mountains, Italy across the Ionian

It's a long haul up the hill from Mykonos market, but old ladies have been doing it for centuries.

Sea, Turkey and Asia on the Aegean's eastern shores, Egypt and Libya to the south.

The northern mountain barrier guards the valleys of Thrace and the plains of Macedonia. To the west, the long Pindus range thrusts through Epirus, while the Ionian Islands act as a breakwater for its coast. Olympus dominates the great eastern plain of Thessaly, protected by another mountain barrier leading down to the Gulf of Corinth. Facing the Aegean, the Attica peninsula has Athens at its heart. Corinth is the eastern gateway to the Peloponnese, almost completely mountainous except for narrow lowlands on the west coast and the Messinian Plain and Laconian Valley in the south. The Cyclades, which include Mykonos, Paros and Naxos, are the mountain tops of a submerged continental plateau. Kythira and Crete extend the ranges of the Peloponnese just as Rhodes continues the Taurus mountains of Turkey.

In fact, mountains cover three-quarters of the whole country. None of them is very big—Mount Olympus, the tallest, is only 2,917 m.—but they very frequently present an illusion of great height with sudden deep valleys and plunging, craggy ravines. Visitors gain a keen sense of this on the awesome, sinuous drive up Mount Parnassus from the Gulf of Corinth to the sanctuary of Delphi. (They may also make their first encounter with the national obsession with politics when they see partisan slogans daubed in blue and white on every available rock face.)

On the mainland, the mountains are largely barren, though Olympus is clad in pines and chestnuts in an otherwise arid terrain. The bare limestone peaks of Parnassus are snow-covered from winter to early June. But the mountains of some of the southern islands, especially Crete and Rhodes, are much greener, in some places almost subtropical in their luxuriant vegetation.

The mountains hold a special place in the popular imagination. As the natural redoubt for the heroic klephts, half bandit, half political rebel who fought Turkish domination in the 1821 War of Independence, the mountains came to symbolize the spirit of resistance and freedom. It was from the mountains again that the partisans came in World War II to sabotage the German invader. "May he live as long as the high mountains" is the ritual blessing of well-wishers for a newborn baby. For an invalid, they pray for "the strength of a mountain". And everybody is still pagan enough to sense the aura of Olympus, abode of the gods; Parnassus, home of the Muses; or Zeus's childhood homes on Crete's Ida and Dikti.

Cheese, Olives and Wine

The sheep grazing the greener mountain slopes provide milk for tangy feta cheese and rich yoghurt. Goats are gradually disappearing, abandoned by government decree to protect the forests whose young shoots they ravage (though deliberate fires of building speculators do far more damage).

Greek farmers have always had a tough row to hoe. Cultivation is limited by the arid, stony soil to olive trees and vineyards—apart from some good tobacco plantations in the north. The olive is the perfect tree for the Greek climate: tough, resistant to excessive heat, fierce winds, hail and frost, capable of surviving years of drought. In the Peloponnese, trees are said to date back to the 17th century, while Attica claims some trees planted in Roman times. Olives of all sorts, green, black, brown, silvery bluemauve, smooth, wrinkled, play a central role in the Greek diet, while olive oil is still the essential fuel for lamps in the churches.

Rather than orderly rows of vines such as those in Burgundy or Chianti, the Greeks often seem to prefer joyously dishevelled vineyards interspersed with wild flowers, fig trees, wild pear or almond trees, which do not always grow there from neglect but are actively encouraged by the peasant, who welcomes their fruit for his refreshment and their shade for his siesta.

The Cities

Athens plays an overpowering role in Greek life, and it has become an almost obligatory exercise to heap curses on it. Phenomenal focus for migration from the islands and the mainland's rural exodus, the national capital has too many people (4,000,000 or two out of every five Greeks live there), too many cars, too much pollution, too much noise. The government might dearly like to call on Hercules' know-how from cleaning out the Augean stables in its efforts to decentralize industry, commerce and government itself. Perversely, the city's sprawling cement, steel and glass makes all the more fascinating the presence in its midst of that perfect emblem of classical Greece, the Acropolis. And a more coherent policy of preservation and restoration has made the museums a suitable complement in which to contemplate the ancient treasures. The Plaka, after years as a tawdry tourist-trap, has been taste-fully renovated with good restaurants and tree-shaded cafés.

In the north, Thessaloniki (the old Turkish name of Salonica is gradually disappearing) presents itself as a brash second city, proud of its gastronomy, its port and museum of Macedonian art.

But in general, Greece is not too pleased with its modern urban develop-ment. After centuries of wars and earth-quakes (most recently in 1953 and 1986), the historic city centres have suffered the

even more devastating indignity of the building speculators' wrecking-ball. The wine in Patras on the Peloponnese and the great Minoan museum in Crete's capital Iraklion are practically the only reasons not to leave these towns in a hurry—and head for the islands.

The Islands
Geographers argue about just how many islands there are, but agree at something over 3,000, of which only 169 are inhabit-ed. The largest are Euboea (just north-

FACTS AND FIGURES

Geography:	Situated at the southern edge of the Balkan peninsula, Greece covers an area of 131,957 sq. km. (50,949 sq. mi.) Its immediate neighbours are Albania, Yugoslavia and Bulgaria to the north and Turkey across the Aegean Sea to the east. The jagged coastline of deeply incised peninsulas faces the Ionian Sea to the west. The islands, of which the largest are Euboea and Crete, number over 3,000 if all the tiniest islets are included, but only 169 are inhabited. With the Pindus range interrupted on its north–south sweep only by the mouth of the Gulf of Corinth, the country's overwhelmingly mountainous terrain leaves a mere 30% suit-able for agriculture. The principal rivers are the Aliakmon winding through Macedonia to the Gulf of Thermaikos, the Acheloos curving south through Epirus to the Ionian Sea, Thessaly's Pinios draining into the Aegean, and the Alfios in the Peloponnese. Highest mountain: Olympus 2,917 m. (9,570 ft.).
Population:	10,089,000, of which only the Turks (0.9%) and Albanians (0.6%) form any measurable minorities.
Capital:	Athens, pop. 1,000,000 in narrow municipal boundaries, 4,000,000 in metropolitan area.
Major cities:	Thessaloniki (440,000), Piraeus (210,000), Patras (160,000), Iraklion (115,000), Volos (110,000), Larissa (108,000).
Government:	Under the 1975 Constitution voted after the overthrow of the Colonels' dictatorship, the country is a parliamentary democratic republic. The president has a largely symbolic role as head of state elected for a 5-year term, with real power in the hands of the prime minister and his cabinet. Parliament has only one 300-seat chamber where the principal political parties are the Panhellenic Socialist Movement (PASOK), the conserva-tive New Democracy party and the Communist party (KKE). In the process of decentralization, the country is divided into 13 administrative regions.
Religion:	Greek Orthodox 97.6%, Roman Catholic 0.4%, Protestant 0.1%, Mus-lim 1.4%, other 0.4%.

east of Athens) and Crete. The others are mostly grouped as distinct archipelagos: the Ionian islands off the west coast; the Sporades north of Euboea; the Cyclades spilling down into the central and southern Aegean; and the 12 Dodecanese dominated by Rhodes along the Turkish coast. The islands have always held a special place in the hearts of this seafaring nation, from the days when Odysseus set out from Ithaca to the modern era of shipping magnates, bred most frequently on islands like Chios and Andros.

The Ionian islands have something of an Italian air to them, most notable in the Venetian buildings of Corfu and Zakynthos. It is the Aegean that furnishes Greece's popular travel-poster image: dazzling white houses and churches squatting round the harbour, like those of Mykonos or Sifnos in the Cyclades, or up on the cliffs of Santorini further south.

But Greek holidaymakers—Greeks take holidays, too—are often puzzled by the northern European taste for these

islands' arid landscape. They prefer to head for the greener islands of Andros or Paros, also in the Cyclades, or further north to Thasos. In the Dodecanese, the old charms of Kos are less easy to enjoy in the package-tours' high season. Attractive Skiathos in the Sporades is threatened with the same fate of mass tourism. If this phenomenon is also creating problems for many of the resorts on the great historic islands of Rhodes and Crete, it is still possible to move away from the throngs to more secluded spots.

The tourist industry, essential underpinning of the national economy, has driven many of the islands' peasants and fishermen into souvenir shops and the restaurant business (or to a new life in the mainland cities). But the natives have remained firmly entrenched in characterful islands like Tinos in the Cyclades, Poros just off the Peloponnese or Chios close to the Turkish coast.

How Greek are the Greeks?

After 400 years of domination by the Ottoman Empire, the Turkish influence is still visible. It would be silly to deny it, though it is a point too sensitive to raise in public. Most mosques and other public buildings clearly Turkish in origin, like bathhouses, have been destroyed and place names Hellenized, but the uniform of the presidential palace guard, if modelled on the heroic rebels of 1821, looks uncommonly "Turkish". In the cuisine, especially the yoghurt dishes and honeyed desserts, it is not clear how much is truly of Turkish origin or how much was merely appropriated by the conquerors from the Greeks themselves. Greek ouzo and Turkish *rakı* are close cousins, and if it is not a good idea to order "Turkish" coffee, your *ellinikó* will be the same thing.

So what is a modern Greek? Just as ancient Greece spread its culture throughout the Mediterranean, so the neighbouring nations returned the compliment by invasion or peaceful com-

Castellorizo is Greece's easternmost island, close to the Turkish coast. In the days of the Trojan Wars, Agamemnon's Mycenaeans occupied what is really just one huge rock. At the top, where the ancients had their acropolis, the Knights of Rhodes perched a castle.

11

merce. Too many Persians, Phoenicians, Egyptians, Serbs, Turks, Albanians and Italians have passed this way and lingered for modern Greeks to bear any resemblance to the ancestors of antiquity. And despite the wealth of sculpture, we have no definite idea of what ancient Greeks looked like either. The male and female figures of ancient sculpture reflected an artistic ideal rather than a biological reality.

The swarthy people of today, flashing-eyed, strong-nosed, seem to have the country's dramatic landscape etched in their faces. In temperament, distinctions can be noted between mainlanders, more volatile and excitable, and islanders, calmer but often more sombre, too.

A third group is formed by the returning émigrés, regarded with a mixture of envy and admiration for their Mercedes from Stuttgart or Chevrolet from Detroit. This is an age-old Greek phenomenon since Spartans, Corinthians and Aegean islanders founded colonies all around the Mediterranean, sitting there, in the words of historian Herodotus, "like frogs around a pond", and returning occasionally to the homeland to show off their new wealth and knowledge. Their return now, in ever-growing numbers since the overthrow of the Colonels in 1974, has brought a welcome fund of intellectual and industrial experience—and hard currency. But many return just to retire to the ancestral home town, building large but not always handsome new houses which change the face of traditional communities.

Whatever differences in temperament may appear, the men—mainlanders, islanders and returning émigrés alike—give free rein to their passions in the all-important café conversations. It is here that you can see how natural it was for this fiercely independent-minded people, always sceptical of authority, to lay the foundations of democracy—even if it has been a struggle ever since to keep it going. The taste for democracy is tempered and not necessarily contradicted

by a preference for strong, almost patriarchal leadership. In those endless debates around the café tables, one man always seems to exert a natural, though sometimes spurious, authority. He leans back in his chair, speaks in a louder voice, leads—and stops—the laughter and ignores any remarks that are not affirmations of what he has just said. He can often be recognized by his distinctive hat, walking stick, and the thick wad of notes with which he ostentatiously pays the bill.

The village's Orthodox priest also plays a prominent role at the café table, smoking, drinking coffee, dispensing advice, listening to local gossip, arbitrating or at least halting heated arguments. Granted a privileged political position under Turkish rule, he remains a revered figure in the community. As he gets on the bus, people rush to pay his fare or help him with his bags, even when he is young enough to handle them himself, often younger than his helpful parishioner.

On rare occasions when they are present, the older women observe their men with a certain amused detachment. Younger girls are not so very different from their European counterparts, though perhaps a little more demure.

With seemingly the whole of the western world sooner or later flocking to what they feel to be their cultural roots, the answer to the question of what is a Greek may be that we all are. When the Greeks entered the European Common Market, a French diplomat greeted them with the comment: "Today we celebrate the fact not that Greece has joined Europe but that Europe has rejoined Greece."

Important affairs are decided not in some musty municipal office but at a comfortable café. Corfu's most respected citizens lay down the law in the Liston arcade.

The Turbulent Journey from One Democracy to Another

The Greeks have rarely had it easy. The drama of their history is played out in alternating scenes of brilliant light and often terrifying darkness. The ancient stand for humanism, reason and democracy has found its modern counterpart in the people's courageous battles for freedom against foreign oppression and homegrown dictatorship. In between is a painful story of the long struggle to keep alive the Greek spiritual and cultural identity.

Scarce natural resources left Stone Age Greece sparsely populated until about 4500 B.C., when migrants from the Balkans and Asia Minor spread south from Macedonia. To Crete, settlers from Anatolia (modern Turkey) brought bronze artefacts and the plough, adding a richer diet of olives, figs and vines to the meagre cereal crops they found when they arrived.

Around 1950 B.C., a new wave of Eastern European invaders assembled on the mainland what may be described as the first Greeks as such, in the sense of a people with a certain cultural unity. Regarded by classical Greece as ancestors of the Ionians, the conquerors from the north readily took to the amiable Mediterranean way of life. They brought with them the horse, but produced no art or luxury comparable to that of their contemporaries in Crete, spared invasion for the time being.

*A*ncient vase found on the island of Euboea.

Crete and Mycenae

With its rich soil and cattle pastures, the great island enclosing the south of the Aegean enjoyed peace and prosperity. Cretans carried on a brisk trade with the Middle East and Egypt, as well as the other Greek islands, with an emphasis on luxury goods: ivory, delicate pottery and finely wrought gold jewellery.

Fearing no enemies, they built their first palaces at Knossos, Phaistos and Malia around 2000 B.C. without fortifications. It is not clear whether war or earthquake caused the palaces' first destruction 300 years later, but they were rebuilt bigger and more splendid. Design was still strictly for pleasure: decorative entrances, roof terraces to face the beautiful surrounding countryside, ornately frescoed bedrooms, sophisticated plumbing for the bathrooms and barbecue braziers in the kitchens.

Crete's Minoan civilization, named after the mythical king Minos of Knossos, was generally on a very human scale. In small sanctuaries or intimate palace chapels, Cretans worshipped female deities, their double axe symbolizing the royal power of life and death. Males were subordinate consorts, with the bull as their emblem. The artwork is characterized by a lively sense of colour, movement and humour.

In 1500 B.C., a new Balkan invasion of Greece drove the Ionians southwards and this time crossed to Crete. The brilliant Minoan civilization went into decline, and a century later the palace of Knossos was destroyed by earthquake. It was probably simultaneous with the erupting volcano that devastated nearby Thera (modern Santorini), the only Aegean island to develop a civilization comparable to that of Crete.

Through commercial contacts, Cretan civilization infiltrated the Peloponnese, dominated from 1400 to 1200 B.C. by the kingdom of Mycenae. But Minoan culture was transformed in the hands of the peninsula's tougher breed of men. Taller, bearded, not clean-shaven like the Cretans, these settlers originally from north of the Balkans had a taste for hunting and raids for cattle and women. Such "masculine" themes dominate the otherwise Minoan-style art, and the

A Fair Amount of Bull
Many a Greek myth has behind it a hard political fact. Historians believe the legend of Athens' obligation to sacrifice seven young men and seven maidens to the Minotaur refers back to a time when Crete reigned supreme in the Aegean, and the city had to pay heavy tribute.

The Minotaur was the offspring of a torrid affair that Minos's wife Pasiphaë had with a bull. Understandably upset, Minos hid the bull-headed monster in a labyrinth. At nine-year intervals, to keep the creature happy—after all, the Minotaur was really family—the powerful monarch fed him those 14 young men and girls from Athens. Athenian hero Theseus put a stop to it. He seduced the king's daughter Ariadne, who gave him a ball of thread to trace his way back out of the labyrinth after killing her monstrous half-brother. On his way back to Athens, without so much as a "Thank you, Ma'am," Theseus left Ariadne, pregnant, stranded on Naxos. Heroes are not always gentlemen.

Miracle of the Baked Tablets
One day in June 1952, Michael Ventris announced on BBC radio that the Mycenaeans spoke Greek. Nobody (except Agamemnon and company) knew this until the young Cambridge linguist deciphered Linear B, his name for inscriptions found at Pylos in the south-western Peloponnese. A palace fire preserved them for posterity by baking the clay tablets on which accountants had drawn up meticulous invoices. Linear B was derived from stylized forms of hieroglyphics in a more primitive Linear A found on Crete. Not yet an alphabet of consonants and vowels, the inscriptions comprised a series of syllabic signs from which Ventris was able to decipher words like *ti-ri-po-de*, the plural for "tripod". The rest, like this, was all Greek to Ventris.

spirit is epitomized in the massive stone lions over the gates to Mycenae palace. The ceramics were not as sophisticated as Crete's, but their work in gold achieved a new level of refinement, as can be seen in the jewellery and death masks now displayed in Athens' National Museum.

Typically, Mycenaeans readily adopted Crete's fertility goddesses, but gave priority to the male deity Zeus they brought from the north—god of the heavens (his name means "bright sky"), of rain, thunder and lightning. Henceforth Greek religion was steadfastly male-dominated.

The most famous of the Greeks' raiding expeditions around the eastern Mediterranean ended in the conquest of Troy (on the Turkish coast) around 1230 B.C. Scholars argue about whether Homer's Agamemnon is a mythical or historical king, but they agree that the raid was real and probably under Mycenae's leadership.

The Archaic Era

Around 1200 B.C., fierce Dorians from the Danube valley swept through the western mainland to the Peloponnese, destroying the Mycenaean civilization, killing or enslaving its peoples. The invasion bypassed Attica, where Ionians had founded Athens a century earlier. Many fled to the Aegean islands and the coast of Asia Minor. The Dorians themselves occupied Rhodes and the southern Aegean.

At the beginning of what is generally called the Archaic Era preceding the great exploits of classical Greece, the country entered a cultural Dark Age. The Dorians installed a tough, warrior-oriented society with little artistic achievement. It promoted the virtues of strength, valour and loyalty, male camaraderie, homosexuality, initiation of young warriors by veterans, and nude athletics, all major features of the great kingdom of Sparta founded two centuries later. In religion, Apollo joined Zeus to complete the male takeover of the Greek pantheon. Just as Zeus displaced his wife Hera as the major deity at Olympia, so did Apollo at Delphi.

It was the combination of the Dorians' somewhat rigid austerity with the Ionians' amiable serenity that created the unique strength and grace of Greek civilization.

By the 9th century B.C., the country began to awake. The post-invasion exodus across the Aegean opened up new commerce with Asia Minor and North Africa, assisted by the introduction of an alphabet borrowed from the Phoenicians. In exchange for imported cereals and raw materials—precious metals, tin, copper, amber and ivory, wood and animal skins—Greek manufacturing talent provided, in addition to wine and olive oil, valued luxury exports of gold, jewellery, perfumes and textiles, tools, weapons and ships. Athens' refined geometric-patterned vases began to challenge Corinth's commercial supremacy in ceramics. The first temples were built in the northern Peloponnese. Crete and Attica produced the first significant bronze sculpture and Homer was composing his epic *Iliad* and *Odyssey*.

The mountainous country divided the people up into independent communities, each constituting a city-state *(polis)*. This was ruled by a powerful aristocracy that had replaced the monarchy everywhere except in tradition-minded Sparta and Thera. The system defied real political unity until Macedonian conquest imposed it. But a certain sense of Greek national identity was fostered by the Olympic Games. From 776 B.C., the religious and sporting festival brought the cities and islands together to the great sanctuary in the western Peloponnese.

As the population grew, it was proving increasingly difficult to eke out a living from the infertile Greek soil on which the aristocracy was appropriating the lion's share. Many looked elsewhere. Overseas colonization was a phenomenon of Greece's mistiest antiquity,

Homer and Homer

It is still not clear whether Homer was one man or two. Supporters of the two-Homers theory, for complex textual reasons, suggest the *Iliad* was composed by a poet from Anatolia, perhaps the Izmir of modern Turkey, and the *Odyssey* by an islander, probably from Chios. Those who argue for just one Homer stress the poems' masterly dramatic unity formed from the patchwork of crazy adventures. Each epic works to one end: the satisfaction of Achilles' anger at being cheated of his rights before the battle for Troy; and Odysseus' long journey to wreak revenge on the suitors tormenting his wife Penelope.

All we can surmise of Homer the man, judging from his abundant rustic similes and his sympathy for the common peasant, is that he was probably himself of humble peasant origin. Was he blind, as sculptures often depict him? Greek bards frequently were. It has been suggested that blindness was an asset in memorizing without distraction the long poems they recited at royal courts.

At any rate, Homer singular or plural was a great crowd-pleaser. Like the tale of Theseus and the Minotaur, the *Iliad* and *Odyssey* may be viewed as pieces of political propaganda. They celebrate the heroism of Greece before the Dorian invasion as if to tell the conquerors they were not the only courageous men around.

when knowledge of the western Mediterranean was revealed in the Odyssey legend, and of the Black Sea in Jason's quest for the Golden Fleece.

Traces of Greek settlement at Taranto in southern Italy date back to the 14th century B.C., but the major effort began around 775, from the Peloponnese and the cities of Megara in Attica and Chalcis and Eretria in Euboea. Agricultural settlements in southern Italy and Sicily were followed by trading posts further west at Marseille and on the south coast of Spain. In the northern Aegean they occupied the Chalcidic peninsula before moving up to the Black Sea. Though retaining religious and cultural attachments to the homeland or *metropolis* (literally "mother city"), the settlements remained resolutely autonomous, not colonies in the modern sense of political dependencies.

Rise of Sparta and Athens

Sparta was founded on the Eurotas river in the southern Peloponnese in the late 10th century B.C., when four or five villages banded together as one formidable city-state.

A rigid social system with a strict hierarchy of three classes set it apart from other Greek cities. At the top, an élite of Equals *(homoioi)*, descendants of the Dorian conquerors, were forbidden to work as farmers, merchants or artisans so as to devote all their energy to military training for the army's officer class. They sat on the councils overseeing their two kings, who jointly commanded the army.

Income derived from the best land of the Eurotas valley, worked by the helots, state serfs who were probably the indigenous population of the conquered region. For the education and enlightenment of the Equals' children, the helots were deliberately oppressed and humiliated; they were forced, for instance, to get drunk to instil in Sparta's future leaders the ideal of sobriety.

The middle rank was held by *perioikoi* ("peripheral dwellers") who farmed less fertile parts of the Eurotas valley, breeding sheep and pigs, and carried on the city's commerce and handicrafts. They formed more or less autonomous communities but had no say in political life.

Sparta at first tried to dominate the Peloponnese by conquest. But revolts by Argos and Messenia in the 7th century B.C. forced Sparta to accept more modest alliances recognizing its leadership of a Peloponnesian League. It remained forever reluctant to launch remote expeditions that left the homeland unprotected.

Suddenly, around 550, Sparta mysteriously closed in on itself, banned all travel beyond its borders and refused entry to all foreigners, apparently fearing the "softening" influence of contacts with the outside world.

Sheltered behind its mountains, Athens avoided the rigidly oppressive regimes that the Dorians imposed elsewhere. Reinforced by Ionian refugees from the Peloponnese, the city developed a supple social system that contrasted sharply with that of Sparta. It

*U*nder the enlightened tyrant Peisistratus, Athenian sculptors developed a refined synthesis of the monumental Dorian style and the more supple Ionian. This elegant kore by Antenor (525 B.C.), now in the Acropolis Museum, anticipates the grace and strength that were to characterize the classical spirit.

was governed by an aristocracy of magistrates overseen by a council of elders and elected by a popular assembly.

In the late 7th century B.C., Dracon gave Athens its first codified laws. The

A Spartan Existence

Life in Sparta was fun for the survivors. Any newborn sons of the Equals' élite considered too sick or puny were hurled into a ravine of nearby Mount Taygetos.

The rest were taken away from the family home at the age of 7 to undergo a gruelling 13-year course of military training under the leadership of older boys. Summer and winter, they wore the same thin tunic, slept on a rough bed of reeds and lived on a grim diet of black wheat porridge. Plus whatever they could steal from neighbouring farms. If they were caught, they were punished—not for stealing, but for getting caught. Physical endurance was the ultimate virtue. Rather than reveal his agony, one boy ran silently through town with his booty, a live fox hidden under his tunic, chewing away at his stomach.

Boys were educated chiefly in the use of arms, physical exercise, learning to live off the land like savages. Minimal time was spared for reading, writing, arithmetic and some music—as food for the soul and future accompaniment into battle. Battle training itself was ruthless, with one clan beating another almost to death in a pitched fight for a sacred island in the Eurotas river. Practice at actual killing was acquired by manhunts staged to slaughter an occasional helot.

Once accepted as officer material—the social disgrace of rejection caused many a suicide—the men, married or not, continued until 30 to sleep in all-male dormitories. Anyone wanting to see his wife had to sneak off in the middle of the night. Even once they were living at home, they still had to have one meal a day—that dreadful porridge—in the officers' mess.

And the women in all this? Girls were bred to become sturdy child-bearers—lots of gymnastics and wrestling, in dresses the more prudish Athenians considered so scandalously short that they scornfully referred to Spartan girls as *phenomeridae*, "thigh-barers". Left to their own devices, grown women enjoyed considerable sexual freedom and proved very able managers of the family fortune. With most of the family out of the house playing at war, luckily the women were there to behave like adults.

law-maker insisted on crimes being punished in court rather than by clan vendetta with its endless cycle of bloodshed. "Draconian" became a synonym for severity when Dracon, asked why he always advocated the death penalty, whatever the crime, blithely replied: "In my opinion, small crimes deserve the death penalty and I know of no severer punishment for the big crimes."

Solon, a champion of social justice, abolished Dracon's more cruel ordinances. The magistrate proposed reforms to protect debt-ridden peasants against arbitrary land-confiscation by the aristocracy. For artisans and merchants, he regulated weights and measures and admitted their guilds to the legislature. But Solon was no democrat. "To the people," he said, "I've given sufficient power without reducing or adding to their rights. For those who had the strength and riches to enforce their power, I have made an effort not to subject them to any indignity."

Paradoxically, it was the advent of a tyrant that set Athens on the road to democracy. In many city-states throughout Greece in the 7th and 6th centuries B.C., tyrants (without the negative sense the word later acquired) won the support of oppressed peasants and artisans to seize power from the aristocrats.

In Athens' case, Peisistratus, a general who had distinguished himself in battle against Megara, came to power in 561 B.C. on a "platform" of Solon's proposed reforms. Personally wealthy from mine-holdings in Thrace, he redistributed land to impoverished peasants, made state loans to repay their debts, and promoted the growth of olives and vines to replace the bad wheat crops. He made a point of touring the country to hear grievances and appease the rich landowners. In Athens itself, Peisistratus organized hugely popular festivals to honour Athena, the city's patron goddess, and Dionysus, god of wine and ecstasy. His ambitious building programme of temples on the Acropolis revealed, particularly in the sculpture, the city's artistic mastery. By 530 B.C., Athenian potters were turning out the black- and red-figure ceramics that finally overcame Corinth's domination of foreign markets.

By organizing the purification of Apollo's sanctuary on Delos—no births or burials allowed on the island—Peisistratus imposed the authority of Athens over the Cyclades. This first step towards empire was reinforced by the end of the 6th century B.C. with victories over neighbouring Boeotia and Chalcis and the establishment in the northern Aegean of Athens' first colonies. An alliance was formed with Sparta's Peloponnesian League.

The 17-year rule of Peisistratus' sons actively fostered the arts, producing the first written edition of Homer. Sparta supported a brief return to power of the aristocrats until another enlightened tyrant, Cleisthenes, emerged in 508 B.C. Himself an aristocrat, he consolidated Athens' growing commitment to democracy by making governing councils and assembly more representative and abolishing privileges of aristocratic birth. He instituted ostracism—banishment without loss of property—as a dignified and bloodless way of dealing with leading citizens who offended the state.

Persian Wars (499–478 B.C.)
The Greeks' first real awareness of their common Hellenic destiny was spurred by the aggressive presence of the Persians in the Aegean. Ionian settlements on the Anatolian coast and neighbouring islands like Samos became Persian satrapies after Lydia's king Croesus was defeated in 546. Heavy taxes imposed by the Persians' military garrisons moved the Ionians to revolt in 499. Fleets from Athens and Eretria provided only token support for their countrymen, but the burning of Sardis, the Persians' Anatolian capital, incited King Darius to launch an all-out invasion.

He crushed the Ionian revolt, but the

Unlucky Runners
In the first of two famous runs occasioned by the battle of Marathon, Athenian courier Pheidippides covered 240 kilometres in two days to request Spartan support. He found the Spartans in the middle of a religious festival and unwilling to march until after the inauspicious full moon. After the battle, another fellow, evidently in less good condition, ran 42 kilometres back to Athens to announce the victory, dropped dead from exhaustion and inspired the most admired of Olympic disciplines.

advance through Thrace and Macedonia was halted by stormy seas wrecking the Persian fleet off Mount Athos peninsula in 492. Two years later another fleet crossed the Aegean, spared the sanctuary of Delos but destroyed Naxos and Eretria. The army landed on the Attica coast a short march from Athens. Miltiades forestalled attack on the vulnerable unwalled city by leading an Athenian army of 10,000 out to the plain of Marathon. Facing a force six times its size, the Athenian army outmanoeuvred the Persians and drove them back to their ships. The Persians lost 6,400 men, compared with the Athenians' 192, whose burial mound is still visible at Marathon today. Before the battle, the revered oracle at the sanctuary of Delphi, always conservative in its inclinations, and playing the safe bet on the apparently stronger side, had predicted Persian victory. Athens' hard-won triumph impressed on its allies the importance of greater Greek solidarity against the Persian foe. (Sparta's contingent of 2,000 men had arrived a day late.)

Darius' son Xerxes raised a new invasion army of 100,000 and this time cut a canal through the neck of the Athos peninsula to avoid the stormy cape. Athens formed a Panhellenic league with Sparta in military command over 31 city-states. In 480, with the Persian fleet sailing down to Euboea, the army pushed south through Thessaly to the pass of Thermopylae, mountain gateway to central Greece and Athens. Sparta was again unwilling to commit significant forces outside the Peloponnese, concentrating instead on blockading Corinth's isthmus approach to the peninsula. The Spartan elders let King Leonidas take only 300 of his royal guard to lead an allied army of at most 7,000. With no hope of victory, the Spartan commander chose to hold Thermopylae ("hot gates") long enough for stronger Greek forces to resist the Persians further south. Leonidas and his élite went to their death displaying all the Spartan virtues of courage, discipline and loyalty. The Persians broke through the pass but their parallel sea engagement against the Athenian fleet at Artemisium proved costly.

With Thebes, capital of Boeotia, deserting the Greek cause to side with the Persians, Athens was left defenceless. The city was evacuated before Xerxes arrived to put it to the flame as a last reprisal for the sack of Sardis 10 years earlier. But Athenian general Themistocles succeeded in enticing Xerxes into a sea battle in the narrows of Salamis Bay. The hemmed-in Persian fleet suffered crippling losses and Xerxes withdrew to Asia.

Classical Age

The Great Fifty Years of Athenian glory extended from the end of the Persian Wars in 478 B.C. to the death of Pericles in 429.

Sparta withdrew from the national scene to consolidate its power in the Peloponnese. Athens' naval supremacy and its courageous wartime defence of the Greek cause made it the undisputed leader of a new alliance of Aegean city-states, the Delian League, keeping its treasury on the island sanctuary of Delos. The league had clearly become the basis of the Athenian empire when, in 454 B.C., Athens blithely transferred the funds to its Acropolis.

Besides ensuring a profitable market for its wine, olives and luxury goods,

Athens exported its democratic system to city-states whose government had often been a tyranny, not always enlightened.

Athens' democracy appealed to an aspect of the citizens' character that remains a constant to this day: visceral hostility to anyone growing too big for his boots. Example: Themistocles, military hero of the Persian Wars, became a popular leader both for his timely strengthening of the navy as backbone of Athenian imperial might, and for constructing fortifications to defend the city itself. But overweening pride and personal greed provoked his ostracism in a vote of 6,000 representative citizens in 472 B.C. Like many disgraced Greek heroes, Themistocles went over to the enemy, ending up in the service of the Persian monarch. His successor at the head of the popular party was Ephialtes, a scrupulous democrat of humble origin who fiercely opposed the return to power of the aristocrats. His crusade to prosecute their corruption ended in his assassination in 456.

He in turn was replaced by an equally fervent assistant named Pericles (495–429 B.C.), who brought members of the lower classes onto the council of magistrates. His idea of paying public officials a salary made it possible for people other than the rich to exercise authority. Salaries for military service in the navy and army made it less of a burden for the lower classes.

Not all Athenian residents had rights of citizenship. Though better treated than elsewhere in Greece, slaves remained, in Aristotle's words, "an animated object of property". Among freemen, aliens were more than welcome in commerce and shipping, as well as the arts and medicine, even dominating the realm of philosophy. But though they served in the Athenian army and navy, aliens could not own land and had no say in the state's political affairs. However, the citizens' political rights entailed, at least for the more wealthy, financial

Pericles, the Great Humanist
The man who dominated Athenian affairs for 27 momentous years came from a family which favoured military toughness and social justice. His father was Xanthippus, a brilliant but ruthless general, and his mother Agariste, niece of the noble democratic reformer, Cleisthenes. With eloquent, powerful-voiced oratory, Pericles championed the weak against the strong, but was himself no natural democrat. He developed social welfare for the poor and promoted the public works programme as much for the full employment it provided as for its embellishment of the city. Yet he disdained the crowd, remaining haughty and unsmiling, and was known to have wept only twice in his life. But his high-minded nature was refined and not insensitive. Of young soldiers lost in battle, he said that they left the city like a "year that has lost its spring".

Friend and pupil of philosopher Anaxagoras, who emphasized the power of the reasoning mind, Pericles was an unashamed intellectual. He made Athens a magnet for artists and thinkers from all over the Mediterranean, with a cosmopolitan atmosphere comparable to 20th-century Paris or New York. He avoided politicians and military men, preferring the company of his cultured mistress Aspasia, a close friend of Socrates. The salon she created for him included master sculptor Phidias, urban-planner Hippodamus, historian Herodotus and tragedian Sophocles. Typically, Pericles' assistance to the poor included free theatre tickets. Protagoras, another philosopher friend, spoke for his own humanism when he proclaimed that "man is the measure of all things".

But Pericles was also an energetic military and political leader, asserting Athenian supremacy in the Aegean and outwitting enemies at home. Unable to impugn his own honesty, they brought trials against his friends on trumped-up charges—his mistress for procuring prostitutes, Anaxagoras for impiety and Phidias for stealing gold allotted to his public statues. The cool Pericles proved ardent in defence of his beloved Aspasia and fiercely loyal to his friends.

burdens in sponsoring musical and dramatic festivals and paying for warships and their crews.

With the Delian League's funds transferred to the Acropolis since 454 B.C., a large portion went into rebuilding the city Xerxes had burned down. The monumental new construction, not only of Athens' Acropolis itself but also the sanctuaries of Eleusis and Sounion, saw the great explosion of sculptural and architectural talent that gave visual expression to the glory of classical Greece.

Peloponnesian War (431–404 B.C.)
Athenian hegemony in the Aegean attracted growing hostility from its rivals. Megara was denied access to the Delian League's markets. Corinth resented Athens' commercial domination and more especially its alliance with the Corinthian colony of Corcyra (Corfu). Thebes was embittered by the Athenians' continuing hostility ever since it had sided with the Persians. Sparta feared a challenge to its own supremacy in the Peloponnese.

War broke out in 431. Sparta launched what it regarded as a pre-emptive strike into Attica, burning the olive groves and tearing up the vineyards. The peasants fled in mass exodus to Athens. Plague from Egypt ravaged the overcrowded capital and killed Pericles in 429. The Athenians had to crush an uprising in Lesbos and slave revolt in the Laurion silver mines of southern Attica. With Sparta continuing its land attacks, it was the navy that again turned the tide for Athens with victories on the west Peloponnese coast, capturing Sphacteria and Pylos. A precarious peace was negotiated in 421.

Six years later, the Athenians' downward spiral resumed with disastrous intervention in the wars of the Sicilian colonies. The expedition cost them 12,000 men captured or killed, crippling the effort to save the empire. At home, the aristocratic party threatened internal stability. The Aegean islands were in revolt. Sparta allied with Persia, sacrificing the Greek colonies of Asia Minor for financial aid to build a fleet. The Athenians continued to resist for nine more years under Alcibiades' brilliant leadership. But Lysander at last gave Sparta naval superiority in the Aegean with

*T*he mass of Greek pilgrims travelled to Delphi as a
pious act of national solidarity, gathering here at the Sanctuary of
Athena before heading for the oracle. For politicians seeking advice
for military campaigns or colonial expeditions, the trip was strictly
business. To keep funds rolling in and protect the sanctuary from
destruction by disgruntled consultants, the priests who handed down
the good word played it very safe. They carefully avoided saying
anything that might upset the touchy Spartans, but occasionally bet
on the wrong horse, warning the Athens-led alliance that it could not
defeat the mighty Persians.

new, looser confederation under Athens' leadership. In 371, Thebes' general Epaminondas smashed Sparta's army, slaying a third of the kingdom's able-bodied males. He occupied the Peloponnese and challenged the revitalized Athenian presence in the Aegean. Lacking sound political underpinning, Thebes' military supremacy collapsed in 362. Greece was left leaderless to face a new power rising in the north: Macedonia.

Philip and Alexander

Macedonia's royal house of Dorian horsemen—the king's name Philippus meant horse-lover—ruled over a rough peasant mixture of Greeks, Illyrians (from what is now Albania and Yugoslavia) and Thracians.

Philip II (359–336 B.C.) had acquired his military training in Thebes as a hostage of Epaminondas, and proved a ruthless warrior. This lusty lover of wine and women was totally unscrupulous in politics. He pursued a divide-and-conquer diplomacy of pitting Athens against its Chalcidic colonies, keeping unrest aboil in Thrace and Thessaly, and exploiting rivalries among Thessaly, Athens and Sparta in the Sacred Wars over the guardianship of Delphi.

Athens' great orator Demosthenes sought to arouse the Greeks to unite against the Macedonian threat. His impassioned appeals to defend liberty and democracy against Philip's monarchy were backed up by very practical reorganization of finances and the navy. His eloquence browbeat Megara, Euboea, Corinth, Achaia, even arch-enemy Thebes into joining Athens in a confederation. In 338, in one last burst of Panhellenic solidarity, they fought bravely at the decisive battle of Chaeronea in northern Boeotia, but lacked generals to match Philip's superb tactics and the ferocious cavalry charges led by his son Alexander.

In victory, Philip was both magnanimous and tough. Athens retained its autonomy and its fleet. Sparta had most of

victories from the Dardanelles to the port of Piraeus, forcing Athens to capitulate in 404.

Vindictive Thebes wanted the city razed and reduced to cattle pasture. Sparta was content for Athens to destroy its fortifications and surrender its fleet and empire.

In the 50-year power struggle after the war, Sparta's brutal military garrisons collecting taxes made the city-states nostalgic for Athens' democratic style of imperialism. The islands even formed a its lands in the Peloponnese laid waste and was excluded from the new confederation led by Macedonia. If most city-states kept their traditional forms of government, Thebes was handed over to an oligarchy under surveillance of a Macedonian military garrison. Three other garrisons were strategically placed around the country. Philip was planning to cement Greek unity with a national expedition against Darius of Persia when he was assassinated at his daughter's wedding by a royal bodyguard.

The grand adventure of his heir Alexander took him beyond Greece's frontiers only two years after his accession to the throne in 336. But Alexander's mission remained always profoundly Greek. From the age of 13, he was tutored by Aristotle, and he took the philosopher's annotated copy of Homer on the journey to Troy and beyond. In his lightning subdual of Greek resistance before setting off for Persia, he destroyed the rebellious city of Thebes—except for its temples and the house of Pindar the poet.

Alexander combined the cool analytical talents of his father and the passionate intuitive powers of his mother, Olympias, claiming descendancy from Hercules through the one and Achilles through the other. Like his father, he was a heavy drinker and, like all Macedonians but contrary to Greek custom, he drank his wine unwatered. His death in Babylon in 323 of malarial fever came after a long and riotous bout of drinking.

For a century after Alexander's death, Greece was a pawn in the wars of his successors. Philip V (221–179 B.C.) made a truly coherent effort to reunite Greece under his Macedonian rule. His initial success provoked Rome's first appearance on the Greek scene in 214, with a fleet north of Corfu to back Greek opposition to Macedonian expansion.

Roman Rule

Flaminius, one of a long line of Roman leaders who smothered Greece with admiration of its civilization, defeated Phi-

Saint Paul in Greece

With its many communities of Jewish merchants, Roman Greece was a prime target for the missionary work of Paul of Tarsus. He crossed from Asia Minor into Thrace in A.D. 49. In Philippi, first European city to be evangelized, local businessmen had him and his followers thrown into jail as Jewish troublemakers. As the New Testament tells it, they sang God's praises in the night and an earthquake awoke the jailer. Paul baptized him and his family and went off to Thessaloniki. There he was well received by the Greeks, but the Jews created an uproar against "these that have turned the world upside down". Slim pickings in Athens. He was upset by a "city wholly given to idolatry", but impressed by the obsessive philosophical curiosity of people who "spent their time in nothing else but either to tell or to hear some new thing." Paul argued with Jews in the synagogue before discussing his "new thing" with Epicureans and Stoics at the Areopagus. The philosophers mocked his talk of resurrection, so, with only a couple of converts, he left for Corinth. He stayed there 18 months, writing, preaching and establishing a church. He got angry again with his obstreperous fellow Jews and gave them up as a bad cause, vowing: "Henceforth, I will go unto the Gentiles."

lip's Macedonian forces in 197 B.C. During the Isthmian Games near Corinth the next year, he proclaimed "freedom" for the Greeks. Fifty years later, Greece had become a Roman province and Corinth was ignominiously sacked. On the dockside, Roman soldiers used the town's treasured paintings as dice-boards—but no more nonchalantly than Greek soldiers carving their names on the revered statues of Egypt.

In general, the Romans assured a certain quiet, if not too proud prosperity. Taxes were efficiently organized and politics remained safely in the hands of foreign rulers. Besides the usual trade in luxury goods, the Greeks exported to Rome their philosophy, theology, political science, coinage, port construction, domestic, civic and religious architecture, sculpture, literature and the Greek language itself—along with well-paid employment for its experts. There was a neat exchange of Roman pragmatism and Greek taste for beauty and truth. In Latin, it was noted, the names of vegetables were of Latin origin and the names of flowers Greek.

Athens was the most prestigious university town in the Roman Empire. Rhodes was esteemed for its studies in literature and philosophy, and Julius Caesar went there to improve his rhetoric. Wealthy Romans organized sightseeing package tours of the great Greek monuments. Among the major attractions were the Olympic Games, by now completely professional, and in Sparta the gruesome spectacle of boys enduring flogging contests in the municipal theatre.

Nero loved Greece. In A.D. 66, he toured the games and won all the music prizes. He was even declared the winner of a chariot race after falling out of his chariot. He repeated the declaration of Greek freedom and dug out the first clod of earth for the Corinth canal, but his plan to follow Alexander's footsteps into Asia was halted by a Jewish insurrection in Judea.

But Hadrian was the sincerest of philhellene emperors, nicknamed *Graeculus*, "little Greek". On his visits to Athens from 125 to 128, he completed the huge Temple of Olympian Zeus begun 250 years earlier and built a whole new quarter, Hadrianopolis, for which the main gate still stands (see p. 76).

In 267, Ostrogoth invaders swept down from the Black Sea, burning and sacking Athens, Corinth, Sparta, Argos and Crete. Thereafter Greece remained a stagnant backwater of the declining Roman Empire until Constantine decided in 324 to move to the east his government of the Balkans, Asia Minor and Greece.

The Byzantine Empire
The Eastern Empire's new capital, founded on the site of Byzantium (later Constantinople), was dedicated in 330 with both pagan and Christian ceremonies. In later years, many of the faithful regarded Constantine (306–337) as the first Christian emperor, converted by divine vision on the eve of a battle to control the empire. For Constantine himself, Christianity was a political instrument with which to unite his empire's diverse peoples. He in fact converted only on his death bed (25 years after the battle) and had a pagan funeral. Greece itself, especially Athens, remained pagan except for pockets of Christian communities where St Paul had passed through on his missions.

Conversion really got underway with Emperor Theodosius (379–395), a pious Christian who encouraged zealots to destroy Greek temples or appropriate them as churches. He banned all forms of pagan cult and stopped the Olympic Games. In 529, Justinian drove a last nail in the Hellenic coffin by closing the Academy of Platonic philosophy in Athens.

Meanwhile, after the horrors of plague and invasion, the Greeks left their homeland in droves. They settled around the Mediterranean and above all in Constantinople (regarded by Greeks right into the 20th century as their natural capital). Goths, Visigoths and Slavs poured through the mainland down to Crete, while Arabs raided the Aegean islands.

The many doctrinal conflicts besetting the Orthodox Church did not greatly affect Greece until 726 when, condemning their worship as idolatrous, Emperor Leo the Iconoclast ordered destruction of all icons. Leo's opponents, known as iconodules, saw these holy paintings as emphasizing the true humanity of Jesus and Mary, refuting the view of them as purely divine. Empress Theodora, devout iconodule, negotiated an end to the bitter dispute in 843, after the death of her iconoclast husband Theophilus. The controversy stimulated Byzantine artists to aim more at spiritual revelation than naturalistic representation of the holy figures.

Basil the Bulgar-Slayer

That terrible title was earned only after more than 30 years of fighting the Bulgarian army, then the mightiest in Eastern Europe. Bulgarian invasions devastated the Peloponnese, Attica and Boeotia until Basil scored a decisive victory in 996 on the Sperkheios river east of Lamia, near the Gulf of Euboea. Carrying the war back into Bulgaria, he inflicted final defeat in 1014. Of the 15,000 prisoners, he blinded all except one in every 100, who was left with one eye so that he could lead the others home. Yet the same man had fostered in Greece the greatest achievements of Byzantine art: illuminated manuscripts and silk embroideries, the mosaics of the monastery church at Daphni (near Athens), Sancta Sophia at Thessaloniki, the monasteries of Mount Athos and Meteora.

The Byzantine Empire reached the peak of its political, economic and cultural power under Basil II (976–1025). But the 11th century was also the beginning of the Empire's long decline. The Orthodox Church was weakened by its schism with Rome in 1054 (over papal authority). Turks of the Ottoman dynasty began their ascendancy with conquests of Byzantine territory in Asia Minor. The Crusades to save Christianity in the east proved more threat than salvation when the Normans tore through Corfu in 1081 on their way to Thessaly. Constantinople called on Venice to come to its aid, but in 1125 Venice helped itself to ports in the Ionian Islands and the Peloponnese. In 1204, the Crusaders sacked Constantinople itself, and the Greeks came under a Latin Empire carved up by the French and Italians into a kingdom of Thessaloniki, duchy of Athens and principality of Achaea. A Byzantine dynasty held on to Epirus.

In the 14th century, Mistra in the Peloponnese had become a grand capital for the last flowering of Byzantine culture. Constantine XI was crowned there in 1448 in time to meet renewed threats from Turkey. Forces of the Ottoman Empire had occupied the north and were now advancing on the Peloponnese. The emperor called on Rome to help, but his military commander, recalling the Crusaders' barbarity in 1204, said he would "rather see the Muslim turban in the centre of town than the Latin mitre".

After a two-month siege, the Turkish turbans took over Constantinople on Tuesday, March 31, 1453, making Tuesday in Greek eyes forever a day of ill omen.

Under Turkish Domination

The Greeks' 400 years of submission to the Ottoman Empire were a bitter experience, but they also toughened the people's fibre in the constant struggle to maintain a national identity.

The sultan's highly centralized system divided Greece into a dozen provinces under military command, but with no civil administration. With a patriarch appointed by the sultan in Constantinople, the Orthodox Church maintained the only direct Greek contact with the Turkish authorities. Although the Church kept alive Greek language and culture through the liturgy and education, its collaboration with the Turks made it suspect when nationalist movements fought for independence.

The Turks' religious tolerance was not disinterested. Heavy taxes on non-Muslims were a source of revenue too attractive to encourage any policy of forcible conversion. Jews settled in major Greek cities—Thessaloniki housed 20,000 expelled from Spain in 1492, joining the Bavarian Jews already there. Orthodox Greeks and Jews were encouraged to engage in commerce, considered undignified for Muslims.

Not that there was no discrimination—some of it minor, like not being allowed to build houses higher than those of Muslims, or to repair their churches and ring the bells without official permission. More ambiguous was the 15th-century "tribute of children", by which one in every five sons in a Christian family was taken to serve as a

Janissary (Turkish *yenicheri* meaning "new force") in the Ottoman infantry. In fact, this proved a source of considerable pride among the peasants. According to their means, they also found it a boon to be able to send a daughter as an odalisque to the sultan's harem.

In Turkey's power struggles with Venice, it was notable that Orthodox Greeks usually preferred Muslim to proselytizing Catholic rule in such places as Tinos, Crete and the Ionian Islands.

Defeat in 1571 by an alliance of Spanish, Venetian and papal forces off the coast of Lepanto (now Nafpaktos) dented the self-confidence of the Ottoman Empire—just five years after the death of its greatest sultan, Suleiman the Magnificent. Not that this was a matter of great concern to the Greeks, who had to row in the galleys of both fleets.

In 1687, the Venetians made one brutal last sally through mainland Greece to Athens. Their captain, Francesco Morosini, bombarded the Parthenon, igniting the gunpowder which the Turks had stored in its inner Sanctuary (see p. 72).

Ottoman rule hardened in the 18th century and the Greeks went once more into mass exile, slowly replaced by Albanians and Serbs. The British ambassador wrote: "A man may ride three or four, sometimes six days, and not find a village able to feed him and his horse." Evading the tax collectors, farmers and shepherds took to the hills in bands of klephts, the rebel-brigands who formed the backbone of the subsequent independence movement.

The French Revolution boosted Greek nationalism, and the Napoleonic Wars aroused international interest in Greek independence by diverting the gentleman's Grand Tour from France and Italy to classical Greece. Most illustrious of this international brigade was Lord Byron, who paid his first visit to Athens in 1809. Less welcome was Lord Elgin, who carved slices off the Parthenon for the British Museum. Greek na-

tional identity was largely ignored in the struggle of Russia, Austria, Britain and France over the fate of the Ottoman Empire. Austrian Chancellor Metternich defied anybody even to define the word "Greek".

Independence

After so many centuries submerged in the Roman, Byzantine and Ottoman Empires, the question of Greek identity was of vital importance. Exiled scholars and diplomats championed the view that a gradual cultural awakening was necessary rather than a violent revolution. Even more vehemently opposed to revolution were the Orthodox patriarch, fearful for his authority, and the so-called Phanariotes, wealthy Constantinople-based merchants dreaming of keeping the Ottoman Empire intact with themselves as its leaders. Far from the Ottoman capital, landowners, local leaders and priests feared for their privileges and indeed for their skins—they had been dubbed "Turkish Christians".

Most enthusiastic advocates of revolution were of course the klephts, who had stayed in Greece to fight: Theodoros Kolokotronis in the Peloponnese (see p. 215), Markos Botsaris in Epirus, others in the mountains of Macedonia and Crete, as well as merchant-pirates operating from the Aegean islands.

Unfavourable Report
Despite their shared faith, there was no great love lost between Orthodox Greeks and Russians. Nonetheless, St Petersburg was a centre for Greek exiles' nationalist ideas and in 1770, Empress Catherine's lover Alexei Orlov led a small expeditionary force to support an uprising in the Peloponnese. The Greco-Russian troops were defeated by an Albanian force that ravaged the land for the next 10 years. The Greeks had expected a more substantial Russian effort, and Orlov wrote home, like some disgruntled modern tour-operator: "The natives here are sycophantic, deceitful, impudent, fickle and cowardly, completely given over to money and plunder."

*B*efore the national flag could be hoisted, the violence of the Greek revolt in the 19th century laid bare the pent-up emotions of 400 years' submission to the Ottoman Empire. The klephts swept down from the mountain redoubts to exact brutal retribution for Turkish atrocities against civilian populations.

of the warriors of Marathon and Thermopylae. The reality was less poetic. Greek forces, however heroic, had also perpetrated brutal massacres. Their various factions were split by bitter political squabbles, assassination and civil war. Greece freed itself of the Turkish yoke, but the price of independence was a monarchy imposed by the great powers. In 1833, a 17-year-old Roman Catholic prince of Bavaria was crowned King Otto of Greece. The Turks vacated the Acropolis and Athens became the capital.

It took another 80 years for Greece to retrieve first the Ionian islands, then its northern territories of Epirus and Macedonia and the key island of Crete. Under its new king, Danish prince William, crowned George I (again a choice of the great powers), the monarchy grew progressively more democratic, accepting a parliament in 1864. But a Greek parliament was inevitably a quarrelsome affair—provoking nine general elections in its first 16 years, 70 different governments in 50 years. Luckily, an outstanding statesman, Eleftherios Venizelos (1864–1936), arrived on the scene to pull the country together before World War I. The Cretan who had led his island's fight for union *(énosis)* with Greece became prime minister in 1910. He combined personal courage, tough pragmatism and a fiercely patriotic vision, the three qualities that Greeks have always demanded of their leaders.

With the Turks progressively weakened by war with Russia and revolt by Ali Pasha of Ioannina, refractory Turkish governor of Epirus, the revolutionary cause gained the day. On March 25, 1821, commemorated now as a national holiday, uprisings spread from the Peloponnese right across the country. Turkish atrocities aroused the protests of Victor Hugo and painter Delacroix in France, Byron and Shelley in England, Goethe and Schiller in Germany. They saw the Greek freedom fighters as descendants

Wars and Peace

When King Constantine I succeeded his father (assassinated in 1913 by a madman in Thessaloniki), Greece faced imminent world war in a highly ambiguous position. Prime minister Venizelos wanted to side with the Western Allies against Germany, Austria and the old enemy, Turkey, but the king, married to the German Kaiser's sister, insisted on neutrality. As commander in chief, he blocked full mobilization and replaced Venizelos with a pro-German prime minister. With the

Balkan situation growing critical in 1917, the Allies forced Constantine off the throne and Venizelos returned to power. By the end of the war, Greek forces marched with the victorious Allies into Constantinople.

But the Greeks' old "Great Idea" of retrieving their Byzantine capital had to be abandoned in their disastrous three-year war against the revitalized Turkey of Kemal Atatürk. The 1923 Treaty of Lausanne imposed a massive exchange of Turkish and Greek populations. Simultaneously with the "repatriation" of 800,000 Turks, more than a million Greek refugees moved to Greece. Bringing with them valuable industrial and agricultural skills, they included prosperous and cultivated merchants from Smyrna (now Izmir), future Nobel prize-winning poet Georgios Seferiades, and pioneers of the Greek Communist Party who settled in the Athens suburb of Nea Smyrni (New Smyrna).

Greek parliamentary life between the two world wars was again a turmoil of unruly factions. In Europe's anti-democratic atmosphere of Mussolini, Stalin, Hitler and Franco, Greece moved inexorably towards dictatorship—under pro-German General Ioannis Metaxas (Constantine's chief of staff in World War I). From 1936 to 1941, he suspended parliament, jailed and tortured Communists and labour leaders and declared unions and strikes illegal. Following Hitler's example, he burned "subversive" books—Heine and Freud, but also Anatole France and Dostoievsky—adding a ludicrous home-grown touch by censoring Pericles' speeches in Thucydides' history of the Peloponnesian War.

Metaxas partially redeemed himself at the outbreak of World War II with a firm stand against Mussolini, driving the Italian army back over the Albanian border in 1940. But British support arrived too late to stop the German invasion (with Italian and Bulgarian allies) and Greece was subjected to four years of brutal occupation. It was estimated that 400,000 died in wartime famine, 200,000 in resistance fighting. Of Greece's 70,000 Jews, 54,000 were deported and exterminated in concentration camps.

Inspired by the grand symbolic gesture of removing Nazi Germany's swastika flying on the Acropolis, the Communist underground was the best organized and most ferocious of the many Greek resistance movements. But the endemic factional infighting, even provoking Winston Churchill to come and negotiate a compromise, pointed towards inevitable civil war after the Allied victory. With the Truman Doctrine bolstering the Greek economy to resist a Soviet takeover, Communists, conservatives and liberals clashed in bloody fighting. The Greek Communists' effort ground to a halt in 1949 after Tito's rift with Stalin stopped the flow of aid across the Yugoslav frontier.

Konstantinos Karamanlis led the most stable of the conservative governments that followed, taking Greece into NATO, conducting the tortuous tractations with Britain and Turkey over Cyprus and ultimately negotiating entry into the European Common Market. Between his two major terms of office came the bitter experience of the Colonels' fascist dictatorship (1967–74). The rule of Colonel Georgios Papadopoulos and police chief Ioannidis inflicted the suppression of civil liberties and perpetrated vicious torture of left-wing leaders in the prisons. In a spurious defence of "Christian morality", the Colonels banned long hair and mini-skirts, deprived film star Melina Mercouri of her citizenship and forbade the songs of Mikis Theodorakis. He was in good company with Sophocles, Aeschylus, Euripides and Aristophanes, whose classical drama was also censored. The dictatorship aroused considerable anti-American feeling when it became known that Papadopoulos had been trained in the CIA and that Washington continued to support the regime against the risk of Soviet intervention.

*F*ilm star *Melina Mercouri rose from persona non grata under the dictatorship of the Colonels to Minister of Culture in the socialist government of Andreas Papandreou.*

In 1981, Andreas Papandreou's socialist party (PASOK) came to power, but did not act on election promises to take Greece out of NATO and the Common Market. The economy was "socialized" rather than nationalized, welfare programmes increased and attempts made to decentralize the government bureaucracy. In 1988, a historic reconciliation between Turkey and Greece was broached with two meetings of their prime ministers. By 1989, the flamboyant Papandreou was embroiled in financial and personal scandals, and after indecisive national elections Greece seemed set for more rounds of factional squabbling. But that's what makes Greek democracy so interesting. Ask Pericles.

HISTORICAL LANDMARKS

Prehistory	4500 B.C.	Mainland settled from Balkans and Asia Minor.
	2700	New wave of Anatolians colonize Crete.
	1950	Ionians invade Greece from Eastern Europe.
Crete and Mycenae	1500–1400	Golden era of Crete's Minoan palaces ending in destruction of Knossos.
	1400–1200	Mycenae dominates Greek mainland.
	13th c.	First buildings on Athens' Acropolis.
	1230–25	Capture of Troy.
Archaic Era	1200	Dark Age after Dorian invasion from Balkans.
	10th c.	Foundation of Sparta.
	c.800–750	Homer composing *Iliad* and *Odyssey*.
	776	First Olympic Games.
	760–700	Greeks colonize southern Italy and Sicily.
Rise of Athens and Sparta	621–593	Dracon and Solon codify Athenian laws.
	6th c.	Sparta dominates Peloponnesian League.
	561–527	Peisistratus enlightened tyrant of Athens.
	499–487	Persian Wars: Greeks fight off invasions by Darius and son Xerxes.
	490	Athenians lead victory at Marathon.
	481	Spartans' heroic stand at Thermopylae.
Classical Age	477	League of Delos under Athens' leadership.
	458–456	Aeschylus' *Orestes*, Euripides' first plays.
	447–438	Parthenon built on Acropolis.
	443–429	Pericles ruler of Athenian Empire.
	442	Sophocles' *Antigone*.
	431–404	Peloponnesian War: Sparta and Thebes end Athens' hegemony.
	399	Death of Socrates.
	387	Plato founds his Academy.
Macedonian Supremacy	356–336	Philip II, king of Macedonia, launches conquest of Greece.
	336–323	Alexander completes domination of Greece and founds empire in Asia and North Africa.
	335–322	Aristotle (Alexander's tutor) in Athens.
	323–276	Alexander's successors carve up empire.
	221	Philip V reasserts control of Greece.
Roman Rule	214	Rome intervenes against Philip V.
	196	Roman general Flaminius proclaims Greek "freedom".
	149–146	Greece made Roman province, Corinth sacked.
	A.D. 49–52	Saint Paul's missions through Greece.
	128	Emperor Hadrian rebuilds Athens.
	267	Ostrogoth invasions devastate Greece.

Byzantine Empire	324	Constantine makes Byzantium (later called Constantinople) capital of Eastern Empire.
	391–393	Emperor Theodosius bans pagan cults, closes Greek temples, stops Olympic Games.
	529	Justinian closes Athens' Platonic Academy.
	6th–8th c.	Slavs invade and dominate Greek mainland.
	726–843	In doctrinal conflicts, iconoclasm launched by Emperor Leo III destroys churches' holy images.
	826	Arabs occupy Crete.
	976–1025	Byzantine art flourishes under Basil the Bulgar-Slayer.
	1054	Schism between Orthodox and Roman churches.
	1081–83	Norman Crusaders rampage through Ionian Islands and Thessaly.
	1204–61	Crusaders sack Constantinople: Greeks under Latin Empire (French and Venetians).
	14th c.	Mistra cultural centre of Byzantine Empire.
Turkish Domination	1453	Turks seize Constantinople, rule Greece through approved Orthodox patriarch.
	1517	Defeat at Lepanto (Nafpaktos) heralds long decline of Ottoman Empire.
	1687	Venetians sweep through Peloponnese to Athens, devastate Parthenon.
	1714	Greeks go into mass exile as Turks bring in Albanians and Serbs.
	1789–1815	French Revolution and Napoleon stimulate Greek nationalism.
Independence	1821	Rebellion in Peloponnese launches Greek War of Independence.
	1832	European powers recognize Greek state.
	1833–62	Otto of Bavaria king of Greece.
	1912–13	Victory in Balkan Wars retrieves Epirus and Macedonia.
	1913	Prime minister Venizelos wins *énosis* (union with Greece) for his native Crete.
Wars and Peace	1914–18	Initially neutral in World War I, Greece joins Western allies.
	1919–22	War with Turkey ends "Great Idea" of regaining Constantinople as Byzantine capital.
	1923	Exchange of 1,500,000 Greeks and Turks.
	1936–41	Dictatorship of General Metaxas.
	1941–44	German occupation with Italian and Bulgarian allies. Communists lead resistance.
	1944–49	Bloody civil war against Communists.
	1955–63	Conservative Karamanlis takes Greece into NATO, long dispute with Turkey over Cyprus.
Dictatorship and Democracy	1967–74	Colonels' coup d'état instals dictatorship.
	1974–80	Karamanlis returns to establish republic.
	1981	Papandreou's socialist party PASOK reluctantly takes Greece into Common Market.
	1989	Indecisive national elections after political and personal scandals.

Choosing Between Musts and Maybes

Deciding on where to go in Greece and how to set about it usually depends on the relative importance you attach to the three basic reasons for heading there in the first place: soaking up the sun and the sea; visiting the ancient and Byzantine monuments; or getting to know the people and the land itself. Some visitors plump for one at the expense of the other two. To enjoy Greece to the full, we recommend a combination of all three. That way, you'll go home browner, wiser and more cheerful.

Our Blueprint is designed to provide years of useful reference and pleasure for several visits, but newcomers to Greece can also concoct from its pages an initial itinerary that gives a broad sense of the country's potential. It is, of course, impossible on a first visit to sample all that Greece has to offer, but we can whet your appetite to return. Before our detailed description of the various regions, we offer you a Short List (p. 42) of what we feel are "essential" things to see in the place(s) you choose as a base. Then, in our Leisure Routes and Themes (p. 45), you will find itineraries that take you from one region to another in pursuit of a particular taste or interest, cultural, sporting or otherwise.

Island-hoppers must be prepared to improvise. If you miss your ferry, you might be able to hitch a ride with one of the local fishermen.

Our eight regional chapters follow a wide loop from Athens out to the Cyclades, south to Crete, across to Rhodes and the Dodecanese, up the eastern Aegean to Thessaloniki and the North, through Central Greece and the Sporades, west across the mainland to the Ionian Islands and south again to the Peloponnese and the Saronics.

Planning your choices, the first and most obvious division you have to make is between the mainland and the islands. Try to combine the two. With, say, three to four weeks at your disposal, you should be able to manage quite comfortably a major mainland region like the Peloponnese or Athens and Central Greece, and then get in a little island-hopping, too.

However forbidding you may imagine ancient ruins to be, the great monumental sites like the sanctuary of Delphi or Agamemnon's palace at Mycenae exert a mysterious power on the most blasé imagination. Quite apart from the mystic attractions of the Byzantine churches and their icons, a quiet moment of meditation there is cooling for body and spirit alike. Taken in small doses before the heat of the day sets in, these ancient or medieval monuments can act as a tonic stimulus if sun-bathing threatens to addle your brain or the sea begins to shrivel your skin to the texture of a dried apricot. One of the advantages of the island of Mykonos, for instance, is the easy accessibility of the Delos sanctuary—even the most hardened beach-addict can visit the ruins in the morning and be back building sand temples in the afternoon.

If you want to avoid the most crowded islands popularized by package tours, you can still find more secluded spots, but hotel accommodation and general tourist facilities will be correspondingly more modest. The answer here is to rent a house and "go native". But even on the most popular islands like Corfu or Rhodes, it is always possible to hike away from the crowd. Peace has its price.

You will find detailed practical information in the Berlitz Info pages at the back of the book, but we want to suggest here some general principles.

Tussle with the Timetable

Once you have a rough idea of where you want to go, study Olympic Airways' domestic route-map to see which connections are possible. You must correlate them to the timetable, because not all flights are daily. Take the trouble to do this yourself as travel agents nowadays don't have the time to work with anything but computers; they will tell you your multiple-destination itinerary is impossible when in fact a little ingenuity can make it work. You'll notice that practically all airports are linked directly to Athens, but there are enough inter-island connections to make island-hopping by air a feasible idea. Advance reservations (and reconfirmations) are necessary, but be prepared to be flexible in case of sudden flight cancellations due to weather or labour problems. In view of the latter risk, give yourself plenty of leeway for your charter or fixed excursion-flight departure date from Athens or wherever.

Which Season?

Greece has a rather short spring, sweltering summer, cooler autumn and a winter that is apparently mild in temperature but somehow wretchedly cold in actual impact—the country is just not built for cool weather. With only minor regional variations (colder winters in the north), temperatures average from 12°C/53°F in January and February to 33°C/92°F in July and August. But extremes can and do drop winter temperatures to freezing point and shoot summer highs up over 40°C/104°F. Summers are slightly cooler on the coasts and islands, but also stickier at night. In general, the west is moister and greener than the east, true both of Crete and of the Ionian and Aegean seas. Corfu gets the most rain, but even that means only 17 rainy days from May to September (compared with Athens' 14). April and October are both quite rainy.

From time to time in the Aegean (but not on the Ionian islands or the mainland's west coast), the sultry stillness of summer is buffeted between mid-July and the end of August by the notorious meltemi wind. Stirred up by a collision of sharply differing atmospheric pressures between the Balkans and North Africa, this north-west wind starts around 8 a.m. and peters out at sunset. Beach-umbrellas take off, the sand flies in your eyes, and aircraft are grounded. Sailors say they love it.

Wherever you find yourself in summer, one institution remains sacred, the siesta. From 3 to 5 in the afternoon, all but the most diligent, yuppified Greeks are resting. Don't phone them. Don't try to beat them, join them.

Mass tourist traffic in the high season makes May, June and September the most attractive months for easy movement around the major destinations. If you can, save your visits to the mainland interior for spring or autumn. You'll find that Athens in August, like Rome or Paris, is increasingly closing down all but its most entrenched tourist centres.

Getting Around

Preparing an itinerary in this small but topographically complex country offers the logistical challenge of a military campaign. It was hell for the Persians, and the Germans found it easier only because they had an air force. As more peaceful invaders, tourists will also find flying the most convenient way of getting from the mainland around the islands and back. It is of course more expensive than by sea but still relatively cheap because of the Greek government subsidy to keep fares down for its own citizens.

Island-hopping by sea is no easy business, but great fun if approached in the right spirit. Timetables of the various ferry lines do exist, available from the National Tourist Organization of Greece (NTOG). They are useful as a general, but by no means exhaustive, guide to what is available, but they do not tell the gospel truth. That is to say, the timetable cannot anticipate the constant changes in routing between islands and frequency of departures. You yourself have to be down at the harbour to ascertain factors like weather conditions, changes in seasonal demand and, most important of all, whims of naturally independent-minded Greek ferry operators. Luckily, this factor often means there are more, rather than less, vessels than officially timetabled.

Try to confirm the next leg of your tour as soon as you arrive. Remember the myriad harbourside agencies are interested only in touting their own boats; to find out what is generally available, particularly when weather conditions are difficult, consult the harbour police. When you have a car to put on the ferry, advance reservations are advisable; even then, be there well ahead of departure time to be sure of getting on.

Trains are by and large too slow—the Athens–Thessaloniki "express" takes 8 hours. Public buses are more fun and faster (Athens–Corinth 90 minutes, compared with 2 hours by train). They are ideal on the islands for getting to and

The Name Game
There is no hard and fast rule for Roman-lettered versions of Greek place-names on signposts and road maps. You should have no problem with Heraklion and Iraklion or Piraeus and Pireéfs, but Greeks prefer Kerkyra to Corfu and Thessaloniki to Salonica, and prudes shy away from Lesbos to prefer Mytilene. Berlitz has decided to be as flexible as the Greeks, but more consistent, using the most familiar English names, with an occasional bracketed mention of the variations and transcriptions of the Greek names you may encounter, when they differ sensibly from the English.

Finding your way around the cities will be much easier if you learn the Greek alphabet (see p. 276 in the Belitz Info section.) All street signs are written in capital letters. The words for street *(odós)* and square *(platía)* are used in conversation but usually omitted from maps and signs.

from the popular beaches, but long-distance mainland trips are usually too complicated to organize for any but the most adventurous. Coach tours with English-language guides are a convenient way of visiting the major archaeological sites.

Taxis are quite reasonably priced, but remember to agree ahead of time on the fare for longer trips out of town. At rush hour in the cities, be ready to share your taxi with a stranger.

The international car rental firms have offices in major mainland cities and some of the bigger islands. Four-wheel-drives are the best choice for leaving the beaten track to reach some of the more desirably quiet beaches. On smaller islands, shop around local portside offices offering battered but serviceable Jap-jeeps, not cheap but often negotiable according to seasonal supply and demand. Motorcycles and mopeds are the most popular motorized transport of all, even more technologically suspect, but great fun for getting to the beach.

Greek driving is extremely Mediterranean—spirited and spontaneous. Most drivers have fast survival-reflexes and

*D*riving inland on the spectacular mountain road to Leonidio in the Peloponnese can be a long, dry run, with villages few and far between. Make it a habit for any excursion into the interior to take a bottle of mineral water.

presume you have the same. Expect the unexpected, stay cool, play Nordic, and you will survive.

Greeks are amazed and delighted to discover any foreigner speaking their language. They usually manage a little English, German, French or Italian themselves, roughly in that order, but will immediately be well disposed to you if you try at least a couple of Greek words to show good will. Berlitz of course proposes some useful phrases at the back of the book (and recommends for more ambitious use its *Greek for Travellers* phrase book). But you are already ahead of the game if you start out just with the following: *ne* and *ókhi* for "yes" and "no"; *parakaló* ("please"), *efkharistó* ("thank you"); *kaliméra* ("good morning"), *kalispéra* ("good evening"). And the ubiquitous *yássas* ("goodbye").

Kaló taksídhi—Bon voyage!

ON THE SHORT LIST

Just the Essentials

You will never get to—or want to—see everything. But for a first trip to each region, here is our list of the major landmarks of Greek sightseeing. It will help you establish your priorities.

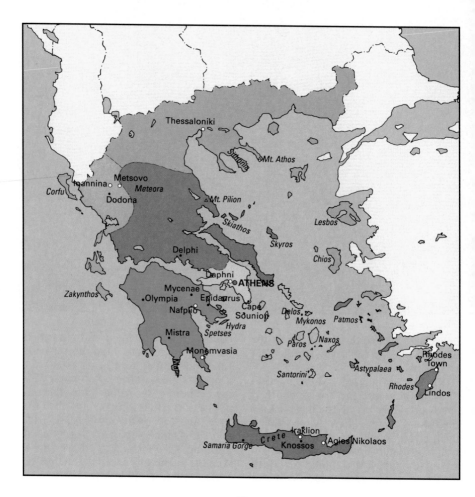

Athens
Acropolis: capital's sanctuary
National Archaeological Museum:
nation's ancient treasures
Plaka: renovated historic
neighbourhood
(2–3 days)

Attica
Piraeus: ancient and modern port
Cape Sounion: Poseidon's temple with
superb view
Daphni: great Byzantine mosaics
(1–2 days)

Cyclades
Mykonos: the swinging island
Delos: Apollo's sanctuary
Paros: superb water sports
Santorini: grandiose volcanic beauty
(8 days minimum)

Central Greece
Delphi: most beautiful of sanctuaries
Mount Pilion: bracing mountain
refuge
Meteora: monasteries on pinnacles
(4 days minimum)

Sporades
Skiathos: great beaches
Skyros: fine handicrafts
(4 days)

Crete
Knossos: Minoan palace
Iraklion: archaeological museum
Agios Nikolaos: most popular resort
Samaria Gorge: spectacular hike
(6 days)

Ionian Islands
Corfu: lively family resorts
Zakynthos: Venetian charm restored
(5–6 days)

North-west Mainland
Ioannina: lakeside bazaar town
Dodona: ancients' oldest oracle
Metsovo: handsome mountain village
(2 days)

Rhodes
Rhodes Town: Knights' Quarter and
bazaar
Lindos: ancient port city and beach
(4 days)

Dodecanese
Patmos: arid beauty, grand
monastery
Astypalaea: haven of peace
(3–4 days)

Peloponnese
Mycenae: palace of Agamemnon
Nafplio: charming resort town
Epidaurus: classical Greek theatre
Monemvasia: fine Venetian town
Mistra: Byzantine monasteries and
mansions
The Mani: wild peninsula
Olympia: sanctuary of Zeus and
Olympic Games
(8–10 days)

North
Thessaloniki: good restaurants and
archaeological museum
Sithonia: best Chalkidiki beach
resorts
Mount Athos: remote monastic
peninsula
(8 days)

North Aegean Islands
Lesbos: pine-covered home of
Sappho
Chios: dramatic lunar landscapes
(4–5 days)

Saronic Islands
Hydra: artist's home from home
Spetses: relaxed family resort
(1–2 days)

43

Going Places with Something Special in Mind

Journeys through Greece open up dozens of different facets of the country's life—sporting, cultural, historical or religious, pleasures for the gourmet, the craftsman or the nature lover. Whether you are island-hopping or travelling around the mainland, you will cross the paths of great travellers of the past—St Paul, Philip and Alexander or Odysseus himself. We propose here some itineraries to follow, and suggest some of the best places to pursue your own personal interests, keyed to the Road Atlas section.

Vineyards

No neatly tailored Burgundy or Chianti country here, but vineyards present a colourful tangle of vines dotted with fruit trees providing welcome shade and refreshment. Outsiders rarely participate in harvests.

CEPHALONIA *10 B3*
The Potamiana region north-east of Argostoli produces reputed Robola white wine.

PATRAS *14 B1*
Important production and distribution centre at heart of Peloponnesian vineyards.

NEMEA (PELOPONNESE) *15 D1*
Famous for its its full-bodied red wines known locally as "blood of Hercules".

CORINTH *15 D1*
Vines here best known for table grapes and currants deriving name from town.

As reminders to drive carefully, roadside shrines often mark the sites of traffic accidents.

MESSOGHIA *13 D1*
Attica's centre for the best resin-flavoured *retsina* wines.

PORTO CARRAS *7 E3*
Sithonia's French-style vineyards producing quite sophisticated reds and whites.

TINOS *16 C1*
Picturesque vineyards surrounded by dovecotes.

SAMOS *17 E1*
Fertile interior produces rich sweet muscatel wines.

SANTORINI *16 C2*
Here it is volcanic soil that makes for some heady reds.

Pottery

The ancient Greek tradition continues both on the islands and the mainland. You will find reproductions of Geometric and Classical patterns as well as more modern designs. Seek out the workshops to watch the modelling and painting.

MAROUSSI *13 D3*
Factories in Athens suburb good place for general overview of regional production.

AEGINA *13 D3*
Time-honoured manufacture of two-handled water jars.

NAFPLIO *12 C3*
Centre of distinctive green glazed Peloponnesian style.

IOANNINA *10 B1*
Find colourful Epirote ceramics in old bazaar.

METSOVO *10 B1*
Cottage industry continues in this mountain village.

SIFNOS *16 B2*
At Vathi, potters model their wares right on the beach.

CRETE *19 C3*
Iraklion workshops reproduce Minoan ceramics.

RHODES *20 C2*
Famous Lindos pottery now produced in Rhodes Town factories.

Rugs and Textiles

The flokati styles are rustic in texture, others continuing the rich ornamentation of the Byzantine era. In the mountain villages you can see the weaving and lacemaking in action.

METSOVO *10 B1*
Proud mountain village turns out best of Epirote weaving.

ARACHOVA *11 D2*
Village near Delphi has become a generic name for bright patterned rugs and wall hangings.

OLIMBOS (KARPATHOS) *20 B3*
Womenfolk weave their shawls and rugs dressed in traditional costume.

KRITSA (CRETE) *19 D3*
Shawls, rugs and laceware hand-made in picturesque village near Agios Nikolaos.

ANOGIA (CRETE) *18–19 C3*
Reputed for its brightly patterned fabrics (and folk dancing).

Colourful Cretan weaving.

Jewellery

Like the princes and princesses of ancient Crete, the Greeks have developed a taste for fine gold and silver jewellery. Ancient and modern styles are sold side by side.

ATHENS *13 D3*
Syntagma, Voukourestiou and Panepistimiou shops have widest range, but not lowest prices.

IOANNINA *10 B1*
People travel clear across country for fine gold and silver in lakeside bazaar.

IRAKLION *19 C3*
First-class copies of ancient Minoan necklaces, bracelets, rings and earrings.

RHODES *20 C2*
Bargain for bargains in capital's Turkish bazaar.

NAFPLIO *12 C3*
Best selection in Peloponnese.

SANTORINI *16 C2*
Stylish boutiques cater to discerning cruise-ship trade.

Woodcarving

Craftwork thrives mainly in mountain areas or regions rich in olive groves.

METSOVO *10 B1*
Intricately carved utensils, boxes and folk-sculpture from Pindus forests.

ANDRITSENA *14 C2*
Near Bassae temple in village built mostly of wood, carpenters have rugged style.

CORFU *10 A2*
Island's millions of olive trees provide wood for finely carved salad and fruit bowls, etc.

SKYROS *13 E2*
Famous for its traditional carved furniture and basketware.

Folklore Museums

Since independence, museums around the country have affirmed regional traditions other than those of classical Greece.

THESSALONIKI *7 D2*
Museum of Ethnological and Popular Art (Vas. Olgas 68) devoted to Macedonia.

IOANNINA *10 B1*
Epirote folklore displayed in Aslan Pasha Mosque.

METSOVO *10 B1*
Folk Art museum in Tossitsa mansion, embroidery, textiles and rugs.

ATHENS *13 D3*
Greek Folk Art (Kidathineon 17) and Benaki Museum (Vas Sofias/Koumbari streets).

SKYROS *13 E2*
Faltaitz Museum in Chorio, costumes, embroidery, copper, furniture and basketware.

NAFPLIO *12 C3*
Peloponnesian Folklore Foundation (Ipsilantou Street).

IRAKLION *19 C3*
Historical Museum (opposite Xenia Hotel), Cretan peasant dwellings and costumes.

RHODES TOWN *20 C2*
Museum of Decorative Arts in Knights' Arsenal.

Military Museums

A fascinating way to link ancient and modern Greek history is through the military museums. They tell a continuous story of prowess on land and sea.

ATHENS *13 D3*
War Museum (Vas. Sofias/Rizari) traces Greek wars from Troy to present day.

PIRAEUS *13 D3*
Nautical Museum (Akti Themistokleous) from Athenian triremes to modern submarines.

MISSOLONGHI *10 C3*
Museum of Revolution (Platía Botsaris) tells story of independence struggle.

CHANIA (CRETE) *18 B3*
Naval Museum emphasizes Crete's special role in Greek history.

Ancient Battlefields

The great battles of ancient times were those that symbolized the unity of the Greek kingdoms and city-states. Two waves of Persian invasions brought the Greek nation together on land and sea under the leadership of Athens and Sparta.

1 MARATHON
Burial mound on the Attica plain marks victory of Greek armies under Athenian Miltiades against Persians in 491 B.C.

2 THERMOPYLAE
Mountain pass in Thessaly where Leonidas led heroic Spartan resistance to armies of Persian emperor Xerxes (480 B.C.).

3 CAPE ARTEMISIUM
During Thermopylae, Athenian fleet held Persian navy off north coast of Euboea.

4 SALAMIS BAY
Themistocles' decisive victory west of Athens drove Xerxes' fleet back across Aegean (479 B.C.).

The Iliad

Tradition and archaeology find precise locations for the lives of Homer's heroes.

MOUNT PILION *11 E1*
Achilles reared by Cheiron as tough outdoorsman.

MYCENAE *15 D1*
Palace of Agamemnon.

PYLOS *14 B2*
Nestor's Palace on Englianos hill.

SKYROS *8 B2*
Odysseus came here to smoke out Achilles disguised as girl.

MT FENGARI, SAMOTHRACE *5 D2*
Share Poseidon's viewpoint of Trojan wars on Turkish mainland.

The Odyssey

Ancient and modern scholars have shared the belief that Odysseus's legendary journey home from the Trojan Wars followed a real itinerary as far as Crete and a more fanciful one for the last leg home. Encouraged by the claims of Greek colonists in the western Mediterranean, some place episodes like Scylla and Charybdis in Italy, others in

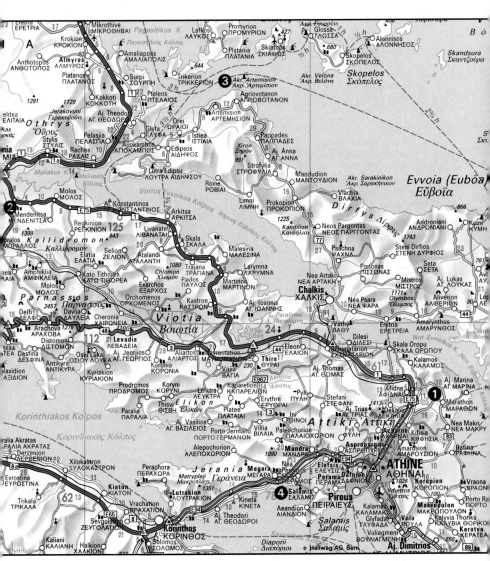

Yugoslavia, Ireland, Norway and the Indian Ocean. Ours is a popularly accepted itinerary through Greek waters.

The Departure From Troy

1 TROY
Battle site discovered by Heinrich Schliemann on Turkish coast, still being excavated by American archaeologists.

2 MARONIA
Odysseus sacks "Ismarus", Thracian city of Cicones.

3 SKYROS
Fleet of 12 ships stops over for 3 days of repairs from storms off Mount Athos.

4 CAPE MALEA
After smooth crossing via Cape Sounion, fierce meltemi wind drives fleet off course south via Kythira, bypassing Crete.

5 CYRENAICA
Libyan coast believed to be land of Lotus Eaters where vegetarian Africans offered crew intoxicating jujube fruit.

6 PALEOCHORA
Peninsula originally island where men hunted goats while Odysseus fought Cyclops in cave on coast of south-west Crete.

Homecoming to Ithaca

7 GRAMBOUSA
Isle of Aeolus off north Crete where ships awaited favourable wind to sail home.

8 MESAPOS
On Mani peninsula, Peloponnesian home of Laestrygonians who destroyed whole fleet except for Odysseus' ship.

9 PAXI
Island where Circe seduced the hero into staying for a year.

10 NEKYOMANTEION OF EPHYRA
Near Parga, oracle of the Dead at Halls of Hades visited by Odysseus.

11 LEFKAS CHANNEL
Passage between Charybdis and man-eating Scylla's cave on mainland Mount Lamia.

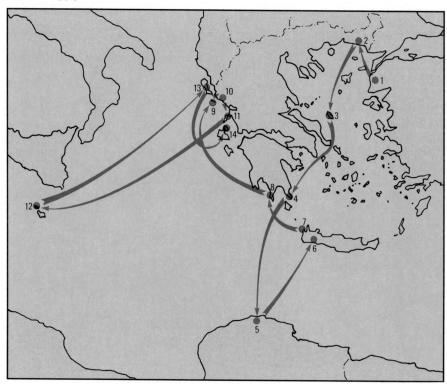

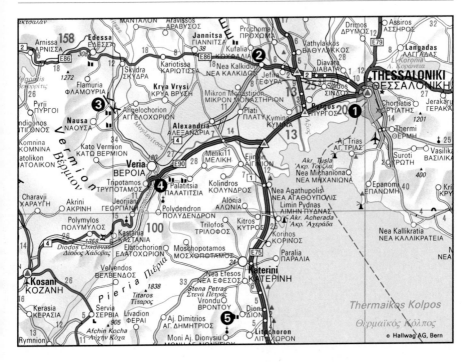

12 GOZO (MALTA)
Calypso's island where hero kept Penelope waiting another seven years.

13 PALEOKASTRITSA, CORFU
Lovely Nausicaa finds Odysseus on beach.

14 ITHACA
Hero rescues Penelope from her suitors.

Philip and Alexander

The horizons of the two great conquerors stretched way beyond Greece's frontiers, but you can trace their beginnings in their kingdom of Macedonia.

1 THESSALONIKI
In archaeological museum, Philip's armour, skeleton and gold funeral casket, Alexander's portrait carved in ivory.

2 PELLA
Philip's capital, Alexander's birthplace; mosaic of Alexander hunting.

3 LEFKADIA
Tomb of one of Alexander's officers.

4 VERGINA
The royal tombs.

5 DION
Garrison town from which Alexander launched his imperial conquest.

Sanctuaries of the Gods

Like Jerusalem and Catholic Rome, the Greeks' sanctuaries were focuses of political power. The gods consecrated regional conquest and national unity.

SAMOTHRACE *5 D2*
Shrine of lords of Underworld.

DODONA *10 B1*
In Epirus, oldest Greek oracle spoke message of Zeus through sacred oak.

DELPHI *11 D2*
Apollo's shrine, most prestigious oracle placed by Zeus at navel of universe.

PARNASSUS *11 D2*
Mountain home of Muses.

51

The Lions of Delos.

ELEUSIS *13 D3*
Mysteries of Demeter, corn-goddess.

OLYMPUS *6–7 C3*
Mountain citadel of all the gods.

DELOS *16 C1*
Apollo's island sanctuary, focus of Aegean alliance.

ATHENS *13 D3*
Acropolis gathered Athenian power around Zeus's Parthenon.

OLYMPIA *14 B1*
National sanctuary for Zeus and Hera, home of Olympic Games.

CRETE *18–19 C–D3*
Zeus's boyhood homes in caves on Mount Ida and Mount Dikti.

The Romans in Greece

The mark left by the conquerors from Italy was most often a homage to their subjects. In each ancient Greek site you will find traces of Roman baths, markets or theatres in Greek architectural style.

Saint Paul in Greece

His Hellenistic education made Greece the natural first target for Paul's missionary work in Europe. Follow his itinerary as described in the New Testament's *Acts of the Apostles*.

PHILIPPI
The ruins of 5th-century church mark site of Paul's first Christian conversion *(Acts 16:14)*.

THESSALONIKI *7 D2*
Paul took Egnatia Road to preach to Jews in synagogue *(Acts 17:1)*.

ATHENS *13 D3*
He harangued sages on Areopagus hill and debated in Agora *(Acts 17:15–34)*.

CORINTH *15 D1*
Paul judged by Roman proconsul in ancient agora *(Acts 18:11)*.

The Venetians

For Venice's overseas empire, Greece provided a series of trading posts. They left their architecture and Catholic religion.

The Ionian sea
The ports here guarded the approaches to the Adriatic.

CORFU TOWN *10 A2*
Old fort and picturesque houses.

ZAKYNTHOS *14 A1*
Campanile on waterfront restored after earthquake.

METHONI (PELOPONNESE) *14 B2*
Massive bastion guarded harbour of principal Venetian stronghold in Ionian sea.

The Aegean
The Aegean possessions acted as way stations on route to Constantinople.

CHIOS *9 D2*
Country mansions with Venetian coats of arms.

ATHENS *13 D3*
Hadrian's Arch, Odeon of Herodes Atticus, Roman Agora in Plaka.

CORINTH *15 D1*
Roman theatre, proconsul's tribune, Peirene Fountain.

THESSALONIKI *7 D2*
Arch of Galerius and his mausoleum (Rotunda of St George).

PHILIPPI
Roman colony founded by Mark Anthony after his defeat there of Caesar's assassins, Cassius and Brutus.

TINOS *16 C1*
Venetian dovecotes dot countryside, iron-balconied houses in island capital.

ANDROS *16 B1*
Castle-ruin in Chora.

PAROS *16 C2*
Venetian citadel, island still most popular with Italians.

NAXOS *16 C2*
Capital of medieval Italian duchy of Archipelago. Catholic cathedral, Venetian tower houses in country.

MONEMVASIA *15 D2*
Elegant balconied houses and campanile from Venetian era.

CRETE *18 B3*
Chania and Rethymnon have attractive reminders of their trading post days. Frangokastello guarded south coast.

The Crusaders

The Normans, Italians, Spanish, Germans and English all left their mark in Greece on their way to and from the Holy Land.

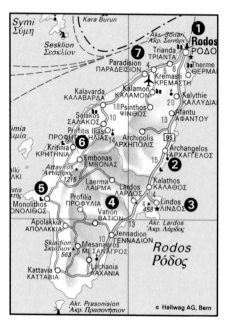

Rhodes
The Knights of St John fortified not only the capital but the whole island with castles along the cliffs and hilltops.

1 KNIGHTS' QUARTER
Capital's headquarters for main garrison, with palaces, hospital and churches.

2 ARCHANGELOS
East coast 15th-century fortress.

3 LINDOS
Commander's Palace built on ancient acropolis.

4 ASKLIPIIO
Fortress built inland in centre of hilltop village.

5 MONOLITHOS
Spectacular 15th-century castle on rocky crag.

6 KAMIROS KASTELLO
Ruined fortress near site of ancient Greek port town.

7 FILERIMOS
Elevated plateau from which Knights launched attack to capture island in 1309.

Byzantine Monasteries

With arrangements in advance, some will receive you as a guest—Mount Athos, for instance. Others can be visited, with proper decorum and dignified clothing.

MOUNT ATHOS *4 B2–3*
Autonomous theocracy within Greek state has 20 monasteries on its peninsula.

METEORA *10 C1*
Monks have perched their refuges on mountain crags in Thessaly.

DAPHNI *13 D3*
West of Athens, renowned for its magnificent mosaics.

KAISARIANI (nr. ATHENS) *13 D3*
Abandoned 11th-century monastery with mill, bakery, bath-house and refectory.

Byzantine art.

54

MISTRA *15 C2*
Beautiful monastery churches amid ruins of Byzantine city in Peloponnese.

PATMOS *17 D1*
Built where St John the Divine wrote Revelations—rich museum of Byzantine art.

Outposts

The country's islands, mountains and isolated peninsulas provided ideal refuges for the zealous robber barons and their sons who never went home.

PARGA *10 B2*
Ruined castle marks Norman bridgehead for 11th-century invasion via Corfu.

FISCARDO (CEPHALONIA) *10 B3*
Norman Crusader Robert Guiscard died here, leaving relic of Norman-style church.

CORINTH *15 D1*
Gothic fortifications on Acrocorinth citadel.

GERAKI *15 D2*
Peloponnesian citadel built in 13th century.

MISTRA *15 C2*
Guillaume de Villehardouin left Kastro at top of Byzantine town.

THE MANI *15 C2–3*
Passava castle of Jean de Neuilly (13th century).

KOS *20 A2*
Knights of St John built castle with temple masonry.

SYMI *20 B2*
French baron Aubusson's hilltop fortress.

Greek Independence

The 19th-century struggle for Greek independence under the Ottoman Empire was a fiery tale of rebellion, massacre and political infighting. It spread north from the Peloponnese and across the Aegean.

AGIA LAVRA *15 C1*
Peloponnesian monastery where Archbishop Germanos proclaimed revolt March 25, 1821.

IOANNINA *10 B1*
Campaign complicated by Ali Pasha's separatism crushed by Turks, 1822.

SPETSES *15 D2*
Regatta commemorates island's victory over Ottoman fleet September 8, 1822.

NEA MONI, CHIOS *9 D2*
Monastery focus in 1822 of Turkish massacres of 25,000, with 47,000 enslaved.

NAVARINO BAY (PELOPONNESE)
British, French and Russians destroy Ottoman fleet in 1827.

NAFPLIO *15 D1*
First capital of independent Greece. President Kapodistrias assassinated here in 1831.

Lord Byron's Greece

The British poet's impassioned campaign for Greek freedom epitomized the European intelligentsia's wide-eyed fervour for the ideals of ancient Greece.

ATHENS *13 D3*
Odós Ágias Théklas 11 was Byron's home in 1809. He immortalized the landlord's daughter Teresa Makris as Maid of Athens.
Benaki Museum: poet's portable writing desk, portrait in Greek costume.
National Historical Museum: his helmet and sword.
National Picture Gallery: painting of Byron at Missolonghi.

CAPE SOUNION *13 D3*
Poseidon's Temple where he carved his initials and wrote of its "marbled steep".

IOANNINA *10 B1*
Remains of Ali Pasha's palace where Byron dined with Albanian despot.

MISSOLONGHI *10 C3*
After death from malaria, poet's heart buried beneath monument in Heroes' Garden. Memorabilia in Museum of Revolution.

Carnival

Pre-Lenten Orthodox and Catholic carnival celebrations are equally pagan, costumed, boisterous and bibulous in the land of Dionysus.

PATRAS *14 B1*
Biggest of Greek processions with elaborate costumes and floats.

ATHENS *13 D3*
Capital drops its sophistication for uninhibited masked dances and procession.

CRETE *18 B–C3*
Iraklion and Rethymnon both make colourful contribution in grandest Minoan tradition.

RHODES *20 C2*
Island celebrates with private and public parties.

Theatre Festivals

If only there could be a full moon every night. In any case, you can recapture something of the classical world's atmosphere with open-air summer festivals of drama or opera in ancient amphitheatres.

ATHENS *13 D3*
Theatre and music festival performed in Odeon of Herodes Atticus.

EPIDAURUS *15 D1*
Performances where Aeschylus, Sophocles and Euripides had their premières.

PHILIPPI
Roman theatre offers superb setting for classical drama.

THASOS *4 B2*
Classical drama performed in theatre dedicated to Dionysus.

THESSALONIKI *7 D2*
October arts festival in modern theatre.

Sound and Light Shows

A painless, even entertaining way of absorbing local history is to watch an English-language audiovisual show in a historical setting.

ATHENS *13 D3*
Ancient story of Acropolis as seen from Pnyx hill.

RHODES *20 C2*
Turkish siege that vanquished Knights of St John, recounted from municipal garden.

CORFU *10 A2*
Island's troubled history narrated in Old Fort.

Skiing

Not the most obvious thing to do in Greece, but a quite exhilarating change from sightseeing in the winter months. And less crowded than Kitzbühel or Courchevel.

PARNASSUS *11 D2*
Ski with Muses and make your base in Arachova or Delphi.

PILION *11 E1*
Achilles is fellow to watch for here, very fast. Best resort facilities at Hania.

OSTRAKINA AND VRISSOPOULOS *14 B1*
Popular slopes in Peloponnese, with Olympia conveniently nearby for accommodation.

Windsurfing and Water-Skiing

Most resorts offer opportunities for one or other of these sports, but some locations have been marked out as superior for aficionados.

PORTO CARRAS (CHALKIDIKI) *7 E3*
Equipment and lessons provided by luxury resort complex.

GERAKINI (CHALKIDIKI) *7 D3*
Well organized by state-run resort.

KOUKOUNARIES (SKIATHOS) *12–13 C2*
Popular but big enough to avoid crowds.

MITHYMNA (LESBOS) *9 D2*
Usually exhilarating wind conditions.

PANORMOS BAY (MYKONOS) *16 C1*
Windsurfers swear this is best in Aegean.

KOLIBITHRES (PAROS) *16 C2*
Boats from Naoussa.

MYRTOS (CEPHALONIA) *14 A1*
Best straight *surfing* in Greece.

Snorkelling and Diving

Diving with oxygen equipment is limited by local regulations. Here are some of the places where you can explore the Greek waters' lower depths.

PALEOKASTRITSA (CORFU) *10 A2*
Good training facility in superb setting.

PAXI and ANTIPAXI *10 A2*
Sail around caves on Paxi's west coast and Antipaxi's Vrika and Voutomi beaches for best diving.

ALONNISOS *13 D2*
Marine conservation park in Sporades, best diving off Kokkinokastro peninsula.

PAROS *16 C2*
Divers head for Langeri, Agia Maria and Platis Ammos beaches.

TELENDOS (KALYMNOS) *17 E2*
See ancient town submerged by 6th-century earthquake.

OLOUS (CRETE) *19 D3*
From Elounda resort, explore submerged ancient city.

MOCHLOS (CRETE) *19 D3*
Swim around underwater remains of Minoan village.

Nature Lover's Islands

Crete

Greece's largest island has a grand variety of landscapes to attract the outdoorsman, whether tough hiker or casual rambler. Spring is the best time for hikes through the wild flowers of the high plains and the pines and cypresses of the mountain gorges.

SAMARIA GORGE *18 B3*
Ramble down to south coast from Lefka mountains.

IMBROS GORGE *18 B3*
Day's walk ending in fishing village of Chora Sfakion.

MOUNT IDA *18–19 C3*
Wild flowers all way from Anogia to Zeus's Idaian cave.

LASITHI PLAINS *18–19 D3*
Citrus and almond trees give way to groves of wild olive and mountain pine.

Corfu *10 A2*

Fortunately, the most popular of package tour islands offers plenty of country walks away from the throng. Dotted among the myriad olive groves, wild orchids, cyclamen, anemones and marigolds are sheer delight.

MOUNT AGII DEKA
Escape noise of east coast resorts to explore wild fruit trees nestling in extinct volcanic crater.

MOUNT PANTOKRATOR
Walks inland from Nissaki to explore island's highest mountain.

MOUNT ARAKLI
North-east of Paleokastritsa are clifftop rambles turning inland via Lakones across groves of cypress and silver olive.

LAKE KORISSION
Among holly oak and juniper, sand dune walk for birdwatchers—look for heron, cormorant oyster-catcher and curlew.

For the Love of the Landscape

Sometimes the interest is just the beauty of the landscape, lending unique flavour

Wild flowers on Crete.
Top: Turban buttercup *(Rananculus asiaticus)*. Bottom left: Pink butterfly orchid *(Orchis papilionacea)*. Bottom right: Cretan lords-and-ladies *(Arum cretica)*.

Corfu: great for all the family.

to a car drive, boat trip or hike. The choice is infinite. Here are a few.

DELPHI *11 D2*
Marriage of ancient sanctuary with awesome natural setting on Mount Parnassus.

SAMARIA AND IMBROS GORGES
Quintessence of Crete's magic mountains.

MOUNT ATHOS *4 B2–3*
Even boat excursion imparts mystic beauty of this world apart.

MOUNT PILION *11 E1*
Unique mixture of alpine landscape and craggy coastline.

METEORA *10 C1*
Monasteries perched on spectacular pinnacles.

NORTH-EAST CORFU *10 A2*
Rugged corniche drive through Lawrence Durrell's dreamland.

THE MANI *15 C2–3*
Savage grandeur of Peloponnesian outpost.

CORINTH: currants.

KALAMATA: smooth, black, almond-shaped olives.

Attica and the North

MOUNT HYMETTOS: renowned for honey since ancient times.

MOUNT PILION: peaches, wild strawberries, pears, plums, chestnuts; cheeses.

MACEDONIA: wild game in autumn—hare, partridge, pheasant; walnuts, hazelnuts, almonds.

THESSALONIKI: *patsás* (tripe soup).

THRACE: wrinkled black olives.

The Islands

CORFU: crayfish, *sofríto* (stewed steak), olives and olive oil.

CRETE: *manoúri, anthótyro* and other cheeses, fresh yoghurt, *stiffádo* (braised beef).

THASOS: honey, fig and walnut preserves.

SANTORINI: *fassouláta* (bean soup).

SIFNOS: *revíthia soúpa* (chick pea soup).

CHIOS: *chelidonópsaro* (flying fish).

NAXOS: honey, fresh yoghurt and cheeses.

SAMOS: olive oil, muscatel wine.

LESBOS: ouzo, olive oil.

Gourmet Landmarks

As you travel around, keep a look out for the best things of the Greek table. Some you will find only in restaurants. Some you can buy for your beach snacks and country picnics like honey, yoghurt, cheeses and olives. Others you may want to take home as tasty souvenirs like olive oil and ouzo.

Peloponnese

DIAKOFTO: honey.

Choosing Your Island

At different times you will choose different islands, depending on whether you are travelling with or without your family; whether you are looking for action, tranquillity, or cultural sightseeing.

Family Islands

The beaches may be crowded but the hotel and restaurant facilities will be good.

CORFU *10 A2*
Easy access from western Europe, green interior, plentiful beaches.

KOS *17 E2*
Lively favourite of the package tours.

RHODES *20 B2*
Good shopping, bustling beaches.

CRETE *18–19 A–E3*
Efficiently run resorts on big island.

SKIATHOS *12–13 C2*
Fine beaches for lazy days.

SIFNOS *16 B2*
Well-organized beach resorts, good family camping, too.

Quiet Islands
Places where you can most easily escape the high-season crowds, though things change fast as places go in and out of fashion.

ANDROS *16 B1*
Green oasis in Cyclades favoured by well-to-do Greeks, in surprisingly easy reach of Athens.

AMORGOS *17 D2*
Most easterly of Cyclades, spectacular cliffs tower over secluded coves.

ASTYPALAEA *17 D2*
Quiet out-of-the-way spot in Dodecanese. Peaceful villages, remote caves and coves.

SYMI *20 B2*
Tiny, charming refuge just off the coast of Rhodes.

PATMOS *17 D1*
Arid, striking island with splendid monastery, appreciated for its coastal villas.

ITHACA *10 B3*
Odysseus' home is blessed with tranquil fishing ports, good seafood.

Trendy Islands
Popular as much for the fauna—artists, would-be artists and their friends—as for the landscapes.

MYKONOS *16 C1*
Most celebrated, lively, cheerful, with authentic charm that resists the crowds.

IOS *16 C2*
Strictly for young rock'n' roll fans.

SANTORINI *16 C2*
Delightful white houses for private accommodation. Volcanic brown beauty for people who vote Green.

HYDRA *15 D2*
Hangout for painters, led by Athens Fine Arts School.

Culturally Interesting Islands
For people who want to mix some culture with their suntan.

DELOS *16 C1*
Sanctuary of Apollo, day trip from Mykonos.

SANTORINI *16 C2*
Ancient sites of Thera and Akrotiri.

CRETE *18–19 A–E3*
Minoan palaces of Knossos, Phaistos, Malia and Iraklion museum.

RHODES *20 C2*
Capital of Knights of St John, ancient port of Lindos.

PATMOS *17 D1*
Monastery of St John the Divine.

SAMOTHRACE *5 D2*
Shrine of gods of Underworld.

THASOS *4 B2*
Summer drama festival in ancient Greek amphitheatre.

Cool Spots
Greece is hot, but it cannot be said there is no getting away from it. Here are a few refreshing places on the mainland where you can cool off.

MOUNT PILION *11 E1*
Exhilarating alpine atmosphere with handsome chalets and mountain rambles.

MOUNT PARNES *13 D3*
Breath of fresh air for Athenians, with chic little casino resort.

IOANNINA *10 B1*
Intriguing lakeside capital of Epirus, good shopping in town of great character.

METSOVO *10 B1*
Handsome mountain village from which to explore forests of Pindus range.

Caves and Grottoes

The cliffs and mountains are riddled with deep caves perfect for exploration.

PERAMA (EPIRUS) *10 B1*
Veritable forest of illuminated stalagmites and stalactites.

PIRGOS DIROU (PELOPONNESE) *15 C2*
Flatboat tour of underground lake in Mani cliffs.

GROTTO OF NESTOR (PELOPONNESE)
Stalagmites traditionally believed to be petrified cattle of old King Nestor.

NYMPH'S GROTTO (ITHACA) *14 A1*
Where Odysseus rested at journey's end.

DROGARATI (CEPHALONIA) *14 A1*
Concerts held in cave's main chamber amid illuminated stalactites.

DIKTAEAN AND IDAIAN CAVES (CRETE)
Zeus's boyhood homes, challenging hike (check when and whether they are open).

Greece Outside Greece

Continue your explorations in museums back home and find traces of Greece in its ancient colonies.

Museums

Greece's archaeological sites, plundered or rescued, have enriched every nation's knowledge of the mother of western civilization. Here are a few of the most important collections.

LONDON
Elgin's Acropolis marbles in British Museum.

PARIS
Venus de Milo, Victory of Samothrace in Louvre.

ROME
Laocoon group in Vatican.

NAPLES
Hellenistic collection in Archaeological Museum.

REGGIO DI CALABRIA
Riace bronzes attributed to Phidias.

TARANTO
Sculpture, ceramics and jewellery in Museo Nazionale.

LENINGRAD
Classical Greek ceramics, jewellery and art of Black Sea colonies in Hermitage.

MUNICH
Aegina marbles from Temple of Aphaia and Apollo of Tenea in Glyptothek.

EAST BERLIN
Sculpture (notably 6th century B.C.), ceramics in Pergamon.

NEW YORK
Ceramics and sculpture in Metropolitan.

BOSTON
Ceramics and sculpture in Fine Arts.

MALIBU, CALIFORNIA
Lysippus bronze in Getty Museum.

Overseas Colonies

The ancient Greeks left colonies that you will find on other travels.

AMPURIAS, SPAIN
Remains of agora and sanctuary of Asclepius in city of Neapolis.

MARSEILLE
Excavated remains of Greeks' fortified port of Massalia in Jardin des Vestiges.

SICILY
Prosperous settlers built theatres and even greater temples than can be found in Greece itself: Agrigento, Segesta, Selinunte, Syracuse and Taormina.

PAESTUM, SOUTHERN ITALY
Superbly preserved temples to Poseidon and Hera.

CYPRUS
Vital Greek colony for trade in eastern Mediterranean revealed by excavations at Curium, Paphos and Salamis.

TURKEY
Most important colonization was on Asia Minor coast. Visit Sardis, Ephesus, Miletus, Halicarnassus (Bodrum), Pergamum and, of course, Troy.

SEBASTOPOL, USSR
Archaeological site of Greek Black Sea colony of Chersonessos.

Heartland of Greece's Grandest Gifts to Western Civilization

This little elongated triangular peninsula ("Attica" probably derives from an old word meaning promontory) provided the heartbeat for the greatest achievements of the classical world. After centuries of drowsy stagnation, it pulsates again, now the industrial, commercial and intellectual centre of modern Greece. Athens' tentacular metropolitan expansion is at last slowing down to give breathing space to the resorts of the hinterland's mountains and beaches.

Attica's particularity owes much to its self-contained geography. The peninsula thrusts out into the Aegean, bounded on the south by Cape Sounion (with its splendid temple) and on the north by a mountain barrier stretching from the Saronic Gulf to the Euboea Channel. In ancient times, this barrier separated Attica from Boeotia and kept it off the track of most invaders pouring down from the north to the Peloponnese. The fierce Dorians passed it by to allow a gentler, more democratic Ionian civilization to evolve. And if the Athenians could not finally keep out the Persians, they did at least gain time to evacuate the city after the Spartans' courageous effort at Thermopylae and their own navy's holding action at Artemisium. Attica's own vestige of the great Persian Wars can be visited in the plain of Marathon.

Today, despite the radar stations disfiguring their summits, the historic mountains of Parnes, Pentelikon and Hymettos are popular with summer hikers and winter skiers. Pentelikon is still rich in the magnificent white marble that graces Athens' Acropolis, and Hymettos welcomes pilgrims to its Kaisariani monastery.

Another fine Byzantine monastery church is at Daphni, north-west of Athens. Further west, mysticism of a more ancient era pervades the sanctuary of Eleusis. South-east of Athens, you can flee the jumbo jets' flight paths to the smart seaside resort of Vouliagmeni. As lively as ever, Piraeus is the major starting-point for island-hopping, while quiet little Rafina over on the east coast has ferries going out to the Cyclades.

The modern capital sprawls out at the foot of the rocky outcrop of Mount Lycabettus.

Athens   13 D3

The miracle is undeniable. The architectural splendours of the ancient city do valiantly resist the stranglehold of the

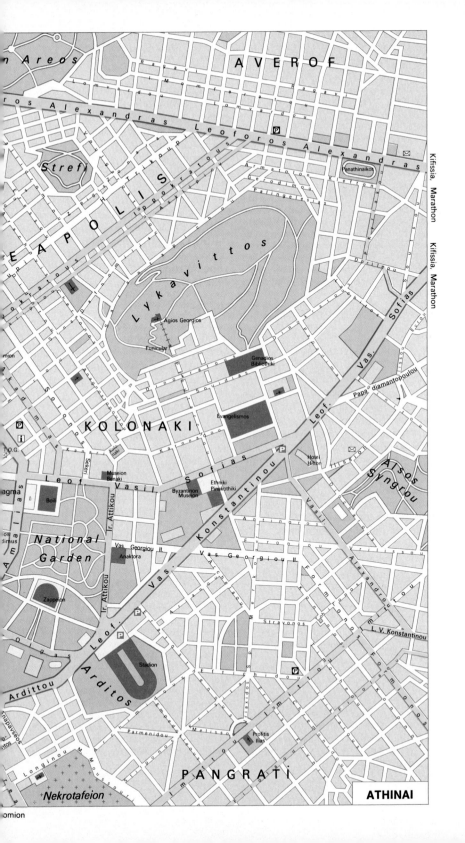

AVEROF

Leoforos Alexandras   Leoforos Alexandras

Ragavi   Ragavi

Panathinaïkós

Strefi

Lykavittos

EAPOLIS

NEAPOLIS

Agios Georgios

Funicular

Gennadios
Bibliothiki

KOLONAKI

Evangelismos

Vas. Sofias

Papa diamantopoulou

Leof. Vas.

Alsos
Syngrou

Hotel
Hilton

Leof. Vas. Konstantinou

Museion
Benaki

Byzantinon
Museion

Ethniki
Pinakothiki

Vasil. Sofias

T.O.G.

National
Garden

Vas. Georgiou II

Anaktora

Vas Georgiou II

Alexandrou

Zappinon

Stravonos

L. V. Konstantinou

Leof.

Arditos

Arditos

Stadion

Ardittou

Parmenidou

Melissou

Profitis
Ilias

PANGRATI

Nekrotafeion

ATHINAI

omion

With an Olive, Please
The Athenians have always claimed their city was founded not by invaders but by an aboriginal population known as Pelasgians. This was underlined by the primeval form, half-man, half-serpent, of their first king, Cecrops, a son of Mother Earth. He acted as judge in the contest between Poseidon and Athena for divine patronage of the city.

The sea-god laid his claim by sticking his trident into the Acropolis hill and causing a well to gush forth seawater. Very nice (still there today, they say, near the site of the Erechtheion temple) but what can you do with seawater? The more practical-minded Athena tapped her spear on the same rock and an olive tree sprouted. "That'll do it," said Cecrops, "the city is yours. How about calling it Athens?"

Greek capital's modern sprawl. The amphitheatre of hills to the north, east and south that provided such a harmonious setting in classical times is now a monstrous atmospheric repository for industrial and traffic pollution eating away at the monumental marble. More than 4,000,000 people (40% of the national population) cram into the metropolitan area with a noise, bustle and fumes that are a million light years away from the fabled serenity summed up in the world's imagination by the name Athens. A new, if belated, national consciousness, supported by the latest techniques of the environmental sciences and the craft of restoration, is fighting back. Meanwhile, the monuments themselves, out on the Acropolis and the Agora or sheltered under glass cases in the museums, seem to retain in their stone enough of their ancient power to make a visit as magical as ever.

But thanks to the verve of the Athenians themselves, the modern city, too, has its attractions. Not, with some exceptions, in its gruesome contemporary architecture, but in the old neighbourhood of the Plaka, refurbished and revitalized in the 1980s. A few august buildings of King Otto's 19th-century capital

survive. To find the Athenians among themselves, head for the food markets and flea markets. And café life everywhere, from broad, bustling Syntagma Square to the tiniest back street, retains all its charm.

Don't even think of driving yourself around the city centre. Leave the hassle to the taxi-drivers or walk, on the shady side of the street. Visit the archaeological sites as early in the morning as possible and save your museum-trips for the heat of the day. After the siesta.

The Acropolis

The historical beginning of the city itself is the logical beginning of any visit today.

The most direct approach is by the 230 bus from Syntagma Square reaching the entrance from the south. Sturdy walkers can take a more interesting route from the back of Syntagma through the old

Give Us Back Our Marbles
In 1801, Thomas Bruce, Lord Elgin, British ambassador to the Sublime Porte, as the Ottoman court at Constantinople was then known, wangled from the Turks what the Greeks have considered a *carte blanche* to plunder the Acropolis. His permit authorized excavation of the ruins, casts and drawings of the sculpture and the right to carry away sculpted figures and inscriptions. At the time, the British envoy argued, much of the monumental masonry was being dismantled by the Athenians themselves for use in their own houses. With an Italian art-scholar to help him pick out the choicest pieces, Elgin took back to London large parts of the Parthenon frieze, attributed to the great sculptor Phidias, and one of the huge Caryatids supporting the Erechtheion temple.

The lord's defenders argue that the British Museum has preserved the artworks from nearly two centuries of war and pollution. Greeks feel that their sovereignty in the matter has been too long ignored, that the very name of the Elgin Marbles betrays an arrogant scorn for the Greeks' rights to the treasures of their own Acropolis, and that their own museums are now perfectly well equipped to receive and protect them.

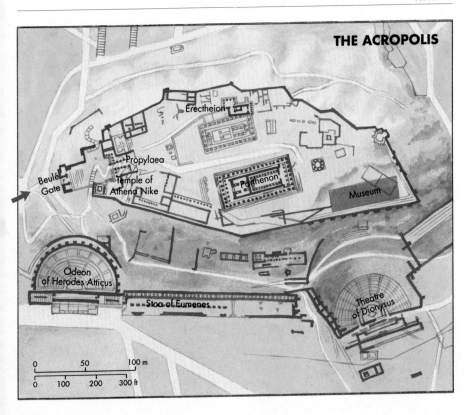

THE ACROPOLIS

Erectheion

Propylaea

Beulé Gate

Temple of Athena Nike

Parthenon

Museum

Odeon of Herodes Atticus

Stoa of Eumenes

Theatre of Dionysus

0   50   100 m
0   100   200   300 ft

Plaka neighbourhood via Mnissikleous Street to view the dramatic north face of the Acropolis. The best time of day, especially for photography, is early morning and late afternoon.

Literally the "city's high point", the Acropolis hill is a great table of grey limestone rock veined with rust-coloured schist rising some 90 m. (300 ft.) above the Attic plain. Inhabited by men of the Stone Age, it became a fortified citadel in the Mycenaean period (13th century B.C.). Seven hundred years later, the tyrant Peisistratus built his palace there, but Athenian democracy made it the exclusive home of the gods. In 480 B.C., the Persians destroyed its temples—and Athena's sacred olive tree—but Pericles replaced them all more splendid than ever.

Despite the additions and ravages of Roman, Byzantine, Turkish or Venetian invaders and the "enlightened" thievery of aristocratic art-lovers, what you see today is essentially Pericles' noble 2,500-year-old conception of a sanctuary for the Greek nation.

Quite apart from the damage caused by air pollution and well-meaning but misguided restoration work with clumsy iron clamps in the 19th century, a major threat to the sanctuary has been the wear of all those millions of tourists' feet clambering unchecked over the site. During the prolonged current period of restoration, moonlight tours have been discontinued and access is now limited to boardwalks and specially paved paths which take you around but not into the temples. No picnics inside the Acropolis limits.

Entrance to the sanctuary is through the **Beulé Gate**, named after the French archaeologist who discovered this

*The Acropolis, symbol and centre of Pericles'
Athenian empire, continues to dominate his capital. The most blasé
of visitors, contemptuous of the urban pollution and unsightly
modern construction surrounding it, cannot but admire its awesome
nobility. Above the demons spewing out their exhaust fumes, the
gods still sit in grandiose residence.*

To the left of the present path is a marble plinth 10 m. (30 ft.) high, which at various times supported a monument of chariots and statues of Antony and Cleopatra. Behind the pedestal is a fine view across to the Temple of Hephaistos on the Agora (see p. 77).

The **Propylaea**, a monumental gatehouse, is the grandest of all surviving secular edifices of ancient Greece. The luxury of its white Pentelic marble aroused protests from Athens' allies when Pericles started to delve into their Delian League defence funds to cover costs. Begun in 437 B.C., it was left unfinished six years later at the outbreak of the Peloponnesian War.

The central building's portico of six Doric columns is flanked by two wings serving as reception halls for visitors to the Parthenon. The north wing became known as the Pinacotheca for paintings described there by Pausanias, a Greek guidebook author of the 2nd century A.D. The Propylaea innovated by adding to the sturdy, unadorned Doric porch a vestibule of more slender Ionic columns with their characteristic scrolled capitals. Restorers have retrieved a fragment of the coffered marble ceiling, originally painted blue with gold stars.

On a terrace over to the right is the graceful Ionic-porticoed **Temple of Athena Nike**. Dedicated to the goddess in her role as "bringer of victory", this work by Callicrates points towards his masterpiece, the Parthenon. During the Venetian invasion of 1687, the little temple was completely dismantled by the Turks to make way for an artillery position on this strategic south-west corner of the bastion. The masonry was gathered up by 19th- and 20th-century archaeologists and painstakingly reassembled, using drawings of another Callicrates temple of similar proportions as their model. Except for cement casts from panels now in the British Museum, sculpted friezes of Athena's legends and Athenian battle-scenes have been rendered "illegible" by years of weathering.

Roman construction of the 3rd century A.D. Its zigzag path replaces a broad straight processional ramp built by Pericles. During the Panathenaic Festival for Athena's birthday, on the night of the midsummer full moon, a wheeled ship bearing a sacred, embroidered saffron robe for the goddess was escorted up the ramp by garlanded priests and priestesses, flute players, cavalrymen and young maidens. She-goats, ewes and heifers brought up the rear—female victims for sacrifice to the virgin goddess.

Oops!
On rare pollution-free days, the Athena Nike temple terrace affords the sea view that poor old Aegeus had while looking out for his son Theseus. He was waiting for the great hero to return from Crete, where he'd gone to fight the Minotaur (see p. 16). The ship carrying the Athenian boys and girls to their ritual sacrifice had put to sea with black sails. If Theseus escaped alive, he was supposed to hoist white sails for his triumphant return. But he had a terrible memory. Not content with "forgetting" to take pregnant Ariadne with him from Naxos, he now neglected to change sails. His father spotted the black sails of death and jumped off the rock in despair. As consolation, his name was given to the Aegean Sea.

The sloping plateau leading up to the Parthenon was originally dominated by a colossal bronze statue of Athena Promachos (the Champion) celebrating the victorious battle of Marathon. Her helmet and spearpoint glinting in the sun served as a welcome landmark for sailors rounding Cape Sounion.

All praise to the goddess, her **Parthenon** (Home of the Virgin) still stands, battered but unbowed by centuries of bombardment and plunder. The wonderment of a first or even umpteenth approach to this most revered of ancient monuments is undimmed by any amount of picture-postcard familiarity.

Inaugurated for the Panathenaic Festival of 438 B.C., the centrepiece of Pericles' new Athens was the supreme architectural achievement of classical Greece. Both shrine and state treasury, it guarded the defence funds of Athens and its allies of the Delian League. The temple's mastermind was Phidias, greatest artistic genius of Athens' golden era. He laid out the overall concept for its construction, executed by Callicrates and Ictinus, and designed the temple's sculptural decoration. He may himself have sculpted part of the frieze between the columns and roof, but his most important personal contribution was a gigantic wooden statue of Athena coated in gold and ivory. She reigned in the temple's inner sanctum, inaccessible to common mortals, until carried off by an unknown plunderer, probably in the 5th century A.D.

A hundred years later, under Emperor Justinian, the Parthenon became the church of Saint Sophia, with galleries added for female worshippers and underground vaults for the bishops' tombs. It was a Catholic cathedral for 13th-century French barons. The Turks used it first as a mosque and then, as Venetian artillery made clear with one well-aimed shell in 1687, a powder-magazine that exploded and burned for 48 hours.

View the temple from the south to take in the peristyle (oblong colonnade) of 46 Doric pillars. The long-gone roof was of marble-tiled wood, but the rest is entirely of Pentelic marble weathering from white to its present honey colour. Sculpture on the pediment gables at either end was largely destroyed by Byzantine church-builders and the Venetian

Mathematical Genius
The marvel of the Parthenon's power and beauty was not achieved just by some intuitive whim. Brilliantly applied mathematics was the subtle servant of architectural harmony, breathing life into the abstract concept of classical equilibrium. The Parthenon is no cold rectangular box of straight drawing-board lines, it has the curves of nature and intricate variations in horizontals and verticals to achieve a semblance of symmetry. The temple's arrangement of 8 columns at each end and 17 along the sides conforms to what was felt to be an ideal width-to-length ratio of 4 to 9—roughly 30 m. (101 ft.) wide to 70 m. (228 ft.) long. Similarly, 4:9 is the ratio between the diameter of each column and the space between any two of them. These spaces vary to accord with the thicker corner columns. Formed by a dozen fluted drums to a height of 10.4 m. (34 ft.), all the columns lean slightly inward and start to swell out a third of the way up (otherwise, an optical illusion would make them look concave). The temple's paving rises gently towards the centre to create a deliberately convex floor.

The celebrated Caryatid Porch is only a small portion of the Erechtheion sanctuary, completed in 405 B.C. just before the final defeat of Athens in the Peloponnesian Wars. It stands on the south side over an earlier temple to Athena. Five of the six original statue-columns are now protected from the elements in the air-conditioned Acropolis Museum.

bombardment, but from ancient accounts and surviving fragments in London and the Acropolis Museum (see p. 74), we know they portrayed the birth of Athena and her contest with Poseidon for control of Athens. Of 92 sculpted metope panels on the entablature topping the columns, only a **western frieze** is still intact and in place. Depicting mythical fights of giants and between Thessalian hunters and brutal centaurs, the friezes were an allegorical celebration of Greek valour against the Persians.

The **Erechtheion** is the last and most complex of the four great monuments on the Acropolis. Dedicated to three deities—Erechtheus, one of the city's mythical snake-man monarchs; Poseidon, to whom Erechtheus is closely associated; and Athena—it is built on two levels over on the north side of the plateau. The Peloponnesian Wars were raging throughout its 15-year construction. It suffered the usual indignities from the barbarians who followed, among them a Turkish military commander who used it as a harem and, particularly voracious here, Lord Elgin. And emerged from it all with considerable grace and elegance.

The temple marks the site of Athena's contest with Poseidon for the patronage of the city (see p. 68). A new, but suitably old-looking olive tree has been planted where Athena's sprouted, outside the west wall, and Poseidon's trident has left marks on a rock hidden in a hole in a corner of the north porch.

The **north porch** is greatly admired for the elegant palm-leaf scrolling of its Ionic columns—one of which was carried off by Elgin, along with part of the marble beam above. Note, too, the doorway's fine moulding, a blue marble frieze and panelled ceiling (all much renovated under the Romans). The sanctuary housed a venerated olivewood statue of Athena, definitely fallen from heaven because, it was said, no Greek artist would have carved anything so primitive.

Most celebrated feature of the Erechtheion is, of course, the southern **Porch of the Caryatids**. Gracefully doing the work of four columns at the front and two at the sides, six maidens unflinchingly hold up the roof, with baskets of fruit protecting their pretty heads from the marble beams. They take their name from the girls of the Spartan village of Caryai, admired for their proud upright posture. But the Athenians gave them long stately Ionian robes rather than the shameless miniskirts favoured by the Spartans. Today's statues are in fact replicas, as five of the originals had to be rescued from the ravages of modern pollution and taken indoors to the Acropolis Museum. The sixth, part of Elgin's loot, is in London.

Save the **Acropolis Museum** for last. In nine galleries, its collection of sculpture covering the whole history of the sacred hill will make more sense after you have visited the sites from which the pieces have been recovered. Just as important for your well-being, its refreshingly cool interior offers welcome respite from that blistering sun.

Galleries 1, 2 and **3** are devoted to pre-classical works of the 6th century B.C., prior to the great building programme of Pericles. You will notice that many of the sculptures have traces of the paint that originally provided bright highlights to costume, face and limbs. Working mainly in limestone, the sculptors were clearly more comfortable with animals, lithe and vigorous creatures from nature or myth, than with human figures, stiff and stylized. Oustanding promise of things to come is the Moschophoros (No. 624), statue of a man purposefully carrying a calf on his shoulders as a gift to the gods. Marble from Mount Hymettos permits better treatment of detail in the man's hair, and more tension and life in the limbs of the man and his animal offering.

Galleries 4 and **5** are principally given over to statues of girls *(kore)*, posted in the temples as handmaidens to the gods. The works here take you to the end of the Archaic period. The somewhat cumbersome Doric robe is gradually replaced by a lighter, more feminine Ionic linen tunic. And you can follow the evolution of the celebrated Archaic Smile, dominating pre-classical statues as an artistic convention rather than psychological observation. This becomes clear when you look at Kore 674, dated around 500 B.C., when the girl's smile is already evanescent, replaced by an expression more intriguingly wistful. Largest of the maidens is the imposing marble Kore of Antenor (681).

Gallery 6 demonstrates a major leap forward in technique expressing a bolder energy. The Kritios Ephebe (698) is an athletic military cadet, agile and confident, released from the heavy archaic posture. No sign of a smile on the melancholy Blond Ephebe (689), so called because of the yellow tints discernible in his hair, or the girl aptly known now as the Boudeuse (609)—French for the Sulker.

Galleries 7 and **8** give excellent close-ups of sculptural fragments from the Parthenon and Erechtheion pediments and friezes. They depict Poseidon, Athena and the Panathenaic procession.

Gallery 9 provides a suitable climax to the museum tour with the originals of the Erechtheion Caryatids. Protected now by air-conditioning, special lighting and a glass screen, they are at last safe, serene but inevitably less exhilarating to behold than in their proper setting.

Ancient Athens

West of the Acropolis are three hills that played a vital role in the city's history. The **Areopagus** *(Ários Págos)* was the hill of Ares, a war god unpopular with the Greeks because he invariably sided with their enemies, notably the Trojans. The hill affords a fine view over the Agora and across to the Propylaea on the Acropolis. The Areopagus was synonymous with the aristocracy's supreme court on the north side of the hill which judged capital crimes of murder and treason. It was here that tragedian Aeschylus set the trial (and acquittal) of Orestes for the murder of his mother. The court became a governing council, a sort of self-perpetuating Senate or House of Lords opposed by Pericles in his fight for democratic government. On the north side of the hill, where St Paul harangued the Athenian sages (see p. 26), are traces of a 16th-century church. It was dedicated to Dionysius the Areopagite, the one council elder who followed Paul back to Rome, where he was converted to Christianity and became Athens' patron saint.

Across the street is the **Pnyx** *(Pníka),* the democratic counterpart to the Areopagus. The terrace of the semi-circular space where the citizens' assembly *(ecclesia)* was held was on a higher level that nosy nobles could not look down on its deliberations. The very impressive **Acropolis Sound and Light show** is held on the Pnyx with an English-language commentary (for times enquire at the tourist information office in the National Bank building, Karagiórgi Servías 2, just off Syntagma).

see p. 26

Caught Red-Handed

With the decline of Athenian democracy, citizens had to be paid to ensure their attendance at the Pnyx, or "crowded place". People passed through a narrow entrance hemmed in by ropes daubed with wet red paint. Thus anyone trying to duck out of his civic duty bore a tell-tale mark which disqualified him from collecting his attendance fee.

The tree-covered **Mousion**, hill of the Muses, is also known as Lófos Filopáppou, after Syrian prince, Roman consul and Athens' benefactor of the 2nd century A.D., Antiochos Philopappos. His tomb is marked by a marble monument. Always an important strategic emplacement for artillery, it provided the Venetian Morosini with his clear shot at the Parthenon in 1687. In World War I, Greek royalists manned the hill to fire on Allied forces, and in 1967 it was a key position in the Colonels' coup d'état. The best shots today are with a camera lens zooming in on the Acropolis or over the city to the Bay of Phaleron and Piraeus harbour.

The **Theatre of Dionysus** stands almost directly below the Parthenon. It was built in the 5th century B.C. to stage the tragedies of Aeschylus, Sophocles and Euripides and the comedies of Aristophanes. Apart from a front row of 67 marble "thrones" for V.I.P.s, the Greeks of classical times—17,000 in a full house—had to content themselves with terraced seating of beaten earth. It was the Romans who installed the hemisphere of marble and limestone. The carved relief of scenes from Dionysus's life is the façade of a raised stage. Next to the auditorium, the double-tiered colonnade of the **Stoa of Eumenes** (2nd century B.C.) was a sheltered promenade for theatregoers before and after the performance (always in the daytime). The original Stoa linked up with a smaller theatre seating 5,000, the **Odeon of Herodes Atticus**. Herodes was a wealthy

Athenian elected to the Roman senate who dedicated the theatre to his deceased wife in A.D. 161. The huge triple-tiered arched façade is typical of Roman theatres. Modern restoration has covered the limestone seating with white Pentelic marble for operas and concerts in the Athens Summer Festival (see p. 256).

At a bend in the main road between the Acropolis and Syntagma, **Hadrian's Arch** (A.D. 132) marked the border between old Athens and the Roman emperor's new city, Hadrianopolis. On the side facing the Acropolis is the inscription: "This is Athens, ancient city of Theseus." The almost petulant vanity of the emperor becomes apparent on the other façade with its inscription: "This is the city of Hadrian and not of Theseus." But he did deserve the ancients' gratitude for completing the great **Temple of Olympian Zeus**, of which only 15 of its 104 majestic Corinthian columns remain. It measured 205 by 129 m. (672 by 423 ft.), the largest temple in Greece, though there were bigger ones in the colonies in Sicily and Asia Minor. Construction of Olympian Zeus had begun under tyrant Peisistratus in the 6th century B.C. It was conceived as a purely Doric edifice. The Corinthian columns were added by Antiochus IV Epiphanes 400 years later. Hadrian's finishing touches included a gigantic statue of Zeus modelled on Phidias' work for Olympia (see p. 239) and one only slightly less colossal of himself.

At first glance, the **Agora** (bus No. 230 to Tissíon terminus) looks like an inexplicable mess of ancient rubble of which only the most hardened archaeology buff could hope to make sense. But with an effort of imagination, it is not impossible to recall that the area sprawling out below the northern ramparts of the Acropolis was "downtown", throbbing heart of the ancient city and the unmistakable ancestor of every city centre and village square in Greece.

From the entrance on Odós Adrianoú, you look down on broken pillars, walls and paving stones that once were shops,

Potted History of Ostracism

Most unprepossessing but nonetheless intriguing exhibits in the Agora museum are shards of pottery *(ostraka)* on which Athenians wrote the name of any prominent citizens who had become unpopular enough to warrant ostracism. By majority vote among at least 6,000 participants, the ostracized man was given 10 days to leave the country for 10 years, after which time he could return to Athens to recover his citizenship, property and honour. Among the most famous to be ostracized were Pericles' father Xanthippus, discredited as a politician but amnestied as a general to fight the Persians; Themistocles, creator of Athens' naval power who was felt to have grown too big for his boots; and Thucydides, who profited from his exile (for losing a battle) to write his historical masterpiece, *The Peloponnesian War*. One important ostracism-candidate, deservedly named Aristides the Just, was asked by an illiterate citizen to help him write down the name "Aristides" on his pottery shard. The statesman obliged but asked why the fellow wished to ostracize him. "Because," he replied, "I'm tired of hearing him called the Just."

banks, market, mint, council chamber, schools, libraries, gymnasium, concert hall, dance hall, temples, the courthouse where Socrates was said to have been tried and the prison in which he committed suicide. A panoramic pictorial reconstruction helps you visualize and situate the original buildings.

Over in the south-west corner is the Horos, marked with the inscription "I am the boundary stone of the Agora". Entering at this point, all were expected to be ritually purified, for the Agora was the sacred centre of the city. Strolling among the ruins, you may catch a distant echo of the major activity here, as is still true of any comparable place around the country today: talk. Near the boundary stone, Socrates held court at the shop of Simon the cobbler, a literate fellow who, long before Plato, began writing down the sage's dialogues. St Paul wandered everywhere arguing with all and sundry. Stoics put up with the man they called "the babbler". To the Epicureans, of course, it was a pleasure. Pericles perfectly defined the rules of the Agora game: "We do not say that a man who takes no interest in politics is a man who minds his own business; we say that he has no business here at all."

The long porticoed gallery closing off the east side of the Agora is a reconstitution of the 2nd century B.C. **Stoa of Attalos** which served as a shady promenade and pavilion from which to watch the Panathenaic Festival procession. It was built as a **museum** in the 1950s by the American School of Classical Studies in Athens, which has carried out excavations of the Agora since 1931. The museum assembles the major archaeological finds from the site: vases, coins, household utensils and an enormous bronze shield captured from the Spartans.

On a small hill above the Agora is the beautiful Doric-columned **Temple of Hephaistos** *(Naós Iféstou)*, first of the major temples in Pericles' building programme after the Persian wars. Although it is more popularly known as the Thesion, because of the Theseus legends portrayed on its frieze (along with others of Hercules), it was in fact dedicated to Hephaistus, goldsmith of the gods and god of all metalworkers. Archaeologists have uncovered traces of iron foundries and workshops near the temple, and 2,500 years later, metalworkers are still sweating away in shops just the other side of the railway tracks. This is the best preserved of Athens' temples, more slender than the Parthenon with its graceful 34-column peristyle. Not the least of the temple's charming features is its garden with myrtles, pomegranates, olives and cypresses, all trees that graced the garden in Roman times.

West of the Agora (along Odós Ermoú) is the **Keramikos** where the ancient Athenians buried their dead, most notably the fallen in battle, in elaborately sculpted tombs. It was here that Pericles made his famous funeral oration for soldiers killed in the first battles of the Peloponnesian War. His exaltation of the democratic values for which they had died became his own political testament (he died a year later): "I declare that our city is an education to Greece. In my opinion each single one of our citizens, in all the manifold aspects of his life, is able to show himself the rightful lord and owner of his own person, and to do this with exceptional grace and exceptional versatility." Some of the best of the sculpture, along with fine funeral vases, are displayed in the cemetery's museum.

Plaka

After a few disastrous years as a tawdry tourist-trap in the 1960s and 70s, the city's most ancient residential area, just north-east of the Acropolis, has retrieved its authentic old charm. Sleepy haven of tranquillity by day, it livens up at sunset, without the blare of now largely banished amplified bouzouki and disco music.

Ancient ruins, Byzantine churches and folk museums recall the neighbourhood's history, but its main charm is the

Urban Oasis

In Athens' chequered modern history, the Plaka neighbourhood is a rare success story of urban conservation. For centuries, it was the nucleus of the village backwater to which the city had dwindled after the departure of the Romans. (The name Plaka is variously interpreted as "flat place", in opposition to the Acropolis, or just "old place" from the Albanian word *pliaka*.)

Patrician villas with handsome garden courtyards mushroomed in the building boom after King Otto reestablished Athens as Greece's capital in 1834. Miraculously, they survived the next building boom that razed most of the 19th-century city after World War II. But a third boom, of mass tourism, nearly proved fatal with the invasion of rowdy bars and cheap but not-so-cheap nightclubs. An alliance of wealthy businessmen with the socialist government of the 1980s turfed out the riffraff and renovated the houses—now chic residences for the 19th-century patricians' successors for whom not even the Greeks have found a word more attractive than Yuppies.

THREE WISE MEN

Just who were the first movers and shakers of our modern thought?

In the Western world, the Greeks were pioneers in formulating ideas about truth independent of a theological creed. They sought the meaning of life not through magic or superstition but in the patient application of man's own reason. The process had begun around 600 B.C. over on the coast of Asia Minor, among men of Miletus speculating on the nature of the universe, probably inspired by contact with Babylon and Egypt. Intellectual method became more refined in Athens of the classical age. Three men stood out.

Socrates (c.470–399 B.C.)

According to traditional accounts, his father was an Athenian sculptor and mother a midwife. As fashioners of life in its ideal and real forms, they were neatly appropriate parents for the man whom the Greeks themselves acknowledged as the "father" of philosophy. It might also be said that his notoriously cantankerous wife, Xanthippe, was an admirable test of the patience necessary for his reasoning.

He is believed to have himself practised as a sculptor for a time. He also served as an infantryman in the army and never had much money. His principal activity was as an unpaid teacher of aristocratic youths

Socrates

in the Agora. In a society where duplicity was the instrument of success, Socrates' personal integrity won their unstinting admiration. His pupil Plato depicts him as ugly but physically powerful with considerable personal charm. More than any brilliant insight into the meaning of existence, his great philosophical legacy, set out in Plato's *Socratic Dialogues*, was his scrupulous method of intellectual inquiry, a perpetual questioning of all certainties. With his young disciples, he explored different avenues to truth by his famous technique of "Socratic irony". By confessing his own ignorance and constant cross-questioning of the other persons' opinions, he exposed their inconsistencies and faults of logic.

The 30 Tyrants who seized power after the collapse of Athenian democracy brought Socrates to trial in 399 B.C. He was charged with having introduced alien gods and corrupting the youth of Athens. According to Platos' account, Socrates gave self-mocking testimony of the Delphic oracle's statement that he, Socrates, was the wisest of all men. This was true, he said, since the Delphic oracle never lies, but only in the sense that Socrates, unlike other more prominent men, had the wisdom to recognize how little he knew, if anything at all. When found guilty, he chose the option of taking poisonous hemlock. He said he faced death with the serenity of a man who "has sought the pleasures of knowledge and has arrayed the soul not in some strange attire but in its own proper jewels—temperance, justice, courage, nobility and truth."

Plato (c.428–347 B.C.)

Son of a distinguished Athenian family, Plato had a more aristocratic turn of mind than his master, Socrates. The latter's death and the rule of the 30 Tyrants turned him away from a career in politics. He was convinced no state could thrive until philosophers became kings or kings philosophers. He spent some time in Syracuse, Sicily, hoping to make its tyrant Dionysius II his ideal philosopher king. But court intrigue made it impossible.

In about 387 B.C., he founded a school near the grove of Academe on the outskirts of Athens. Here he hoped to form young

Aristotle

Plato

men in science and philosophy as essential training for the service of the state. How this might work was set out in his utopian *Republic*. Convinced that democracy could only engender disorder, he divided society into three classes: workers, soldiers and rulers. For the last-named, he conceived a rigorous educational system—gymnastics from 17 to 20, mathematics 20 to 30 and the study of ideas 30 to 35. The best pupils were to become active leaders from 35 to 50 and then to return to study.

The Republic was one of the Socratic Dialogues which Plato wrote to expound the master's dialectic method of constant questioning of all assumptions, but principally to test his own theories. Man's senses, he argued, are an obstacle to understanding ideal beauty and truth. Ordinary man lived in a state of ignorance chained in a dim cave world of shadows. The philosopher casts off his chains and progresses through dialectics towards the light of day—knowledge.

Plato's Academy continued nine centuries after his death, and Platonic theories of universal ideas have had continuous influence on the thought of Judaism, Christianity, Islam and Renaissance Humanism.

Aristotle (384–322 B.C.)
Born in Macedonian Chalkidiki, Plato's star pupil at the Academy was the son of a doctor. Bald and thin-legged, Aristotle had a taste for fine clothes and jewellery. He spoke with a lisp and his small beady eyes had a formidable mocking expression.

Though he never became a statesman himself, he did use what he learned at Plato's training school for the élite in preparing Alexander to rule an empire. He taught the 13-year-old boy Homer, Greek drama and some elements of political science.

Aristotle was more interested in the practical sciences than abstract theory. Just as Socrates and Plato had developed dialectics for philosophical inquiry, so Aristotle laid down the ground rules for scientific method. He travelled through the northern Aegean in search of specimens for his favourite science of zoology. Alexander financed his museum and sent him contributions gathered by his hunters and fishermen from all over the empire. Paying tribute to his classification system, Charles Darwin said: "Linnaeus and Cuvier [zoologists of the 18th and 19th centuries] have been my two gods, but they were mere schoolboys to old Aristotle."

At his school and library in Athens, Aristotle organized large-scale research into music, theology and the other sciences. He extended his passion for classification from animals to constitutional history, listing all the various state-forms of Greek cities. More realistic than Plato, he saw all political systems as subject to the selfishness of the rulers: monarchy becomes tyranny, aristocratic rule deteriorates into unscrupulous oligarchy, and democracy into vicious demagogy. Neither aristocrat nor democrat, he himself might be labelled a middle-class liberal. He was a man who preferred common sense to dogma and extremes.

unique atmosphere of the streets themselves, narrow winding lanes, often climbing steep stairways to follow the original paths of ancient Athens. Amid all the charted wonders of the city, Plaka is a place of serendipity, the chance discovery of concealed beauties: vines curling around a pink-, ochre- or whitewashed villa with blue or lime-green shutters, a garden of hibiscus, jasmine, roses and a fragrant pot of holy basil. Early morning is the best time to explore. In the evening, you can return to enjoy the open-air cafés and restaurants and souvenir shops.

Without formally defined boundaries, Plaka roughly covers the area south of the Odós Ermoú shopping street. But the heart is closer to the Acropolis. You may well prefer your own adventurous itinerary through the Plaka maze. If not, we suggest the following: starting out from Syntagma, head down Odós Filellínon and turn right into Kidathinéon. The houses here were built in the earliest years of the Bavarian monarchy. At No. 17, now the **Museum of Greek Folk Art** (*Mousío Laïkís Ellinikís Téchnis*), see the fine display of Byzantine gold, silver and jewellery and embroidery from the islands.

Further down Kidathinéon, turn left into Farmáki to visit the 12th-century **church of St Catherine** (*Agía Ekateríni*) set in a sunken palm-shaded courtyard. In front, two Ionic columns, believed to be the remains of a Roman bath, were incorporated in an earlier church on the site.

Nearby is the **Monument of Lysicrates** (*Mnimíon Lisikrátous*), erected to commemorate a prize won in 334 B.C. by a boys' chorus. Lysicrates was their sponsor. It is celebrated in classical architecture as the first building to make exterior use of Corinthian columns. The six columns support a dome formed from a single marble block carved to imitate fish-scale tiling. On top stood the prize, a three-legged bronze cauldron known as a tripod. A frieze shows Etruscan pirates

being turned into dolphins by Dionysus, at whose festival the prize was won. Several such monuments once lined the Street of Tripods (Odós Tripódon). This one was incorporated in a monastery (later burned down), where Lord Byron stayed in 1810, sitting among the columns to write part of his *Childe Harold*.

Follow Epichármou off to the left from Tripódon towards **Anafiotika**, a remarkable whitewashed village within the city. To cope with Athens' severe housing shortage after Greek independence, a

The Roman-era Tower of the Winds was in reality a water clock. This major landmark of the Plaka district measured the passage of time by the level of water rising and falling in a cylinder housed inside the white marble tower. In medieval times it was imagined to be the tomb of Socrates. The Turks used it as a convent.

law granted occupancy to anyone who built a house—or at least managed to get the roof up—between sunset and sunrise. First to occupy were two stonemasons from the little Aegean island of Anafi (east of Santorini). Other Anafiot masons followed, building and restoring houses and churches in their native style. Today, Anafiots living here on the heights of Plaka outnumber the 300-odd residents back on their island. One of the churches, at the top of the village, **Ágios Simeón**, is guarded by a stately cypress and offers a splendid view of Athens.

Further west, Odós Klepsídras takes you over to the **Roman Agora**. Over to your right is Plaka's best-known landmark, the **Tower of the Winds** *(Aérides)*, built by astronomer Andronicus in the 1st century B.C. It once housed an elaborate water clock fed by a spring on the Acropolis and was topped by a triton—half man, half fish—serving as weather vane. Bas-reliefs on each side of the octagonal marble tower represent the eight points of the compass and the corresponding wind: Notos, the rainy south wind, pours water from an urn; Zephyr, west wind heralding spring, scatters flowers; and, all too familiar to summer visitors, Sciron, the searing north-west meltemi wind of July and August, carries a bronze brazier of charcoal.

In the marketplace north of the tower, the **Turkish Mosque** was built to celebrate the Ottoman capture of Athens in 1456. Minus its minaret, it now houses an archaeology workshop.

Just four Doric columns remain from the original entrance to the Roman Agora, the **Gate of Athena Archegetis**, built in the 1st century B.C. One of the door supports, protected by a rusty iron grille, is inscribed with Emperor Hadrian's edict taxing olive oil which cast doubt on just how much of a Grecophile he really was.

North of the old Roman marketplace, a colourful modern **flea market** flourishes on Platía Monastiráki and along Odós Pandrósou, site of the old Turkish bazaar. It is most active on Sunday mornings when the hurdy-gurdy plays a welcome change from eternal bouzouki cassettes of *Zorba the Greek*. Even if you are not in the market for antiques or old brass, embroidery, rugs or leatherware, the stalls of fresh drinks and cool coconut should be very welcome. The square's monastery church dates back to the 10th century but suffers from its modern restoration. More interesting is the 18th-century **Tzistarakis Mosque**, built with the marble of one of the massive Corinthian columns from the Olympic Zeus temple. After the usual retaliatory removal of its minaret in 1821, it was commandeered first as a prison and then as a Folk Art Museum. Climb up to the open loggia for a good view over the Plaka neighbourhood.

On your way back to Syntagma along Pandrósou, you will pass the 19th-century **Mitrópolis**, cathedral of the Greek Orthodox Church after the split with Constantinople. The hybrid curiosity, allegedly inspired in its interior by Venice's basilica of St Mark, was built from parts of some 70 other demolished churches. If you return to Syntagma by way of Odós Ermoú, you'll see the **Kapnikaréa**, a Byzantine church in the middle of the busy street.

Modern Athens

Get your bearings of the modern city with the fine panoramic view from the 277 m. (908 ft.) summit of **Mount Lycabettus** *(Likavittós)*. Take the cable-car from Odós Ploutárchou in Kolonaki. Planted there in the Attic plain, the conical peak was created by a rock that Athena dropped when frightened by an owl on her way to building the Acropolis.

At the very top is a 19th-century chapel dedicated to St George, scene of a candlelight procession on the eve of the Orthodox Easter. Just below it, a visitors' pavilion provides refreshments and an unbeatable view (at least early in the morning before the traffic smog rises) of the Acropolis and the city over to

Piraeus harbour. On the terraces, consult the orientation maps in marble indicating all the important sights. Cannons on the western slopes are fired on Greek Independence Day (March 25).

The hub of the modern city is **Syntagma** (Constitution) **Square** *(Platía Sintágmatos)*. Its name refers to the charter of Greek statehood voted in 1844. Big business has its offices here, the airlines their agencies. Miraculously, orange trees, palms and cypresses survive the exhaust fumes of traffic from the eight streets that converge on Syntagma. On the square's smart (and so more expensive) terrace cafés, take the pulse of Athens' big and little decision-makers who, even in the shade, hide behind dark glasses. They take a solitary coffee with their morning newspaper, rendezvous with their lovers or business partners at midday, disappear for the afternoon siesta and return to argue politics and divorce settlements in the evening. The square boasts the city's grandest hotel, the **Grande Bretagne**, a monument in its own right, noble example of the city's 19th-century neoclassicism. Treat yourself to a drink in the plush bar of what was originally the home of Danish architect Theophil von Hansen, designer of Athens' University, Library and Academy.

Across the east side of the square is the national **Parliament** *(Voulí)*, until 1935 the royal palace. Sentries *(évzones)* in traditional white uniform guard a memorial to the nation's unknown soldier in the forecourt. A formal changing of this Republican Guard is held on Sundays at 11 a.m. Engraved on the monument as an epitaph are texts from Pericles' funeral oration in 430 B.C., honouring Athenians killed in the first year of the Peloponnesian War.

Beyond the flower stalls and members' entrance to the Parliament, take refuge from the downtown traffic with the ducks and peacocks in the **National Garden** *(Ethnikós Kípos)*. You will find blessedly cool shade in this quiet oasis of flowers, greenery and ornamental ponds.

The busts are of modern Greek poets and political heroes. Open-air concerts and plays are performed at the Záppion exhibition halls.

Nestling in the hollow of Arditos Hill is the marble **Olympic Stadium**, where the first modern Olympics were staged in 1896. It stands on the site of an ancient stadium built in 330 B.C. for the games of the Panathenaic Festival. It has the traditional U-shape to be seen at Olympia and Delphi, with a length of 184 m. (about 606 ft.), i.e. the ancient Greek measure of one *stadion*.

North-west from Syntagma, take the broad avenue, **Panepistimíou,** past the most imposing of the city's surviving 19th-century neoclassical buildings devoted to the nation's higher education. These piles of Pentelic marble pay rather heavy-handed tribute to ancient Greece, jolting modern taste with their façades painted and gilded in the classical tradition. Distant echo of the Acropolis's Erechtheion, the Ionic-columned Academy *(Akadimía)* has statues of Plato and Socrates sitting rather uncomfortably at the entrance. It stands next to the University *(Panepistímion)*, where British visitors recognize a statue of Gladstone and Greeks point out their own great statesman, Ionannis Kapodistrias, assassinated (by Greek rivals) in the fight for Independence. Beyond is the National Library *(Vivliothíki)*, with nearly a million books and manuscripts, among which you may be shown beautifully hand-illuminated versions of the Gospels of the 10th and 11th centuries.

Opposite the University, take Odós Koraí over to Klafthmónos or Sobbing Square, so named because citizens came here to register their complaints with King Otto. His modest two-storey palace with a balcony on the south-east side of the square is now a **Museum of the City of Athens**, illustrating his reign. But the more important attraction here is the 12th-century church of **Ágii Theódori**, the finest of Athens' few Byzantine monuments.

Stadíou's broad avenue of shops takes you on to **Platía Omónia**, linking the capital to its mainland provinces. Its streets run north to Thebes, Macedonia and Thrace; south to Piraeus; east to Marathon and west to Corinth and the Peloponnese. Main station, too, of the municipal subway, this is where Greeks pour in from the countryside and mill around the subterranean shopping centre.

South of Omónia are the bustling **city markets**. Nothing tragic about the fruit, vegetable and herb markets on Sophocles and Euripides Streets. Poultry, rabbits and other wild game hang out on Armodíou. Liveliest of all are the fish and meat markets along Eólou and Athinás. The counters of these covered refrigerated halls are of course in finest marble.

Amid the city's largely unimaginative, not to say downright hideous, buildings of the 20th century, two modern edifices, coincidentally both American commissions, are worth your attention. East of the National Garden on Vasilíssis Sofías Street, the white-façaded **Hilton Hotel** is a handsome work by Greek architect Vassiliadis. Notice the "graffiti" painted by Iannis Moralis to symbolize Greek culture. Even more distinguished is the **United States Embassy** (1961), one of the last designs of Bauhaus master Walter Gropius. His thoroughly modern structure renders homage to classical Greece with a peristyle of marble-faced columns surrounding a two-storey steel-and-glass rectangular core.

National Archaeological Museum

At Odós Patisíon 44, not far from Omónia, is the great treasury of ancient Greek art. Though the exterior is understandably neoclassical, the museum provides inside an admirably modern setting, easy of access for works from all over the Greek world.

With the exceptions of Crete, Delphi, Olympia and Thessaloniki, all archaeological finds were brought here. But an

increasingly decentralized cultural policy will leave works in regional museums close to their original sites. Thus, the Thera frescoes (see p. 86) are due to be removed one day to a museum on Santorini.

From prehistoric times to Greece under Roman rule, the exhibits cover some 7,000 years. Give yourself at least half a day to see the highlights.

Mycenaean Room (No. 4). Of all the treasures recovered in 1876 from the royal chamber tombs at Mycenae, the most

84

*I*t is once more respectable, even chic, to live in the
Plaka. The noise of its formerly notorious bars and nightclubs has
been eliminated or subdued to preserve a pleasant residential
neighbourhood. Stroll around the lanes for a rare moment of
tranquillity before returning to shop or dine here after the siesta.

That Takes the Apple

Donating a golden apple as the prize, the gods let Paris organize a beauty contest between Hera, Athena and Aphrodite anyway he liked. So the young Trojan herdsman told them to undress. Aphrodite was first to strip. Hera complained she had kept on her magic girdle, which made everyone fall in love with her. Aphrodite agreed to remove it, "as long as Hera takes off her helmet. She looks ghastly without it."

To stop the bitchiness, Paris asked to see them separately. Hera was first, slowly turning around to show off her splendid figure. She promised he would rule all Asia and be the richest man alive if he gave her the prize.

He refused her bribe and called Athena. In typical pragmatic, soldierly manner, she told him it was only common sense to declare her the winner and promised him victory in all his battles. Paris told her he was not very keen on war, but would not hold that against her.

Last and determined not to be least, Aphrodite moved so very, very close to Paris that they almost touched. "What's a handsome young fellow like you doing tending cattle? Find yourself a real lady, like Helen of Sparta. She's almost as beautiful and passionate as I am, and yours for the asking."

Aphrodite got the golden apple, Paris got Helen, and Troy got a lot of trouble.

---

famous is Agamemnon's gold death mask (16th century B.C.). Scholars immediately insist there is no proof or even historical likelihood that this is the facial imprint left by the man who led the Greeks to Troy. But look at the kingly brow, haughty mouth with moustache and beard, and you may share with its finder, German archaeologist Heinrich Schliemann, the conviction that here indeed is Homer's sad and stubborn hero. Or a close relative.

Look, too, for the grand silver bull's head with golden horns and rosette showing it ready for sacrifice. And the two gold Vaphio cups (15th century B.C.) from a tomb near Sparta, portraying the capture of a wild bull in a net, luring him with a cow and then roping him in.

Room 9. Among marble sculpture of the Archaic era is the exquisite Attic maiden Phrasikleia (540 B.C.)—her name is on the base, along with the sculptor's signature, Aristion of Paros.

Room 13. Here the Kroisos tomb-statue of 525 B.C. is a more sturdy and fleshy figure than earlier Archaic work.

Room 15. One of the museum's proudest possessions is the towering bronze Poseidon (460 B.C.) poised to hurl his trident. Probably looted 2,000 years ago, the god took a Roman ship down to his watery realm and was found on the seabed off Artemision (at the northern tip of Euboea island) in 1928.

A fine sculpted Eleusian frieze shows the goddess Demeter giving a youth ears of corn to initiate him and all mankind into the mysteries of cultivation.

Room 21. Found at the same time as Poseidon, the bronze Jockey of Artemision (2nd century B.C.) is urging on his steed with all the excitement of the race. Only spoilsport art-scholars suggest that the boy is much too small in scale for his horse and was originally part of another sculpture.

Room 28. Another Roman theft, in the infamous plundering of Corinth (see p. 220), the Youth of Antikythira (340 B.C.) is a superb study in grace and balance, left arm swinging free and right leg lightly poised. He is thought to be young Paris offering the prize apple to Aphrodite.

Room 30. Later Hellenistic bronzes here show a keenly observed psychology, notably the head of a philosopher (3rd century B.C.) with his furrowed brow and piercing gaze framed by unruly hair and beard. From Olympia comes the bronze head of a boxer, complete with cauliflower ears, flattened nose and championship laurels.

Room 48 (upper floor). Excavations at Akrotiri on Santorini delivered the Thera frescoes from 3,500 years of burial under volcanic ash that shrouded the island's Minoan civilization. With neighbouring Crete's own treasures kept in its museum at Iraklion (see p. 118), Athens has a rare opportunity to see the life and

Zeus, 200 B.C.—father of the gods and of men.

Other Museums

The **Benáki Museum** (corner of Vasilíssis Sofías and Koumbári streets) was installed in the family mansion of a wealthy Greek art lover. His eclectic collections include Mediterranean art of prehistoric times, Byzantine art, traditional Greek costume and jewellery, and historical memorabilia particularly from the war of Independence.

The **Byzantine Museum** (Vas. Sofías 22) houses in an elegant villa a vast collection of sacred sculpture, panel paintings and jewellery from the 9th to the 15th centuries and icons from the great revival of the 14th and 15th centuries. Three rooms present reproductions of churches from the earliest (5th century), middle and post-Byzantine eras.

The **National Gallery of Painting** (Vas. Konstantínou 50) presents Greek painting of the 19th and 20th centuries, much influenced by the classical, Byzantine and folk art traditions. France has donated a series of paintings by Picasso, Utrillo and Picabia to honour Greece's liberation in 1945.

The **War Museum** (corner of Vas. Sofías and Rizári) is the cultural contribution of the Colonels' military dictatorship from 1967 to 1974. Models of ships and aircraft, weapons, uniforms, flags and medals trace Greek warfare from Mycenae to World War II.

grace of that culture. Scenes include a naval expedition, a naked fisherman carrying strings of fish, boys boxing, a spring landscape with clumps of lilies growing in the ravines and swallows darting in and out.

Also on the upper floor, the **Vase Collection** traces Greek ceramics from the first painted pottery of the Bronze Age (2000 B.C.) through the stylized Geometric patterns (10th to 7th centuries B.C.) and Attica's rather stiff black-figure vases (6th century B.C.) to the triumph of classical Athens' lively red-figure vases of the 5th century B.C.

Attica 13 D3

The region's main attractions are each an easy day excursion from Athens. Some of them can be combined in one long day's tour, for example, visiting the temple at Cape Sounion in the morning and then relaxing on the beach at Vouliagmeni in the afternoon. Or, even better, reverse that with a swim in the morning, siesta after lunch and then head down to the cape for its magnificent sunset.

However you plan your trips, start out as early as possible. Except for the mountain resorts, it's only going to get hotter as you go, and archaeological sites have little shade.

Piraeus *(Pireéfs)*   *13 D3*

Three superb natural harbours, for commerce, fishing and leisure, sustain the town's position as the Mediterranean's third most active port city (after Marseille and Genoa). Piraeus has a population of half a million when considered independently of metropolitan Athens. And that is the way it has always preferred to be considered. Founded in prehistoric times by Minyan warriors, it built its strength in classical times on its cosmopolitan population—Egyptian, Phoenician and Jewish merchants, as well as the boldest entrepreneurs from Greek overseas colonies. Their descendants sit today in gleaming marble banks and shipping offices, eclipsing the world of tipsy philosopher-seamen and golden-hearted tarts made famous by Melina Mercouri's film, *Never On Sunday.*

But the town remains a delight for anyone lured by the romance of ships big and small. Built on a peninsula thrusting into the Saronic Gulf, the town's chequerboard street plan was laid out by Pericles' urbanist Hippodamus (behind the railway station, Platía Ippodámias pays him tribute). On the peninsula's west shore where the town hall clock provides a traditional meeting-place for travellers, the bustling **Great Harbour** serves international freighters, cruise liners and major inter-island vessels. Behind the town hall, the boisterous

bazaar draws a colourful crowd of islanders stocking up with vegetables, fruit and spices.

Across the peninsula on the east shore, **Zéa Harbour** is the haven for luxury yachts and fishermen, nimbly mending their nets with fingers and toes serving as a loom. The **Nautical Museum** (on Aktí Themistokléous) traces maritime history from models of ancient Athenian triremes to 20th-century submarine conning towers and torpedoes. Graphic displays provide detailed explanations of the great naval battles of Salamis against the Persians (480 B.C.) and Lepanto (Nafpaktos, 1571) pitting papal forces against the Turks. Incorporated in the museum building is part of the Long Wall fortifications built by Themistocles to protect Piraeus and Athens against Persian and Spartan attack.

Further east is the most attractive of the three harbours, **Tourkolímano** (officially changing its name on signposts to Mikrolímano), where the sleekest Mediterranean racing yachts have their berths. Its basin describes an almost perfect circle with only the narrowest of outlets. Many of the region's best seafood restaurants line the quay and provide delightful vantage points from which to watch the bobbing masts and brightly coloured sails and pennants.

Ancient shipwrecks around the harbours have yielded some surprising art treasures to stock a fine **Archaeological Museum** (Chariláou Trikoúpi 31). Pride of place, on the upper floor, goes to three magnificent bronzes dredged up in 1959:

*P*oseidon's temple on the promontory of Cape Sounion remains a handsome landmark for sailors rounding the Attic peninsula on their way to or from Piraeus. A beacon was lit on this clifftop to signal Agamemnon's return home from Troy.

a stunningly graceful Apollo (530 B.C.) as handsome as his legend; Athena (350 B.C.) with Athenian owls and griffins on her helmet; and the huntress Artemis with a quiver on her shoulder.

Drive up the **Kastela Hill** cliff-road for a superb view over the whole peninsula and out to the Saronic Islands (see p. 244).

Attic Peninsula   *13 D3*

Athenians spend their weekends at the seaside resorts down the coast, beyond the international airport. Weekday traffic is much easier. Elegant **Vouliagmeni**, just 22 km. (14 mi.) from the capital, has some beautiful bathing beaches around its peninsula with the not-to-be-snubbed advantage of shady pines. At the marina, the local yacht club, you can take lessons in water-skiing.

Go down to the southern tip of the coast to **Cape Sounion**. On a promontory overlooking the Aegean, stand by the marble columns of **Poseidon's Temple** (c. 440 B.C.) to watch the sun set or rise among the islands. The best way to catch both is to camp overnight. Only 16 of the temple's original 34 Doric columns still stand. The Ionic friezes have been largely obliterated by time but are believed to have depicted battles of the giants and exploits of Theseus (like Athens' Temple of Hephaistos, probably the work of the same architect). Some 60 m. (197 ft.) above the sea, the precipice looks out over seven islands, with Milos visible on the clearest days.

Lord Byron couldn't resist carving his name on one of the pillars. He was better inspired when he wrote:

Place me on Sunium's marbled steep,
Where nothing, save the waves and I,
May hear our mutual murmurs sweep;
There, swan like, let me sing and die.

North-east of the cape, across rolling wooded hills, lies **Lavrion**, an industrial town no less grimy than in ancient times when tyrant Peisistratus developed its silver mines. Expedient exception to Athenian democracy, the slave-labourers furnished Pericles with finances for the Athenian fleet until they revolted during the Peloponnesian War. Today, French companies extract cadmium and manganese from the mines and lead from the ancient slag heaps.

If you are sailing to the Cyclade islands from the east coast port of Rafina, spare some time to drive down to **Brauron** *(Vraóna)*. There, amid attractive pine trees and marshland, is the mysterious **Sanctuary of Artemis**, lying in ruins below a 15th-century Byzantine chapel. According to local belief, the goddess rescued Iphigenia, daughter of Agamemnon, from sacrifice here by substituting a bear. Little girls disguised as bears danced in the sanctuary's ritual. In the **museum**, they are portrayed by exquisite marble sculptures of the 4th century B.C.

If you prefer to stick strictly to historical fact, head for the **Plain of Marathon**, battlefield of the Athenians' most famous victory over the Persians (see p. 21). For those who do not feel like running the statutory 42.195 km. (26.219 mi.) all the way from Athens, buses leave from Odós Mavromatéon. A pleasant ride takes you through the pines and plane trees of the smart residential suburb of Kifissia, at the foot of Mount Penteli. (The mountain's heights are disfigured by the ancient marble quarries.) Named after the fragrant fennel *(márathos)* gathered there, the crescent-shaped **battlefield** curves 10 km. (3 mi.) around the bay of Marathon from Cape Kavo up to the Kynosura promontory. At night, imaginative souls have heard the phantom clank of swords and neighing of horses—very imaginative indeed, as there was no cavalry present. Signposted inland is the moving monument of the Athenians' **burial mound**, collective tomb of 192 soldiers who fell in 490 B.C. Near the mound, a marble memorial of the "Warrior of Marathon" is a copy of a bas-relief in the National Archaeological Museum, in fact executed before the battle took place. A **museum** displays prehistoric pottery and funeral vases from the battle tombs. On the outskirts of Marathon village, flags around a marble platform mark the start of the battle-messenger's brave and foolhardy run back to Athens. Try it.

Daphni and Eleusis 13 D3

Two celebrated sanctuaries, Byzantine and pagan, fight off a dismal industrial environment of oil refineries and shipyards. The **monastery of Daphni** protects its celebrated mosaics behind battlemented ramparts that date back in part to the earliest Christian settlement of the 6th century. The walls and the church of 1080 include masonry from an Apollo sanctuary destroyed in A.D. 395—the god's sacred laurels *(dáfni)* grew here in abundance. The temple columns offer a fascinating juxtaposition with the Gothic arches of Cistercian monks installed in the 13th century by the Crusaders.

Two cypresses and an olive tree mark the church's south entrance. Inside, you will be transfixed by the piercing, demanding gaze of the **Christ Pantocrator mosaic** in the central dome. He is surrounded on the vault's drum by the 16 prophets of the Old Testament. The best preserved of the other mosaics, on the south side of the narthex (vestibule), portray the *Presentation of the Virgin Mary* and the *Prayers of Joachim and Anna* (her apocryphal parents).

To penetrate the most sacred mysteries of ancient **Eleusis**, you must leave the westbound highway after Aspropyrgos and take the old Corinth road to Elefsina. Of old, priests and their initiates walked in their September procession from the Athenian cemetery of Keramikos, along the Sacred Way, *Ierá Odós* as it is still named. Today, only well-versed classical historians could make detailed sense of the sanctuary destroyed by the barbarians after the pagan cult was banned by Emperor Theodosius in A.D. 395. But laymen can at least get a feel of its mystic aura. With a model of the original site, ceramic paintings and marble reliefs, a little **museum** illustrates the focus of the cult: humanity's blessed gift of corn from the goddess Demeter. Indeed, more knowledge would be sacrilegious since the shrine's rituals were ever shrouded in secret. Tragedian Aeschylus and military commander Alcibiades were both severely condemned on suspicion of having respectively revealed or ridiculed aspects of the holy rites. All we know, from Roman initiates like Cicero, Hadrian and Marcus Aurelius, is that the experience was spiritually exalting.

Mounts Hymettos and Parnes 13 D3

These two mountains close to Athens offer welcome escapes from the summer heat.

Approached via the eastern suburb of Kaisariani, **Mount Hymettos** *(Ímettos)* is treeless but fragrant with lavender, juniper, thyme, sage and mint, and popular with bees for a honey appreciated since ancient times. The mountain takes on a bewitching mauve colour at sunset. **Moni Kaisariani** is a fine 11th-century monastery standing at the source of the Ilissos river at the end of a ravine shaded by planes, pines and cypresses. Spring water above the monastery is said to cure sterility. The monks have gone, but the monastery is kept up as a national monument and the centre of a colourful Ascension Day procession. Visit the monks' mill, bakery, bath house and refectory, with its imposing vaulted kitchen. The church has some noteworthy 17th-century frescoes, and its dome is supported by Roman columns.

North of Athens, pine and oak forests among rocky ravines make **Mount Parnes**, 1,413 m. (4,635 ft.), popular for summer hiking. As well as a casino, nightclub and cinema, the mountain's smart resort hotel has facilities for swimming and tennis, and a cable-car for trips higher up the mountain (the summit is an off-limits military zone).

A Profane Ring of Hedonism Around the Sacred Isle of Delos

They scatter out into the Aegean east of the Attic peninsula as if, understandably, fleeing the hustle of the metropolis. The Cyclades encourage a carefree life among easy-going islanders who refuse to be hurried. These islands are first port of call for those chasing the Greek holiday dream of lazy, hazy mornings down by the harbour with blue-doored, brilliant white houses and chapels climbing the hill behind. And, after a few hours on the best of the Aegean beaches, just a little cultural stimulus or bouncy nightlife to avoid total torpor.

The name comes from the circle *(kyklos)* which a dozen islands describe around the sanctuary of Delos, birthplace of Apollo. In modern times, the archipelago has extended its name over another 20 islands as far south as Santorini (slowly resuming its ancient name of Thira). The modern administrative capital is Syros, an industrialized island (cotton and tanning) west of Mykonos.

Cypresses and olive groves, orange and lemon trees blossoming beautifully in spring lend their colour to the largely arid brown landscapes. Man has added his dovecotes, windmills and castles.

Their all too obvious attractions have made much of the Cyclades easy prey to the package-tour trade. But secluded corners remain for the adventurous to discover, and the charms of the most

Few gateways to self-indulgence achieve their promise so faithfully as the port of Mykonos.

popular, like Mykonos or Santorini, are powerful enough to withstand the commercial onslaught—even despite the summer meltemi blowing at its fiercest in this south-west corner of the Aegean.

Some of the Cyclades, like Mykonos, Paros and Santorini, have direct air links with Athens and other islands. Major ferry lines start out from Piraeus or Rafina. (For island-by-island details of air and sea transportation from mainland ports with inter-island connections, see the Island-Hopping directory in the blue pages of our Berlitz-Info section, p. 286.)

Mykonos
16 C1

The miracle of Mykonos is that it still manages to live up to the expectations of those who want the perfect hedonistic holiday. It attracts everyone from the smart yachting fraternity to more modest backpackers, as well as lovers of classical Greece who come for its easy access to the Delos island-sanctuary.

93

Story of an Archipelago

Settling in the Cyclades in 4000 B.C., the Aegean's first island-hoppers were farmers and fishermen from Asia Minor.

Milos (whence the Louvre Museum's *Venus*, much, much later) attracted a lively Mediterranean trade with its sought-after glassy obsidian stone, vital in the Bronze Age for knives, razors and other tools. These cosmopolitan contacts and prolific skills in stone and clay sculpture made the Cyclades more civilized than the mainland. With a leading role in Crete's Minoan empire, Thera created a society probably as rich and sophisticated as Knossos itself, until the great volcanic eruption and earthquakes of 1500 B.C. buried both under lava and cinders.

During the rise of Athens and Sparta, Naxos was the dominant political and economic force in the Cyclades, a major target of the Persian invasion. But Apollo's sacred island of Delos was the symbolic centre of Athens' Aegean empire. As a sanctuary commanding the allegiance of the surrounding islands and protecting their war treasury, it was the "Brussels" of a NATO-like alliance. It became one of the wealthiest trading posts in the eastern Mediterranean.

In the post-classical era, the Cyclades went up for grabs, abandoned by the Byzantines first to the Arabs, then the Venetians, who set up a Duchy of the Archipelago under Marco Sanudo, Duke of Naxos. In the 17th century (already), English aristocrats looted the islands' sculpture for the rival collections of Charles I and the Duke of Buckingham (with much of it ending up in the Ashmolean Museum in Oxford). Before anyone else could do any harm, the Cyclades were the first of the islands to be included in the independent Greece of King Otto.

The canny visitor will find antidotes to the island's many superficial symptoms of the dread surfeit-of-tourism disease. For every overcrowded beach within easy access of Mykonos town, there's another off the beaten track offering peace and good swimming to which any enterprising visitor can get by boat or motor-scooter. (If you rent a car here, make sure it has four-wheel-drive for the many unpaved roads down to the beaches.) If the main town centre is indeed chock-a-block with boutiques, bars and restaurants, they are bright and not at all tawdry, with good quality merchandise, especially the locally handwoven linen. With the cruise traffic in mind, the tone is definitely "upmarket". The island's trump card has been to avoid hideous jerry-built blockhouses by strict enforcement of a traditional-architecture ordinance, so that even its most recent hotels may look like a series of fishermen's cottages.

The islanders themselves remain remarkably friendly and have overcome a

tendency to baldness noticed by Strabo, Greek geographer of the 1st century B.C. But the landscape of the interior is as barren as ever.

Mykonos Town

Surrounded by low hills on the west side of the island, the town hugs its harbour with narrow winding lanes and alleys deliberately laid out in a labyrinth to confuse medieval pirates.

Three landmark windmills loom above the **port**, at its best early morning

The pelican is a most appropriate mascot for Mykonos. In keeping with the habits of the rest of the island's fauna, it remains an essentially lazy creature—except when it's going for dinner. Ornithologists pay tribute to its gregarious qualities, again admirably suited to this party-loving place.

and late afternoon outside the hours of the cruise-passengers' daily invasion. Small boats handling the Delos excursion traffic are moored along the natural jetty of the harbour's north arm. Bigger boats dock round to the east. The quay is shared by cafés, fishermen and an occasional tame pelican, languid island mascot since the languid hippy 60s. With the water often lapping below their portside windows, the balconied houses of the **Alefkándra quarter** have earned it the nickname of "Little Venice".

Above the port, the spotless white-washed **Paraportianí church,** more backdrop than building, seems more revered by pagan photographers than devout Christians.

The little **Archaeological Museum** out on Agios Stefanos is devoted principally to tomb-sculpture and ceramics from the Rhenia cemetery where the dead of Delos were buried after the sanctuary's purification in the 5th century B.C. Most notable are a statue of Hercules and a *pithos* or jar (7th century B.C.) decorated with scenes from the Trojan War.

Beaches
The island boasts more than a dozen above-standard beaches. Unless you like the bustle of a crowded beach, the best are the remotest on the north coast or at the east end of the island. As you hunt down your ideal location, remember that on an island where winds blow up in the summer without a moment's notice, fine-sand beaches can prove more troublesome than pebbles or coarse-grained sand.

Closest to town and accessible by road are **Ornos, Tourlos** and **Agios Stefanos**. Almost as convenient, just an inexpensive 15-minute taxi or bus ride from town, are **Psarou** and **Platis Gialos**. These are more conventional than the secluded coves and beaches further along the coast, where people begin to ignore the English sign: "Is forbidden for the undressed people in order of the police."

Paranga and the sandy cove of **Agia Anna** are relatively tranquil spots with pleasant shaded tavernas. Most popular of the nudist beaches are **Paradise**, a long, gradual arc of grainy tan sand backed by gentle rocks and scrub-covered hills, and its companion in Karkinagri Bay, **Super Paradise**.

You need a boat or four-wheel-drive car to get to **Elia** beach and its fashionable tavernas. But a taxi can take you over to the long, curved **Kalafatis** beach at the eastern end of the island. Little caïques sail out to the isle of **Dragonisi**, famous for its seals and caves.

On the north shore, **Panormos Bay** is much appreciated by wind-surfers, with remote **Agios Sostis** the best of its beaches.

Ano Mera
Standing proudly aloof from the coastal resorts, this inland village is worth a bus-trip for the quiet little **Tourlianí monastery** and 16th-century openwork steeple. It is one of some 360 churches and chapels dotted around the island.

Delos *(Dilos)* 16 C1

The island-sanctuary is the site both of great temples and the most complete residential quarter surviving from ancient Greece. At the hub of the Cyclades, the island was not only spiritual focus of the ancient Greeks' ethnic identity but also a highly prosperous grain port and slave

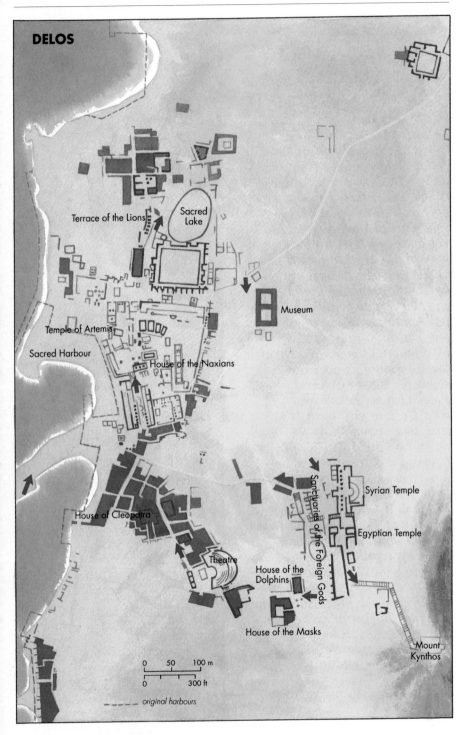

DELOS

Terrace of the Lions

Sacred Lake

Museum

Temple of Artemis

Sacred Harbour

House of the Naxians

Sanctuaries of the Foreign Gods

Syrian Temple

Egyptian Temple

House of Cleopatra

Theatre

House of the Dolphins

House of the Masks

Mount Kynthos

0   50   100 m

0   300 ft

— — — original harbours

97

This headless statue of a Delos resident dates from the late Hellenistic era when the island was a thriving commercial port as well as a national sanctuary. Walking around this hot and barren rock today, you may find it hard to believe that Delos was chosen as a birthplace by Apollo's mother Leto because she had to find some shade. She and his father, Zeus, always looking for variety to spice up his romantic tangles, had made love disguised as quails, reputedly most lascivious birds. Forbidden by Zeus's ever-jealous wife Hera to give birth in the sun, Leto laboured on the shady north side of Mount Kynthos, between a date palm and an olive tree. Four days later, the baby felt big and strong enough to take off with bow and arrow for Mount Parnassus and Delphi to hunt down and kill his mother's reptilian enemy, Python. Apollo became the god that best epitomized the Greek ideal: if on the practical side he was identified with archery and herdsmen, he was most appreciated as art's image of youthful, manly beauty, patron of music, philosophy and the highest values of civilization itself.

market. At its height, the latter had a "turnover" of 10,000 slaves a day. The religious festival became a veritable trade fair and Delos was as cosmopolitan a port as Piraeus.

To honour the birthplace of Apollo, pilgrims from the surrounding islands and city-states of the mainland built great monuments and brought rich gifts and treasure. Their rulers and warriors consulted its oracle. The island was twice "purified" on Athenian orders: no births or deaths were permitted there and all graves were exhumed and transported to neighbouring Rhenia. The purification is likely to remain in force for some time to come as accommodation on the island is minimal—one hotel of only seven beds.

Those with queasy stomachs should be prepared for a frequently choppy sea on the 30- to 40-minute motor launch ride from Mykonos (longer excursions from Tinos, Naxos and Paros). Take good walking shoes for the hike up Mount Kynthos.

Sanctuary of Apollo

If poor weather does not force a landing around Cape Kako on the north-east coast at Gourna, the average three-hour morning visit begins on a landing immediately beside the old **Sacred Harbour**, now silted up. Follow the pilgrims' path left along the paved Sacred Way to the shrines dedicated to Apollo. On the north side of the **House of the Naxians** is the huge base on which Apollo's colossus was erected in the 7th century B.C. An inscription tells that the base and statue were constructed from one solid block, with graffiti added by Venetians and some 17th-century tourists. The statue proved too big for the Venetians to carry off (in 1422), and you will find some of the pieces they dropped—pelvis and torso—over to the left behind the **Temple of Artemis** (2nd century B.C.). A hand is displayed in the local museum and a foot ended up in London's British Museum.

Terrace of the Lions

These majestic protectors carved from Naxian marble have become the sanctuary's most celebrated symbol. Five of the original nine lions sit up on their haunches, mouths open to roar, guarding the **Sacred Lake**. Until it was dried up in 1926 (because of malarial mosquitoes), the lake was the home of swans and geese, descendants of the shrine's holy birds. Now a lone palm tree has been planted in the middle to symbolize the place of Apollo's birth.

Museum

On a hot day, the museum's airy pavilion makes a cool and pleasant pause before tackling Mount Kynthos and the rest of your tour of the archaeological site. The best of the Delos sculpture is in Athens' National Archaeological Museum, but the seven rooms here include a fine sphinx, a lion's body with woman's head from Paros (6th century B.C.), Aegean Geometric vases and Mycenaean figurines. Particularly fascinating are objects of everyday life from Delos's days as a commercial port: medical instruments, utensils, knives, jewellery, keys, combs, anchors and weights.

Sanctuaries of the Foreign Gods

Along the stone mountain-path, you pass shrines built by overseas merchants living around the port. The **Syrian temple** (128 B.C.), honouring weather god Adad, giver and destroyer of life, was the scene of violent orgiastic rituals until toned down by an Athenian high priest. **Egyptian temples** were dedicated to Serapis, god of healing, Isis, goddess of fertility, and Anubis, jackal-headed lord of the dead.

Mount Kynthos

Beyond traces of a small temple to Hera, the climb is worth the effort for the magnificent views. From a platform halfway up, you take in the whole sanctuary and ancient port-town, and at the summit, 112 m. (367 ft.), look out over the

Cyclades that paid the island ancient allegiance. The mountain was inhabited during the Stone Age; shrines were built for Athena and Zeus in the 3rd century B.C. It was from here that the supreme god watched the birth of his son.

Theatre District

Coming back down the mountain, turn left towards the sea to the port town's main residential quarter surrounding the ancient theatre. On your right as you enter the town is the **House of the Dolphins**, so called for its mosaic of dolphins ridden by cupids. Across the street, the **House of Masks** has mosaics of theatrical masks and a splendid Dionysus riding a panther. Best viewed from the top overlooking the stage, the fine marble **theatre** (3rd century B.C.) sat an audience of 5,500 on its 43 rows. Beyond the theatre follow the signs over to the left to the **House of Cleopatra**, an Athenian lady whose headless statue, beside that of her husband, welcomes you into their courtyard with its 2,200-year-old well still in working order.

Andros
16 B1

Quietest and greenest of the Cyclades, the first stop on the Rafina ferry-run to Mykonos is a favourite of Athenians baffled by the foreigners' obsession with the other, arid islands. Shipping magnates have luxurious villas along the east coast while others have houses with delightful gardens up in the hills, hidden among pine groves and looking down on vineyards and olive trees in the valleys. Like neighbouring Tinos, the island is dotted with Venetian dovecotes in square towers. Gourmets love the local omelette, grilled octopus and a crushed-almond dessert known as *amygdalotá*.

Batsi and the Beaches

The ferry stops on the west coast at Gavrion, but the main resort is just to the south at Batsi, built around a charming fishing and sailing harbour with some good hotels and pleasant beaches. Over on the cooler east coast, the best beaches are at **Nimborio** and **Korthion**.

Andros Town

Also known as Chora (just "town"), like many island capitals, Andros Town is built along the ridge of an east-coast promontory. Attractive 19th-century neoclassical houses line the main marble-paved street, joined by bridge to a Venetian castle-ruin out on a rock. The Goulandris shipping magnates have endowed the town with three new art institutions: a **Museum of Modern Art**, principally home-grown talent; an **art gallery** for temporary exhibitions; and an **Archaeology Museum** housing finds from the excavations of the ancient settlement of Zagora at the southern end of the island. They include ceramics, household objects and sculpture, notably a statue of Hermes.

Tinos
16 B–C1

The great charm of this mountainous island is in its sparkling white villages, medieval dovecotes, windmills and farmers' terraces. When its serenity is disturbed, it is not by packages of foreign holiday-makers, but by thousands of Roman Catholic pilgrims. Ruled by Venice from 1207 to 1714, Tinos has always been the most Catholic island of the Cyclades.

Around Annunciation Day (March 25) and Assumption (August 15), devout invalids are drawn to the port capital of Tinos by the curative powers attributed to an icon discovered in 1823.

Tinos Town

The capital's pretty **harbour** describes an almost complete circle, and its waters seem (miraculously?) clean enough to attract some very good fish right up to the dockside. The island caters much more to its Greek visitors than foreigners, but

Lacking the sandy beaches and more spectacular attractions that bring in the throngs, Andros is an island for connoisseurs. The Greek bourgeoisie has long sought it out as a haven of peace away from the mainland bustle and foreign tourist traps. Pull into the harbour of Gavrion and you can explore a verdant interior that contrasts sharply with the dazzling but arid landscapes of the other Cyclades.

hind high walls in a marble and tile court-yard with nine cypresses and a lone palm tree. A monumental staircase leads to its porch, which commands a grand view over the harbour and across the water to Mykonos, Delos and Syros.

Greek Orthodox tastes have clearly influenced the modern church's highly ornate interior. The ceiling is hung with over 100 silver candelabra. Dominating everything is the **icon of the Virgin Mary**, gold-framed and ablaze with jewels. Scores of pilgrims' offerings are placed around it to conjure up its curative powers.

Down the main boulevard from the church, an attractive **Archaeological Museum** exhibits Geometric vases of the 10th century B.C., huge amphorae from the 8th and 7th centuries B.C. and an ancient sun dial.

Interior

Many of the islands fifty-odd villages are reachable only by donkey-paths—though buses seem quite happy to tackle them. An excursion is a hilarious adventure. Take, for instance, the afternoon bus from Tinos to **Komi**. Within minutes you are sweeping up, over and around spectacular mountain ridges, past carefully cultivated terraced fields. The rough narrow road takes you past dozens of the island's characteristic landmarks, the tall stone **dovecotes** of which the Venetians built over 800 here.

The bus stops at **Exombourgo hill**, worth the 90-minute hike to its summit (565 m., 1,853 ft.) with its ruined Venetian castle and fine view over the Cyclades. Other pretty villages are **Loutra**, **Pirgos** and **Falatados**, where you can see nuns of the Kehrovouníou Convent making traditional lacework and embroidery.

Beaches

Closest and most popular is the long strand of **Agios Fokas**, an easy walk east of Tinos harbour. To get away from the crowd, head north of Komi (rough road

the pilgrimage trade has created an abundance of hotels and a bustling bazaar. Restaurants and cafés are unsophisticated, decidedly not tourist-traps but with the concomitant problem of menus, like the street-signs, all in Greek. In the cobbled back streets, the old iron-balconied houses recall the centuries of Venetian rule.

Target of the pilgrimage is the vast **Panagía Evangelístria** church, reached by a broad street sweeping directly up from the harbour. The church stands be-

and donkey-path) to **Kolimbithra**, an attractive, secluded sandy beach with a pleasant restaurant up on the hill behind. Even further away, practically at the end of the bus route, is **Ormos Isternion**.

Sifnos 16 B2

For long a haven of calm, being off the main ferry-routes, the sparsely populated island has attracted increasing attention to its well organized resorts and beach villages, popular with campers.

In ancient times, the island was famous for its gold and silver mines and in 526 B.C. built the most opulent treasury at the sanctuary of Delphi (see p. 189). Now, it claims, the conscientious Christian can worship each day of the year in a different place, touring the island's 365 churches and chapels.

Ferries dock at **Kamares**, the main port and a centre for the island's thriving pottery. A bus will take you inland around Mount Profitis Ilías to the inland capital of **Apollonia**. Its classically white Cycladic houses sprawl across the slopes of three terraced hills. On the north coast, **Kastro** is a gently decaying medieval village on the site of what was probably the island's ancient capital. A little museum displays finds from Mycenaean and Archaic-era excavations, including a few clay horses of Geometric design.

On the south-east coast, **Platis Gialos** and **Faros Bay** are the best known of the beach resorts. For more secluded bathing, the long, sandy beach of almost land-locked **Vathi Bay** is reachable by caïque or a 60-minute walk.

Paros 16 C2

One of the loveliest Aegean islands, Paros also has a reputation for being the friendliest. This and its excellent facilities for water sports have made it very popular with Italians and anyone else in love with *dolce far niente*, sweet idleness.

Parikia

On the quayside of the ferry-harbour, signs are posted forbidding nude bathing. More inviting beyond is the delightful village of narrow stone walkways. Shops, archways, churches and houses are all the requisite dazzling white, with shutters blue and green, and courtyards of sweet jasmine and basil, honeysuckle and lemon trees, and canaries in the vine arbour. A particularly exquisite corner of town is the sleepy little quarter around the hilltop **Kastro**, a 13th-century Venetian citadel. Enjoy the view from the church of Saints Constantine and Helen overlooking the bay, with Antiparos and other islets close offshore and Sifnos looming on the western horizon.

*N*obody quite knows why there are so many dovecotes on Tinos, though the white doves are certainly not complaining. Scholars suggest the Venetian's proliferation of these crumbling square towers, some decorated with patterned tiles, was indulging a common medieval taste for towers like those in Tuscany's San Gimignano. Less fanciful local peasants come up with the equally convincing argument that the dovecotes just provided a useful way of piling up the stones littering the farmland.

The town's cathedral, **Panagía Eka-tontapilianí**, or the "Church of 100 Doors", owes its name to its complex structure. It is said to stand over a 4th-century shrine founded by St Helen, mother of Constantine the Great, on her quest for the True Cross in Jerusalem. Earthquakes and modern restoration have subjected it to many changes, most recently from Venetian Baroque back to a hybrid version of its early Byzantine form. In the outer courtyard, notice five church bells hanging from a tall cypress tree that has served as belfry ever since the original tower tumbled down in an earthquake in the 18th century. Inside, to the left of the choir, the 6th-century chapel of **Ágios Nikolaós** is built on Doric columns from an ancient Roman building. A fine bishop's throne stands in the apse of the central Temple of the Virgin. The baptistery, to the right of the main church, has a sunken font.

The little **Archaeological Museum** nearby houses an engraved marble slab that is part of the mysterious Parian Chronicle *(Marmor Parium)*, found in Paros in 1897. A larger fragment, discovered in Smyrna, is now in Oxford's Ashmolean Museum. The whole purported to narrate the history of Greece from Cecrops, first king of Athens, down to 264 B.C., with a strange mixture of political, military, religious and literary events. Fifth-century sculpture in Parian marble includes a large lion and calf relief, a Victory and a winged medusa with snakes. A Roman mosaic in mauve, yellow and blue depicts the labours of Hercules.

Villages and Beaches

Take a bus over to the fishing port of **Naousa**, where the gaily coloured cottage-doors on the quayside have to compete with the yellow and russet nets and blue, white and orange boats cramming into the tiny harbour.

Motor launches take bathers across the broad bay to the sandy beaches and carved rocks of **Kolibithres**. Further around the island's north-east peninsula, Naousa boats also ply between the fine beaches of **Langeri, Agia Maria** and **Platis Ammos**.

Start out from the village of **Marathi** to explore the ancient marble quarries briefly revived in 1844 to furnish the marble for Napoleon's tomb in Paris.

The bus for Marathi continues to the pretty mountain village of **Lefkes**, singled out by the twin-towered, orange-roofed marble cathedral and reputed for its fine ceramics.

At the top of **Kefalos hill** is a gleaming white monastery with splendid views around the island. Down on the east coast, the beach of **Piso Livadi** is popular with wind-surfers. Further south, long sandy beaches stretch on either side of **Dryos**.

Snorkelling is good almost everywhere, but best of all over on **Antiparos** (40-minute boat-trip from Parikia). The main island's little sister is also noted for its vast cave with stalactites, a half-hour walk (slightly faster by donkey or bus) up the slope of Mount Ágios Ilías.

Naxos   *16 C2*

The largest of the Cyclades has much of what you need for the sweet life: groves of orange and lemon trees, figs and pomegranates, good honey, tangy cheeses, and a wine that made it a centre of ancient Dionysian orgies and pretty good parties today. The island also boasts the highest peak in the Cyclades, Mount Zas, 1,001 m. (3,284 ft.).

If Naxians are a little cooler in manner than their neighbours on Paros, could it derive from a natural pride in their august history? The island was reputed for its fine white marble and was a leader in early monumental sculpture and Ionic architecture. It was the dominant island power in the Aegean until its destruction by the Persians in 490 B.C. It returned to prominence centuries later as the capital of the medieval Venetian Duchy of the Archipelago.

Naxos Town

Looming over the harbour is the town's imposing landmark, a giant **gateway** to the 6th-century B.C. Temple of Apollo destroyed by the Persians. It stands 5½ m. (18 ft.) tall among gleaming white marble ruins on an islet joined to the port by a causeway.

Ignore the port's dull modern construction and head up to the old **citadel** *(kástro)*. You climb easily through a delightful warren of whitewashed cobbled lanes, arches and cheerful tunnels, with the boutiques sandwiched between butchers, vegetable shops and tavernas. Inside the citadel, coats of arms above the doorways bear witness to the island's Venetian heyday. The church of **Panagía Theosképastos** has a fine 14th-century icon of the Crucifixion. The **Catholic Cathedral** boasts an even older icon from the 10th century, a rare full-length portrait of the Virgin Mary and Child.

Nikos Kazantzakis, author of *Zorba the Greek* and *The Last Temptation of Christ*, was a pupil in the school that is now the town's **Archaeological Museum**. Among its prize exhibits are early Cycladic figurines, bowls and pitchers excavated from nearby 4,500-year-old tombs. Look, too, for the Mycenaean vases and gold leaf jewellery, as well as Geometric and Archaic pottery.

Climb **Aplómata hill**, just north of town, site of ancient cliff-edge tombs and a memorial to a World War II resistance hero, to share with the goats a magnificent view of Paros, Delos and Mykonos.

Excursions and Beaches

Peaceful **Tragéa valley** in the middle of the island is the best of the inland excursions. Stop off at the village of **Chalki** with its old Italian tower-houses. In front of the fine 17th-century Grazia palace, the Protothrónis church has some notable wall-paintings. From here, stroll out into a serene countryside of olive groves, cypresses and lemon trees and, nestling among them, white Byzantine chapels.

Jilted on Naxos

The story so far: greatly excited by the blood-covered Theseus just after he killed the Minotaur (see p. 16), Ariadne, daughter of King Minos of Crete, had succumbed to his embraces outside the Labyrinth. On their way to Athens, she asked him to stop off at Naxos because she was very seasick and rather pregnant and worried she might have a miscarriage.

After Theseus sailed on the next morning without her, who should pass by but that lovable wino Dionysus, who claimed he was born on Naxos from the thigh of Zeus. At least he did the decent thing by Ariadne and married her so that her bastard son Oenopion could have a proper upbringing and manage the family wine-business. Ariadne stopped trying to live up to a name that meant "most pure" and became a fertility goddess. She bore Dionysus half a dozen children. Theseus later married her sister, the hot-blooded Phaedra.

The road through the mountains to the north takes you to the remote little fishing village of **Apollon**. Up on the hill a colossal statue of Apollo (some claim it's Dionysus) lies where its sculptors left it 2,600 years ago, unfinished because faults in the marble cracked it open.

Many of the island's best beaches are south of the capital. Closest to town is **Agios Georgios**. You will find the best sand and most solitude further out at **Agios Prokopios**, the tiny port of **Agia Anna**, and coves around the **Mikri Vigla** promontory. On windy days, head over to the north coast where the beautiful marble pebbles of **Lionas** beach will not blow in your face.

Amorgos *17 D2*

This narrow island, just 18 km. (11 mi.) long, attracts seekers of the quiet life, and is also popular as an excursion from Naxos. Sailing around the south coast, you will see some of the most spectacular cliffs in the Aegean.

The charming island-capital of **Chora**

*A*s ancient Thera, the volcanic island of Santorini was an important bridgehead for the Minoan civilization of Crete in its commercial and cultural conquest of the Aegean. Today, with its capital at Fira on the west coast (viewed here from the north end of its crescent-shaped bay), Santorini challenges Mykonos' claim as the most popular of the Cyclades.

with its little white houses nestling against a Venetian fort is a 45-minute drive inland. North-east of the capital, on a cliff overlooking the Aegean is the 11th-century **Chozoviótissa monastery**, boasting a celebrated icon from Cyprus.

The most accessible beaches are on the north-west coast—**Ormos Egiali** and **Katapola** with its harbour. Others like **Kalotaritissa** and **Pharos** are accessible only on foot or by caïque.

Santorini
16. C2

Volcanic eruptions and earthquakes have made of this island one of the most spectacular in all the Aegean. The biggest of all its explosions, in 1500 B.C., took a bite out the originally round, bun-shaped island and turned it into the croissant you see today. The bay is the volcano's collapsed crater, a gigantic caldera 11 km. (7 mi.) long.

What's Its Name?
Greek place-names are never easy to get right, but Santorini is a case apart. The government, Olympic Airways, and some, but by no means all ferry-operators are gradually reverting to the island's ancient name of *Thira* (or Thera), after a Spartan colonizer of the 8th century B.C. Thera is the name, too, of the ancient excavated capital in the south of the island, while *Firá* or *Thíra* is the modern capital on the west coast. The name Santorini comes from the Byzantine Saint Irene.

Sailing into the caldera is a memorable experience. Sheer cliffs exposing starkly etched volcanic layers rise over 300 m. (1,000 ft.). Two formidable black islets jut out in the middle of the bay, forced to the surface by modern eruptions, most recently in 1950 (an earthquake devastated the west coast six years later). The nearly deserted Thirasia, part of the original "bun", now blocks off most of the western horizon as you reach the port of Fira. The gleaming white buildings of the island's capital are strung out along the top of the dark cliffs like an ivory crown.

Fira and Ia

From the tiny landing stage, by foot or donkey, it is 587 stone-ramped zigzagging steps to the top, but only a 2-minute ride by cable-car. (You might like to take the donkey back down to the boat-excursions around the bay.)

Fira has been quite well reconstructed since the 1956 earthquake, and the boutiques, especially the jewellery shops, are much appreciated by visiting cruise passengers. A small **museum** houses early Cycladic figurines, some Geometric and Archaic pottery and statuettes from the site of Ancient Thera (see p. 111). There are also some finds from the local Akrotiri excavations, kept here prior to completion of a new museum down at the site.

Further up the coast, above its tiny fishing harbour, the clifftop village of Ia has done an exquisite job of rebuilding. Highly regarded for its handwoven fabrics, it is generally a much quieter place in which to try and find private rooms, or at least to come to for a café-terrace view of the grandiose sunset.

Interior

Much of the island is covered with layers of pumice and lava, over 40 m. (140 ft.) deep. But under a light that is, even for the Cyclades, exceptionally dazzling, the plain sloping east away from the cliffs is unexpectedly green. Tomatoes and grapes producing a very heady wine thrive in the volcanic soil. Quiet inland villages like **Pirgos** make a pleasant change from the main tourist haunts. Up on a hill on cobbled streets, its white houses and green-doored chapels cluster around an old Venetian fortress.

The best vantage point overlooking the whole island and south to Crete is the summit of **Profítis Ilías**, 566 m. (1,857 ft.). Sidestep the towering TV and radio antennae and visit the **monastery** with a notable 15th-century icon of the prophet Elijah (Ilias) to the right of the main church altar. A little **museum** displays icons, illuminated manuscripts and other illustrations of monastic life (with explanations in English and German). If you have a taste for such things, you can peek at the ossuary of monks' bones. Others prefer the sweets and *tsikoudiá* liqueur made from the island's grape leaves.

Akrotiri

Intensive excavation at the south-west end of the island is gradually revealing a remarkably intact city founded by settlers from Minoan Crete. Take a bus, bike, motor scooter or organized tour for a rare view of a momentous dig in progress.

Protected now under the archaeologists' vast corrugated iron roof, the site lay under a crust of volcanic lava for 3,400 years. Buried by the 1500 B.C.

eruption and later ravaged by earthquakes, traces of the city first emerged in the 19th century during the mining of pumice as construction material for the Suez Canal. But proper excavations began only in 1967, to reveal a civilization as flourishing and accomplished as that found at Knossos in Crete. The works of art uncovered include the great frescoes presently in Athens' National Archaeological Museum awaiting transfer back to the island.

But as you take the signposted tour of the site, its major appeal is the vivid view it gives of the town as a place to live: houses built of massive hewn ashlar stone, many of them with walls still standing up to the third storey; fireplaces, handsome door and window frames, stone stairways, toilet and drainage pipes. Greek archaeologists wryly acknowledge that the system of winter heating is better than that found in most Greek houses today. Among the artefacts left in place are some massive millstones and, in the pantry of the tall House of the Ladies, some huge decorated storage vessels.

Ancient Thera

Without the benefit of a protective layer of volcanic lava, the old hilltop capital is less easily discernible than the much more ancient Akrotiri, but the site remains evocative and worth a visit. Let the local guides show you around.

Though some of the tombs are 600 years older, the ruins date mostly from the 3rd century B.C., when it was a garrison town for the Ptolemies, Macedonian rulers of Egypt. Past the Byzantine chapel of Ágios Stéfanos is the Artemidorus Shrine, erected in honour of the Ptolemaic admiral. (Following Alexander, many Macedonian leaders raised themselves to quasi-divine status.) As you tour the houses, guides like to point out the sculpted relief of a phallus with the inscription: "For my friends". Make your way up to the **Festival Terrace**, a dance-floor for the rites of Apollo, with a fine view over the southern tip of the island to Akrotiri. At the far south end of the site is the Gymnasium.

Beaches

After the first visual shock, you quickly grow accustomed to the black volcanic sand and pebbles of Santorini's beaches on the east coast. The pebbles, when polished, make handsome substitutes for worry beads. Appreciated for its snorkelling, **Kamari** has a pebble beach at the foot of rocky cliffs. **Perissa** has the best sand and **Monolithos**, least frequently served by bus, is by the same token blessedly less crowded.

Ios

This island, Nio to the natives, is strictly for kids—kids, that is, from 18 to 30 who like the day-long, night-long blast of disco music on the beach, in the boutiques and inside and outside the bars and cafés. Even when it was a hippy paradise in the 60s, amplification technology did not have today's decibel level. On a clear day, you can hear Ios from Santorini.

After busting their eardrums in the bright white island-capital, **Ios Town**, the college fraternity and apprentice-yuppies like to sleep it off in rented rooms and tents around the west coast harbour of **Ormos Iou** with its nearby beach of Gialos. The beautiful, big, but unshaded and very popular sandy beach of **Milopotamos** is a 30-minute walk down the coast. Others, accessible by boat, are on **Manganari Bay** at the southern end of the island. Heavy dates head over to the east coast to the remoter beach of **Agios Theodotis**.

The closest the island gets to anything cultural is the claim of a 18th-century Dutch digger to have uncovered Homer's grave in Plakotós creek at the northern end of the island. It is prehistoric, but not Homer's, so the story that the bard was killed by the island's noise is spurious.

Greece's Biggest Island Where It All Began

Crete is its own country. At a crossroads between the Middle East, Africa and the western Mediterranean, its civilization is the oldest in Europe. After centuries of often violent struggle against the Turks to achieve union with Greece, it stands resolutely apart from the rest of the country. The largest Greek island is a Texas with a pride more ancient, a Sicily but more smiling, a Scotland but warmer. Independent-minded people? Who else would name their sons *Eleftherios*—Freedom?

As a holiday destination, this richly varied island is as self-contained as its people are self-assured. On their best days, they even refer to their beloved Crete as a "continent". Nowhere is it easier to combine beach-bumming with cultural enrichment, or to indulge yourself with the best of Greek seafood, cheeses and wines, and then work them off with a bracing hike through the lovely meadows and mountains of the interior. So you may well be happy to spend your whole holiday on Crete, though good sea and air connections with Santorini, Paros or Mykonos enable you to get a taste of the very different Cyclades, too.

Crete rounds off the Aegean Sea. Its mountains prolong the south-eastern sweep of the Peloponnese's Taygetos range in the stepping stones that contin-ue with Karpathos and Rhodes to the coast of Asia Minor. Do not be surprised to see subtropical flora on a land closer to the equator than Tunis or Algiers. Libya is only 320 km. (200 mi.) from Crete's south coast.

The long, narrow island—250 km. (155 mi.) from west to east but only 60 km. (37 mi.) across at its widest point —is divided lengthways by a series of mountain ranges: to the west, the Lefka or White Mountains, in the centre, Ida and Dikti.

The population of more than half a million is concentrated mainly along the plains and gentler mountain slopes of the north coast and is scattered only very sparsely on the south coast where the mountains drop abruptly into the sea. As a result, most tourist facilities are clustered along that north coast, around Chania and Rethymnon, outside Iraklion (the capital), and in Agios Nikolaos, all linked by the island's only major highway. On the south coast, with Ierapetra the lone substantial town, you will find secluded spots at isolated fishing

Crete is an island of infinite variety, not least of all in its breads.

After it had dominated the Aegean with its brilliant Minoan civilization (see p. 15), invasion and earthquake removed Crete from Greek history's centre stage. Some coastal dwellers migrated into remote mountain refuges while others embarked on an overseas exodus that took them as far as Palestine, where the Israelites referred to them as Philistines. The island stayed out of Greece's Persian and Peloponnesian Wars, but attracted Alexander's attention as a source of brave and energetic mercenaries.

The Romans made the inland city of Gortys their provincial capital. In A.D. 59, Paul dropped by with his disciple, Titus, Crete's first bishop, and was most unkind.

"One of themselves," he noted, "even a prophet of their own, said: 'The Cretans are always liars, evil beasts, slow bellies.' This witness is true."

But the Byzantine Empire found Cretans to be enthusiastic supporters, remaining loyal to the Orthodox Church throughout the Arab occupation of the island from 824 to 961. The Arabs systematically destroyed the churches and turned the island into a pirate base and one of the Mediterranean's major slave markets. Their fortified capital was at Rabd-el-Kandek (Candia to western Europe and now Iraklion). When recapturing the island, the Byzantine general was no more tender-hearted. To impress the Arabs holding out in the fort, he catapulted his prisoners' heads over the wall.

When Byzantium fell to the Crusaders, Crete was given to Boniface of Montferrat who sold it for cash—1,000 silver marks—to Venice. Crete thrived under the 465 years of Venetian occupation (1204–1669). The ports and fortifications of Chania, Rethymnon and Iraklion bear witness to the Venetians' ambitious public building programme. Crete was a refuge for artists fleeing the Turkish conquest of Constantinople in 1453. In the 16th century, one of the most accomplished of Greek icon-painters, Michaïl Damaskinos, combined Byzantine convention with a more audacious technique he had studied in Venice. Another local boy, Dominikos Theotokopoulos, began with icons and went off to Italy, then Spain, to make his name as El Greco.

The Turks waged a titanic struggle to wrest Crete from the Venetians. The latter had strengthened fortifications of what they saw as the last Christian bastion against Turkey's advance on the western Mediterranean. But Chania and Rethymnon fell in 1645. Three years later, the Turks began a siege and assault of the capital, Candia, that was to last 21 years. After the first 15 years, the Turkish commander, Hussein Pasha, was summoned back to Constantinople and publicly strangled for his failure to take the city. In the end, Candia's capture cost the lives of 30,000 Venetians and 118,000 Turks. As the conquerors entered the city gates, the Venetians fled with the head of St Titus, the island's patron saint (which was returned only in 1966).

Turkish rule (1669–1898) was a period of cultural and economic stagnation. The darkness was broken only by outbursts of revolt, culminating in the 19th-century struggle for union with Greece *(énosis)*. Violent insurrection provoked equally ferocious massacres in retaliation. In 1898, Britain, France, Russia and Italy forced the Turks to grant the island autonomy within the Ottoman Empire. But it was only in 1913, under the leadership of its great statesman, Eleftherios Venizelos, that *énosis* was achieved with a final Turkish evacuation of the island ten years later.

But Crete's pains were not at an end. In 1941, the retreating Allies staged a desperate effort to fight off German bombardments that devastated the island. With a centuries-old tradition of resistance to foreign invaders, Cretans maintained constant guerrilla warfare to make the German occupation costly and uncomfortable. Today the island of Minos has retrieved its rightful place in the sun.

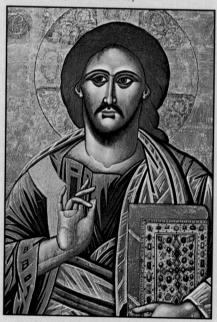

Icon from Toploú Monastery

villages like Paleochora and Chora Sfakion or the slowly developing resorts of Matala and Agia Galini.

Nature-lovers have many a field day here. For amateur botanists, Crete boasts some 130 species of plant life unique to the island. Ask at the main tourist offices about guided tours. In early spring, you will spot orchids and listera, fields of crocus and anemone, later narcissus and wild tulips, and whole carpets of buttercup in the upland meadows of the Ida and White Mountains. Oleander heralds the summer. While the city markets are full of oranges that connoisseurs write poems to, figs, apricots, almonds, pomegranates and every kind of olive, you can also find all of them wild in the hills and valleys.

Bird-watchers come for the spring migration: egrets, golden orioles, kingfishers and falcons. Birds for whom Crete is home include eagles, buzzards, lammergeiers (bearded vultures), blue rock thrush, and owls at nightfall. You may spot ibex in the mountains, weasel and the odd badger. Nastier, but not frequent, are scorpions and vipers.

Iraklion   *19 C3*

With its busy airport only 4 km. (2½ mi.) from the city, the island capital is a lively but also noisy centre of commerce and industry. Its population of 115,000 places it fifth among Greek cities, first in terms of per capita income. If it does not invite a prolonged stay, it certainly has plenty to repay a visit: the Venetian legacy of harbour, castle and ramparts; the church of Agía Ekateríni with its great icons by Michaïl Damaskinos; above all, the Minoan treasures in the Archaeological Museum, second only to Athens' national museum. The best way to enjoy them is to make excursions *into* the town from a coastal resort. Reserve one day for the museum and other cultural sights and perhaps a second day to shop for jewellery and ceramics or visit the market to

make up a picnic for the mountains. The fellows you see in traditional Cretan costume—black scarf around the head, blouse and cummerbund over breeches tucked into knee-high boots—are the real thing, not a tourist-office gimmick.

The Town

The city centre's charm has not been enhanced by centuries of earthquakes (the last major one in 1926), World War II bombardment and unimaginative modern building in reinforced concrete. So start out at the **port**. The new outer harbour bustles with ferries and freighters. The inner Venetian harbour is now reserved for fishing boats, yachts and caïques. Towering over them out on the jetty is the grand **Venetian Fort**, *Rocca al Mare* to the Italians, and to the Turks, *Koules*, as it is still known today. Built between 1523 and 1549, its massive buffstone walls provided the main bulwark of the Venetians' heroic resistance to the Turks' prolonged 17th-century assault. Climb up to the battlements for a fine view over the harbour and the Aegean. Emblazoned on a fortress wall facing the sea is the best preserved of three sculptured lions of St Mark, proud emblem of the Adriatic city-state. On the quay across the street from the harbour authority are the lofty arcades and storerooms of the 16th-century **Arsenali** where ships were repaired and fitted out for battle on the high seas.

From behind the harbour bus station, the well-preserved Venetian ramparts run south past a pleasant public park to the **Martinengo Bastion**, burial place of Crete's great novelist Nikos Kazantzakis (1885–1957). Born in Iraklion, the author of *Zorba the Greek* and *The Last Temptation of Christ* wrote his epitaph for the gravestone here: "I hope for nothing. I fear nothing. I am free."

The busy **Platía Venizélou** (Venizelos Square) is a good place to buy your souvenirs or read a newspaper at one of the many cafés. In the centre, four lions support the ornate **Morosini Fountain**

(1628), named after a Venetian governor and father of the man who blew up Athens' Parthenon (see p. 29). The Turks destroyed the fountain's Neptune statue, but nymphs, bulls, dolphins and musicians still frolic around bas-reliefs on the basins. Walk north along Odós 25 Avgoústou towards the church of **Ágios Títos**, converted back from a Turkish mosque and dedicated to the island's patron saint, whose skull is kept there in a reliquary. A Syrian Greek from Antioch, Titus was the key test-case in St Paul's campaign to convert Gentiles to Christianity without circumcision.

Downhill on the other side of Odós 25 Avgoústou, children (and their parents even more) will be grateful for the playground in **El Greco Park.**

From Platía Venizélou moving away from the harbour, take the main shopping thoroughfare of Leofóros Kalokerinoú towards the three churches on Platía Agías Ekaterínis. On the west side of the square, the 19th-century cathedral and the more charming little church next to it are both dedicated to St Minas. But the main attraction is the 16th-century **church of St Catherine** *(Agía Ekateríni)*. Linked to St Catherine's desert monastery at Mount Sinai, the church and its seminary provided a haven for artists and theologians fleeing the Turks in Constantinople. The church is now a museum including six icons of Michaïl Damaskinos, true masterpieces of the art. Profiting from five years in Venice (1577–1582), the painter infused his traditional Byzantine art with the Venetian school's renowned energy and bold use of colour. In the central nave you will find his *Adoration of the Magi; the Last Supper; the Virgin with Moses' Burning Bush; Christ with the Holy Women; Constantine with the Bishops;* and *Christ Celebrating Mass with the Angels.*

The **Central Market**—and, logically enough, the city's best restaurants—are located on and around Odós 1866. Stalls of fruit and vegetables, exotic spices and the island's great honey and fresh yo-

ghurt are succeeded by meat and fish markets of astonishing variety. At the top of the market street, on Platía Kornárou, take a rest at the café whose centrepiece is a kiosk formed from an old Turkish fountain. Behind is the 16th-century **Bembo Fountain** with its headless Roman statue.

If the fountain makes you long for a swim, the closest, but crowded place is **Florida Beach** out at Amnissos, handily but noisily near the airport. Be patient and head back to a resort.

*T*he port of Iraklion attracts freighters and cruise liners from all over the Mediterranean and beyond, but that doesn't scare off amateur fishermen. The commercial catch on display in the local market is among the richest in the Aegean.

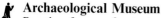

Archaeological Museum

People often prefer to tour an archaeological site before visiting the museum displaying its excavated artworks. In the case of Knossos, Phaistos, Agia Triada and Crete's other Minoan sites, you will more easily appreciate their significance if you first visit Iraklion's magnificent Archaeological Museum (off the noisy Platía Eleftherías opposite the tourist office). The elegance and vitality of life in the days of King Minos will seem more real after seeing the beautifully exhibited Minoan treasures, along with scale-models of how the palaces probably looked in their heyday. In fact, for a complete sense of the sites, many visitors like to make a quick preliminary tour of the museum on their first day and then a second, more leisurely tour at the end of their stay.

More preoccupied with resisting earthquakes than appealing to the eye, the museum is an uninspired concrete blockhouse. But its collection of Minoan art in 20 galleries is the most complete in the world—Athens has nothing to match it. Here are the highlights:

Gallery 1: ceramics, figurines, jewellery and weapons from the first 3,000 years of Cretan settlement (5000–2000 B.C.) down to the period immediately before the building of the first palaces.

Gallery 2: from the early palaces (1900 to 1700 B.C.), look for the town mosaics, small earthenware plaques from Knossos bearing models of Minoan houses up to three rising storeys—like those you can see at Akrotiri on the island of Santorini (see p. 111).

Gallery 3: also from the early palace period, the famous Phaistos Disk from the south Cretan palace. The clay disk, 16 cm. in diameter, is covered on both sides with a so-far undeciphered hieroglyphic inscription spiralling to the centre. Its 241 miniature figures include vases, animals, birds, fish, insects and ships as well as men, women and children. What may be a religious hymn or magical incantation you can now see reproduced in all the souvenir shops as earrings, key chains or cocktail coasters.

The ceramics include red-and-white patterned Kamares vases and the first eggshell ware from Knossos, so called because of its exceptionally thin fabrication.

Gallery 4: from Knossos's golden "Neopalatial" age (1700–1450 B.C.), two polychrome faïence figures of Snake Goddesses or priestesses, perhaps mother and daughter. In the carefree Minoan fashion, the dresses leave the breasts bare. Snakes coil around mother's tiara, breasts and waist, while daughter has a small leopard on her cap and brandishes a snake in each hand.

The ivory statue of a Bull-Leaping Acrobat shows him in full flight in an audacious athletic ritual involving the bull, a central figure of Minoan culture. The bull, symbol of virility, is represented here in the striking black serpentine Bull's Head Chalice, or *rhyton*, used for sacred libations poured through the mouth and the crown of the head. The gilded wooden horns have been reconstituted from a sketch found on base, but eyes and nose are formed by original incrustations of rock crystal, jasper and mother-of-pearl.

Gallery 7: also Neopalatial, stone vases from Agia Triada are remarkable for their vivid carving. The tall Boxer Vase of dark green serpentine is decorated with four scenes depicting boxers wearing helmets, and a bull-leaper. The Chieftain Cup shows a chief receiving a gift of animal hides from a hunt or sacrifice. Liveliest of all is the Harvester Vase, shaped like an ostrich egg, which has a rustic scene of peasants laughing and singing behind a priest and musicians in a ritual autumn harvest procession.

Gallery 14: in this **Hall of Frescoes**, among the most significant is the series decorating the Sarcophagus of Agia Triada, cut from a single limestone block. One side shows, to the right, a funeral procession in which a personification of the deceased receives offerings of calves and a model boat, probably for his voyage to the Land of the Dead; to the left, women perform a purification rite between two pillars topped by the sacred Minoan double-headed axe while a musician plays the lyre. Along the opposite side is a bull-sacrifice performed by women, accompanied by a flute player. At each end, in poorer condition, are scenes of goddesses with chariots.

From the frescoes found at Knossos, a priestess or goddess has been nicknamed by archaeologists La Parisienne, no doubt because of her elaborate coiffure, big eyes and sensual red mouth. More demure are the pretty Ladies in Blue. The delicate Prince of the Lilies with peacock feathers in his hat does not look as if he would do very well in the bull-leaping depicted in the Toreador Fresco. Whereas men are shown sun-tanned, women, who also participated in this rough, tough sport, dressed in male attire, apparently kept their complexion milky white.

Historical Museum

On the other side of town, across from the Xenia Hotel, the Historical Museum continues Crete's story beyond the Minoan civilization. The collections include Early Christian sculpture from Gortys; Byzantine icons, frescoes and bronze liturgical instruments; sculpture from the 17th-century Venetian loggia and the coat of arms of a Venetian Jewish family with a motto in Hebrew; Turkish tombstones; a typical Cretan peasant dwelling, with traditional costumes and fabrics; and a reconstruction of Kazantzakis' study, with his desk, library, photographs and personal memorabilia.

Central Crete   18 C3

In valleys between the Ida and Lasíthi mountains, the Minoan nobility built their earliest road linking their summer residence at Knossos and winter homes at Phaistos and Agia Triada. Roughly the same route is followed today to the island's principal archaeological sites, including the old Roman capital of Gortys—and beyond to the seaside resorts on the south coast. Knossos needs a day to itself. The others can be comfortably combined in one excursion (tourist agencies run guided tours), with the bonus of a swim at Matala or Agia Galini at the end of the day.

Knossos   19 C3

Just 5 km. (3 mi.) south of Iraklion, you enter the excavated palace of King Minos under an arcade of magenta bougainvillea. There on the **West Court** is a bronze bust of Sir Arthur Evans, the man who uncovered and reconstructed—some say excessively—the Minoan world of Knossos. On the left of the court are three well-like walled pits that

The Diggers
Director of Oxford's Ashmolean Museum, Sir Arthur Evans (1851–1941) began scratching around Knossos in 1894. Hoping to solve the linguistic riddles of Greece's earliest settlements, he was looking for clay tablets with pictographic inscriptions and engraved seal stones like those found on Mycenaean sites in the Peloponnese.

Some 16 years earlier, a local amateur archaeologist with the appropriate name of Minos Kalokairinos had unearthed what Evans later identified as the Minoan palace's storerooms. The Turkish authorities stopped the excavations, but the discovery attracted the attention of the eccentric German digger Heinrich Schliemann, the man of Troy and Mycenae (see p. 226). Like some latterday Agamemnon avid to hold on to the spoils of past battles, he haggled over the price of the land, even the number of olive trees, and abandoned the site in high dudgeon in 1886.

Evans arrived with money, energy, vision and a little more diplomatic skill than Schliemann. He had pleased the Greeks with his anti-Turkish articles in the *Manchester Guardian* and after Crete won its autonomy was given a free hand to dig at leisure. From 1900 to 1940 he toiled away on the hillside he bought in the Kairatos Valley. He turned up relatively few clay tablets and seal stones, but managed to content himself with the stupendous treasure trove of King Minos's palace.

in fact served as sunken granaries. Notice how the stone blocks of the palace's western façade are blackened by the fire of its destruction, probably by earthquake around 1500 B.C.

Within minutes, tourists penetrating the palace precincts arrive at a conclusion that students of antiquity took years to reach. The palace of Knossos is itself laid out like the kind of labyrinth in which King Minos imprisoned the Minotaur. Broad corridors, narrow zigzagging passages, stairways with L-shaped, T-shaped and X-shaped landings lead up and down and in and out of courtyards and vestibules among the palace's approximately 1,200 rooms. Just when you think you have got to the heart of the palace, the great central court, the corridor deviates away from it. Once you have arrived, you will find that a stairway leading out will just double back, and you will swear you hear Minos snicker. Various theories suggest that the intricate layout was a deliberate plan to foil invading enemies or evil spirits. Some gloomy scholars have suggested that Knossos was not a palace at all, but a giant mausoleum like the Egyptian pyramids, in which following the complicated pattern was part of a sacred ritual. Or is the maze a natural creation of the Minoans' sense of play so wonderfully depicted in their art?

Adopting the last theory as the most attractive, the game, then, is to get to the central court. It can be done. Leaving Sir Arthur behind you, turn right to the south and take the **Corridor of Processions.** The frescoes here, like others on the site, are "recreations" by the Gilliérons, a Swiss father and son, of originals preserved in Iraklion's Archaeological Museum. Some feel that the paintings, like Evans' reconstructions of columns and other masonry, have been overdone and detract from the ancient palace's mystery. But they do serve to clarify the functions and settings of what would otherwise be very anonymous, unadorned stones. Here, like others on ceremonial occasions, two curly-haired, dark-skinned Minoans in loin cloths are shown carrying vessels towards the centre of the palace.

Turn left (east) towards the columned vestibule of the **South Propylaea.** Note the characteristic downward taper of the reconstructed columns. A grand staircase leads north up to what Evans called the **piano nobile**, borrowing a term from the Italian Renaissance for the loftier reception rooms of an upper storey. A balcony here gives you your first view of the central court.

The earthquake has left several paths down, but we suggest continuing north via the palace's **Sanctuary.** In keeping with the intimate, human scale of their lives, the Minoans did not have monumental temples for their worship but preferred the small shrines and chapels you will see here. Immediately north (left) of a stairway leading into the central court is the entrance, via an antechamber with a marble basin, to the **Throne Room.** Frescoes of griffins guard a small gypsum throne, probably not the royal seat of Minos but the ritual chair of the high priestess known as the Lady of the Labyrinth. In front is a sunken area for purification rites. On the other side of the sanctuary's staircase is a columned **crypt and treasury** where various cult objects were excavated, including the snake-goddesses now in Iraklion's museum. It is believed that the sacred snakes had their home here.

Time now to stroll around the grand **Central Court**, 53 m. (174 ft.) long and 26.5 m. (87 ft.) wide, and imagine the scenes witnessed here 4,000 years ago. This is where they held the athletic contests and great bull-leaping ritual so vividly depicted in the frescoes and sculpture. Picture the buildings surrounding the court topped by symbolic bull-horns. Tiers of spectators gather in open-air galleries supported on blood-red, gold-banded columns. Festive throngs of Minoan women spectators fan themselves with white ostrich plumes, their doe-eyes

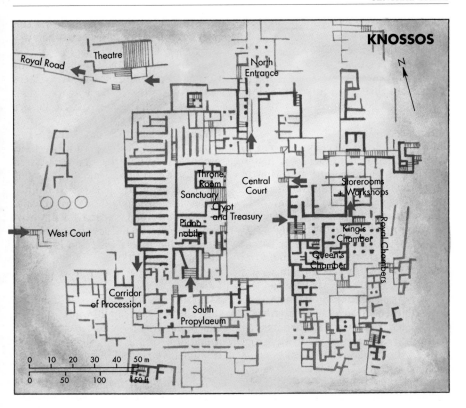

KNOSSOS

Royal Road

Theatre

North Entrance

N

Throne Room

Central Court

Sanctuary

Storerooms + Workshops

Crypt and Treasury

Piano nobile

King's Chamber

Queen's Chamber

West Court

Royal Chambers

Corridor of Procession

South Propylaeum

0 10 20 30 40 50 m

0 50 100 150 ft

outlined and shadowed with green malachite, their reddened lips highlighted against white face paint. In their elaborately curled hair, jewels and pendants sparkle in the sunlight. Long, brightly coloured dresses conceal their legs but leave their breasts bare. The Minoan men are relaxed and casual—not stiff and formal like the later Greeks—their coiffures, equally elaborate and bejewelled, framing eyes also accentuated by makeup. Deeply tanned, their lithe, muscular bodies are covered only by loincloths with tasselled codpieces.

Music spills across the courtyard to accompany the dancers and cartwheeling acrobats. Leather-helmeted boxers fight in the blazing sun. Fans toss flowers into the ring for the victor.

A hush falls over the spectators. Across the courtyard, the doors of the sanctuary open and a wide-eyed priestess emerges with writhing snakes in each hand. She intones an incantation, a blessing for the day's main event: the bull-leaping. The priestess withdraws, and athletes enter the arena with the first bull. The nervous creature is steadied by two female athletes standing at the head and tail. Hoisting himself up by grasping the bull by the horns, the first acrobat leaps headlong over the beast's back and then propels himself off its haunches for a final somersault onto the ground. The crowd roars its appreciation as one after another lands on his feet. Then, suddenly, a chorus of gasps as the bull balks and tosses his head and the acrobat is impaled on his horns, a terrible, but honourable death. Others triumph, others are sacrificed. The bulls themselves are sacrificed. Later, by torchlight, the divine beasts are roasted for the evening feast, honouring the quick and the dead.

On the east side of the court, opposite the sanctuary, a staircase leads down to what Evans identified as the **Royal Chambers**. These are the palace's best-preserved rooms. Set into the slope of the hill, the quarters were built on four floors, two above and two below the level of the central court. Lighting was channelled down to rooms on lower floors through an ingenious system of spacious light-wells. Shields in figure-eight shape and signs of the Minoan double axe mark the walls of what was probably the guardroom adjacent to the **King's Chamber**, where Evans found a wooden throne. A narrow passage leads across to the **Queen's Chamber**, decorated by a lively fresco of dolphins and flying fish. Next to it is a room with a clay bathtub, but scholars now feel this was the queen's bedroom, the bathroom probably being located down a dark spiral-frescoed corridor next to her dressing room. The toilet was originally equipped with a wooden seat and a still visible flushing system much admired by modern plumbers.

North of the royal quarters are the **Storerooms and Workshops** of the palace's tailors, goldsmiths, potters and stone-masons. Notice the enormous earthenware jars *(pithoi)* for storing grain, oil and wine and big enough for a man to

Stop Playing Around, Minos
Life in Minos's Royal Chambers was not all sweetness and honey. The name Minos meant "moon-being", and the ubiquitous double-headed axe was regarded as the waxing and waning moon joined back to back—symbolizing the king's power of creation and destruction. But it was Minos's excessive taste for philandering to which his wife Pasiphaë decided to put a stop. After her shocking affair with a bull that produced the Minotaur, she found an even more dastardly way of punishing her husband's persistent infidelity. She cast a spell on him so that he discharged not his seed, but serpents, scorpions and centipedes, which rather upset his mistresses.

hide in—or drown in, as Minos's son Glaucus found out to his cost when trying to help himself to some honey.

Leave the main palace-grounds through the **North Entrance**. It was here that Evans situated a customs house. North-west of the palace is a **theatre** seating some 500 spectators for ritual dances and perhaps boxing and wrestling matches. Leading away from it, probably to link up with a main road to Knossos's port at Katsambas is an impressively built **Royal Road** with rain-gutters running along the central paving. Imagine the road bordered with two- and three-storey houses like those depicted in the Town Mosaics in Iraklion's museum (see p. 118).

Gortys   19 C3
Make an early start if you are combining this old Roman capital with Phaistos and Agia Triada in one excursion, a round trip of 160 km. (100 mi.) from Iraklion if you include a swim at Matala. Leave Iraklion from the western gate *(Chanióporta)*.

The well-marked road passes through valleys of olive groves, cypresses and vineyards—the town of Daphnes produces some of the island's best wine. The landscape is dotted with rock outcrops and small rounds of rock known locally as "wheels of cheese". After the Pass of Vourvouliti, the rich farmland of the Plain of Messara opens up before you, with the Asterousia mountain to the south-east and the Libyan Sea gleaming in the distance. In spring, nature-lovers will be so entranced by the array of wild flowers here that they may never get to Gortys. In the village of **Agia Deka**—"Ten Saints"—the 13th-century church is built in part with fragments of Gortys's Roman ruins.

The **archaeological site** of Gortys is scattered over a large area. The Italian excavators have chosen not to try the kind of imaginative reconstruction carried out by Evans at Knossos. So the capital established on an ancient Dorian settlement by the Romans in 67 B.C. now presents the columns and statues of its temples and administrative buildings in a charming wilderness of trees and flowers. The site's major find, near the Roman Odeon, dates from around 500 B.C., when Dorian settlers carved their Code of Laws on massive blocks of stone. In 17,000 characters in rows to be read alternately from left to right and right to left, the code lays down the laws for adultery, seduction, rape, divorce, inheritance, property mortgage and the treatment of slaves. You can also see the Praetorium, residence of the Roman governor built of marble- and stone-faced concrete. There is a Temple of Isis and Serapis, Egyptian gods that were popular with the Romans; the Temple of Apollo has an interesting pyramidal altar.

From the post-Roman city, a centre of early Christianity, you can see the shell of the 7th-century basilica of **Ágios Títos** built in Greek-cross form and destroyed by Arab invaders in the 9th century.

Phaistos   19 C3

Of all the Minoan sites in Crete, the kings' winter palace and retreat of the priesthood enjoys the most enchanting setting. From the ruins, it commands a magnificent view over the long sweep of Messara flecked with olive groves and vineyards to the Libyan Sea. It is framed by Zeus's childhood playgrounds, Mount Dikti and Mount Ida, snow-capped in spring.

The palace was built and abandoned at the same time as Knossos. It was excavated by Italian archaeologists and, like Gortys, has not undergone Knossos's elaborate modern reconstitution of brightly painted columns and frescoes. As a result, the site's pristine ruins, resurrected but bearing all the marks of time and the elements, evoke more readily the palace-sanctuary's mystic qualities. Cretan monarchs, we remember, were both king and priest.

Phaistos has the same labyrinthine layout of corridors and stairways among the rooms as Knossos, with a similar central court, but all on a less massive scale. Start from a stairway down from the **North Court**, leaving on your right, outside the main palace grounds, a **theatre** with an elongated narrowing shape like a grand piano and similar to the one at Knossos.

Another, grander staircase leads left up to the **Propylaeum**, monumental entrance to the palace proper. Left again, across a hall where you can see the bases of its peristyle colonnade, are the **Royal Chambers**. What was probably the queen's suite has preserved its alabaster paving. East of the royal quarters are commoners' dwellings where the Phaistos Disk was found (see p.118). From the queen's rooms, a small courtyard and corridor lead back south to the long **Central Court**. It had porticoes along its east and west sides. Most of the eastern part of the court has collapsed down the hillside, but the column bases of the western portico are all still visible. Walk to the far end to see the **well** and then double back past what was the **Sanctuary** where you will see a two-pillared crypt and a hall with stone benches around its walls. Beyond the sanctuary, turn left down the **Corridor of Storehouses** and **Workshops** used for metal smelting and pottery. The last house on the right has some huge earthenware **storage jars** *(pithoi)* that held oil or wine—a receptacle is set in the ground to catch spillage. Notice the jars' many handles through which ropes were passed to haul the gigantic vessels around.

The palace originally covered far more ground, probably including a Minoan village. Now farms and houses stand over the area where Minoan structures are suspected to lie.

Agia Triada   18 C3

The Minoan **Royal Villa**, with a later Mycenaean-age village below it, is a 45-minute walk or 3-km. drive from the palace of Phaistos. Its Minoan name

Till the onslaught of earthquakes and Dorian invaders around 1400 B.C., life at the Palace of Knossos was easy-going. Excessive energies were devoted to sports rather than warfare, and the good things of life—especially food and wine—were plentiful. With their highly developed decorative sense, the Minoans turned even mundane storage containers like this giant pithoi *into ornate works of art.*

At Matala, a fine white sand beach slopes down to the Libyan Sea, while the famous caves provide some welcome shade.

remains a mystery, so it is known by that of a nearby Venetian church (not to be confused with the 14th-century Byzantine church of Ágios Geórgios directly above the excavations).

Scholarly guesses are that the site was the residence of the king's relatives or a summer hideaway for the king himself. With a splendid view out over Messara Bay, the villa is spacious but more intimate than the palaces, without a central court or monumental staircases. Its elegance is hinted at by fine alabaster paving.

It was here that Italian archaeologists unearthed, among several of the most valuable examples of everyday Minoan life, the great stone vases with their *Boxer*, *Chieftain* and *Harvester* motifs now on display in the Iraklion museum.

Of the later town (14th–12th century B.C.), you can see the main square *(agora)* bordered by what were originally arcades of shops.

Beaches
18 C3

Diligent explorers of archaeological sites deserve a good swim. The expanding resort of **Matala** offers a refreshing, if sometimes crowded, bathe in the Libyan Sea just 10 km. (6 mi.) south of Phaistos. The beach has fine, white sand and the sea is green and gentle. You may also want to visit the famous **Matala caves** *(Spiliés Matálon)*. They have had a varied career. First hewn out of the cliff by Romans for use as catacombs, they were subsequently inhabited by early Christians. After Germans set up artillery positions there in World War II, peace and love once more prevailed with the hippy troglodytes of the 1960s.

Agia Galini, 18 km. (11 mi.) north-west of Phaistos, is a booming tourist resort. A steep, winding road leads down to the resort, situated in a narrow crevice between high cliffs. Camping facilities are available and it offers good fishing and excellent seafood restaurants.

Eastern Crete   *19 D–E3*

Moving away from the centre of the ancient Minoan civilization, the island's attractions for the foreign visitor are more straightforwardly hedonistic. You will find first-rate beach resorts along the north-east coast, and the tourist industry has offered itself the ultimate accolade of dubbing the winding corniche coast road the "Cretan Riviera".

Barely an hour's drive east of Iraklion airport, Agios Nikolaos is the main resort, but there are smaller, less-crowded spots on either side. Inland, you can explore caves, hike in the Lasíthi mountains, wander around villages proud of their handicrafts. The south coast's main town, Ierapetra, is increasingly popular as a resort. Indefatigable archaeology buffs can visit the Minoan village of Gournia and the palaces of Malia and Kato Zakros. Toplou's monastery has a masterly icon. The region takes good care of body and spirit.

Agios Nikolaos   *19 D3*

Nestling at the heart of the splendid bay of Mirabello, this undoubtedly beautiful resort fights gamely to protect its natural charm against the onslaught of the package tour. The climate is rather dry, the winters mild, and the sports facilities excellent.

You must avoid July and August to enjoy the relaxed atmosphere of the fishing harbour. Elegant boutiques border the town's main (but short) street, Leofóros Koúndourou climbing from the harbour to the traffic circle of Platía Venizélos.

A man-made channel connects the harbour to **Lake Voulisméni**, once reputed "bottomless" but in fact 64 m. (210 ft.) deep, still a surprise for anyone casually dropping in. From its landward cliff, which has an aviary, you get a great view of lake and harbour. A *vólta* or evening promenade along the lake's quayside— the equivalent of the Italians' *passeggiata*—is almost a social obligation.

The town's **Archaeological Museum**, on Odós Paleológou leading away from the lake, boasts an admirable collection of Minoan ceramics and gold jewellery from regional sites. Most notable are the so-called "teapot" and "frying pan" vases and a distinctive libation vase with two orifices, known as the Goddess of Myrtos.

The **beaches** lie north of the harbour. Further along, the smarter hotels hiding among bougainvillea, olive and palm trees command a lovely rocky promontory. Occasional international exhibitions of modern art are held at the Minos Beach.

Mirabello Bay   *19 D3*

Explore this loveliest of Cretan bays with a boat excursion from Agios Nikolaos or a tortuous drive along the spectacular coast road. **Elounda** is a charming little fishing village on the bay's western shore. On the adjacent Spinalonga peninsula is **Olous**, a Greco-Roman settlement mostly submerged beneath the sea and a fascinating target for skindivers. On dry land an Early Christian church has been excavated to reveal a 4th-century dolphin mosaic. The nearby island of **Spinalonga** has an impressive 16th-century Venetian fort, captured by the Turks and used briefly at the beginning of this century as a leper colony (no health risk today).

On the east side of the bay, you will see ruins of Minoan settlements on the tiny islands of **Psira** and **Mochlos**, the latter opposite a very pleasant resort village of the same name.

Commanding a fine natural harbour, **Gournia**, 18 km. (11 mi.) from Agios Nikolaos, is the island's best preserved Minoan town. Excavated by American archaeologist Harriet Boyd Hawes, it reveals a clear ground plan of multistorey houses and shops around an Agora leading to the palace. The construction of modern Cretan villages is not so very different from the designs of 3,000 years ago.

127

These graceful windmills dotting the Lasithi Plains do not serve to grind flour and should more properly be known as wind pumps. Their sails draw subterranean water to the surface to irrigate the fields of cereals and potatoes, as well as apple orchards. The upland plateau in the Dikti mountains, difficult of access, made the region and ideal redoubt over the centuries for klephts fighting Venetians, Turks and Germans.

the steeply sloping streets, villagers sit in their doorways selling their shawls, rugs and table-linen.

In an olive grove on the edge of the village, the small white church of the **Most Holy Virgin** *(Panagiá Kerá)* is a treasury of 14th- and 15th-century frescoes that are among the most admired in Crete. The dome is decorated with four scenes from the gospel: the Presentation of Jesus at the Temple, the Baptism, the Resurrection of Lazarus and Christ's Entry into Jerusalem. On the vault of the nave you can see the Last Supper. Frescoes in the south aisle depict scenes from the life of the Virgin and her mother Anna, while those of the north aisle show the rivers and garden of Paradise, St Peter at the gate, and Abraham, Isaac and Jacob beside the enthroned Virgin.

If your car can take the rough road, follow the signs below Kritsa leading up to **Lato**, a Doric settlement founded in the 7th century B.C. Its spectacular site up in the mountains overlooking the Aegean is in any case worth a 45-minute walk. Students of antiquity will be interested to identify the city gate at the western end of the site, the agora in the

Tough Baby

Cretan tour-operators and scholars of Greek mythology argue about whether the Diktaean cave or the one on Mount Ida (see p. 134) was Zeus's birthplace. Another version, equally authoritative and popular with Peloponnesian tour-operators, suggests Zeus was in fact born on Mount Lycaeon, in the heart of the Peloponnese. His mother, Rhea, sent him off to Crete to save him from his father's plan to eat him. Because of a prophesy that he would be dethroned by one of his offspring, Cronos, Lord of the Titans, had already devoured his other five children. When he came looking for Zeus, Rhea fooled him with a stone wrapped in swaddling clothes, which he promptly swallowed. Zeus grew up in the Diktaean Cave, weaned on goat's milk and good Cretan honey. He spent his teens with shepherds on Mount Ida. When he was big enough, he went off and smote his father with a thunderbolt, a twist popular with Sigmund Freud.

Lasithi Plains   *19 D3*

This fertile plateau some 850 m. (2,800 ft.) up in the Dikti mountains offers pleasant excursions from Agios Nikolaos. The plains are dotted with orchards of apple and almond trees; a few remaining white-sailed windmills drive the irrigation system where they have not yet been replaced by oil-powered pumps.

Perched on a mountainside 12 km. (7½ mi.) from Agios Nikolaos, the almost excruciatingly picturesque town of **Kritsa** is celebrated for its weaving. Along

centre and a temple and theatre to the east. Others will be content to sit among the olive and almond groves and dream antique dreams.

Take your best walking shoes and a pocket torch for your visit to the **Diktaean Cave** *(Diktéon Ántron)*. The entrance to Zeus's old home, beyond the village of Psychro 75 km. (47 mi.) from Agios Nikolaos, is a steep and tricky descent and the cave is damp, slippery and dimly lit—just the way caves should be. There are some impressive stalactites. Bronze votive offerings and stone altars found here and now in Iraklion's museum revealed that the cave was a sanctuary during the Minoan era.

Malia and Limin Chersonisos   *19 D3*

These resorts owe their popularity to their long sandy beaches, among the finest in Crete, a wide range of accommodation and easy access to Minoan sites on or near the north coast.

The **Minoan palace** on the eastern outskirts of Malia dates from the same era as Knossos and Phaistos. The French excavators did little restoration, and you can ramble around the evocative ruins with a superb view over the sea. Next to the ceremonial staircase just off the south-west corner of the Central Court is a remarkable circular **kernos** or ritual table. Set in the limestone slab are 34 small depressions around a central hollow. One theory is that fruit seeds or grain were placed in the hollows as offerings for a good harvest. Another suggests it was used for gambling, comparable to certain board games found in Africa. A short walk north of the palace is the **Chrysolakos** (pit of gold), a royal burial chamber where clay idols and an exquisite gold honeybee pendant were found, now deposited in Iraklion's Archaeological Museum.

Ierapetra   *19 D3*

East of Gournia, the road cuts across the island at its narrowest point, just 14 km. (9 mi.) to a resort proclaimed to be Europe's southernmost town. Certainly it is the only large town on Crete's south coast, and its mild climate and year-round fresh fruit and vegetables make it an attractive spot, even or especially in winter when the crowds have gone. It has a good beach, and a **Venetian fort** dating back to the 13th century adds character to the fishing harbour. A Turkish fountain and minaret still stand in the town centre. In summer, boats go out to the little island of **Chrysi** for a quieter swim and meal in the taverna.

East Coast   *19 E3*

The heady drive from Agios Nikolaos to the eastern end of the island winds along a mountain road with plunging views over the sea. This is the corniche they call the Cretan Riviera. Between orchards and olive groves, it passes white villages perched precariously on steep slopes, clearly ready to topple into the ravine at the first hint of an earthquake. This was the frequent fate of **Sitia**, a Venetian port much plundered by Turkish pirates and now an attractive port of call for boats from Rhodes and Santorini. The beaches are good and the restaurants very good. Visit the **Archaeological Museum** before going to the Minoan palace of Kato Zakros, from which it exhibits many of the most recent finds.

East of Sitia, a short, rough road after a turn-off leads to the 14th-century **Toploú Monastery**. Its icon, *Lord, Thou Art Great* (1770) by Ioannis Kornaros, is a hallowed masterpiece of Byzantine art.

Further north, cool off from your strenuous mountain drive with a dip in the sea at the fine sandy beach of **Vaï**. The name means "palm" in Greek—the (very popular) beach is surrounded by groves of palm trees said to have grown from date stones spat out by Arab invaders.

At the far eastern end of the island is the fourth of the great Minoan palaces: **Kato Zakros**. The road crosses a high plateau with views across a vast gorge and Karoubes Bay before winding through banana plantations down to the sea and a delightful little beach with pleasant tavernas. The **Minoan palace** was enriched by its flourishing port trade with Egypt and the Middle East. Its ceramics and stone vases, ivory and bronze artefacts (now displayed in Iraklion and Sitia) are among the finest found in Crete. The palace layout is similar to those at Knossos, Phaistos and Malia, but with the rare distinction of a well-defined kitchen area north of the Central Court. Climb up to the ancient town above the palace for a good view over the whole site.

Western Crete   *18 A–C3*

This quieter end of the island affords a great opportunity to explore small inland villages, sleepy fishing ports and the secluded beaches of the south-west coast. But in Rethymnon and Chania, it also has two popular resorts with good water sports facilities and colourful reminders of the Venetian and Turkish past. Ramblers with a taste for the great outdoors head for Zeus's cave on Mount Ida and the Samaria and Imbros gorges in the White Mountains.

Rethymnon   *18 B3*
Well-established tourist facilities are now being enhanced by a steady programme of restoration in the attractive old quarters of the town's Venetian heyday and the Turkish years.

Down on the seafront a long sandy beach curves lazily around the bay. The Venizelou promenade is lined with outdoor cafés, restaurants and shops, the natural venue for Rethymnon's evening stroll, the *vólta*.

But to plunge into that dual historic ambience, park your car by the public gardens (scene of the July Wine Festival) and pass under the arched Venetian gateway, **Porta Cuora**, to take the narrow streets meandering down to the harbour. Shops installed in the old houses offer an enchanting combination of Venetian façades with Turkish overhanging wooden balconies. A minaret and domes have turned the church of Santa Maria into the **Mosque of Neranzies** *(Djamí ton Neranzión)*. You get a fine view of the city from the balcony where once the muezzin called the faithful to prayer. Nearby, the lion-headed **Arimondi Fountain** is the strange fruit of a similar involuntary collaboration of Venetian and Turkish craftsmen.

The town's small **Archaeological Museum**, housed in a 16th-century Venetian loggia, displays prehistoric clay sarcophagi, stone and clay figurines, tools of bone and obsidian, Bronze Age jewellery, and ritual artefacts from Zeus's Idaian Cave (see p. 134).

Dominating the town's western promontory is the imposing Venetian **Fortétza** (1574), reached by an ancient stairway from Odós Melissinoú. The outer wall, worth the visit for its fine view over the harbour, once enclosed warehouses, garrison, artillery placements, a church and hospital. Today, near the main gate, only part of the governor's residence remains standing.

Monastery of Arkadi   *18 C3*
A 45-minute drive south-east of Rethymnon (via Platanias) takes you up along a spectacular gorge to one of the

*V*iewing the colourful, relaxed life along Chania's harbourfront, people can scarcely guess the violent past of what was a kingpin among Venice's fiercely defended trading posts in the south-eastern Mediterranean. Only a fragment remains of the ramparts stormed by the Turks in 1645. The harbour suffered further heavy bombardment in World War II. *(Pages 132–133)*.

most revered sites of Crete's resistance to Turkish occupation. Perched on a rugged mountainside, the monastery became in 1866 an armed bastion of revolt, with hundreds of villagers taking refuge within its walls. Rather than surrender to the besieging Turkish troops, Abbot Gabriel waited for them to break into the monastery and then blew up the gunpowder magazine, killing hundreds of enemy soldiers and nearly 1,000 villagers.

The 16th-century monastery has been restored to something of its former ornate Venetian self. You will notice that the refectory is still pockmarked with bulletholes. A **museum** preserves relics of the suicidal massacre with an ossuary displaying the victims' bones, as is the Orthodox custom. Every November 9 in Rethymnon and Arkadi, solemn memorial services and festive fireworks, music and dancing celebrate the anniversary of this supreme demonstration of the Cretan slogan: "Freedom or death".

Idaian Cave   18 C3

It was easy for Zeus. He was whisked up here on a cloud. For us ordinary mortals, the mountain road to his childhood home is a rough but manageable drive—remember that Pythagoras made the pilgrimage on foot. But the scenery alone makes the trip worthwhile. (Before you set out, check with Rethymnon's tourist office, as the cave is sometimes closed because of archaeological excavations.)

From Rethymnon, drive 52 km. (33 mi.) east via Perama to the little hill village of **Anogia**, where the residents like to put on a traditional dance or two and sell their brightly woven fabrics—save the local wine for later, there is a little hike from the car park.

Just beyond the village the mountain road turns off south up to **Mount Ida,** locally more commonly known as *Psilorítis,* "the high one", in fact Crete's highest one—2,456 m. (8,058 ft.). It is snow-capped till late spring, but in May and June, the wild flowers along your route are a sheer joy, with a veritable explosion of colour when you get to the **Plain of Nida**, 1,400 m. (4,593 ft.). The road forks left to a café and car park, and the famous cave is a further 20-minute walk.

Whatever the competing claims of the Diktaean Cave (see p. 130), the Greeks certainly treated the **Idaian Cave** as a sanctuary. Italian excavators found votive offerings, jewellery and ceremonial bronze shields and a bronze drum now on display in Iraklion's museum.

Chania   18 B3

The buildings of this resort cover the post-Minoan city of Kydonia, and show an agreeable mixture of Venetian and Turkish influences. To keep the charm intact, make a conscious effort to ignore the garish modern neighbourhoods.

The town's outstanding feature is the grand loop of the **Venetian Harbour**. At night, viewed from the lighthouse at the end of the long breakwater of golden stone, the lights of the shops, cafés and taverns can be pure enchantment. At the west end of the loop is the Firkás, a restored section of the Venetian ramparts, housing the **Naval Museum** *(Naftikó Mousío)* with ship models and scenes of key episodes in Greek naval history. Facing it is the Mosque of the Janissaries (1645), now a tourist information centre.

The heart of ancient Kydonia is buried beneath the **Kastélli quarter** behind the mosque. Some of it came to light after the bombardments of World War II and, as you will see in an occasional trench or pit, archaeologists ever since have been pottering around until chased away by new builders.

The neighbouring **Splánzia quarter** to the east is dominated on the waterfront by the Arsenals, where the Venetians built and repaired their ships. Behind them you can walk back to the Orthodox church of **Ágios Nikólaos**, ecumenically sporting a Venetian Catholic bell-tower and Turkish Muslim minaret.

In the **Topaná quarter** behind the

Firkás, explore the narrow lanes where the houses have Venetian stone façades with wooden upper storeys added by the Turks. Stroll along Odós Theotokopoúlou for good local craftware.

For a wide range of leather goods, including handmade shoes and boots, head for Odós Skridlof in the old Jewish quarter, Evréïka. Housed in the Venetian monastery church of St Francis in Evréïka, the **Archaeological Museum** has interesting Minoan clay coffins and tomb sculpture.

A covered **market** *(Dimotikí Agorá)* dominates the centre of town. Bustling but clean and efficient, the stalls, overflowing with Cretan fruit and vegetables, show just how fertile an island it is. Get the olives, tomatoes, salad and goat cheese here for your picnic.

Away from the city centre, at Odós Sfakianáki 20, the **Historical Museum** is interesting to anyone curious about the pungent flavour of modern Greek and more especially Cretan patriotism. It exhibits the earnest, flashing-eyed portraits of rebel chiefs throughout the struggles for independence and documents the resistance to Turks and Germans. A special room is given over to the career of Chania's most illustrious son, Eleftherios Venizelos (1864–1936).

Akrotiri   *18 B3*
The peninsula east of Chania makes an easy excursion. First stop is a hill, **Profitis Ilías**, scene of the Cretan insurgents' heroic resistance to the Turks in 1897. From beside the impressive **tomb of Eleftherios Venizelos** (Greek prime minister, see p. 31), you get a panoramic view over the Gulf of Chania.

Drive through the peninsula's cheerful countryside, bright with wild flowers in springtime, to visit three monasteries. The fine 17th-century **Agía Triáda** (Holy Trinity) with its nest of domes is a major pilgrimage centre welcoming visitors. Just a few kilometres further (an hour's hike) is the older and more isolated **Moní Gouvernétou**. It's another bracing 1-hour

hike down to the abandoned monastery of **Katholikó** built beside a bridge at the foot of the cliffs. The caves were inhabited by pagan and Christian hermits, with stalagmites to hang their clothes on.

Samaria and Imbros Gorges   *18 B3*
For a truly indelible impression of Crete as a force of nature, take one or both of the excursions we propose, a drive and hike through gorges of the Lefka Mountains south of Chania.

The landscape is of that awe-inspiring quality that forces meditation—gentle orange groves in the valleys giving way to pine trees overhanging sheer ravines, wild flowers sparkling in dramatic plays of sun and foreboding shadow, colours changing from silvery morning haze to brilliant gold at noon, softening to pink and purple at the end of the afternoon.

There are two approaches to the more popular **Samaria Gorge**, 18 km. (11 mi.) long. One way is to take a taxi or bus to Omalos, 42 km. (26 mi.) from Chania, then hike down to the sea at Agia Roumeli, where a boat takes you to the bus (or pre-arranged taxi) at Chora Sfakion. Or drive directly to Chora Sfakion for the boat to Agia Roumeli to explore just the bottom of the gorge in the early morning before the day-hikers reach it.

If you are hiking right through the gorge, **Omalos** is a good place to breakfast at a café and stock up with picnic goods. You will find springs, drinking troughs and a couple of toilets down in the gorge. Take along a bottle of water, all the same, and a hat, as the sun beats down strongly and there's little shade. You'll also need good walking shoes.

The descent to the gorge begins on a wooden staircase *(xylóskala,* which is also the name of the bus terminus). Park wardens give you a ticket (no charge) to be given up at the other end as a means of checking that no one is stranded in the gorge at the end of the day.

With the huge rock wall of **Mount Gingilos** towering on your right, the staircase dwindles into a path dropping

135

sharply 1,000 m. (3,280 ft.) to the upper gorge bed in the first few kilometres. Take it easy and keep to the designated path. The route is considerably less steep once you reach the chapel of Ágios Nikólaos tucked away among some majestic cypresses and pines on your right. Among the blues, greens and greys of the rocks, the pools are invitingly cool and clear, but swimming is strictly forbidden. But nobody will stop you scrumping the fig trees.

The hamlet of Samaria and the little Venetian church of Ossia Maria (Mary's Bones) mark the halfway point. Beyond it is the gorge's narrowest point, the famous Iron Gates (Sideróportes) hemmed in on either side by rock walls 300 m. (1,000 ft.) high. From here, the gorge opens up in its approach to the sea. Paddle across the shallow Tarraios River and you are almost there. At Agia Roumeli, the Libyan Sea awaits you for a relaxing swim. If you are fresh enough, you may like to visit the church of the Panagía built over an ancient temple to Apollo whose black, white and red mosaic floor can be seen in the forecourt.

A 90-minute bus ride on the deliciously hair-raising Chania–Chora Sfakion road brings you to the village of Imbros, the start of an 11-km. (7-mi.) hike through the Imbros Gorge almost to the sea, in an easy 5 to 6 hours. If you are taking a taxi, ask your driver to stop for a moment at Vryses to sample what connoisseurs consider to be the best yoghurt and honey on the island. To start the hike, at the end of the village of Imbros take a sharp left down to the dried-up river bed and then turn right towards the sea. This hike offers a gentler descent

than Samaria but with equally spectacular scenery, notable for its wild flowers, including the lovely purple blooms of Jerusalem sage.

The gorge ends at the village of Kommitades, where a bus takes you down to Chora Sfakion, with its beach for swimming and seafood restaurants bordering the harbour. Some 15 km. (9½ mi.) to the east is the stark silhouette of the massive 14th-century Venetian fortress of Frangokastello. Its fine sandy beach is accessible by boat or road. At dawn in mid-May, climatic conditions create an eerie mist around the castle's four great towers, and Cretans see the ghosts of Sfakiots who died defending the fort against the Turks.

Western Beaches   *18 A–B3*

West of Chania, the facilities for water sports or plain lazy beach-bumming vary from sophisticated to the very simple. On the north coast are the elaborate modern resort complex of Maleme and long, sandy beaches of Kastelli Kissamou. On the west coast is the splendid curving bay of Falasarna, an important trade port in the 4th century B.C. Down the coast, visit the delightful little fishing village of Sfinari and bathe at its pebble beach.

On the south coast, Paleochora is a busy little port with plenty of accommodation and lively taverns. It is a good base from which to take sea excursions out to the coral pink beaches of the Elafonisi islands or further south to Gavdos, where Odysseus dallied with fair Calypso while his poor wife Penelope was patiently weaving and unravelling her tapestry.

*I*t can be strenuous going down to the Iron Gates of the Samaria Gorge, where the hardy hiker is soon sorted out from the casual tourist. But it's well worth the effort, and the reward, not far beyond, is a refreshing dip in the sea at Agia Roumeli.

ART IN ANCIENT GREECE

Bull-leaping fresco from Knossos (Iraklion Museum)

Under the influence of southern Mediterranean and northern European cultures, the artistic pendulum of ancient Greece swings back and forth between warm hedonism and cool, orderly sobriety.

Minoan Civilization (1600–1400 B.C.)
Light and colour are the dominant features of art in Minoan Crete, as we can see at the palace of Knossos and the museum collection at Iraklion, and also in the frescoes of the Minoan settlement on Santorini (currently displayed in Athens). The overall tone is of a warm-blooded sensuality drawing inspiration from the island's Egyptian and other Middle Eastern neighbours.

The convivial **architecture** reflects the Minoans' taste for easy living: no massive fortifications to fend off invaders, palaces and villas that emphasize the human scale—small decorative rooms, brightly lit, terraces and verandahs from which to enjoy a sunset and the landscape.

Palace **frescoes** are vibrant with life, depicting plants, animals and people with a great sense of movement, humour and individuality that set Minoan art apart from the later more formal and intellectual art of classical Greece.

The intimate scale of Cretan palace life did not lend itself to monumental statuary, and **sculpture** takes the form of elegant polychrome figurines, most notably the bare-breasted snake-goddesses of Knossos. Wheel-turned **ceramics** produced eggshell-thin pottery glazed in high-temperature kilns and delicately painted with motifs similar to those of the frescoes. As the Cretan civilization declined, human and animal forms became more stylized without losing their finesse. **Jewellery** was also highly sophisticated, using gold, silver and ivory with incrusted gems.

Mycenae (1400–1200 B.C.)
The early art of the Peloponnese shows a clear Minoan influence, but with a tougher, more "masculine" edge to it, brought into Greece by the first wave of northern invaders. This is apparent in the earliest Greek monumental **sculpture**, the powerful Lion Gate at Agamemnon's Mycenae palace. Other art of the age can best be seen in Athens' National Archaeological Museum.

Picking up on the late Minoan stylized figures, Mycenaean **frescoes** disdained naturalism but preferred manly themes of war and the hunt to Minoan dances and butterfly-chasing. **Ceramics** were less delicate and ornate, but the Mycenaeans proved themselves masterly **goldsmiths**. With subtle techniques of etched and inlaid damascene, embossing and chasing, they produced splendid goblets, vases, seals, swords and the kings' famous funerary death masks.

From Geometric to Archaic
(900–500 B.C.)

Archaeologists define Greek art between the fall of Mycenae and the dawn of the classical era by its most visible forms, the styles of painted **ceramics**. Highly stylized late-Mycenaean figures of animals and humans gradually evolved into zigzagging, wavy or swastika-like geometric patterns. Simple, even crude in Boeotia and the Cyclades, the Geometric pottery of Attica and Athens is ornate and elegant, reflecting the wealth of Athenian aristocrats and already suggesting an intellectualized sense of beauty.

In **architecture**, the first temples appeared between 850 and 750 B.C. in the Peloponnese at Perachora (near Corinth) and Argos as simple hairpin-shaped or rectangular wooden shelters for the god's statue. A temple was the house of a god, not of his worshippers, who observed his statue from afar and left their offerings on the altar erected outside. The stone edifices that followed in the 7th century B.C. derived their structural elements from the wooden temples. The fluted stone columns imitated the old pillars of trimmed tree trunks. Beam-ends for the roof became triple-grooved blocks (triglyphs) between the carved panels of the metope. The latter were originally just terracotta slabs blocking gaps between the roof-beams so as to keep birds out of the temple.

Two basic styles of Greek architecture emerged. The Doric order of the Peloponnese was marked by power, sobriety and rigour. More graceful, ornate and fanciful,

Archaic Sphynx
(Keramikos Museum, Athens)

the slightly later Ionic order spread through the Aegean islands in the 6th century B.C. from the coast of Asia Minor. Athens achieved a synthesis of the two, using Ionic suppleness to modify Doric severity.

The differences are most easily seen in the temple columns. The robust Doric column, inspired by the sturdy oaks of the Peloponnese, has sharp-edged fluting, no base and a simple, slightly curved capital to support the entablature. The more slender Ionic column usually has less pronounced fluting, but its most distinctive feature is the elegantly scrolled capital. Beneath the roof, Ionic entablatures have ornate detail framing a continuous sculpted frieze rather than the individual metope panels of Doric entablatures.

Among the major Doric edifices of the Archaic period are the Temple of Artemis at Corfu (a Corinthian colony) and the treasury shrines of Olympia. Ionian temples like the Heraion on Samos are often more colossal, on the Oriental model.

With the evolution of the temple, **sculpture** developed to monumental size. Female caryatid statues double as pillars. Life-size male *kouros* and female *kore* figures represent deities, priests and priestesses. In all the major museums you will usually find examples of these males naked and females in light tunics, most often standing upright with the left leg forward, almond-

Agamemnon's Death Mask from Mycenae
(National Museum, Athens)

shaped eyes and rather thick lips set in the famous enigmatic "archaic" smile. Notice the stylized decorative hairdress, often with a braid and "snail shell" curl on the forehead. At the end of the Archaic period, you will find more realism in the muscles, knee joints, pubic hair. The smile has faded into a more serious, sometimes even frowning expression.

Again there are Doric and Ionic distinctions. Doric figures tend to be massive, rigid and severe. Females have a solid stability, with heavy long robes draped over scarcely delineated breasts to fall in folds resembling Doric columns. Ionic sculpture is more voluptuous. There is a taste for animals and mythical creatures, like the lithe lions of Delos. The *kouros* is less athletic, more decorative; clothed and even frankly corpulent, he is often seated and apparently enjoying the good life—not so pious. The *kore* is more lively, sensuous, her robe coquettishly emphasizing the curves of her body. Firmly muscled in Naxos, softer closer to the Asian coast, cheerful in Paros, positively merry in Chios.

Though early sculpture in Athens was less adventurous, a real style emerged at the end of the 6th century B.C. Beginnings of the Athenian synthesis can be seen in the greater psychological depth of a melancholy youth and his sulking sister, both in the Acropolis museum.

Ceramics flourished with the growing luxury trade in perfumes, wines and oils. Oriental influence is apparent in the bright colours and animal and plant motifs, most notably on Rhodes and the adjacent coast. Dominant in the 7th century B.C., Corinthian pottery, pale yellow with animal and human figures in black varnish, gradually lost markets to the more sophisticated red and black production of Athens.

The Classical Era (500–400 B.C.)
In the arts, the period of the Persian Wars (499–478 B.C.) should more properly be called pre-classical when, in the challenge for national survival, the prevalent tone is one of severity. The **sculpture** of this period is stern, stiff-upper-lip stuff, four square in the austere Doric tradition. The mood of Ionic figures is subdued rather than serene.

Under Pericles, Athens fulfilled the classical ideal of combining Ionic harmony and grace with Doric order and discipline. Phidias, the great sculptor and Pericles' "Minister of Culture", achieved the synthesis in overseeing the new **architecture** of the Acropolis. The Parthenon of Callicrates and Ictinus combined strong Doric columns and heroic metopes on the exterior with more

Poseidon, Apollo and Artemis from Parthenon frieze (Acropolis Museum)

140

ornate Ionic friezes on the interior peristyle. And we should not forget that the temple was originally completed by Phidias's own gold and ivory colossus of Athena. The Propylaea gatehouse is in the grandest Doric tradition, while the caryatid columns of the Erechtheion, completed in the Peloponnesian Wars, add a more gracious Ionic touch.

Classical **sculpture** perfected the athletic figure. Myron produced his famous *Discus Thrower*, known to us only in Roman marble copies of the bronze original. Polyclitus was the master of the ideally proportioned figure, surviving in copies of his *Doryphoros* (Youth Holding a Spear). But we can better judge the refinement of classical technique in the National Archaeological Museum's *Poseidon* (and the great Riace bronzes of two soldiers, probably by Phidias himself, in Reggio di Calabria). As the sculptor of gods and of men on a divine scale, Phidias gave his statues a new suppleness and freedom of line, and facial expression infused with a calm, very human spirituality, very much the classical ideal.

The humanism of the age influenced **ceramics**, too, refining the decoration and producing more psychological portrayals of its figures. The later motifs show a more relaxed Ionic ambience, more florid, indolent reclining figures in shimmering colours.

The 4th Century B.C.
The collapse of the Athenian empire ushered in an era of anguish. Socratic inquiry imposed an intense realism in the expression of emotions. In **sculpture**, the serenity of Phidias was replaced by the sensual languor of Praxiteles. Scopas of Paros is renowned for the passion and pathos of his hunting and battle scenes. The gods are portrayed with less exaltation, more of a sense of humanity and understanding of suffering. Lysippus, whose athletes have a more elongated beauty than those of Polyclitus, became court sculptor to Alexander, who liked his leonine but gentle portraits.

In **architecture**, the major development was the Corinthian column with the acanthus leaf motif on its capital. It first appeared on the the interior columns of the *tholos* (rotundas) at Delphi and Epidaurus and the Philippeion at Olympia. The theatre at Epidaurus is significant for its strict application of mathematical principles to achieve a thing of beauty.

The art of **ceramics** declined rapidly in a spate of tasteless facility. Athenian red-figure motifs disappeared by the end of the century.

Thereafter, with the advent of the Roman Empire, Greece was no longer master of its own art. But its legacy is eternal.

Corinthian columns, Temple of Olympian Zeus, Athens

Crusaders Have Made Way for Pilgrims Broiled Lobster-Pink

Rhodes' divine protector is Helios, god of the sun, still doing a pretty good job, on the premises 300 days a year. Fair-skinned worshippers from darkest northern Europe flock to his island. And he has plenty of time to spare for the Dodecanese archipelago along the Turkish coast. Crusaders' massive ramparts are a cool reminder of the rattle of battle with Turkish buccaneers. With luck, on remoter islands, the loudest sound you will hear is the crack of a pistachio nut.

If you are seeking an essentially peaceful holiday in this south-east corner of the Aegean, your best bet is to visit Rhodes as a side trip from a base on one of the smaller islands. There is no getting around it—Rhodes is a major destination for mass tourism. Despite new policies to spread people more evenly across the island, most of the beaches remain very crowded—although with a little perseverance you can hunt down more secluded spots off the beaten track. Nonetheless, the flowery gardens and historical sites, particularly in the old quarters of Rhodes Town itself and the village and ancient acropolis of Lindos, are still enormously rewarding. You just have to be an early enough bird to beat the mob. Similarly, the island of Kos, green and pleasant out of season, is fun for holiday-makers who like their holidays loud and boisterous.

Odós Ippotón, Street of the Knights, is the historic centre of the Crusaders' capital.

The quieter islands are rugged Patmos, something of an aristocrat, with its handsome coastal villas and private houses up in the capital around the hallowed monastery of St John the Divine; Kalymnos, proud home of the sponge divers and a mecca for underwater fishing; Astypalaea, remote and so still sedate, cultivating a rough chic; Karpathos, where villagers wear traditional costume for their own comfort rather than tourist postcards; and closer to Rhodes, the charming little Symi and Chalki, which avoid the masses by just not catering to them (yet).

The Dodecanese, as the Greek name *dodeka nisi* indicates, were 12 islands, united in 1908 against discriminatory Turkish legislation and subsequently joined by Rhodes and Kos. The islands came under Italian rule from the Italo-Turkish War of 1912 until 1947, when they formed a Greek administrative region covering some 200 islands of which only 14 have any sizeable population. How to get there? For island-by-island details of air and sea transportation

143

from mainland ports with inter-island connections, see the Island-Hopping directory in the blue pages of our Berlitz-Info section, p. 286.

Rhodes   20 B–C2

The joy of Rhodes is its smiling climate. More than living up to its name of the rose *(ródos)*, the island charms its visitors with the flowers adorning its courtyards: besides the rock rose, you will see and scent jasmine, hibiscus, bougainvillea and honeysuckle. The hills (apart from Mount Attaviros, 1,215 m. or 3,986 ft., Rhodes is rarely more than hilly) are fragrant with lavender, sage and marjoram. Its butterflies have a valley all their own. If you hear of the Rhodes Dragon, try to discourage your little boy from playing St George to slay the poor creature—it is only a green lizard measuring at best 18 inches long and very rarely breathing fire.

With the frequent wind, most often just hair-ruffling but sometimes quite gusty, most of the sheltered beaches are on the leeward east side of the island.

Rhodes is just 20 km. (12 mi.) from the Turkish mainland, and the Turkish heritage is still apparent in the capital at the north end of the island, where half the 90,000 population is concentrated. But the strongest cultural influence there—and elsewhere in the Dodecanese—remains that of its medieval masters, the crusader Knights of St John. Of the island's three ancient Greek trading ports, Lindos and Kamiros retain interesting archaeological sites, while Ialissos is now a beach and hill resort (modern Trianda and Filerimos). Island-hoppers should set aside three or four days to "do" Rhodes.

Rhodes Town   20 C2

The capital is two towns, the old and the new. The latter, with the exception of the harbour area, is without great charm—modern hotels, restaurants and shops.

The heart of the town, in all senses of the word, lies behind the fortifications in a maze of narrow streets where the wily wanderer can always duck away from the crowds and find a piece of authenticity and calm. Here again, there are two main areas: the Knights' Quarter with its medieval monuments, and the Turkish Quarter with its bazaar and mosques and old Jewish enclave.

The Knights of St John

Also known as Hospitallers, the Knights of St John were originally attached to a Catholic hostel and hospital founded in the 11th century by Italian merchants in Jerusalem. In their Rhodes bastion, they never numbered more than 600, all members of the noblest families in Europe. They took monastic vows of chastity, obedience and poverty, but their thirst for Muslim blood was decidedly un-Christian.

They divided into eight groups, according to "tongues": English, French, German, Italian, Aragonese Spanish, Castilian Spanish, Provençal French and Auvergnat French. Each group lived within a compound called an inn under an appointed prior. The security-conscious knights walked in pairs and left their walled domain only on horseback. About 5,000 Rhodian Christians staffed the forts and hospital.

Supported by Auvergne and Provence, the French outnumbered the other tongues when it came to electing the lifelong post of grand master. Thus, 14 of the 19 grand masters were French, and French was the order's spoken language (Latin for official documents). The Italians' natural maritime talents made them the obvious choice to command the knights' fleet, while other tongues each defended a section of the city walls, known as a "curtain".

Outside the city, the knights extended their system of defences with some 30 fortresses strung across the island and yet more on outlying islands. They were linked by an elaborate communications network of bonfires, smoke signals and homing pigeons.

After the Turkish invasion, the knights found a home on Malta until Napoleon drove them away to seek the Tsar's protection in St Petersburg, then the Pope's in Italy, ending up with "branches" of charitable, unbelligerent associations in the United States and Britain.

MERCHANTS AND KNIGHTS

Rhodes' destiny is marked by its proximity to Asia Minor and the Middle East. Carians from Anatolia and Phoenicians from Lebanon were its earliest settlers. Driven from Crete by earthquake and invaders from the Greek mainland, Minoan merchants set up shop in the ports of Lindos, Kamiros and Ialyssos to continue at closer quarters their lucrative trade with Egypt and the Levant. For the Greeks accompanying Agamemnon, Rhodes was a stepping stone between Crete and the Asia Minor coast where they were to conquer Troy. According to Homer, nine Rhodian ships sailed with the fleet.

By 700 B.C., Rhodes' three cities set up a trading league with the island of Kos and the Asia Minor ports Halicarnassus (now Bodrum) and Knidos. Looking westward, their merchants colonized the Costa Brava in Spain, Gela in Sicily, and Naples.

In the ancient conflicts, these inveterate navigators trimmed their sails according to the winds of their trading interests, but with varying success. Siding with the Persians, they went down to defeat at Marathon and ten years later lost 40 ships at Salamis. They supported Athens, then Persia again, against Macedonia, before seeing their advantage on Alexander's side in the trading concessions with Egypt. Turning against Alexander's Ptolemaic successors, they had to face and courageously withstand the brutal assault of Demetrius the Besieger in 305 B.C. From the huge amount of battle equipment he left behind him, they amassed the bronze to build the port's famous Colossus (see p. 153).

Under the Romans, they showed abominable political judgment, backing Macedonia against Rome, Pompey against Julius Caesar. Even when they resisted demands for support from Caesar's assassins, it cost them the plunder of 3,000 statues, with the lean and hungry Cassius leaving them "nothing but the sun".

But their scholarship commanded Rome's respect. Rhodian law inspired both Augustus and Justinian. Students at Rhodes' School of Rhetoric included Cicero, Julius Caesar and Mark Antony, who acquired what Latin scholars describe as a florid Asian style captured by Shakespeare's "Friends, Romans, countrymen, lend me your ears."

With the fall of Rome, Rhodes was constantly plundered by barbarians and pirates. Among the many Crusaders stopping off on their way to Palestine, Philippe Auguste of France and Richard the Lion-Heart recruited mercenaries in 1191. A century later, Genoese pirates sold the island to the equally ferocious Knights of the Order of St John, retreating from their role as defenders of pilgrims in the Holy Land. For the next 200 years, they turned Rhodes and its neighbouring islands into a maritime fortress to fight off Muslim assaults, occasionally sallying forth to carry the battle to the Turkish mainland. They also ran a hospital.

Sultan Suleiman the Magnificent seized the island in 1522, and under Turkish rule the island sank into four centuries of stagnant neglect. Things picked up under the Italians, occupying Rhodes as part of the Dodecanese ceded to them after their victory over the Turks in 1912. Ancient Greek sites were excavated, medieval buildings and monuments restored, new roads, homes and public buildings constructed. Mussolini's Fascists tried to suppress the Greek language and Orthodox Church, but they also made Rhodes a more accessible island to promote the development of tourism. After German occupation in World War II, the island was liberated by the British and united with Greece in 1947.

Palace of the Grand Masters

Fortifications

To get an overall view of the Old Town, it is a good idea to start with a walk along the top of the **ramparts.** The section open to the public (usually Monday and Saturday afternoons, tickets in the courtyard of the Grand Masters' Palace) covers about a mile, a third of the perimeter.

Quite apart from the historical interest, the walk along the walls starting from the monumental Amboise Gate is attractive for the wild flowers bordering the path and lush vegetation in the moats. The massive fortifications are themselves a major work of military art, evolving over the centuries as weapons changed from arrow and spear to cannon and gunpowder. The walls grew constantly more massive, often over 12 m. (40 ft.) thick, and were curved to deflect cannonballs. The southern section of ramparts allotted to the English and Spanish knights was particularly difficult to defend because the land rises outside the walls, making them more vulnerable to attack. The fortifications here are noticeably more extensive with extra towers and double moat. The moat between inner and outer walls never contained water but served to discourage invaders from putting up siege towers. You will see cannonballs down there serving as goalposts for schoolboys' football games, as well as others around the old town, neatly piled in pyramids. The iron ones were fired by the Turks, while those of limestone and marble, more handsome but less deadly, were catapulted over in an earlier epoch.

Knights' Quarter

Start your tour at the north-east corner of the Old Town, through the **Freedom Gate** *(Píli Eleftherías),* so named by the Italians who saw themselves as liberators of the island from Turkish oppression. The name remained valid for the Greeks when they took over after World War II. On Platía Símis, the little square just inside the gate, are some of the rare vestiges of the ancient Greek city, shafts of

columns and fragments of entabulature from the Temple of Aphrodite, 3rd century B.C.

Up the slope to the south, on Platía Argirokástrou, the curious **fountain** is a Byzantine baptismal font brought here by the Italians from a church in the south of the island. To the left, housed in the Knights' Arsenal, is the **Museum of Decorative Arts**, exhibiting local costumes, embroidery and ceramics and the reconstructed interior of a traditional Rhodian house.

Originally containing 158 rooms, of which about 15 are now open to the public, the Palace of the Grand Masters was a lavish home indeed for leaders who had taken vows of poverty. Destroyed by a gunpowder explosion in 1856, the palace was restored by Italian archaeologists and architects, to provide a summer residence for Mussolini—overthrown before he could use it.

Also facing onto the square is the **Inn of Auvergne**, built in 1507 with a fine Gothic doorway at its main entrance and now, like many of the other inns, housing administrative offices.

Continuing south past a shopping arcade, you come to the **Panagía tou Kástrou** (Virgin of the Fort). Originally the Knights' cathedral, it had its steeple transformed into a minaret and became a Turkish mosque (known to Rhodians as the "red mosque" because of the Christians executed here in 1523), and is now the Byzantine Museum.

Bypass for the moment the famous Odós Ippotón (Street of the Knights) to visit on Platía Nosokomíou (Hospital Square) the august **Knights' Hospital**, noble pretext for the island's massive defences and indeed the order's raison d'être. It was built on Roman ruins in the 15th century. Above the grand Gothic doorway of the main entrance, with its bas-relief of the Order of St John's coat-of-arms, was the hospital's chapel. Other ground-floor arches around the courtyard lead to storerooms now used by local merchants. Among the stone missiles piled in pyramids are some said to have been used in the siege of Rhodes by Demetrius in 305 B.C. A marble lion of the 1st century A.D. sits in the centre.

The infirmary along the upstairs gallery had canopied beds and isolation cells for a hundred patients. Surgeons tended pilgrims, often quarantined from recurring plagues. But in a bizarre vicious circle, most of the patients were the knights themselves, wounded defending the hospital. They in turn had to make room for their companions who had continued the battle. And so on.

The hospital now houses the **Archaeological Museum** with its fine collection of ancient sculpture, Mycenaean vases and jewellery. The marble Aphrodite of the 3rd century B.C., popularly known as the Marine Venus on which writer Lawrence Durrell wrote his *Reflections*, was netted off the coast of Rhodes by fishermen in 1929. The kneeling Aphrodite of Rhodes (1st century B.C.), sculpturally more graceful, holds out her long wavy hair to dry in the sun after emerging from the sea. Other sculpture includes a tombstone bas-relief (5th century B.C.) of a daughter taking leave of her mother, and a striking head of the island's sun god, Helios (2nd century B.C.).

Across Hospital Square stands the **Inn of England**, reduced to rubble by earthquake and the 1856 gunpowder explosion (see p. 149) and restored a century later by the British. But already in 1533, three years after their fellow knights had found a new home on Malta, the English left the Order following the Pope's excommunication of Henry VIII.

Now stroll up the narrow cobblestoned **Odós Ippotón**, one of the most remarkable medieval thoroughfares in Europe, for which we must thank the Italians' meticulous restoration work completed in 1916. On the right opposite the hospital, the **Inn of Italy** is the first you come to, with the emblem of 16th-century grand master Fabrizio del Carretto sculpted over the doorway. Next door is the mansion of Villiers de l'Isle-Adam, who as Carretto's French successor had the sad task of surrendering to Sultan Suleiman in 1522.

Opposite the mansion, the hospital's original main gate led directly to the infirmary. Just beyond the hospital, behind a wrought-iron gate, is a charming shady garden with a Turkish fountain and the museum's marble relics stored among the palm trees and shrubs.

Facing the garden, with the royal fleur-de-lis among the coats of arms, are the splendid late-Gothic façades of the **Inn of France**, its chapel and the chaplain's residence. The doorway inscription dates the inn back to 1492, but the chapel, with Virgin and Child in a niche, is much older, bearing the escutcheon of one of the earliest grand masters, Raymond Béranger (1365–73).

Linked by the first of two arches spanning the street, the simpler **Inn of**

Provence stands to the right and the **Inn of Spain** to the left (divided into two for the knights of Aragon and Castile). The Church of St John, originally on the left just beyond the street's second archway, was blown to smithereens by the gunpowder explosion of 1856.

From the top of Ippotón, look back down the street to appreciate the orderly sobriety of its perspective. The Italian restorers did a marvellous job of removing the colourful but clumsy clutter of ramshackle wooden balconies added when the Turks billeted their troops in the inns.

The reconstruction of the **Palace of the Grand Masters** on the long tree-lined esplanade of Platía Kleovoúlou is more controversial. Admittedly it looks better than the prison to which Suleiman reduced it before it was gutted by the great gunpowder explosion. But Greek scholars would have liked the ruins razed in order to dig for the ancient temple they believed to be lying underneath. As it was, Mussolini ordered the palace rebuilt in the 1930s as a summer residence, but World War II interrupted his vacation plans. What he bequeathed looks nothing like the original medieval palace but presents an intriguing hodge-podge of Roman and Byzantine columns, Italian Renaissance wood-panelling and floors paved with Roman and early Christian mosaics brought from the island of Kos. Among the statuary in the courtyard, notice the bronze she-wolf, mother of Rome's Romulus and Remus, which originally guarded the entrance to Mandraki harbour, now repaced by a Rhodian deer (see p. 151).

In keeping with this symbolic "change of management" at the end of World War II, notice two inscriptions near the palace courtyard entrance. One is dated 1940, "the 18th year of the Fascist era". The other, carved in Greek in 1947, honours the "unconquered Dodecanese people" for preserving "under all foreign occupation that inexhaustible fount of eternal Greek civilization: the ideal of freedom".

Turkish Quarter

From Platía Kleovoúlou, walk south beneath the plane trees of Odós Orféos down to a clocktower. It replaces a Turkish watchtower from which an inner rampart once ran east to the port, separating the Knights' Quarter from the rest of the fortified town.

Continue down to the **Mosque of Suleiman**, built in honour of the sultan soon after his conquest of 1522, renovated 300 years later and still in use today. It stands on the site of a Church of the Apostles from which it is believed the handsome Venetian Renaissance portal was taken. The mosque is spacious and peaceful, quite the best-preserved on the island; unfortunately its elegant minaret collapsed and is awaiting restoration. Opposite is the **Turkish Library**, possessing many valuable Arabic and Persian manuscripts, including two exquisitely illuminated Korans of the 15th and 16th centuries.

Double back to **Odós Sokrátous**, where the bustle of tourists and merchants captures much of the boisterous atmosphere of the old **bazaar** of which it was always the main focus. Among the

Kaputt!

Shortly after capturing Rhodes, the army of Suleiman the Magnificent hid a stockpile of gunpowder somewhere under the Palace of the Grand Masters and the Church of St John. And forgot all about it. One night in 1856, lightning struck a turret of the palace and fire broke out. Flames spread through the passageways and tunnels joining the palace to the church. Suddenly, an enormous explosion rocked the entire island. Fire spread all the way to the harbour, leaving about 800 dead. Among the many medieval treasures destroyed, the Church of St John and the Inn of England were levelled and the Grand Masters' Palace was left a burnt-out shell. As for the Inn of Germany, it vanished completely; now nobody even knows where it was in the first place.

*T*he Turkish cemetery in Rhodes' New Town is one of the few monuments of the Ottoman Empire left relatively unchanged by the Greek authorities. It was the burial place of the Turkish élite. Murad Reis was interred here in 1522, after rising from pirate to become admiral of the Turkish fleet. Other notables include a Shah of Persia.

150

Back on Sokrátous, head down (noting some good seafood restaurants for the evening) to Platía Ippokrátous. On the far side of the square beyond the Turkish fountain is the **Castellania**, medieval courthouse and stock exchange. The sockets in the façade once held banners to proclaim the court in session.

Facing the harbour, turn right on Aristotélous along the northern edge of what was the old **Jewish Quarter**. From the earliest centuries, Rhodes' Jewish community played an important role in the island's commercial life. Its neighbourhood east of Pithagóra was notoriously noisier than the somnolent adjoining quarter of the Turks. Of the 6,000 Jews living in the old town in the 1930s, two-thirds of them had emigrated at the outbreak of World War II. When the Germans occupied the island in July, 1943, the remaining 2,000 were assembled in what is now **Platía Evréon Martíron** (Square of the Jewish Martyrs). From this square, quiet now and adorned by a cheerfully kitschy modern fountain of bronze seahorses, the Jews were deported to the Third Reich's extermination camps. Only 50 survived. Half a dozen Jewish families remain on the island today. The crumbling **synagogue** with its rusty, barely distinguishable Hebrew plaque above the gate can be found on nearby Odós Dosiádou.

New Town
Under Turkish rule, the Greeks moved outside the walled city into what came to be called the Néa Chóra or New Town. The area surrounding the Old Town was first settled in ancient times and new construction today still unearths remains of old civilizations. But the commercial section at the north tip of the island—hotels, shops, administrative buildings, banks, cafés and restaurants—is less than 100 years old.

Mandraki Harbour, Rhodes' historic port where the knights moored their galleys and modern tour-operators dock their excursion boats, is a natural link

array of ceramics, icons, daggers, pots, jewellery and junk, you will find as many fakes and bargains as there ever were.

South of the bazaar, make your way to the pleasant Platía Aríonos and relax at one of the cafés. Better still, drop in at the **Turkish baths** to steam away the worst aches in sightseeing muscles (bring your own soap and towel; closed on Sundays). The 1765 construction, bombed in World War II, has been rebuilt to something of its old marble-floored splendour.

between the Old and New towns. (Emborio, the commercial harbour at the foot of Old Town, is used for larger ships.) Derived from its shape, the name Mandraki means "sheepfold", but its "gates" are guarded by bronze statues of a stag and doe. The latter, on the harbour's seaward arm, has replaced the she-wolf that symbolized Italian rule, now in the courtyard of the Grand Masters' Palace. Deer have long been a feature of Rhodes, introduced in ancient times at the prompting of the Delphic oracle to combat the island's snakes, said to be repelled by their odour. In the modern era, the deer died out but the island was re-stocked by Italians who had read their classics. But snakes are notoriously irreligious and still hang around the island.

The three drum-shaped stone **windmills** were built during the Middle Ages to mill grain for departing cargo boats. Sea breezes still turn their jib-like sails, but the millstones have long since ground to a halt. Go to the end of the pier for the view from the 15th-century **St Nicholas Fort**, now a lighthouse with a chapel inside, Nicholas being the Orthodox patron saint of sailors.

The dull administrative buildings along the harbour—courthouse, harbour-master's office and post office—are pompous contributions of the Italian regime. Opposite, and equally uninspired, is the Italian attempt to reproduce the **Church of St John** destroyed in the Old Town. It is the seat of the archbishop of the Dodecanese. Just beyond it, the **Governor's Palace** is a pastiche of the Doge's Palace in Venice.

South of these sad errors in Italian taste, and much more lively, is the **New Market** *(Néa Agorá)*, a Turkish-style seven-sided building. Its arcades surround an inner courtyard with stands of fresh fruit, vegetables, meat and fish. The cafés and restaurants make good vantage-points from which to watch the action.

North of the harbour, past the chic but private Nautical Club, the public **beach** stretches around the tip of the island and down the western shore. The Elli Club charges a small admission fee for its changing facilities.

Inland from the beach club along G. Papanikólaou, a slim white minaret marks the **Mosque of Murad Reis** and the **Turkish cemetery.** The Turks' chief buccaneer, Murad Reis died in the victorious assault of 1522 and is buried in a circular mausoleum next to the mosque. In a peaceful setting of fragrant eucalyptus and pine trees, the cemetery's women's graves are marked by sharp-angled stones, while the men's headstones are topped by carved turbans. Dignitaries are buried beneath ornate porticoes.

Standing alone at the northern end of the island, the **Aquarium** *(Enidrío)* displays its octopus, spotted moray, triggerfish and other exotica in an underground room designed to look like the seabed.

Monte Smith

On the west side of town, the hill where British Admiral Sydney Smith monitored the movements of the Napoleonic fleet makes a pleasant excursion at the end of the day. The view of the Turkish coast and the island of Symi in the late afternoon sun is a sheer delight. Amid olive groves, Rhodes' hilltop acropolis is crowned by the Doric **Temple of Apollo**. It was destroyed by the same earthquake that toppled the Colossus around 225 B.C. (see p. 153), and three columns have been somewhat haphazardly resurrected by Italian archaeologists. Below the temple is the rebuilt theatre, in which only the three bottom rows of marble seats are 3rd-century originals, together with a partially restored stadium.

Rodini Park

The Italians landscaped a beautifully wooded park on the southern outskirts of the capital where scholars believe Rhodes' famous School of Rhetoric once stood. Today, the setting inspires meditation rather than oratory. Streams

Colossal Error

Sorry, the Colossus of Rhodes, one of the Seven Wonders of the ancient world, did not bestride the harbour entrance. Its 20 tons of bronze would have sunk immediately into the seabed. The statue of Rhodes' protector, sun-god Helios, 32 m. (105 ft.) high, probably stood near the Palace of the Grand Masters, site of an ancient sanctuary.

Sculptor Chares of Lindos took 12 years to cast the Colossus. Extracting bronze from battle-machines and tools left after Demetrius's abortive siege (see p. 145), he finished the work around 290 B.C. He committed suicide after discovering a mistake in his calculations. An assistant tried to correct it, but to no avail. During an earthquake around 225 B.C., the Colossus cracked at the knees and crashed to the ground.

The Delphic oracle warned Rhodians not to restore the statue, and the crumpled bronze lay where it had fallen for nearly 900 years. Arab pirates shipped it to the Lebanon and sold it as scrap to Jewish merchants, who needed 90 camels to carry it away.

meander among oleander bushes, cypress, maple and plane trees. A rock-carved **Hellenistic tomb** with Doric half-columns is wrongly known as the Tomb of the Ptolemies.

East Coast to Lindos   *20 C2*

Sheltered from the island's blustery wind, the east coast offers pleasant excursions among beach resorts and orchards. A high point is Lindos, historic trading port of ancient Greece and still one of the most beautiful villages in the Aegean, with the bonus of a splendid beach in its bay.

First stop, less than 10 km. (6 mi.) south of the capital, is **Kallithea**, where the small bay offers excellent swimming and skin-diving. The Italians tried to launch it as a spa for rheumatism, gout, kidney and liver ailments. Even the claim that Hippocrates, Greek father of all physicians, came over from Kos to take the waters, failed to draw the crowds, and the buildings have fallen into disrepair.

Rheumatism and gout are not major worries for the young crowd on the long sandy beach of the booming resort of **Faliraki**. Even the older set look pretty limber driving and putting on the 18-hole golf course down the road overlooking the Bay of Afandou. The village of **Afandou** makes a living from its apricot orchards and carpet weaving.

At Kolimbia, an artificial waterfall pours down as part of the local irrigation system. Turn inland here for **Eftá Pigés** (Seven Springs), the source of the waterfall. Its pine-shaded restaurant has tables perched on rocks in the middle of the stream.

Back on the coast road, a turn-off leads to the relatively quiet sandy beach at **Tsambika**. Stretch your legs with the climb to the town's white hilltop monastery with a fine view across to Rhodes' highest peak, Mount Attaviros. In early September, local women make this pilgrimage to pray for fertility.

Archangelos lies at the heart of the fruit-growing country amid groves of oranges, lemons, figs, olives and vines. Towering above the lush vegetation is a 15th-century fortress, one of the many defences which the Knights of St John built along the coast to fend off the Turks. The town is reputed for its splendid leather boots, handmade knee-high but worn Puss-in-Boots style folded down to the ankle. The peasants have worn them since ancient times to protect against snakes. They make to measure if you have the time.

Lindos

This ancient port-city possesses the island's only natural harbour. Its population estimated at 17,000 in antiquity has dwindled now to 700—though it can look like 17,000 when the tour buses roll in. The golden rule, as always: get there early. It really is worth getting up at dawn for that first view over the wonderful sweep of the bay and the gleaming white village hugging the hillside crowned by dark medieval ramparts.

Most of the winding streets are just wide enough for donkeys. (You can hire one for the uphill climb on the main square.) From the bus terminal, foot-sloggers take the one main street to-wards the acropolis. You pass first the 15th-century Byzantine **Church of St Mary** *(Panagía)*. It has some fine 18th-century frescoes. Its black-and-white pebble mosaic floor, known as *chochláki*, is a characteristic feature of the Aegean, and you will see it in houses and court-yards throughout the village.

But save your stroll around the village until after tackling the **acropolis**. The an-cient sanctuary is built on a triangular rock outcrop above the village. Hewn in the rock at the foot of a long stairway is the carved relief of a Greek warship (2nd century B.C.) At the top of the stairs is the main gate to the fortress first built in the Byzantine era and reinforced by the

Three cities of Lindos climb the hill to its acropolis:
—modern, medieval and ancient. Facing the rich markets of the
Middle East, it was the most prosperous of Rhodes' three ancient
trading posts. The reputed ornamental Lindos pottery is in fact of
Asian origin, with the town serving only as its distribution centre.
Today, it is manufactured in Rhodes Town. Lindos merchants sailed
across the Mediterranean to found an Italian colony that was to
become the city of Naples.

155

knights. Their Commander's Palace and the ruins of a Byzantine church precede a Doric portico leading to the acropolis proper. Take in the view from the portico over the main harbour. At the top of the sanctuary's broad monumental stairway, the terrace of the entrance hall, or *Propylaea,* opens out to a forecourt and the little **Temple of Athena**, standing at the edge of a precipitous cliff. It was rebuilt after a fire in the 4th century B.C. From the cliff, look down on the rocky harbour where St Paul is said to have moored in A.D. 51 on his way to Syria. A small white church marks the spot.

Your tour of the charming village will take you through a maze of beautifully refurbished patrician houses, many of them with Gothic-arched doorways and windows. Peek in at the flowery courtyards and fine staircases. On top of some of the houses are "captains' rooms" with lookouts for passing ships.

South of Lindos   *20 B3*

Continue south along the coast road from Lindos to Metamorfosi and turn inland to the lovely old hilltop village of **Asklipiio**. Visit its ruined fortress, and you will usually find the priest hanging out in the café and happy to give you a guided tour of his 11th-century church adorned with some notable frescoes.

The beaches along this south-east coast are fewer but blessedly uncrowded. The best are along the wide cove running from **Plimiri** to the tip of **Cape Viglos**. People who like going to the end of things should trundle on down to the perfect tranquillity of **Cape Prassonisi**, where a lighthouse marks the island's southernmost point.

West Coast   *20 B–C2*

With fewer beaches on this more exposed side of the island, the most attractive excursions are inland up in the hills.

The ancient Minoan settlement of **Trianda** is now a booming beach resort. Above it, on the plateau of **Filerimos**, only a few temple fragments and a Doric fountain of the 4th century B.C. remain from the great trading city of Ialyssos. The Knights of St John exploited its strategic position above the coast to launch their assault on the island in 1309 before making the Genoese pirates an offer they could not refuse (see p. 145).

The **Church of Our Lady of Filerimos**, originally built in the 14th century, has been many times restored. Behind it, the cloisters of the monastery beautifully set among the cypresses invite a moment of meditation. Visit the underground chapel of St George to see its 14th- and 15th-century frescoes.

Continuing along the coast road through Kremasti, notice the American colonial style of the schoolhouse, donated by the town's emigrants to the United States. Hurry past the airport to turn inland to the **Valley of the Butterflies** *(Petaloúdes)*. Besides being used for church incense, the vanilla-scented resin of the valley's storax trees attracts hundreds of thousands of Quadrina butterflies *(Callimorpha quadripunctaria)*. They come to the valley to mate between June and the end of September. From a camouflage of dark brown to blend with the rocks or storax bark, the butterflies in flight open out to a flutter of black, brown, white and red. They earn their name Quadrina from four spots and a Roman numeral IV on each wing. A word of warning: they are a nocturnal species and, like any self-respecting Greek, do not appreciate being awoken from their daytime siesta. To protect their declining numbers, clapping hands or blowing whistles to see them in flight is strictly forbidden.

To get away from the heat of the coastal plain, take the inland fork at Kalavarda up to the cool pine-shaded resort on **Profitis Elías**, 798 m. (2,618 ft.). Its two mountain lodges, Elafos ("stag") and Elafina ("doe"), are entirely surrounded by forest.

Kamiros, third of Rhodes' ancient city-states, was probably founded by Cretans fleeing their devastated island. It prospered from eastern Mediterranean trade well into the classical era in apparent serenity, judging by the absence of any fortifications on the site excavated by the Italians in 1929. With the dig interrupted by World War II, the surrounding hills still conceal a much vaster city.

Preceding the entrance to town is a **Doric sanctuary** of the 3rd century B.C. Footprints on the empty pedestals were left by statues probably carried off by Cassius in 42 B.C. (see p. 145). But begin your visit of the town itself by walking up around the peripheral ridge to take in the whole settlement sloping gently towards the sea. Viewed from above, the residential area is situated to the right of the main street running through the middle of town. The Hellenistic houses have inner courtyards with peristyle colonnades. On the agora (marketplace), six Doric columns have been resurrected from the portico that once shaded the shops.

The town's modern fishing port, **Kamiros Skala**, has some good quayside seafood restaurants. If you prefer a hike and a picnic, turn west off the main road up to the knights' 16th-century hillside fortress, **Kamiros Kastello**, for a delightful view of the sea and small islands off the coast. For a more ambitious hike, take the loop road around **Mount Attaviros**, at 1,215 m. (3,986 ft.) the island's only real mountain. From the village of **Embonas**, surrounded by vineyards and tobacco fields and famous for its women folk-dancers, the mountain path to the summit takes two hours, passing remains of an ancient temple to Zeus on the way.

The main road from Kamiros continues south to the 15th-century castle of **Monolithos**, named after the soaring monolith on which it is precariously perched, 236 m. (775 ft.) above the valley. Inside the battlements are two cisterns and a chapel, but the view alone, along the coast and out to Chalki island, makes the climb worth while.

Symi and Chalki   20 B2

An easy day-excursion from Rhodes (daily ferry from Mandraki harbour and Kamiros Skala), these two rocky islands offer a charming escape from big brother's crowds. Although not so famous as the sponge divers of Kalymnos (see p. 159), the Symiotes are recognized in the trade as the most skilful.

Chalki

If this little snippet of an island, just 16 km. (10 mi.) west of Rhodes, is so peaceful, it is because its sponge divers emigrated to the United States to work in the shallow waters of Tarpon Springs, Florida. There they earned enough money to pave Chalki's only real road, from the port to the almost abandoned hill town of **Chorio**, and named, of course, Tarpon Springs Boulevard. **Pontamos** has a sandy beach, but all the sponges are in the souvenir shop.

Symi

The island's pretty harbour of **Gialos** lies at the end of a fjord. Some of its elegant pastel yellow and white neoclassical houses have been converted into stylish hotels. A 15-minute walk takes you up to the hilltop capital, **Ano Symi**, with its castle (1507) bearing the French Aubusson coat-of-arms on the gate. On either side of Gialos are the seaside resorts of **Emborio** and **Pedi**, a fishing village with shingle beach. At the southern end of the island, **Panormitis Monastery** has some fine frescoes and icons.

Patmos   17 D1

The little island where St John the Divine had his apocalyptic vision of the struggle of good against evil is these days a haven of peace. Among its sheltered bays on the rugged coastline, elegant clifftop villas and Chora's immaculate white houses nestling up against the fortified monastery, good has triumphed, with a smile. Practically all the fruit and vegetables have to be imported, and bottled water is preferable to the local stuff, rather brackish, but the simple life has great style.

Skala and Chora

Sheltered from the open sea on an isthmus in the middle of the island, the ferry harbour of Skala is also the easygoing commercial centre serving the island capital up on the mountain. Hotels, cafés and restaurants line the quayside.

Behind the port, a road winds up the mountainside past the **Convent of the Apocalypse**. Here, below three chapels of the 17th and 18th centuries and a theological college, is the **Cave of St Anne** where St John is said to have had his revelation. A stone ledge is pointed out as his desk.

Three windmills line the ridge leading into Chora, with its immaculate white houses 300 and 400 years old.

Crowning the mountain, the **Monastery of St John** has all the foreboding towers, battlements and ramparts of the fortress it was obliged to be, considering the treasures it had to protect from pirates. The monastery was founded in 1088 by the powerful Abbot Christodoulos from Asia Minor and subsequently amassed its riches from commercial shipping and a little rakeoff from piracy, too. A stairway zigzags up to the pebble-paved central courtyard, with the monastery church off to the left, built over a temple to Artemis. To start construction off on the proper footing, Christodoulos smashed the pagan goddess's statue. His marble sarcophagus is in the **Founder's Chapel** to the right of the church entrance. North of the nave, over the door to the outer treasury, is an icon of the Apocalypse (1625). The 12th-century **Chapel of the Virgin**, opposite, has an exquisite wooden icon-screen (1607). On the east wall are austere, profoundly solemn icons painted around 1190, fine examples of the unadorned early Byzantine style. Note the superb Virgin with Christ on her lap, flanked by the archangels Michael and Gabriel. Above them is Abraham serving three holy guests, symbolic of the Holy Trinity.

Behind the chapel and left across the inner courtyard, the 11th-century refectory has long marble-faced stone tables with hollows for the monks' cutlery and pewter. The 13th-century frescoes are in a livelier, more emotional style than the chapel paintings. Just beyond, the kitchen has some splendid high-domed ovens.

Climb up to the roof terrace for the view of Samos to the north and sometimes as far west as Mykonos.

In what is one of the wealthiest monasteries in Greece, the **library** has a magnificient collection of illuminated early Christian and Byzantine manuscripts. Among the most precious are a 6th-century codex of St Mark's gospel, with silver letters on purple parchment and the titles and sacred names in gold, and an 8th-century Book of Job. In the equally impressive **treasury** are 200 icons from the 11th century to the modern day, 300 pieces of silverwork, amulets and gold medallions given to the monastery by Peter the Great and Catherine II of Russia, bejewelled bishop's staffs and richly embroidered liturgical vestments.

"The Time Is At Hand"

Patmos is not much easier to get to now than when the Romans chose it as a penal colony for political prisoners sentenced to hard labour. Among them, in A.D. 95, was John the Divine (i.e. the Theologian), a Christian activist in Asia Minor. He was condemned, as he wrote, "for the word of God and for the testimony of Jesus Christ" in opposition to Rome's enforcement of emperor-worship. Between shifts of quarrying stone on the mountainside, John had his mystic visions of the Apocalypse, "a great voice as of a trumpet" foretelling Christianity's terrible trials and ultimate triumph. His powerful, enigmatic poetry composed in a Patmos cave became the last book of the New Testament, the book of Revelation.

Beaches

The best sandy beach on the island, some say in the whole Aegean, is on the east coast at **Psili Ammos**. Unless you are sailing, you must bike or hike to get there. **Grikos Bay** is an easily accessible beach resort, with ancient cave dwellings to visit. **Meli** and **Lampis** are good for windsurfing and water-skiing.

Kalymnos   *17 E2*

Diving and underwater fishing are appropriately major attractions on an island that continues its ancient profession of sponge diving. Largely arid and mountainous in the interior, the island has a dramatic coastline of coves, cliffs and caves.

Set against a dark mountain backdrop, the shuttered houses of **Pothia** make a colourful splash of white, green, blue and yellow. During the last years of Italian occupation, when the Fascists tried to suppress the Greek language and Orthodox worship, Kalymnotes turned their house-painting into an act of political resistance by restricting the colours to patriotic blue and white. A green mermaid sits on the breakwater to comfort the departing sponge divers.

From Seabed to Bathtub

Each spring, carrying on a 3,000-year-old tradition, some 200 Kalymnotes sail around the Mediterranean, in recent years along the North African coast, to scour the seabed for that luxurious marine animal, the sponge. The departure from Pothia harbour for five or six months is blessed by an impressive quayside religious ceremony, and the return of the fleet, decks laden down with sponges, is received with great festivities. There is a veritable explosion of joy and relief that the men have survived the considerable risk of death or paralysis, most often due to decompression sickness. Shallow-water sponges have been overfished, but among the deep-sea varieties, the most desirable is Venus's flower basket.

Further up the east coast away from the bustle of the island's capital, the lovely inlet of **Vathi** protects in its transparent blue waters the ghostly remains of an Italian warship sunk by British aircraft in World War II. A fertile oasis in an otherwise barren interior, the valley behind the tiny port makes delightful picnic country. The volcanic soil nurtures vineyards and rich groves of mandarins and oranges, figs and olives. Among the ancient remains on the hillsides are a throne cut out of the rock at **Rhina** and sturdy walls of rough-hewn stone at **Platanos**.

The best accessible beaches are over on the west coast. **Kantouni** is a good family beach, while the narrow strands of **Mirties** and **Masouri** are more popular with the singles crowd. A quick ferry takes you out to good swimming, snorkelling and nudist beaches on **Telendos**. When an earthquake split this islet off from Kalymnos in A.D. 535, it submerged an ancient town, still visible under the water.

Kos   *17 E2*

For mass-market package tours, this island is Paradise or Hades, depending on your point of view. Even if the crowds sardined along the beaches or pouring into and stumbling out of the harbour cafés are not usually your glass of lager, you may be tempted to come for a brief perverse moment of anthropological observation.

Greener than most of the Dodecanese, Kos could be very nice. Its fishermen boast of the best catch in the Aegean, and it produces fine wines—Gláfkos white and Apélles red—delicious table grapes and a famous lettuce. The local hot springs are strong in iron for all that ails you, heartily recommended by the island's ancient physician, Hippocrates. The "Father of Medicine" was born here in 460 B.C. How to beat the crowds? Rent a bicycle and ride a little further.

Kos Town

The port and Italian-style island capital are pleasantly tree-shaded. Overlooking Mandraki harbour, the grounds of the 15th-century **Knights' Castle**, built with masonry from the Asclepium, are littered with the flotsam of the island's ancient and medieval history—marble statuary, vases and rusty cannons.

Near a Turkish mosque of the 18th century, a huge plane tree propped up on crutches and in need of a tree-doctor, is very old—but not old enough to justify the tour guide's claims that Hippocrates taught in its shade 2,500 years ago. Life and death meet at the fountain, whose basin is an ancient sarcophagus. The doctor is of course also prominent, in sculpture and mosaic, in the town's little **museum** on the main square.

Between Mandraki harbour and the ancient acropolis, the colourful **Turkish quarter** reminds us that half the town's population is Muslim, close to 5,000.

Doctor Hippocrates

Understandably seeking to boost the qualities of the island's spa waters, but without historical justification, local tradition claims that the great physician born in Kos in 460 B.C. lived at least 100 years. In fact we know only for sure that he was a contemporary of Socrates, active in the late 5th century B.C., that he was short in stature, travelled a lot and died at Larissa on the Greek mainland.

In his medical teaching, we know that he broke away from old magic towards more modern therapy based on empirical reasoning. He examined the effects of climate and environment on man's psyche and physiology, rejecting, for example, the "divine" explanation of epilepsy, known then as the sacred disease. His treatise on the dislocation of bones was still in use in the 19th century.

The doctors' famous Hippocratic Oath began: "I swear by Apollo the Physician and Asclepius god of healing to respect my teacher as I do my parents, ... not to give poison, though I be asked," nor procure abortion, to abstain from seducing male or female patients and to observe professional secrecy.

Excursions

The **Asclepium**, a terraced sanctuary and medical school founded in the 4th century B.C. after Hippocrates' death, is 4 km. (2½ mi.) out of town at the end of an avenue of cypresses. At the lower level are remains of a Roman bath (1st century A.D.) exploiting the island's sulphur- and iron-rich waters. You will see some fine Ionian column-capitals on the middle terrace, but the principal Doric Temple of Asclepius is on the upper terrace. From here you have a good view of the Turkish mainland, the Knidos peninsula to the south and Bodrum (ancient Halicarnassus) to the north.

Further west, high on the north slopes of Mount Dikeos, **Asfendiou** is a charming commune of white stone houses where the bread is baked in stone ovens out in the courtyard among the fig trees.

Beaches

The most popular beaches are along the north coast at **Tigaki** and the fishing village of **Mastichari**. The distinctive feature of **Agios Fokas** on the south-east coast is its black sand. At the west end of the island, Club Med has planted its flags on **Agios Stefanos Bay**. Nearby **Kefalos** has good sandy beaches, lively tavernas and a working flour windmill.

Astypalaea 17 D2

Still hard to get to and unprospected by the tour-operators, this island is particularly beloved of the French, acquiring in the process a certain romantic and snobbish cachet. Many of the sharply indented coves at the foot of tall cliffs are accessible only by boat and still blessedly anonymous for each to discover and protect. The handsomely restored white houses of the island's one real town spill down the hillside from **Kastello**, with its 13th-century Venetian citadel, past a row of windmills to the little harbour of **Perigialo**. Down the coast, the charming seaside hamlet of **Livadia** has a nudist

*O*ut in the islands, the faces defy classification as "Greek", "Turkish" or "Slavonic". Etched into every feature are elements from the whole Mediterranean, the sum of the country's turbulent history.

beach, and the French clientele keeps up the quality of the tavernas. At the northern tip of the island, explore the caves of **Vathi**.

Karpathos 20 A–B3

The island's population is concentrated in the fertile southern end around **Pigadia**, the modern capital surrounded by orchards and vegetable fields. **Kyra Panagia Bay** has a monastery and pleasant beach. The real charm of the island is to

be found in the more isolated north, a broad elongated promontory separated from the south by two mountains. Boats will take you along the dramatic coastline, with cliffs topped by stunted pine trees, to the little port of **Diafani**. From there, continue by donkey past dozens of windmills on the slopes of Profítis Ilías (1,140 m.; 3,740 ft.) to **Olimbos**, oldest and most enchanting village on the island. Continuing age-old folk crafts, the women dress in traditional costume to please themselves, not the tourists (there are not that many).

Window on the Balkans From the Home of Alexander

The frontier lands of the north have an identity quite separate from the rest of Greece, tinged by their Balkan neighbours Albania, Yugoslavia and Bulgaria as well as the historic enemy, Turkey. Scholars argue whether Macedonia, country of Philip and Alexander, was ever truly Greek. The monks of Mount Athos rule an autonomous theocratic republic. To the east, Thrace has always been ethnically and linguistically distinct. The islands, too, from Samothrace down to Samos, remain very aware of the Anatolian coast on their horizon.

Far from the national capital, with slow train and ferry connections, the north has long remained a tourist backwater. But now that better-known destinations are saturated, that is a real asset. The increase of direct flights to the northern capital of Thessaloniki from major European cities has opened up the resort potential of the Chalkidiki peninsulas. Largely untouched by the mass assault of package tours, the islands of Limnos, Lesbos, Chios and Samos can be reached from both Athens and Thessaloniki.

Even if the old Byzantine districts of Thessaloniki itself have practically disappeared in the smoke of war, earthquake and fire, Greece's second city is a busy modern centre of commerce well worth an excursion from your resort for its

The east coast of Chalkidiki is far enough off the tourists' beaten track to remain unspoiled.

great museum of Macedonian treasures and some of the best meals in Greece.

The north is a region of religious mysticism. The ecstatic cults of Dionysus and the gods of the underworld have left their mark on the island sanctuaries of Thasos and Samothrace. Zeus's Mount Olympus straddles Macedonia's southern boundary with Thessaly. After years of decline, the Orthodox Church is reaffirming the monastic tradition and scholarship of Mount Athos, its peninsula accessible to male visitors only but visible to women taking a boat excursion along the coast.

Inland, forbidding mountain ranges form natural barriers with Greece's Balkan neighbours, but the plains of Macedonia and Thrace are fertile for grain-farming and high-quality tobacco. Lion hunts are a thing of the past, but September opens the season for pheasant, partridge, hare and wild boar in the Macedonian forests. In springtime, birds and birdwatchers flock to the eastern marshlands of Thrace. The northern mainland

163

is subject to a Balkan continental rather than Mediterranean climate, and so winters are colder, summers more torrid, with more rain in autumn and early spring.

Thessaloniki   7 D2

Named after Alexander's sister Thessalonikeia, the bustling business capital of the north has gone through a lot of changes since it was founded by the great conqueror's general, Cassander, in 316 B.C. Its importance in the Byzantine Empire, second only to that of Constantinople, is attested by the many monumental Orthodox churches still being painstakingly restored after recent earthquakes. Under Ottoman rule, the city's population became predominantly Jewish in the 16th century after Jews expelled from Spain joined those from Bavaria already settled here. In World War II, nearly all the city's 60,000 Jews were deported and killed in German concentration camps. Today, underlined by an international trade fair each September, the city is again prospering from its focal position at the centre of the old Byzantine maritime triangle of the Black Sea, the Aegean and the Adriatic.

The City

The natural and indeed most attractive place to start a tour of the town is at the waterfront. It is there on the broad, airy square of **Platía Aristotélous** that the bourgeoisie of Thessaloniki congregates in tree-shaded cafés to conduct its business, romantic liaisons and political intrigue. The square is the starting point for the ritual evening stroll—the *vólta*—along the sea promenade to and from the not very **White Tower** *(Lefkós Pírgos)*. The Venetians built this massive battlemented landmark for the Ottoman rulers as part of the harbour fortifications in the 15th century. Executions performed there earned it the title of "Tower of Blood", which the Sultan hoped to wipe

A Boyhood in Macedonia

Alexander had as simple a boyhood as could be imagined for someone destined to conquer the greatest empire the world had seen. Much of his childhood is obscured by the embellishments of legend—understandable for a man who convinced himself as well as followers and enemies that he was a god.

He was born in Pella (see p. 173) in 356 B.C., son of King Philip of Macedonia and Olympias, princess of Epirus. The Persians explained his astounding conquest of them by claiming he was in fact of Persian blood, his mother having been secretly seduced by the king of Persia and then sent back to Macedonia because she had such terrible bad breath.

As a 10-year-old, he played the lyre and recited poetry at Philip's banquet for Greek ambassadors, who were warned to curb their amorous interest in the pretty fellow. But he also developed an early taste for hunting birds and foxes. At the age of 12 he was given Bucephalus, the legendary black horse he rode for the next 20 years. The stallion bucked, reared and refused all commands until young Alexander, realizing he was shying away from his own shadow, turned him to face the sun. He quickly soothed and mounted Bucephalus and father Philip wept for joy.

The next year, at a time when the rough-and-tumble Macedonian court was eager to acquire some of the polish and culture of Athens, Philip sent for Aristotle, then a research fellow at Plato's Academy, to become Alexander's tutor. For two years, the philosopher, himself a Macedonian from Chalkidiki, kindled in Alexander an undying passion for Homer. Identifying himself with Achilles (whom his mother claimed as an ancestor), Alexander carried Aristotle's annotated edition of the *Iliad* throughout his travels. Efforts to teach him some politics were less successful—"young men," the tutor wrote later, "are not a proper audience for political science, they have no experience of life." The conqueror was more responsive to Aristotle's interests in zoology and botany, later sending him back rare animals and plants from all over his empire.

In a royal court where fathers like Philip were away on long military campaigns, boys often turned to strong personalities as substitute father-figures. Alexander's closest boyhood companion, a royal page named Hephaestion, became his gruff but faithful lifelong lover and his most trusted general. Homosexuality was not incompatible with an active family life. Father of three children, Alexander had three wives and four mistresses.

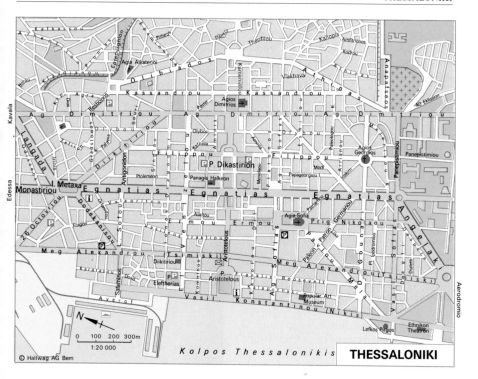

Kolpos Thessalonikis **THESSALONIKI**

© Halwag AG Bern

0 100 200 300m
1:20 000

out at the end of the 19th century with a coat or two of whitewash. The tower now houses a **museum** documenting local history from early Christian to late Byzantine times.

Back on Platía Aristotélous, walk north to the small brick church of **Panagía Chalkéon** set amid pleasant gardens at the south-west corner of Platía Dikastírion. Its name, "Our Lady of the Coppersmiths", refers to the trade practised, today as in centuries past, in surrounding streets, ablaze with glowing copper pots and pans. Founded in 1028 with one of the city's earliest Greek-cross ground plans, the church was heavily restored in 1934; when current reconstruction is completed, you will once again be able to go inside and see its 11th-century frescoes.

Opposite the church on the same square is a 15th-century **Turkish bathhouse**, serving the Greeks under the evocative name of *Loutrá Parádeisos*.

Work your way east along Odós Egnatía, named after the great Roman road running from the Adriatic to Neapolis (modern Kavala), in fact bypassing the north-west corner of the city. North on Odós Agía Sofías, **Panagía Achiropíitos** is one of the city's oldest churches, probably completed in the 5th century. The name, "Not Made by Human Hand", refers to an icon believed to be of divine origin. Note the fine Theodosian capitals

Patience, Men at Work
Despite the ravages of time and the elements, Thessaloniki still has the most complete range of Byzantine monuments outside Istanbul. Unfortunately, the damage of the 1978 earthquakes necessitates elaborate ongoing reconstruction which may make temporarily inaccessible much of the artwork we describe. To avoid disappointment, we suggest you contact the tourist information centre at Odós Aristotélous 8 for up-to-date information.

of its columns, so called because of the wind-blown acanthus leaf motif popular under Byzantine Emperor Theodosius II. In the south aisle are 13th-century frescoes of church martyrs.

Egnatía continues east, past little shops still practising the ancient art of icon painting, to the Roman **Arch of Galerius** *(Apsída Galériou)*. This commemorates victory over the Persians in A.D. 297 by Galerius Maximianus, military commander of the Eastern Empire. The brick structure, faced with stone reliefs, is crowded with scenes of men and horses. Best preserved, on the second zone from the bottom, is a sacrifice scene showing Galerius (in soldier's uniform) and Emperor Diocletian (in imperial robes) giving thanks at the altar.

On a rise above the arch, the **Rotunda of St George** was built in the 4th century as a mausoleum for Galerius but was converted into a church—and later a mosque. After its restoration as a museum of Christian art, you will be able to admire the magnificent mosaics of angels and martyrs in the eight recesses of the peripheral wall.

Make your way back west again to the city's largest Byzantine church, **Ágios Dimítrios**, which also has the best preserved (and currently most accessible) mosaics. It is dedicated to Saint Demetrius, a noble executed by Galerius, and its crypt (entrance in the south transept) has remains of the shrine built over the martyr's tomb and the Roman baths where he was detained and killed. Using columns with finely carved capitals from other churches, the main structure is a good reproduction of the 5th-century basilica destroyed in the great fire of 1917. Five superb 8th-century mosaics of Demetrius with church benefactors are mounted on pillars flanking the iconostasis (icon-screen).

South of the church is the **Bezesténi**, a bazaar-style street market of clothes and household goods. Adjoining it, the covered arcades of the **Central Food Markets** *(Stoá Modiáno)* are the town's live-

liest daytime spot, with the most cheerful bunch of butchers, fishmongers and greengrocers you could wish to meet.

One more church worthy of your attention, a quick taxi-ride to the west, is the 14th-century **Ágii Apóstoli**. The complex patterns of its brick façades have the intricacy of mosaic work. Inside in the barrel vaults are some splendid Nativity mosaics showing a handmaiden preparing the baby's bath with the midwife carefully testing the water while Jesus shies away in his nursemaid's arms.

*T*he jewels of Thessaloniki's Byzantine architecture have had to contend with the twin menaces of earthquakes and tentacular urban expansion. Some, like this tiny chapel on the corner of Egnatía and Germanoú streets, are staging a last ditch effort to resist strangulation and in the process provide a welcome oasis of tranquillity amid the city bustle.

167

Archaeological Museum

Even if you have little time for a thorough tour of the city, you should spare a morning or afternoon for the astounding riches coming to light from the tombs of the kings of Macedonia.

Just up the road from the White Tower, near the main entrance of the International Trade Fairgrounds, the museum houses ancient and prehistoric finds from all over northern Greece. The handsome Stone Age vases from Thrace, elegant Geometric vases, jewellery, delicate spectacle-frames, swords and knives from Macedonia would be a credit to any collection.

But even the most seasoned museum-visitor is dazzled by the **Treasures of Vergina** excavated from the Macedonian royal tombs some 80 km. (50 mi.) west of Thessaloniki (see p. 174). Highlights include: exquisitely wrought gold laurel wreaths worn as necklaces by the kings and queens; the king's armour—bronze helmet, iron cuirass for the chest with gold lion's head, bronze greaves for the shins; a massive gold and ivory shield with its bronze casing; small carved ivory reliefs that decorated a wooden bed, tiny heads of Dionysus, a satyr, and a bearded man, perhaps Philip himself holding forth to a reclining Alexander. But certainly the most chillingly exciting exhibit of all comes from one of the two magnificent solid gold funerary chests, embossed with a 16-point star, emblem of the Macedonian dynasty. It contained the slightly charred skull and bones of Philip, displayed nearby in almost complete skeletal form. Traces of a terrible eye wound sustained in battle have persuaded scholars that these are well and truly the remains of Alexander's father.

Chalkidiki 7 D2

This centrally located region has plenty of new beach resorts that make ideal bases from which to explore the northern mainland and nearby islands. Around its mountainous interior, fertile plains form a rich grain belt with fine beaches rimming much of the coastline. To the south, three peninsulas jut out into the Aegean like the prongs of Poseidon's trident—Kassandra, Sithonia and Mount Athos.

Just 29 km. (18 mi.) around the coast from Thessaloniki, **Agia Triada** remains a characterful Macedonian village while offering a holiday resort's fine sand, camping and good hotel facilities along **Thermaikou beach**. Hugging the coast road to Kassandra Bay, you pass the archaeological site of **Olynthos**, one of the region's most important ancient cities rebuilt by Greek colonists in the 5th century B.C. Its allegiance to Athens brought about its destruction by Philip of Macedonia. Built on two table-top mounds, the town's ruins present the classical gridplan laid down by Pericles' urbanist, Hippodamus. Its artefacts and mosaics are on show in Thessaloniki's Archaeological Museum. Nearby is the bungalow beach resort of **Gerakini** in a refreshing green setting of lawns, flower gardens and olive groves.

Explore the interior mountain country via the regional capital of **Poligiros**, with its interesting little archaeological museum (fine sculpted head of Dionysus) and a hilltop view from Profitis Ilías over all three of Chalkidiki's peninsulas. The road east winds up through pine forests to the hill town of **Arnea**, where the women spin and weave handsome rustic tapestries, carpets and long-pile flokati rugs. You will see the natural wool hanging out to dry on the balconies of the houses. You can buy either direct from the loom or from one of the small shops around the main square.

En route to the east coast, any travellers philosophically inclined visit a little garden on the outskirts of **Stagira**, birthplace of Aristotle, who is "honoured" by a dreadful modern statue looking understandably disgusted with his sculptor. Sympathize with the sage who said: "Misfortune unites men when the same thing is harmful to both." And

*P*ainting icons for the Greek Orthodox Church is still performed within specific doctrinal constraints, but the style has evolved from rigid formalism to a modern line of greater fluidity.

hurry on through the rolling hills to the fishing and boat-building village of **Ierissos**. Just 7 km. (4 mi.) down the coast, the road from Nea Roda to Trypiti marks the narrowest point of the isthmus leading to Mount Athos. This follows the course of **Xerxes' Canal** of 480 B.C., from which mounds, depressions and other infrastructures are still discernible. The Persian king cut through the isthmus to avoid the treacherous route around the peninsula which devastated the Persian fleet 11 years earlier. (You will see what bothered him if you try to cruise south around Cape Ákrathos today.)

Gateway to Mount Athos, **Ouranopolis** is growing in importance as a smart beach resort with fine hotels and first class sandy beaches. The waterfront

watchtower was built in the 12th century to guard against pirates, but the town itself was founded in 1922 by refugees from Turkey. Local hand-knotted Byzantine-patterned rugs are also a recent innovation, thought up by a Grecophile Australian.

Kassandra 7 D3

The long, sweeping beaches of the western peninsula have been developed into large-scale holiday centres by the Greek National Tourist Organization. The resorts of **Sani, Kalithea, Kriopigi, Chanioti** and **Paliouri** are ideal for family vacations. Facilities include protected swimming areas and swimming pools, bars, restaurants, discotheques, boutiques, tennis and volley ball courts, mini-golf and horse riding. Sports equipment can be hired on the spot. Non-residents can participate for a small fee. Smaller hotels and rooms in private houses are also available. The government-run camping grounds are impeccably clean and efficient. Trees and hedges lend privacy to individual grassy sites.

Named after Alexander's general, Kassandra was settled from ancient times, largely by cattle farmers, until the Turkish Pasha of Thessaloniki massacred the inhabitants and destroyed their houses during the struggle for independence. The peninsula was resettled with refugees from Turkey during the great population exchange of the 1920s, but full-scale development is recent.

Sithonia   7 E3

This is undoubtedly the prettiest and most cheerful of Chalkidiki's three peninsulas. A corniche coast road winds along bays and creeks past occasional fishing ports amid sea pines, olive trees and newly developed vineyards. Tiny beaches afford absolute privacy and perfect calm. Inland, the fragrant pine forests of **Mount Lóngos** are dark and cool with streams and springs.

You find fine beaches from **Metamorfosis** down to **Toroni** and a superb natural harbour further south at **Koufos**. From **Kalamitsi**, look east to the dramatic pyramidal silhouette of Mount Athos. West coast camping facilities are first class at **Paradissos** and **Neos Marmaras**.

Near the latter, Sithonia boasts one of the country's best resort complexes, **Porto Carras**. It comprises two hotels and a village inn, two theatres, an 18-hole golf course, excellent beach and a marina for luxury yachts and smaller craft. The complex is backed by a large estate run as a model farm, producing fruit, olives, almonds and an honorable wine drawing on vine-cuttings and wine-growing experts from Bordeaux. It is the brainchild of shipping magnate John Carras, whose other contribution to upgrading Greek tourism was to promote renovation of Athens' Plaka district.

Mount Athos   4 B2–3

If our only access to ancient Greece is through the stones of ruined cities, sanctuaries, palaces and tombs, Mount Athos presents living testimony to the spiritual world of Byzantium. The Holy Mountain *(Ágion Óros)*, as Athos is known to the Orthodox church, is a world apart. Within the Greek state, the monks of Mount Athos form an autonomous theocratic republic controlling all access to the peninsula.

Many women feel slighted at not being allowed to visit this totally male preserve. Yet even male visitors should remember, however hospitably they will be received, they are in essence intruders into the natural rhythm and sense of monastic life. Nobody comes as a mere tourist. The consular letter of introduction required of foreign visitors is a guarantee of their seriousness of purpose. During the short stay (usually a maximum of four days), the peninsula's wild, unspoiled beauty and the art treasures of the churches are memorable enough, but it is the fascinating insights into monastic life and the place's all-pervasive spirituality that make the greatest impact.

For those, then, who have presented their consular letter of introduction to the Greek Foreign Ministry in Athens or the Ministry of Northern Greece in Thessaloniki, the Mount Athos boat leaves early morning from Ouranopolis. Travel lightly, with a small backpack, good walking shoes, sweater for cool evenings on the mountain, and a pocket torch—the monasteries have little or no electricity after dark. The boat itself is already an exclusive community of men—Greek locals delivering monastery supplies, visiting priests or resident monks, and only a sprinkling of foreigners. On the quayside, women wave goodbye with a bemused smile.

They and others without residence permits can get at least a sea view of the Holy Mountain's west coast monasteries on **boat cruises** (from Ouranopolis or Ormos Panagias on Sithonia). The cruises follow the same route as the Athos launch, but at a more respectful distance from the coast. The launch pulls in to drop supplies and monks at the monasteries' ports—simple landing-stages with old watchtowers and little warehouses. The first monastery you pass is **Docheiariou**, a cluster of russet-roofed houses dominated by an 18th-century watchtower lying snugly against a green hillside. Its church has some splendid 16th-century frescoes in the decorative Cretan manner. Further down the coast, amber onion-bulb domes behind tall tenement-like shorefront houses announce the Russian monastery of **Ágios Panteleímon**, a 12th-century foundation locally known as the *Rossikón*. Visitors will find a gaily coloured church built in 1812, with green lantern-domes and white, blood-red and ochre walls inspired by the Baroque architecture of St Petersburg. The halls have heavy Russian furniture, monumental samovars and portraits of the Tsars. Other monasteries visible from cruise boats on the west coast include **Simonopetra** and **Dionysiou**, both audaciously perched on rocks above the sea.

All visitors pass through the main port of **Dafni** to take a bus to administrative headquarters for the residence permit *(diamonitírion)*. In **Karyes**, the peninsula's capital and only town, try to hitch a ride with monks visiting from outlying monasteries. In their Byzantine world, they know how to handle jeeps, lorries and caïques with outboard motors. But you may also try mule-back or join up with a fellow hiker: loners get lost in the dense forests.

Before setting off, visit the town's **Protáton** church, built in the 10th century but much restored since. It has a fine 16th-century iconostasis (icon-screen), but is most admired for frescoes (1300) by the great Byzantine painter, Manuel Panseleinos. He depicts in very personal style, angular and forceful, the *Nativity, Presentation at the Temple, Washing of the Feet,* and the *Baptism.*

Nights and Days on the Holy Mountain

The first religious men to seek refuge on Mount Athos were hermits hiding out in caves during the persecutions of the iconoclasm controversy in the 8th century (see p. 28). The monks' cells were organized into communities by Athanasius, counsellor to Emperor Nicephorus Phocas and founder of the Great Lavra monastery in 963. In its 15th-century heyday, the Holy Mountain numbered 40 monasteries, each with up to 1,000 monks. Good relations with the Sultan after the Turkish conquest meant that while Constantinople remained "political" capital of the Orthodox Church, Mount Athos was its spiritual centre. But support for Greek independence brought Turkish oppression in the 19th century and numbers dwindled drastically. In 1926, Mount Athos was made a theocratic republic under Greek suzerainty.

Of the 20 monasteries left today, 17 are Greek and the other three Russian, Bulgarian and Serbian. Each has a deputy on the Holy Council, led by the First of Athos, ruling in the village capital, Karyes. The monastic communities are either *cenobite,* the monks "living in common", observing strict discipline and an austere diet; or *idiorrhythmic,* each monk "going his own way", less rigid in discipline.

With one "modern" exception, the monasteries observe the Julian calendar, 13 days behind ours, and the Byzantine clock, by which midnight is at sunset. The day is dominated by the liturgy, most of it after dark. Worship begins with twilight *hesperinón,* vespers; then *apódipnon,* after dinner; *nykterinós,* the main nocturnal service; *agrýpnion,* sleepless vigil; and *ýrthros,* at dawn.

In addition to the monasteries, there are smaller dependencies *(skíti)* where monks live in groups of two and three. Vagabond beggar monks *(gironákes)* wander through the forests while solitary anchorites live in the most austere simplicity in isolated caves or tiny cabins perched on a cliff ledge. In all, some 1,200 monks live on the Holy Mountain, plus about 500 laymen providing manual labour and services.

Progressing from novice to monk, the Athonites exchange a short gown for the long black *zostikón* with leather girdle. From their arrival on Mount Athos, to distinguish them from the outside world, they leave hair and beard uncut, ultimately winding their hair into a bun tucked inside their hats. Promulgated in 1060, the celebrated ban on women, female animals, children, eunuchs and smooth-faced persons is officially still in force, but today beardless visitors are permitted, tabby cats, hens and sows, too.

North of Karyes is the most modern of the monasteries, **Vatopedi**, with telephone and electricity. Built around a triangular courtyard, the refectory and housing overlook some slick little motor boats in the harbour. The relaxed idiorrhythmic community is the only one on the peninsula to observe standard European time and calendar. The 15th-century bronze doors on its basilica come from Thessaloniki's Agía Sofia. There are good icons of Peter and Paul in the northern chapel of St Demetrius.

Further north, the Serbian monastery of **Chiliandari** lies hidden from the coast in a beautiful green valley surrounded by wooded hills. Visit the church, built in

splendid multicoloured brick in 1197, the year of the monastery's foundation when there were 1,000 monks. The 30-minute walk among chestnut, oak, maple and eucalyptus to the pebble **beach** has even atheists believing God is in his heaven.

Down the east coast, **Stavronikita** is a battlemented fortress monastery dramatically positioned on a rock overlooking the sea—it was under constant pirate attack in the 13th century. Its prize treasure, in the church, is a mosaic icon of patron saint Nicholas.

Iviron or Iberia (meaning Russian Georgia, not Spain and Portugal) is now a fully Greek monastery. This hamlet by the sea serves as a hospitable port of call for travellers between Karyes and the Holy Mountain's oldest and biggest monastery, **Great Lavra** *(Megísti Lávra)*. At the foot of Mount Athos itself, this veritable fortified village—*lávra* means large-scale monastery—has alone escaped unscathed from the peninsula's countless fires. Its diligent idiorrhythmic monks work away in the carpentry shops, gardens, fields and vineyards, each planted with a red wooden cross to bless the crop. Tradition insists that the gnarled, split but unbent cypresses in the spacious courtyard were planted in the year of Lavra's foundation, 963. The **church** possesses in its nave the Holy Mountain's finest frescoes, executed by the Cretan artist, Theophanes, in 1535. In front of the church is an elegant 17th-century Holy Fountain *(Phiale)*, a basin of porphyry stone and sculpted bronze under a domed canopy decorated with the baptism of Christ. The handsome refectory with superb semi-circular stone tables is graced by more Theophanes frescoes, most notably the *Last Supper*.

Of Lavra's numerous dependencies to the south, perhaps the most forbidding is

Visitors' Etiquette

If you are approaching a monastery by mule, dismount before you reach the entrance. Present your residence permit at the visitors' hostel *(archontária)*, where the guest-master will receive you with a welcoming glass of ouzo or other potent home-made liqueur and a *loukoúm* sweetmeat. Lodgings are of monastic simplicity. Do not expect hot water for shaving, this is a land of beards. At the end of the afternoon, a wooden-beam gong is sounded for dinner. Refectories have a handsome austerity; the massive stone tables set in the floor have dips in the top as receptacles for olives. Served on pewter, a typical meal may be chickpea soup, bread, olives, feta cheese and fruit with strong retsina wine or water. Breakfast, very early, may be a spicy vegetable stew, feta, fruit and again that wine or water. Stricter monasteries ask non-Orthodox visitors not to enter the church during services and to take their meals after the monks. A donation to monastery funds is entirely voluntary.

Karoulia at the south-west tip of the peninsula. This group of flimsy wooden dwellings clinging to the cliff-face is accessible only by ropes and ladders, but visible from the sea—when weather permits.

Mount Athos, 2,033 m. (6,670 ft.) bears the name of a rebel giant buried here by Poseidon. Alexander's architect-sculptor Deinocrates proposed to carve the whole white limestone mass into a statue of the great conqueror. Alexander declined. In 1948, Britain's Captain John Hunt shinned up the tough western slope as training ground for his team's historic conquest of Mount Everest five years later. From the south-east, via the *skíti* of Kerassia, the summit, with its magnificent view beside a little chapel, is a perfectly manageable day's hike.

Western Macedonia

This mountainous region was the stronghold of the ancient kings of Macedonia. Their palaces and tombs make a good one-day round trip from Thessaloniki.

Pella, Philip's capital and Alexander's birthplace, lies some 40 km. (25 mi.) north-west of Thessaloniki. It was the home of Macedonian kings from about 400 to 167 B.C. Today, excavations have not yet located the palace, but the city is re-emerging among columns from a classical temple, traces of the theatre where Euripides saw the première of his tragedy *The Bacchae*, and wide streets where Aristotle walked in the shade of colonnaded buildings. The **House of the Lion Hunt** (300 B.C.) still has its patterned pebble mosaic floors, but the great pictorial mosaic that gave the house its name is now displayed in the site's **museum**. The scene is believed to show Alexander in Sidon (Lebanon) being rescued from the clutches of a lion by his faithful officer, Craterus. Other museum mosaics depict *Dionysus Riding a Panther*, a *Gryphon Attacking a Deer* and a *Battle of Amazons*. North of the main road at the western end of the site, two mosaics have been put back in place in their house: the *Rape of Helen* and a *Stag Hunt*.

Cool off with a 40-minute drive west to the foothills of Mount Vermion. Several bubbling streams run through **Edessa**, a town of refreshing parks and greenery. The waters converge into a grand **cascade** dropping 24 m. (80 ft.) down cliffs thick with fig trees, pomegranate and nut trees.

Turn south 18 km. (11 mi.) to the site of an ancient Macedonian cemetery, near **Lefkadia**. Most impressive of three monumental mausoleums is the **Great Tomb** or Tomb of Judgment (3rd century B.C.). Sheltered by a hangar, the limestone mausoleum comprises two rooms of two storeys with frescoes of the dead man's judgment in the Underworld. Sculpted battle friezes on the tomb's façade suggest he participated in Macedonian campaigns in Asia.

Continuing south, you pass through the peach orchards and vineyards of prosperous **Naousa** to the ski resort of **Veria** on the eastern slopes of **Mount Vermion**, offering some pleasant summer rambles among the chestnut, hazel, oak and beech trees. Just 11 km. (7 mi.) south-east of Veria are the **Royal Tombs of Vergina** unearthed by Professor Andronikos in 1977. The treasures of Philip and other Macedonian kings have been transported to Thessaloniki's museum (see p. 168), but frescoes decorating the tomb walls are being prepared for public display.

Kastoria   6 B2

This charming lakeside town, capital of Greece's fur industry, is off the beaten track but well worth a visit. Prettily located on a promontory jutting out into Kastoria lake, it has direct flights from Athens, reliable bus and train services from Thessaloniki. If you are in the market for a fur coat, stole or hat, the price savings will go a long way to paying the fare. In any case, you should see the grand 17th- and 18th-century **patrician** mansions *(archontiká)* with their ground floors, once stables, converted now to furriers' workshops. Resisting the creeping modernization, many of the best houses are in the old cobblestoned Kariadi neighbourhood around the southern lakefront. Beneath an overhanging roof, the corbelled upper storeys have handsome casement windows with dark wood shutters. Inside are wooden ceilings, carved wall panelling and imposing fireplaces. One of them, the **Nerandzis house,** is now a folklore museum. Most

of the fur shops are on the main street, Mitropóleos.

"Kastoria" is Greek for the beaver that populated the lake until the 19th century. Started by Jewish furriers from eastern Europe, the fur trade continues to flourish with imported mink, fox, squirrel and stone marten. The pelts are worked into garments and sold worldwide, promoted by an annual fur fair in March.

Most of the town's 70 churches, more than 50 still in use, were originally the patrician families' private chapels. But

There are no beavers left in Kastoria's lake, but the abundant frogs stage daily choral recitals free of charge during the summer months.

take a walk around the south shore of the lake to visit 11th-century **Panagía Mavriótissa**, one of the more attractive, with frescoes both outside and inside. The fine *archontiká* house opposite is also worth a look.

Notice on the lake the strange snub-nosed, flat-bottomed fishing boats, an ancient form unchanged since the troubled Orestes came here and gave the lake its official name, Orestiada.

Mount Olympus 6 C3

Tackling the home of the gods is strictly for seasoned mountain-climbers. Anyone driving from Thessaloniki to Athens can get a close-up view of the country's highest mountain by turning off south of Katerini to the climbers' base-camp village of **Litochori**. The summit, 2,917 m. (9,570 ft.), is named Mítikas (the Needle). Zeus's Throne stands 8 m. (26 ft.) lower.

*B*ird-watchers head for the countryside around
Lake Koronia and nearby Volvi. With luck you may spot a flamingo.
More plentiful are the herons, pelicans, storks and cormorants.
The cooler, greener landscape has a more Balkan than
Mediterranean atmosphere.

177

Eastern Macedonia

The drive east from Thessaloniki around the **Koronia** and **Volvi lakes** leads through orchards and tobacco plantations. North of Koronia from April to June, you may see nesting herons rising from the plane trees in the red soil landscape. Attractively surrounded by hills, Volvi lake offers a hot springs resort at **Nea Apolonia**, good for rheumatism. If you prefer fresh sea water, head down to the beach resort of **Asprovalta**. Where the Strymon river reaches the sea from the Bulgarian mountains, the great **Lion of Amfipolis** (4th century B.C.) guards the bridge. The stone burial monument was washed downriver from the nearby Athenian colony.

The scenic coast road passes several fine beaches, the best located between **Nea Peramos** and **Kalamitsa**. Camping is excellent at **Batis**.

Kavala   4 B2

Macedonia's second-largest city, centre of the Greek tobacco industry, rises in tiers from the waterfront up the slopes of Mount Symvolon. The harbour's fishing boats and the houses behind share a taste in bright reds, yellows and blues. This was the port of Neapolis where St Paul landed on his way to Philippi to bring Christianity to Europe (see p. 26).

The town's dominant feature is a huge Roman-style Turkish **aqueduct** built in the 16th century to carry water to the old citadel *(acropolis)* out on the eastern promontory. Walk along the Byzantine ramparts for superb views over the harbour and city. Head down past the Imaret, a 19th-century enclosure of domes, courtyards, and terraces established as an almshouse by Mohammed Ali, founder of the modern Egyptian dynasty that ended with King Farouk. Close by is **Mohammed Ali's house** with his swashbuckling equestrian statue in front. The monarch, son of a rich Albanian tobacco merchant, was born here in 1769. A caretaker will show you the Pasha's quarters

and lattice-shuttered harem above the stables and kitchens, and an attractive garden behind the house. A belvedere nearby looks out over the island of Thasos.

The **Archaeological Museum** has interesting local finds, notably a stone frieze of fighting soldiers carved in the 5th century B.C.

Philippi

Conquered and renamed by Philip of Macedonia, the town's **ruins** are of Roman and early Christian interest. It was here that Julius Caesar's assassins, Cassius and Brutus, were each defeated by Octavius and Antony in two famous battles that ended the Roman Republic in 42 B.C. The town was promptly elevated to the status of a Roman colony. On the north side of the modern road, you can see the excavated Greek theatre (4th century B.C.) where Roman gladiators fought and where classical tragedy is again performed today. Nearby are ruins of a sanctuary dedicated to the Egyptian deities Isis and Serapis. Beside the road is Basilica A, a 5th-century church near where Paul made his first European conversions. Opposite is the forum, its outline still clearly visible. Much of its masonry went into the building of the adjacent Basilica B, a 6th-century church left unfinished when its dome collapsed. Equally impressive in its own way is the neighbouring ancient public lavatory, reached via a portal and a flight of steps down to its splendid marble seats.

Thasos   4 B2

Famous of old for its fine white marble and heady wines, when Dionysus led the dance, this most northerly of the Aegean islands still cultivates a taste for the good life, albeit less orgiastic. (Wine is now imported from the mainland.) A good ferry service from Kavala brings you to a serene island, green with graceful pines and chestnut trees, with a silver filigree of olive trees and sandy beaches. You will find people much more friendly and easy-going than on the mainland.

The modern port town of **Limin** is built among ruins of the classical city, still using a rampart from the 5th century B.C., including towers and gates. The wall rises steeply from the harbour to the ancient theatre, a lovely creation with a proscenium dedicated to Dionysus where classical drama is performed in summer. Further up, a rock-hewn shrine to Pan has a carved relief of the god piping to his goats.

The **Archaeological Museum** near the old harbour has some fine sculptures in the local marble, notably a colossal *kouros* (temple statue, 6th century B.C.) of Apollo carrying a ram, and a handsome head of Dionysus (3rd century B.C.).

Just 2 km. to the south-west, sandy **Makriamos** is a luxury beach resort providing almost every sport under the sun and a few in the shade, but especially skin-diving, fishing and sailing. **Chrisi Amoudi** is the favourite beach for the snorkelling fraternity and has some good seafood restaurants, too. Head south to **Kinira** for some gentle surfing. In the old quarries down at **Aliki**, the marble still bears the scars of ancient picks. On your tour of the island, taste the honey and Thasian preserves *(glyká tou koutalioú)* of green figs or green walnuts, cooked in the gardens in giant cauldrons over glowing wood fires.

Thrace

Bounded on the north by the Rhodope mountains, what is really only western Thrace extends from the Nestos river to the Evros river frontier with Turkey. The atmosphere and architecture of the towns are noticeably more "eastern", ethnically more Bulgarian and Turkish. The town of **Xanthi**, centre of the region's finest tobacco-growing, has some delightful traditional houses and little shops on a hill north of the modern quar-

ters. The university town of **Komotini** has a distinctly Oriental bazaar, but also an impressive modern **Archaeological Museum**, boasting a gold bust (2nd century A.D.) of emperor-philosopher Marcus Aurelius.

Swimming is pleasant down at the pebble beach of **Fanari** backed by its tree-shaded campsites. Birdwatchers head for the eastern **Evros Wetlands** to spot herons, wild swans, storks and cormorants among the tamarisk, poplars and willows. **Alexandroupolis**, the region's capital, has a wine festival in August, but gourmets come for the mussels and caviar, working the meal off along the charming harbourside promenade.

Samothrace   5 D2

It isn't hard to believe that the gods of the nether regions live on here in the deep shadows of the rugged granite mountains, fleeing the blinding sunlight like the island's eternal goats. Of old, Aristophanes, Plato and monarchs, too, from Philip of Macedonia to Rome's Emperor Hadrian, came to be initiated into the mysteries of Samothrace's cult of the Underworld. Today, after a short ferry ride from Alexandroupolis via the port of Kamariotisa, you can retrace their pilgrimage to the **Sanctuary of the Great Gods** at Paleopolis.

Ask at the Xenia hotel for admittance to the archaeological site, set in a wilderness of rocks and olive trees. Leaving the museum till later, take the path left to the Anaktoron (500 B.C.), an initiation hall with a small adjoining room where novices changed into their sacred robes and later obtained their certificate of initiation. The Arsinoion rotunda was erected in the 3rd century B.C. by Egyptian Queen Arsinoe. Built of marble from Thasos and combining all three orders—Doric entablature, Ionic cornices and Corinthian columns—it was the largest circular edifice in ancient Greece, 20 m. (64 ft.) in diameter. To the south,

*P*hoenician merchants are popularly believed to be the earliest settlers on the island of Thasos. Their wide-ranging journeys around the Mediterranean and beyond nurtured a vigorous boat-building industry, for which many of the techniques have not needed modification since the classical age of the trireme.

Temenos frieze of musicians and dancing girls performing for a wedding of the gods.

On the north coast, the green and pleasant spa of **Therma** claims to cure infertility. The women's pool is much hotter than the men's. If such is not your problem, then use the spa as base camp for the 5-hour climb up **Mount Fengári**, 1,600 m. (5,250 ft.). From what Homer described as the "topmost peak of wood-ed Samothrace", you, like Poseidon, can see the battlegrounds of Troy.

sacrificial feasts were held in the en-closed courtyard of the Temenos (4th century B.C.). Several Doric columns have been restored to the porch of the grand Hieron, where the culminating ritual was held.

On a hill above the theatre is a foun-tain marking the site of the *Winged Vic-tory of Samothrace* that was carried off in 1863 to Paris where it is now the emble-matic statue of the Louvre.

In the sanctuary's more modest **mu-seum**, see in the sculpture collection the

Limnos

8 *Bl*

Facing the Turkish islands of Gökçe and Bozca (Imbros and Tenedos to the Greeks) and the Dardanelles beyond, the island is of strategic importance, and its natural sheltered harbour of **Moudros** is a major military base. It was from here that the British launched their World War I attack on the Dardanelles; 900 British Commonwealth soldiers lie in the cemetery.

But the island's charm derives mainly

The Divine Smith

Limnos is the island of Hephaistos, the only god on Olympus who ever did any serious work. The son of Zeus and Hera was so ugly and feeble as a baby that his mother dropped him into the sea off Limnos. He was saved by a couple of sea-goddesses, Thetis and Eurynome, who nurtured him in an underwater grotto and gave him a smithy as a playroom. He began making little jewels, in particular a wonderful brooch for Thetis that Hera noticed one night at a party. When she found it was made by her own son, Hera took him back up to Olympus and fitted him out with a real god-size workshop. With 20 bellows going day and night, he branched out into weapons, armour, chariots and furniture. But he got into trouble again by trying to stop Zeus mistreating Hera. Dad did not like that and hurled him out of heaven, this time onto dry land at Limnos, breaking both his legs. But feisty Hephaistos soon fixed himself up with a pair of golden leg supports and hobbled back up to Olympus. Now that he had to ease his workload, he made self-propelled trolleys to convey his tools around the smithy and fashioned golden women robots as his assistants.

from its tree-shaded capital of **Myrina** on the west coast. It has two harbours divided by a promontory guarded by a Venetian fortress. Traditional sailors' houses with wooden balconies line the stone-paved streets. The town's well-organized **museum** displays finds from the archaeological sites of Poliochni and Hephaestia. North of town, at the end of the beach, is one of the Aegean's major luxury hotels. The best beaches around the south coast, none of them over-crowded, are at **Ziniatha, Thanos** and **Plati**.

🏃 *Lesbos*   9 D1

Greece's third-largest island (after Crete and Euboea) is bustling and prosperous. Covering 1,632 sq. km. (630 sq. mi.), it offers lazy days on good pebble or sand beaches, and delightful rambles through the hilly interior of pine forests with olive groves in the valleys.

The island of poetess Sappho—along with fellow poets Arion and Alcaeus, and the father of Greek music, Terpander—has an enduring cultural tradition among modern Greek artists, too. From all over the world, pilgrims seek out the island that inspired Sappho's exalted verse about the young women she loved. More down-to-earth, at Petra on the north coast, the government's Secretariat for Sex Equality has set up a thriving women's agricultural cooperative.

The island takes an alternative name from its capital of **Mytilini**. The sophisticated modern port-town has a boisterous bazaar-like shopping street running behind the harbour, with its obligatory but unflattering statue of Sappho. For a good overall view, head up to the **kástro**, the Genoese-Turkish citadel. At the **Archaeological Museum**, see the Roman villa mosaics (3rd century A.D.) portraying Athenian playwright Menander and scenes from his comedies.

Inland from the capital, **Agiassos** is a lovely hill town on pine-clad Mount Olympos. It is reputed for its ceramics and woven fabrics. Up on the north coast, **Mithymna** (also known as Molyvos) is an increasingly popular fishing

The Tenth Muse

Plato wrote: "Some say the Muses are nine, but how carelessly! Look at the tenth, Sappho from Lesbos." Born in 612 B.C., she was forced into exile as a child with her aristocratic family, but returned from Sicily to marry and bear a daughter, Cleis. At Eressos, she lived in a commune of women devoted to music, poetry and the worship of Apollo. Her odes and elegies treated love with simple tenderness and passion, praising her companions' beauty and goodness in very direct and unaffected manner. But the family, too, is important:

Evening, you who bring all,
All that light-giving dawn scattered;
You bring the sheep, you bring the goat,
You bring the child to its mother.

port with a maze of tall tower-houses climbing steeply from the harbour to the Genoese castle. It has a great beach.

On the west side of the island, between Sygri and Eressos is a fascinating **petrified forest** of conifers and redwoods buried by volcanic ash and solidified by rainwater and underground springs. Sappho's home is believed to have been at the port, **Skala Eressos**, not the more modern inland town. In any case, its sandy beach makes the pilgrimage more rewarding. Only fragments of stone wall remain from the days of the great lady.

Other beaches, on the south coast, are at **Vatera** and **Plomari**, famous for its ouzo.

⚓ *Chios*   *9 D2*

Proud without being aloof, the island's striking personality owes much to its Italian past and tormented relations with Turkey (now the object of peaceful day-excursions to Çesme, 30 minutes by ferry). It competes with Turkey's Izmir as the birthplace of Homer. In sharp contrast with the north's dramatic lunar landscapes around a historic monastery, the south is green with orange and lemon groves, almond and olive trees.

Chios Town

The busy port capital tingles with excitement when the evening ferry comes in from Piraeus and local citizens mingle with travellers for the *vólta* along the waterfront. The most rewarding of the town's art collections is in the **Argenti Folklore Museum** on Plátonos Street, with its superb display of old costumes and exquisite painted porcelain statuettes of the island's Greek and Turkish peasants. The **Byzantine Museum** in an old mosque combines church art with relics of the Venetian and Genoese past. The **Archaeological Museum** (Odós Míchalou) exhibits distinctive Chian ceramics and terracotta figures from the 7th to the 4th century B.C.

The beach suburb of **Vrontados** boasts a "master's stone" where people like to imagine Homer recited his verse. South of Chios Town, **Karfas** has a popular sandy beach.

Nea Moni

Take the exhilarating excursion west of Chios Town winding up to this 11th-century monastery hugging the mountain side. A few nuns replacing the hundreds of monks that once lived here will show you the Byzantine mosaics in the church. See, too, the handsome refectory with a marble table 18 m. (59 ft.) long, and a grim ossuary containing skeletons of Chians massacred by the Turks in 1822. More than any other, it was this event that roused foreign writers and artists to support Greek independence.

Further into the mountains is the mysterious half-abandoned village of **Anavatos**. Byzantine ruins straggle up to a precipice from which women and children jumped to avoid slaughter in the 1822 massacre. Today, the hilltop church is a shell, its frescoes intact. Elderly people occupy a couple of houses, a few fig trees and pomegranates still bear fruit, and the bakery's smoke-begrimed oven stands empty.

North Coast

The island's many prosperous ship-owners live up in the pleasant little village of **Kardamyla**, claiming that Homer preceded them. Their villas look down on the charming port of **Marmaro**. You will find a couple of good pebble beaches nearby at **Nagos** and **Giossonas**.

South of Chios Town

Beyond Chios airport, old mansions with Italian coats of arms on estate walls enclosing citrus orchards, olive groves and cypress trees remind us of the island's Genoese and Venetian masters. Thereafter, you begin to see the bush-like lentisk trees from which Chians since antiquity have been tapping a resin of wondrous powers called *mastícha*.

Magic Mastic

The people of southern Chios boast that theirs is the only real mastic region in the world—even a few kilometres north, the "gum tree" cannot produce the proper resin (Portuguese claims are dismissed as humbug). So what is so terrific about mastic? Midwives use it as an antiseptic in childbirth. Hunters stuff mastic twigs into gutted hares to preserve them. It was a staple aphrodisiac in the Turkish sultan's harem. It makes good toothpaste, hygienic chewing gum and a "killer" alcoholic drink.

Centre of the "mastic country" is the delightful town of **Pyrgi**. Unique grey and white geometric patterns adorn its houses, a subtle touch of colour added by ropes of tomatoes and peppers hanging from the balconies to ripen. To the west, **Mestra** is an equally charming medieval village where the streets are shaded by arches and tunnels linking the houses from one roof-patio to another. At **Emborio**, 10 minutes' drive south of Pyrgi, is an attractive black pebble beach. Nearby are ongoing (currently off-limit) excavations of a town that occupied the site from Trojan to classical times.

Samos   17 D–E1

This fertile island just 3 km. (2 mi.) from the Turkish mainland is renowned for its sweet red muscatel wine and a much admired olive oil. Mystic mathematician Pythagoras was born here in the 6th century B.C. but fell foul of tyrant Polycrates and went off to square his hypotenuse in southern Italy. Before him, another great Samian traveller, Colaeus, sailed through the Straits of Gibraltar—Pillars of Hercules in those days—to explore Spain's Atlantic coast. Today, many have gone clear across to Massachusetts.

The sleepy port resort of **Pythagorio** stands on the site of Polycrates' ancient capital of Samos. North-west of town, take a torch to explore the **Tunnel of Eupalinos** built in the troubled 6th century B.C. to provide clandestine passage under the city walls. Along the coast west of Pythagorio are the ruins of the **Heraion sanctuary**, with what was the largest temple in the Aegean—one and a half times the size of the Parthenon. One surviving column and pillar stumps defining the ground plan are all that remain. The nearby beach resort pays homage with its name **Colonna**.

The modern capital is over on the north coast. **Samos Town** has a spacious harbour serving the northern islands. In the **museum**, sculptures from the Heraion sanctuary include a giant *kouros* (6th century B.C.), 5 m. (16.5 ft.) tall, and a seated female statue, perhaps of Hera herself. Up on a hill behind the port is the old Turkish capital of **Vathi** with charming old houses and a view across to Turkey. North coast beaches include **Kokari**, **Avlakia** and **Karlovasi.**

On the west side of the island, the characterful hill town of **Marathokampos** preserves its leafy tranquillity among impossibly steep narrow streets, overlooking **Ormos**, its little beach resort.

*T*he distinctive geometric patterns on the façades of *Pyrgi's buildings are achieved by a technique known as* sgraffito. *Walls are covered with layers of plaster which are scraped to reveal the contrasting grey and white forms.*

From Delphi's Ancient Enigmas to Meditation on the Meteora

The centre of Greece was for Zeus the centre of the world, the site he fixed for the sanctuary of Delphi. After consulting the oracle, you can seek respite from the baking sun in the cool greenery of Mount Pilion. Or, further north, the respite which monks sought from worldly cares in precarious eyries atop the Meteora crags. Less ascetic refuge can be found at the beaches and yachting harbours on the Sporades islands from Skiathos out to Skyros.

Apart from the sanctuary of Delphi, attracting as many pilgrims now as in antiquity, this region is blessedly uncrowded. Of old and in more recent times, Boeotia's mountain barrier has protected the north-western approaches to Attica and Athens. To the north, the famous Pass of Thermopylae was the last redoubt defended by the Spartans before the Persian advance. Behind Delphi, Mount Parnassus was a perfect hideout for the klephts rebelling against Turks and Germans alike. In Thessaly, it was the very inaccessibility of the Meteora rocks that attracted monks fleeing Turkish oppression. Mount Pilion, increasingly popular among skiing enthusiasts, has in summer the quiet Alpine charm of Switzerland, with a bonus of first rate seafood and good beaches. Out in the islands of the Sporades, you can choose between the lively crowds of

Recluses know as stylites once perched on man-made columns. Meteora's monks found God had done the job for them.

Skiathos' modern resort and the remoter, more traditional atmosphere of Skopelos, Alonnisos and Skyros.

The Road to Delphi

The spectacular natural location chosen by the ancient Greeks for their most important sanctuary, on the southern slope of Mount Parnassus, is best appreciated if we follow the land route taken by pilgrims coming from Athens.

Thebes

It is purely for history's sake that we make a first stop at Oedipus's Boeotian capital, *Thiva* in modern Greek, apparently still beset by the king's ancient curses. Two 19th-century earthquakes and equally devastating building speculation have left the city "reeling like a wreck", as Sophocles put it. Archaeologists haunt building sites like sophisticated vultures, hoping to scavenge treasures from Mycenaean palaces buried beneath office buildings. If you do find yourself downtown for car repairs or something, visit the **museum** at the north end of Pindárou Street. Relax in the garden and courtyard among fragments of sculpture, mosaics and Turkish tombstones. Inside are some very phallic terracotta figures, Mycenaean ceramics and, in this ancient warrior state, carved gravestones of Boeotian soldiers. If the car is still not ready, ask the children the riddle which the Sphinx of Thebes put to Oedipus: "What creature, with only one voice, has sometimes two feet, sometimes three, sometimes four and is weakest when it has the most?" Oedipus, who had just killed his father, replied, without the slightest complex: "Man—he crawls on all fours as an infant, stands firmly on his two feet as a youth, and leans upon a staff in his old age." Spared the punishment for a wrong answer—being strangled and devoured on the spot—Oedipus became king of Thebes and married his mother.

Levadia   *11 E3*

This pleasant town of shady plane trees is much appreciated for its brightly coloured handspun cotton fabric and succulent roast lamb, especially at Easter. It has two landmarks: a **clocktower** left by Lord Elgin (nice, but not a patch on the marbles he lifted from the Parthenon); and a pretty **Turkish bridge** across the Erkina river.

Osios Loukas   *11 E3*

After Levadia, turn south via Distomon to the 11th-century **monastery**, a masterpiece of Byzantine architecture with splendid mosaics and icons. Dedicated not to the Apostle Luke but a local hermit, it stands on a hill commanding a grand view over the Helikón mountain range. Above the refectory, the two adjoining churches, **Katholikón** and smaller **Theotókon** to the north, present richly varied exteriors. Brickwork and roughhewn ashlar stone, enhanced by rust-red mortar, frame elegantly mullioned double and triple windows. In the Katholikón (1022), the narthex vaults have glow-

ing mosaics of the *Washing of the Feet*, the *Crucifixion* and *Resurrection*. In the apse is a *Virgin and Child* beneath the vault's *Descent of the Holy Ghost*. In the body of the church are 16th-century icons by Cretan painter Mikhaïl Damaskinos. Inside the Theotókon, notice the columns' fine Corinthian and two Islamic-style capitals.

Mount Parnassus   *11 D2*

The home of Apollo and the Muses, shared with Dionysus and his nymphs, has two peaks, *Lyákouri*, "Wolf's Mountain", 2,457 m. (8,061 ft.), and *Gerontovráchos*, "Old Man's Rock", 2,435 m. (7,989 ft.). Climbers and good hikers can make it to the top in the snow-free months of July and August from **Fterolaka**, a ski-resort from December to April. (Inquire about mountaineering guides at the Alpine Club in Athens.) The view takes in Olympus and Mount Athos, the Sporades and Cyclades, and south to the mountains of the Peloponnese.

Arachova   *11 D2*

With cool streams running down its narrow streets, this charming terraced mountain village is a good place to stay

Water and Wine

While Noah was landing on Ararat, Deucalion ended up on Parnassus. The Greek story has a familiar ring to it. Zeus decided to destroy humanity because of the impieties of Greece's first inhabitants, the Pelasgians. Warned by his father, Prometheus, that the earth was about to be flooded, Deucalion built an ark and sailed with his wife Pyrrha for nine days. He, too, sent out a dove to reconnoitre and bring back an olive twig as a sign the flood was over. The biblical and Greek stories were both apparently inspired by a Mesopotamian flood in the 3rd millennium B.C.

Like Noah, Deucalion invented wine—his name means "new-wine sailor"—but the Greeks transferred the patent to Dionysus, who also held sole rights to Parnassus until Apollo arrived with the Muses.

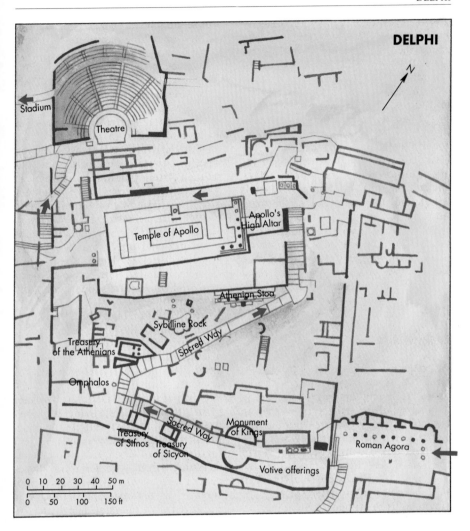

DELPHI

Stadium

Theatre

Temple of Apollo

Apollo's High Altar

Athenian Stoa

Sybilline Rock

Sacred Way

Treasury of the Athenians

Omphalos

Sacred Way

Treasury of Sifnos

Treasury of Sicyon

Monument of Kings

Roman Agora

Votive offerings

```
0   10  20  30  40  50 m
0       50    100    150 ft
```

overnight so that you can, like the pilgrims of old, get an early morning first view of Delphi as you arrive from the east. The villagers make excellent flokati rugs and good wines. Try the local fried cheese speciality, *formaéla*.

Otherwise, most hotel accommodation is 1 km. west of the archaeological site in the modern town of Delphi. Until excavations began in 1892, the town, then named Kastri, had stood for 12 centuries directly over the sanctuary.

Delphi   *11 D2*

Anyone finding it hard to capture the essence of the Greek religious experience among broken pillars, entablatures and monumental pedestals may see things more clearly in Delphi. If the sheer beauty of the site of the ancient oracle inspires awe in the most blasé modern traveller, imagine what it did for the believing pilgrim. Amid cypresses, olives and pines on the southern slopes of Parnassus, a walled enclosure of temples and treasury shrines stands at the foot of two soaring crags, the **Phaedriades**. Some 600 m. (2,000 ft.) below is the sparkling Gulf of Corinth.

With steep paths to tackle, take the visit in easy stages: early morning start on the sanctuary; relax for the view from the theatre; a slow walk to the stadium; cool off at the museum; then the sacred Castalian Spring and Athena's sanctuary at nearby Marmaria. Purists follow ancient pilgrims by visiting Athena's temple and the spring *before* the main sanctuary.

For ancient Delphi's magnificent reconstruction by French archaeologists, and our knowledge of lost features such as the statues stolen by Nero and company, thanks are due to detailed descriptions by Pausanias, a Greek traveller of the 2nd century A.D. His 10-volume *Description of Greece* was the world's first real guidebook.

Sanctuary

Start at the courtyard of the Roman **agora** where pilgrims bought supplies in shops behind the portico or washed in the public baths. No secular buildings were allowed inside the sacred precincts.

Four steps lead up to the beginning of the **Sacred Way**. Inscriptions in the paving come from masonry that the Romans recycled from ruined shrines. The road climbs to Apollo's temple past remains of **votive offerings** donated by the city-states, free-standing statues or elaborate treasury shrines *(thesauroi)*. Immediately to the right of the entrance, for instance, is the base of a bronze bull statue offered by the people of Corfu in gratitude for an exceptional tuna fish catch. Opposite was a series of 37 statues donated by Sparta to celebrate its destruction of the Athenian fleet in 404 B.C. This was considered arrogant and in bad taste because it concerned a victory over fellow Greeks. But, 40 years later, the Arcadians retaliated by commemorating their defeat of Sparta with a

bronze monument of nine gods and roes on the oblong platform next to Corfu bull.

Just beyond, a well-preserved s circular wall marks the enclosure of gos's **Monument of Kings** to honou alliance with Thebes.

The Sanctuary's treasury shrines ter around a bend in the Sacred V First on the left is the **Treasury of Si** (ancient city-state west of Corinth rotunda of tufa (volcanic stone) bui 500 B.C. whose friezes of the Argo expedition are now in the museum p. 194). The neighbouring **Treasur Sifnos**, financed by the Cycladic isla silver and gold mines, was among sanctuary's richest. The museum sh splendid remains of its sculpted p ment and entablature supported by caryatids.

At the road's elbow is the **Omph** stone navel of the universe that stood in the temple. Scholars a whether it is Roman or Helleni Zeus's two golden eagles crowned original.

North of the Omphalos, the **Trea of the Athenians** was the grandest of phi's shrines. Built of white Parian ble, this miniature Doric temple is al masterpiece of archaeological re struction, pieced together from 80 cent of its original materials. The sc tured friezes are cast copies of origi preserved in the museum. The shrine erected around 507 B.C. by the new enian Democracy and rededicated the defeat of the Persians in 490 B.C inscription on the south terrace wall claims: "From the Athenians to Ap the Persian spoils from the battl Marathon."

Beyond a rectangular building was probably an assembly hall for phi's administrators is the **Siby Rock**, a clump of boulders fallen the Phaedriades crags marking the si the pre-Apollonian oracle. To the rig a smaller rock on which goddess Let holding her little boy Apollo whil

190

THE ORACLE'S SMOKY TRUTHS

Zeus chose the site by having two eagles fly towards each other from the eastern and western edges of the world, meeting at the centre. There, the world's "belly" or "womb"—Delphi—was marked by a stone *omphalos* (navel). The sacred flame that burned there became the "common hearth of all Greeks", to which the remotest outposts of Hellenic civilization sent pilgrims to consult the oracle and athletes to compete in games second in importance only to the Olympics. The Delphic oracle came into its own in the 8th century B.C., playing a vital role in the colonization of Sicily and southern Italy. Emigrants from islands and city-states began by consulting the oracle on where to go and which deity to choose as patron of the enterprise. Three sacred wars were fought for control of the sanctuary—and the treasure brought by the city-states.

But Delphi was sacred ground long before the arrival of the Dorian Greeks. Earlier inhabitants worshipped a dragon or serpent god guarding a cave entrance to the Underworld. The spot had been discovered by a herdsman whose goat was overcome by the cave's mephitic fumes. Everyone who approached was reduced to weird mumbling. Henceforth a prophetess or Sibyl sat at the cave to pass on messages from the Underworld. The Greeks took over the sanctuary after baby Apollo, symbol of the conquering Dorians, had come from Delos to slay the serpent (see p. 98). Deferring to existing tradition, a woman, Pythia, was kept on to murmur oracular incantations—incoherent until interpreted by a male priest, representing the new power. Originally, Pythia was a young virgin, but after the priests and oracle-seekers took too many sexual liberties, she was replaced by an old hag, dressed as a young virgin and seated on a tripod.

After purification, sacrifice to Apollo and a gift to the Delphic treasury, the pilgrims questioned Pythia via the male prophet—on marriage, childlessness, commercial enterprises or affairs of state. Enveloped in a smoke of burning laurel twigs and barley flour, Pythia worked herself up into a frenzy, chewing bay leaves, sipping holy springwater, babbling away. The priest composed his interpretation in hexameter verse. Like established religion everywhere, the Delphic oracle was generally conservative. Moral precepts inscribed in Apollo's temple preached: "Know thyself" and "Nothing in excess". But a concession was made in the winter months when the sanctuary was handed over to the ecstatic worship of Dionysus, who shared Mount Parnassus with Apollo. Political interpretation of Pythia's mumbles sided, often wrongly, with what were considered the most powerful forces

of the day. Delphi championed the aristocracy (generous donors), discouraged Greek resistance against mighty Persia, defended Sparta against Athens and supported Philip of Macedonia.

In doubtful cases, the oracle hedged its bets. To gain acceptance in the Greek world, King Croesus of Lydia poured gold into the Delphi treasury. Should he attack Persia? If you do, the oracle replied, you will destroy a mighty empire. He attacked, and the empire he destroyed was his own.

After centuries of decadence, Roman Emperor Julian tried to revive its fortunes in A.D. 360, but Delphi sent its last pathetic oracle:

Tell the king the well-wrought hall has
*   fallen to the ground.*
No longer has Pythia a hut or prophetic
*   laurel,*
Nor a spring that speaks. Quenched is
*   the speaking water, too.*

Incantation to Apollo

fired off his arrows at the Python. The column drums strewn around here are part of the monument that supported the Sphinx of Naxos now in the museum.

Up against the polygonal wall which surrounded Apollo's temple, the **Athenian Stoa** was a seven-column marble portico with a wooden roof to shelter naval trophies captured from the Persians in 478 B.C.

The Sacred Way climbs sharply to **Apollo's High Altar** (5th century B.C.) at the entrance to the temple, donated by the island of Chios. As the inscription explains, the donation gave the people of Chios priority in questioning the Pythia. Before the pilgrim had his goat sacrificed on the altar, the priest sprinkled water over the beast; if it trembled in all its limbs, the signs were favourable for a good oracle.

The **Temple of Apollo** in its present state dates from 330 B.C. Originally there was just a hut of laurel branches (laurel is Apollo's sacred tree) sheltering a wooden cult statue. You can still see lying around the temple Parian marble column drums from the great edifice of classical times destroyed by earthquake in 373 B.C. The temple now has 6 Doric columns at each end and 15 along the sides. Imagine it housing huge statues of Apollo and Dionysus surrounded by the pilgrims' votive offerings. A bronze relief of Homer bore the inscription of the oracle he received.

Skirt the north side of the temple—where the famous Charioteer statue (see p. 194) was buried by the polygonal wall—and take the stairway up to the **theatre**. Built in the 4th century B.C. and enlarged by the Romans, it seated an audience of 5,000 on the limestone terraces. From the topmost seats, the view over the ruined temple and shrines and the dramatic Pleistos ravine beyond reveals the ancients' genius in marrying their sanctuary with the grandiose beauty of its natural setting.

West of the theatre, the path winds up through a grove of olive trees to the

stadium where athletes from all over the Greek world gathered for the prestigious Pythian Games. Notice at the east end of the arena the runners' starting blocks, or rather grooves, set in marble slabs and, 178 m. (195 yds.) down the track, the finishing line. On the north side of the stadium is the judges' box, the only seats with backrests. Delphi also had its hooligans: an inscription on the south wall specifies penalties for drunkenness but warns spectators not to take wine *out* of the stadium.

*T*he Temple of Apollo was the heart of the Delphi
sanctuary, housing the oracle itself. Apollo's pre-eminence in the
handing down of oracular advice derived from the elevated moral
example attributed to him. He prescribed purification and penance
for crimes committed and discouraged vengeance. Criminals hoped
for the clemency Apollo typified when defending Orestes against the
vindictive Furies.

Museum

Housed in a bright and airy modern building, the sanctuary's surviving statues and superb architectural reliefs have been assembled by the French School of Archaeology.

The marble **Omphalos** on the staircase leading to the exhibition halls was found in the temple precincts. Early Roman or Hellenistic, it has a carved relief of the woollen net draped over the sanctuary's original stone "navel".

Hall 4, though known as the Sifnian Room, is dominated by the Sphinx of Naxos (560 B.C.) seated on an Ionian capital that topped a 12-m. (40-ft.) column. It has a woman's head, with characteristic Archaic smile, bird's chest and wings and lion's haunches. Among the sculpture from the Sifnian Treasury (6th century B.C.), notice the Homeric frieze. On the right, Trojan heroes Aeneas and Hector fight the Greeks Menelaus and Aeas, watched on the left by the gods, with Zeus in the centre (headless). The shrine's eastern pediment shows Hercules and Apollo fighting for the Delphic tripod on which Pythia was to sit. The Caryatid, one of two statue-pillars supporting the treasury entablature, was originally bejewelled, in the holes around her headband.

Hall 5: see here the *kouroi*, two monumental Archaic statues (580 B.C.), perhaps of Argos heroes Cleobis and Biton. The blurred remains of the Sicyon frieze show adventures of the Argonauts.

Hall 6: the wealth of Delphi's treasury is hinted at by fragments of a silver bull (6th century B.C.) once mounted on gold plate, and figures of gold, silver and ivory, found discarded in storage pits.

Hall 7 is devoted to the Treasury of the Athenians. The sculpture includes eight metope friezes of the *Labours of Hercules*, the best preserved being the first, of the hero fighting a stag. Theseus is shown with Antiope, Queen of the Amazons, and in his fight with the Minotaur.

Hall 13 boasts the museum's finest treasure, the magnificent bronze Char-ioteer, one of only half a dozen bronzes surviving from the classical era. It was dedicated by Polyzalos, tyrant of Gela, Sicily, in 470 B.C. after his man won the chariot race at Delphi's Pythian Games. Portrayed on his victory lap, the charioteer (left arm missing) has a winner's ribbon around his head and a subtle expression of contained triumph. The eyes are of white enamel and brown and black onyx with tiny bronze wires for the lashes. Notice the superbly moulded feet. The body's disproportionate length may be a deliberate effect to correct optical distortion when viewed from below. The statue was part of a group with four-horse chariot and what was probably a groom. Shown separately are three horse legs, a tail, reins and the groom's arm.

Hall 14 has a particularly elegant example of the countless sculptures of Antinoüs which Emperor Hadrian had made after his beloved companion died in Egypt in 130 A.D. They had visited Delphi together to consult the oracle.

Castalian Spring

Named after the nymph Castalia who drowned escaping from the clutches of Apollo, the ice-cold waters have their source in the ravine dividing the two Phaedriades crags. The large stone-paved basin in which pilgrims purified themselves can be seen at a sharp bend in the road running past the sanctuary. Purification before consulting Apollo's oracle generally meant rinsing the hair, imitating Apollo, reputed adept of frequent shampoos. Murderers had to wash from head to toe.

Marmaria

Still known by its pre-excavation name, the **Sanctuary of Athena Pronaia** lies just down the mountainside south of the road back to Athens. In fact, this was the pilgrims' first stop on their way via the Castalian Spring to the Oracle. The Doric **Temple of Athena** (6th century B.C.) stands opposite the entrance to the site. Beyond are the remains of two treasuries, the larger perhaps Athenian and the smaller erected by Greek colonists from Marseille. But the site's most striking monument, in fact, architecturally the most noteworthy in Delphi, is the **Tholos**, a marble rotunda of 390 B.C. On a raised platform, 20 Doric columns, three still standing with their cornice, encircled an inner shrine that had 10 Corinthian half-columns around the interior wall. Scholars have not yet determined what form of worship was performed in this and two other similar rotundas at Epidaurus and Olympia.

Coast West of Delphi

For a more profane dip than the Castalian Spring, head down to the beach resort of **Itea**. Some 20 km. (12½ mi.) along the coast is the old port town of **Galaxidi**, sleepy now but once a thriving shipbuilding centre, as you can see in the local **maritime museum**.

The Battle of Lepanto

It was a short, bloody rerun of the Crusades, Christianity versus Islam. To halt further westward expansion of the Ottoman Empire, Spain, Venice and the Papacy gave up their squabbles long enough to present a common front against a Turkish fleet supported by Egypt and Algeria. At sunrise on October 7, 1571, Don Juan of Austria, half-brother of Spain's Philip II, drew up 208 ships of war to face the Turks west of Lepanto at the entrance to the Gulf of Corinth. The Turks outnumbered Catholic forces by 22 vessels but were already exhausted from months of pillaging in Crete and the Adriatic. Massive Venetian galleys proved in the front ranks to be veritable maritime fortresses which, with Spanish discipline, heavy cannon and long-barrelled arquebuses, overwhelmed a Turkish fleet that still relied in large part on bows and arrows. The Turks escaped with only 30 ships, and the sea did indeed run red. Muslim casualties numbered 30,000 dead and wounded, the Catholic forces 8,000 dead and 21,000 wounded. Among the injured was Miguel Cervantes, who crippled his left hand but saved the right one to compose *Don Quixote* 30 years later.

Nafpaktos *11 C3*

The fortified port the Venetians named Lepanto, scene of Christian Europe's momentous naval victory over the Turks in 1571, is now little more than a tranquil yachting harbour with a square of pleasant jacaranda trees. To appreciate the port's strategic importance, follow the ramparts up to the old pine-shaded Venetian **citadel** for the view over the entrance to the Gulf of Corinth. The fortifications contain ancient masonry from the 5th century B.C. when the port was a major Athenian defence against Sparta in the Peloponnesian War.

The Road to Pilion

The cool mountains of the Thessaly region come as a welcome relief. On the Volos road north from Athens (or from Delphi via Levadia), history buffs may like to stop at the **Pass of Thermopylae**. Most celebrated for its desperately courageous defence to the death by the 300 Spartans of King Leonidas (see p. 22), it has been regarded throughout history as the military gateway to Athens and southern Greece. It was a route taken by the Goths and the Crusaders, besides the Persians. The pass is 6.5 km. (4 mi.) long, narrow at either end and widening out in the middle. The Spartans' valour is honoured by a modern white marble

Taking a Pass

In 1941, British officers with too much Classics and not enough modern geography thought they could defend Thermopylae against the advancing Germans. They would do a better job of holding the byroad on higher ground that the Persians had taken for their front-and-rear attack on the Spartans. Trouble was, as the British realized when they put down their Herodotus and went to look at the terrain, the coast that was close by in ancient times had silted up. The sea was 5 km. (3 mi.) out, giving a land attack all the room it needed. The British abandoned the indefensible position before the enemy arrived.

When all are sweltering down in the plain, the wild flowers and orchards around villages like Portaria (alt. 1,968 ft.) make the peninsula of Mount Pilion a cool delight. If you do try the heady local wine, let someone else do the driving along the winding mountain roads.

monument topped by a bronze statue of Leonidas, opposite the soldiers' grave mound. Today, the waters of Thermopylae ("Hot Gates") cure a common complaint of veteran soldiers, sciatica.

Volos   *12 C2*
Thessaly's chief port is a modern town frequently ravaged by earthquake, but it provides an ideal gateway for tours of the Pilion peninsula (and ferries to the Sporades islands). It has good hotels and an extremely agreeable harbour prome-

Mount Pilion *11 E1*

Cool summers, luxuriant vegetation and charming alpine villages with good hotels make the Pilion peninsula a bracing change from the familiar Greek landscape. Highest peak in what is in fact a mountain range rises to 1,651 m. (5,417 ft.). The hills are green with forests of chestnut, beech and oak, and orchards of apple, cherry and peach. Botanists have catalogued over 2,000 sorts of plants. The villages, about 20 in all, hug the slopes and hilltops and nestle in ravines, a few sitting down on the coast by sand or pebble beaches. Plane trees lend a welcome shade to the village squares; courtyards are fragrant and bright with basil, gardenias and geraniums. Notice the houses' timber-framed gabled upper storey and beautifully weathered greystone-tiled roofs. The churches have distinctive external galleries and free-standing belfries.

The mountain roads from Volos around the Pilion peninsula are mostly well paved, but give yourself plenty of time to negotiate the hairpin bends. Head north-east to **Anakassia**, where a characteristic house has been transformed into an **art museum** of works by the popular 20th-century naïve painter Theophilus. At **Portaria**, pause in the delightfully shady village square to sample the local wine and cheese. Then take the side road north to **Makrinitsa** up on a green mountainside overlooking the Bay of Volos. Several tall, traditional

nade. Volos olives are a gourmet favourite, as is the local delicacy of *spetsofái*, a sausage stew with tomatoes and red and green peppers. The ancient site of Iolkos, the port from which Jason took his Argonauts in search of the Golden Fleece, has turned up some important finds for the local **museum**. They include Stone Age jewellery, figurines and Mycenaean vases from the heroic age of Jason. From ancient Demetrias, south of Volos, comes a remarkable collection of 300 painted tombstones.

Better Than Anabolic Steroids

Mount Pilion's invigorating climate was the source of Achilles' strength. Abandoned by his mother, he was brought here to be reared by the centaur Cheiron. At the age of 6, he killed his first wild boar and brought it proudly to his foster father, who told him to go away and eat it. To nurture his bravery, Cheiron fed the boy on a special diet of lion's and boar's tripes and bear bone-marrow, supplemented with honey and fawn bone-marrow to give him extra speed.

houses have been turned into comfortable inns around a square with carved marble fountain. Notice the sculpted chancel of the little 18th-century **church**, which also has some good icons inside.

Double back to Portaria and continue through chestnut forests to the mountain pass of **Hania**, a ski-resort at 1,350 m. (4,429 ft.). Further on, at **Zagora**, the old houses are prettily scattered among orchards of pears, peaches and plums. The town also boasts a heady red wine. Time for a swim down at the sandy beach of **Chorefto**, a fishing village and resort with good seafood taverns. You will find another beach resort down the coast at **Agios Ioannis**, framed by green hills.

The houses of **Tsangarada** stand amid majestic oak forests with splendid views over the Aegean. A winding 8-km. (5-mi.) drive takes you down to a dazzling white beach at **Milopotamos**.

If you are looping back to Volos, stop off at the hill resort of **Milies** with a side trip to the old houses of **Vizitsa**.

𝄆 Meteora 10–11 C1

Unlike those on Mount Athos (see p. 170), Meteora's **monasteries** are accessible to everyone, man, woman and child—if you can get up there. It is a long climb. The monks' astounding isolation on top of barren crags in the remote northern reaches of Thessaly epitomizes the fierce eastern spirit of asceticism. *Meteoros* means "high in the air", and these huge pillars of grey rock, creviced, streaked and eroded by wind and rain, rise up to about 530 m. (1,740 ft.) above the Valley of Meteora. After living for years in caverns at the foot of the rocks, holy men built their monasteries on the pinnacles as refuges from the Turks and Albanians in the 14th century.

By the 16th century, there were 24 monasteries, of which a dozen remain, but only a few are still inhabited. (They no longer provide accommodation for visitors, so you should plan on staying at nearby **Kalambaka**. If you have time, visit the **cathedral** to see its 12th-century frescoes and a rather strange marble pulpit.)

Monastery opening hours are irregular, so check in Kalambaka before you start your visit. Strict clothing regulations are enforced: skirts for women, long trousers for men, no sleeveless tops. In the old days, monks clambered up rope ladders or were pulled up in a netted basket-lift by a brother monk working a hand winch. Today, there are power winches to haul up supplies, and steep but negotiable stone stairways for people.

For the less adventurous, one of the monasteries, **Ágios Stéfanos** (now a convent and orphanage) is directly accessible by a footbridge spanning a ravine from the road (turning off south-east of Kalambaka). See the fine icons and frescoes in its 14th-century **church**, but you are likely to be most impressed by the sweeping view across the Thessaly plain.

Those prepared to climb stairs should set out west of Kalambaka, skirting the village of Kastraki. On the left, you will pass the abandoned ruins of two monasteries perched on the **Doupiani column**. Three km. (2 mi.) from Kalambaka is **Ágios Nikólaos Anapáfsas**. Partially ruined and uninhabited, it is accessible for those hell-bent (heaven-bent?) on climbing up to see the church's well-restored 16th-century frescoes by Theophanes of Crete, notably of *The Last Supper*. To the east, admire but do not even dream of tackling the needle-like rock to ruined **Agía Moní**, one of the valley's earliest monasteries, built in 1315.

The road continues round to the **Great Meteoron** *(Megísti Meteóron),* crowning the tallest rock in the valley, 534 m. (1,752 ft.) up. Slowly but surely, take the 115 stairs to the richly endowed 14th-century monastery. The **Church of the Transfiguration** *(Metamórfosis),* with its impressive 12-sided dome, has a fine iconostasis and austere frescoes of the 15th and 16th centuries. The refectory has been arranged as a museum for the church treasures. In the library is a collection of rare editions and monastic manuscripts.

At nearby **Varlaam** (1517), the flowers and butterflies of the lovely walled monastery garden are almost reward enough for the 195-stair climb. Notice the winch that once hauled up supplies and visitors. In the two adjoining churches, **All Saints** and the smaller **Three Hierarchs**, see the elaborately ornamental gilded iconostasis and 16th-century frescoes by Frangos Castellanos of Thebes. For many, the monastery's most handsome building is the guest house, sadly no longer in use.

The Sporades

The Sporades, literally "scattered" islands east of the Pilion peninsula, are an attractive mixture of well-organized (sometimes almost too well) beach resorts and traditional, old-fashioned places that the Greeks themselves like to relax in. Though there are plenty of fine sand beaches, in a region where the meltemi can blow quite fiercely, you will quickly appreciate the advantages of the smooth pebble beaches, too.

For island-by-island details of air and sea transportation from mainland ports with inter-island connections, see the Island-Hopping directory in the blue pages of our Berlitz-Info section, p. 286.

Skiathos 13 C2
This is *the* beach resort island. It boasts over 60 beaches, fine sand and smooth pebble, and several bays and harbours for yachts and small craft. Dense forest blankets the interior with beech, evergreen oak, chestnut, hazel, pine and the low arbutus strawberry tree—its berries are pretty but inedible.

Skiathos Town
Surrounded by wooded hills, the island capital has plenty of cheerful cafés and souvenir shops. Cross the causeway to **Bourdzi** islet for its view of the harbour.

Beaches
Buses run west from the capital to the beaches on **Kalamaki peninsula**, the most popular being **Kanapitsa**. At the west end of the island, the celebrated **Koukounaries** beach has fine sand stretching over half a mile. More secluded around on the west coast is **Agia Eleni**, facing Mount Pilion. Nearby is the nudist **Banana Beach** *(Krássa)*. Further north, amid beautiful pine trees and backed by russet cliffs, are the sand dunes of **Mandraki**. The best of the pebble beaches is on the north side of the island at **Lalaria**.

Kastro
To get away from the crowds, head out to this ghost town, now in ruins on its north coast promontory. Islanders built their refuge here in 1538 while the Turkish pirate Barbarossa Khair ed-Din was slaughtering the population of neighbouring Skopelos. There are guided boat tours, but you can also drive north-west of the capital and take a delightful 30-minute walk through the forest out to the coast. The fortified town, with only a drawbridge linking it to the rest of the island, once had 300 houses. Of the 20 churches, two remain. One of them, the **Church of Christ**, still contains icons and a carved wooden altar screen.

Skopelos 13 D2
The islanders here are remarkably friendly, and the women especially proud of their traditional costume—flowered silk skirt, velvet jacket with billowing sleeves, and light silk kerchief on their heads. The capital, **Chora**, is a typical Aegean town of dazzling white houses with blue-slate or greystone-tile roofs, with a **Venetian castle** at the top of the hill. Its craftsmen produce some fine black pottery. Visit the 17th-century **Church of Christ** to see the icons and altar screen. The island's hilly interior is dotted with monasteries and chapels.

Beaches

The best are on the south and east coasts. **Limonari** has the best reputation, with some good tavernas, too. Nudists undress over at **Velanio**. The nearby beach at **Stafilos** is named after the Cretan general believed to have colonized the island after the collapse of Minoan civilization. His grave was found here in 1927 with a gold crown, weapons and burial offerings now displayed in Volos museum.

Alonnisos   *13 D2*

This simple little island of herdsmen and fishing folk has great appeal for swimmers and snorkellers, but also for hikers tackling its pine-clad, thyme-scented hills. The island's limpid waters have been declared a marine conservation park. The best pebble beaches of the **Kokkinokastro peninsula** are a 30-minute boat excursion from **Patitiri**. The tavernas in the little yachting harbour of **Steni Vala** serve the island's best seafood.

Skyros   *13 E2*

Out on its own, further east, the largest of the Sporades splits into two distinct halves on either side of an isthmus. To the south, oak, beech and pine forests cloak rugged mountains, while the north is pleasantly green and fertile with farmland and cattle pastures. The famous Skyrian miniature ponies, descendants of an ancient breed known as Pikermic, are kept in a hillside pasture near the port of **Linaria** from late autumn until late spring.

The island capital, **Chorio**, is an attractive town of white houses, many of them veritable museums of the island's traditional handicrafts. One such house

That Was No Lady

Achilles was made to look very silly during his short stay on Skyros. His mother Thetis, apparently feeling guilty about abandoning him in early childhood (see p. 197), decided he should dodge the draft for those dangerous Trojan Wars by coming here disguised as a girl. Under the name of Aïssa, Achilles mingled with the ladies at the court of King Lycomedes. But cunning Odysseus smoked him out. He brought gifts to the palace, a pile of jewels, robes and other finery for the ladies to rummage about in. Then he ordered a battle trumpet blown outside the palace, along with the clash of arms. One of the ladies immediately stripped to the waist and grabbed a shield and spear which just happened to be in the pile of gifts. Odysseus had his man.

has been turned into the **Faltaitz Museum,** displaying embroidery, furniture, copper and basketware. The **Archaeological Museum** has some good Mycenaean ceramics. The hilltop **fortress**, part Byzantine, part Venetian, stands on the site of the ancient acropolis from which King Lycomedes is believed to have pushed Athenian hero Theseus to his death.

Just north of town is the popular **Magazia beach**. Among the best of the others is the sand and pebble cove of **Pefkos** on the west coast.

Lovers of English poetry will find **Rupert Brooke's grave** amid olive trees on Mount Kokhilas above Tris Boukes Bay; the 28-year-old bard of World War I died offshore in 1915 on his way to fight in the Dardanelles. His poem for all English soldiers served as his own epitaph:

If I should die, think only this of me:
That there's some corner of a foreign
   field
That is for ever England.

*G*reek peasants insist that the ass's proverbial stupidity is really a misinterpretation of his stoical resistance to the stupidity of his master.

Cricket on Corfu and Dolce Far Niente Everywhere

The merchants of Venice, the soldiers of Napoleon and colonial officers of Queen Victoria have all passed through the Ionian Islands and left their mark. Corfiotes play cricket and drink coffee in a decidedly Parisian arcade. After the earthquake, Zakynthos rebuilds its *campanile*. The proximity of Albania lends a more Balkan note to mainland Epirus. But the realm of Odysseus is also here, as nobody in Ithaca will let you forget. And Dodona's oracle is older than Delphi's. We are still in Greece.

"The scene," says Shakespeare's stage-direction to *The Tempest*, believed to be set in Corfu, "an uninhabited island." Things have changed. Closest to western Europe, the Ionian islands of Corfu, Ithaca, Cephalonia and Zakynthos (formerly Zante) are most convenient targets for the package tours. The resorts are crowded. But the richly varied countryside and plentiful beaches are equally good reasons for their popularity—and for individual travellers to come out of high season.

Do not be frightened when they tell you it rains more in western Greece than elsewhere. It is still a totally marginal phenomenon, leaving more than enough spring and summer sun to go round. The advantage is that the landscape is greener, the climate gentler than in the Aegean. The meltemi does not blow in the Ionian Sea. While Corfu seems to be outside the seismically sensitive area, other islands have been frequently ravaged by earthquakes, most recently in 1953. Historical monuments have suffered, and rebuilding has sometimes been more hurried than tasteful, with the notable exception of Zakynthos. (For island-by-island details of air and sea transportation from mainland ports with inter-island connections, see the Island-Hopping directory in the blue pages of our Berlitz-Info section, p. 286.)

The mainland can be tackled as a two- or three-day excursion from the islands. Cool off in the forests and caves of the Pindus mountains. Unscramble your beach-battered mind with a visit to Dodona's ancient theatre and sanctuary. Romantics may want to make a separate pilgrimage down to Missolonghi, last resting place of Lord Byron's heart.

Much of the pleasure on Corfu is to be found away from the crowded beaches, shopping with the locals.

Corfu *(Kérkira)*   *10 A2*

The most popular of all the Ionian Islands is understandably so. People may curse the mob scenes at the beach resorts in high season, but the island is big enough for you to find more isolated corners and coves for a quiet family picnic or solitary snooze. Certainly the beaches, fine sand and smooth pebble or shingle, are among the best in the whole of Greece.

The island has the elongated form of a

*T*he Venetians, French and British have come and gone, but the Orthodox priests remain the most influential members of the community.

Corfu Town 10 A2

Known like the island itself as Kérkira to the Greeks, the bustling, sophisticated island capital is built on its own peninsula ending in a fortified promontory.

The **Esplanade** *(Spianáda)*, the town's main social focus, catalogues the foreign cultural influences that have shaped the city and indeed the whole island. The broad green expanse was levelled by the Venetians as a parade ground for their garrison. Inspired by the arcades that Napoleon put up along Paris's Rue de Rivoli, the French built the elegant **Liston** arcade to shelter the town's best cafés (lively in the evening, but perfect for a quiet early morning breakfast). They provide only a distant view—for many, ideal—of the **cricket field** on the northern half of the Esplanade. The field is grassy enough, with a few treacherous Greek bumps, but the pitch itself is of coconut matting. At closer quarters, the July games pitting Corfiotes against visiting Englishmen and a "touring side" from Malta are most appropriately

Cosmopolitan Island

Except for its legendary golden era as the kingdom of Phaeacia which received Odysseus on his way home, Corfu has been a constant target for colonizers. In the 8th century B.C., the Corinthians founded a colony here, but relations between the island and the mother-city were always tempestuous. Corfu's sea battle with Corinth was a major cause of the Peloponnesian War, with the island supporting the Athenian cause. In the modern era, the island's stepping-stone position between Italy and the Balkans exposed it regularly to invasion—Norman Crusaders, Venetians, the French during the Napoleonic Wars and the British in the 19th century (holding on to its protectorate for more than 40 years after Greek independence). Typical of the island's cosmopolitan history, Corfu-born Count Giovanni Antonio Capo d'Istria served as Russian foreign minister in St Petersburg before returning to become independent Greece's first president in 1827. When he was assassinated by political rivals four years later, his name was Ioannis Antonios Kapodistrias. Greek at last.

scythe—64 km. (40 mi.) long but rarely more than 15 km. (9 mi.) wide except in the north, region of its tallest mountain, Pantokrátor, 906 m. (2,972 ft.) The interior is rich in orange and lemon groves and fig trees, with cypresses in ranks across the rolling hills. But most impressive of all are the literally millions of olive trees amassed by the lucrative planting policies of the Venetians who ruled here from 1386 to 1797. They also left their language, still widely spoken on the island.

watched while sipping another British legacy, ginger beer.

North of the Esplanade, the neoclassical **Royal Palace** was handed over to the Greek monarchy in 1864 by the departing British High Commissioner. It houses a **Museum of Asian Art**, exhibiting ancient Chinese, Thai and Khmer ceramics and sculpture bequeathed by Greek diplomat Grigorios Manos.

The Venetians' *Fortezza Vecchia*, **Old Fort**, stands out on a promontory east of the Esplanade. Part of it is now a Military Academy, but you can climb up to the rather dilapidated fortifications for the view across to Epirus and the mountains of Albania. An evening **sound-and-light show** in the summer traces the island's history from Odysseus to modern times.

Much more characteristically Italian is the jumble of narrow winding streets and piazzas of the **Old Town** between the Royal Palace and the ferry port. As you wander around this "little Venice" minus the canals, look out for a charming square with carved stone fountain (1699) and romantic restaurant.

South of the main Old Town area is the 16th-century church of **Ágios Spirídon**, Bishop of Cyprus in 319 and Corfu's patron saint since his remains were smuggled into the island from Constantinople in the 15th century. Kept in a brilliant silver coffin beside the high altar, they are the object of great veneration for the healing powers attributed to them. The coffin is paraded through the town on major holidays—Orthodox Palm Sunday; Easter Saturday; the saint's day, August 11; and the first Sunday in November. Call out "Spiros" and half the boys around you will come running.

On an island with few remaining ancient monuments, the **Archaeological Museum** is worth a visit for its mostly pre-classical sculpture and ceramics (Vraíla Street 5, just off the waterfront south of the Esplanade). Highlight of the collection is the Gorgon pediment (590 B.C.) from the island's Temple of Artemis. Snake-haired Medusa (one of three Gorgon sisters) turns on the famous petrifying glare, much fiercer than that of her guardian panthers. The Lion of Menekrates is a splendidly carved tomb sculpture for a warrior of the 6th century B.C. (The ancient tomb is south of the museum in the garden of the police station.)

Achillion

A short drive south of the capital is one of those magnificent follies imagined from time to time by the idle rich to fight off boredom, where normal criteria of beauty or ugliness no longer apply. In this case it was Elizabeth of Austria who in 1890 built this dreadful, grandiose villa to honour her Greek hero Achilles, so unlike her old fogey husband Franz Joseph. In the really very pretty **Italian landscaped gardens**, it is not an entirely perverse joy to wander among cypress trees and gloomy Homeric statuary and imagine Sissi walking barefoot through the dewy grass to watch the sunrise. One sculpture at least has some artistic merit, Ernst Herter's *Dying Achilles*.

After the Empress's assassination in 1898, Kaiser Wilhelm II of Germany bought the house, coming each spring from 1908 till the outbreak of World

---

Pack Your Bag, Gladstone

Britain's William Gladstone was a pretty good prime minister, but before that, in 1858, he was a wretchedly inept Lord High Commissioner Extraordinary on an abortive mission to give Corfu a new constitution. He was mistrusted by everyone. Islanders were convinced (wrongly) that he wanted to annex Corfu to the British Empire. The British military command suspected (rightly) that his major concern was to deepen his knowledge of Homer and the *Odyssey*. For his part, Gladstone voiced dismay at the Corfiotes' "complete and contented idleness" and proceeded to turn it into complete and utter rage by making all his speeches to them in Italian.

War I in 1914. After a spell as military hospital, it has been restored as a casino by descendants of the famous Red Baron von Richthofen. The villa's ground-floor **museum** has Austrian and German memorabilia, including a portrait of Sissi by Franz Winterhalter and the Kaiser's saddle-seat from his study.

To see the whole of the Achillion and its grounds—and the rest of the island—take the pleasant drive inland up to **Mount Ágii Déka**, 576 m. (1,890 ft.). Directly below on the east coast, you also have as good a view as you need of the hugely popular **Benitses**, a once pretty fishing village and now favourite resort of the beer fraternity.

Kanoni

The natural beauty of the peninsula south of Corfu Town has been sadly diminished by the airport and surrounding resort hotels. But tour-operators are so insistent, you may be curious to know what the excursion offers. It starts with a side-trip to **Anemomilos** to see the 12th-century Byzantine **Church of Saints Jason and Sosipatros**, who brought Christianity to Corfu 1,800 years ago. They are depicted in icons (16th century). You pass **Mon Repos,** a villa on the site of the ancient city of Corcyra but better known as the birthplace of Britain's Prince Philip in 1921. Since you can peep but not visit, here at least is some dynastic trivia: grandson of Prince William of Denmark, crowned King George I of the Hellenes, Philip Schleswig-Holstein-Sonderburg-Glücksburg took his mother's name, Mountbatten, before he married Princess Elizabeth in 1947. Like his wife, he is a great-great-grandchild of Queen Victoria. You can look down on the villa and its gardens from nearby **Analipsi**, the hill of the ancient acropolis.

The reward at the end of the peninsula is a picture-postcard view of the two islets of **Vlacherna**, with its red-roofed, white-walled monastery, and **Pondikonissi** (Mouse Island), its monastery half hidden in the cypress trees.

Paleokastritsa   *10 A2*

Quite the loveliest spot on the island, the west coast resort attracts droves of admirers in high season. But from autumn to spring it remains a glorious place to start a new romance or patch up an old one. Swimming, snorkelling and sailing attract the energetic to the turquoise waters of its coves. Dreamers prefer a clifftop stroll or siesta among the olive, lemon and cypress trees. To take in the full beauty of the scenery, drive up to the precipice to which the village of **Lakones** clings. From the *Bella Vista* café, the **panorama** is truly stupendous. Paleokastritsa's six coves fan out below you. You look out, too, over the town's 16th-century **monastery**. This is worth a separate visit, for the peace of its gardens and terraces more than its icons and old manuscripts. But remember to observe the strictly enforced dress code—no swim suits, shorts or sleeveless tops.

Paleokastritsa is frequently identified as the spot where Odysseus swam ashore from his shipwreck on the last lap of his homeward journey. Just off the coast is the faintly ship-shaped **Kolovri** rock.

Sorry, My Wife is Waiting
Homer is not all blood and thunder. The episode which Corfiotes believe is set at Paleokastritsa is one of blushing lyricism. Swimming for two days before reaching one of the coves, Odysseus fell asleep in a thicket. At a river nearby, the beautiful princess Nausicaa and her court ladies were washing their linen. While the laundry dried on the rocks, they bathed in the river, rubbed their bodies with olive oil and played with a beach ball. Suddenly, the ball soared out of reach into the sea, causing Nausicaa to shriek and wake up Odysseus. He leapt up, saw the girls and grabbed a leafy bough to cover his nakedness. The girls fled behind the sand dunes at the approach of this fellow begrimed with the salt of the sea. Only Nausicaa stayed, though her legs trembled. She offered to wash the caked salt off his body and give him an oil rub. Ah, women! First Calypso, then Circe, now Nausicaa. How was Odysseus ever going to get back to his Penelope? He declined the offer and bathed himself in private.

Those familiar with the legend assert it is the ship petrified by Odysseus's enemy, Poseidon, for having dared to take the hero back to Ithaca.

Beaches

Just below Paleokastritsa, boats take you to the less crowded beaches on **Liapades Bay**, one of the prettiest being the cypress-framed **Gefira**. Further south, also accessible only by boat, are the secluded pebble and sand beaches of **Homous** and **Stiliari**, lying at the foot of soaring cliffs striped by an eternity of wind and waves.

Most popular of the family beaches on the west coast is **Glifada**. To get away from the crowds, pedal a pedalo around a rocky promontory to the bewitching little sandy beach of **Mirtiotissa**, backed by rugged cliffs and romantic greenery. Both beaches can be reached overland via Pelekas. Above this hill village is the **Kaiser's Throne**, a lookout point where Wilhelm II sat to watch the sunset.

Easier to get to from Corfu Town is the west coast beach of **Agios Gordis**, long and sandy, approached through an attractive landscape of orchards, olive groves and vegetable farms. Snorkelling and spear-fishing are particularly good at the southern end of the beach.

North of Paleokastritsa, the beaches of **Agios Georgios Bay** are worthwhile as much for the trip itself as for the soothing swim at the end. The countryside of this north-west corner of the island is blessedly unspoiled, with scarcely more than the sheep and goats to disturb your contemplation of the olive groves and majestic cypresses. Dressed in traditional blue and white costume, the peasants in the villages of **Arkadades** and **Pagi** are friendly and refreshingly unpreoccupied by the "tourist trade".

On the north coast, **Sidari** is an attractive beach and cove area notable for its curiously bevelled sandstone cliffs. Once more, the drive is half the pleasure. Between the hamlets of **Mesaria** and **Agios Athanasios**, the road coils through some

of the island's most ancient olive groves, with thick fern hugging the contorted trunks. To the east, the little beach of **Agios Spiridon**, especially safe for children wading far out in shallow water, is a favourite of the Greeks who crowd in here at the weekend.

North-east Coast

Facing the mysterious coast of Albania, this was the stamping ground of writer Lawrence Durrell, whose *Prospero's Cell* is a romantic evocation of pre-package Corfu. Since his day, resorts have sprung up at **Ipsos** (Club Med), **Barbati** and **Nisaki**. His own house at **Kalami** is now in part a thriving taverna.

But the coast still makes a beautiful excursion, if you drive the winding corniche along the rugged green mountain slopes. Better still, hire a little outboard motorboat at **Kouloura** and coast along the limpid blue-green waters, rounding **Cape Varvara** to the lively harbour resort of **Kassiopi**. Be careful not to drift into Albanian waters—the mainland is only a couple of kilometres away, with armed patrol boats there to remind you. In the waters of the Corfu-Albanian channel, archaeologists have spotted amphoras from a ship wrecked in classical times, but exploration is strictly forbidden.

Paxi and Antipaxi   *10 A2*

The perfect refuge from Corfu's crowds (outside high season), these two tiny islands to the south offer very little hotel accommodation but plenty of private rooms. The major attraction here is snorkelling or scuba-diving, particularly in and out of the caves in the towering cliffs along Paxi's west coast. The sea depth off these sheer rocks plunges from 30 to 100 metres. **Gaïos** is Paxi's port capital with charming old Venetian houses. You will also find pleasant tavernas at **Lakka** and **Logos**. The local claim to the Odyssey industry is that Paxi was the island of the enchantress Circe who turned the hero's crew into

*T*he olive harvest is particularly prolific on Corfu,
with much of the crop gathered in the north-western corner of the
island between Paleokastritsa and Sidari.

pigs. Not so much as a sausage to be found on neighbouring Antipaxi's **Vrika** and **Voutoumi** beaches, so take along a picnic.

Lefkas
10 B2

The mainland is linked directly by bridge to this mountainous island, making it a convenient transition route for road travellers from Igoumenitsa to Cephalonia. In recent years, archaeologists have tried to demonstrate, much encouraged by local tour operators, that Lefkas, rather than its allegedly misnamed neighbour, is really Odysseus's original homeland of Ithaca.

Although the west coast has more sandy beaches, those on the east are bet-ter sheltered from the wind at the foot of tall rugged cliffs. The best of the resort towns is **Nidri**. Offshore to the east is the private island of **Skorpios**, where Ari Onassis wooed Jackie Kennedy. The Cephalonia ferry leaves from the southern fishing port of **Vassiliki**, which has a pleasant beach for a swim while you wait. On the island's south-west cape is the dramatic **Lefkatas cliff**, with a drop of 72 m. (236 ft.) and famous in ancient times as a "lover's leap". Lesbos poetess Sappho (see p. 182) was said to have jumped to her doom here when jilted by Phaon, a handsome ferryman. In Roman times, criminals could gain their freedom by surviving the jump. Ponder all this before you fall asleep on the fine beach of **Porto Katsiki**, just around the cape.

Ithaca

10 B3

The island of Odysseus? The topographical evidence is convincing. Several of the small natural harbours, creeks and coves are exactly the kind of spot where the hero might have landed and hidden the treasures gathered on his voyage. Archaeologists claim to have found the homes of Odysseus, his wife Penelope and son Telemachos. For the modern traveller, Ithaca is a tranquil place of hospitable people. Though relatively barren, the interior is attractively fragrant with herbs and shrubs. Clumps of myrtle and oleander add their bright splashes of colour. The wines are good and the roast hare excellent. The charming sleepy white capital of **Vathy**, founded only 400 years ago, has been quite nicely rebuilt since the 1953 earthquake. In the north of the island, you will find two enchanting little fishing harbours at **Kioni** and **Frikes**, both with good seafood restaurants.

Many scholars and most of the tour-operators locate the famous **Nymphs' Grotto**, where Odysseus was left to recuperate at the end of his long voyage, at **Marmarospilia**, just a few kilometres west of Vathy on the Bay of Dexia. Besides the nymph-like stalactites, the cave meets Homer's specifications of two openings, one for men and one for the gods. You will find a gap in the rocks wide enough for a man to squeeze through and a hole in the roof for the gods. In the cave, says Homer, Odysseus hid the gold, fine fabrics and 13 copper tripods given him by the Phaeacians (see p. 205) as a going-away present. A century ago, British archaeologists found 13 copper tripods in a cave near a villa they were excavating at **Pelikata** in the north of the island, visible in the site's **museum**. Unfortunately, although the Mycenaean-age villa would fit in chronologically with the Odyssey's Trojan era, scientists set the tripods' manufacture 400 years later. Tour-operators have had to settle for declaring the villa to be "Odysseus's Palace".

Cephalonia *(Kefallinia)*

14 A1

The largest of the Ionian Islands has some magnificent mountainous landscapes and rugged coastlines. Below mountainsides covered in dense forests of dark firs peculiar to Cephalonia, the vineyards produce one of Greece's finest white wines, Robóla. The network of good roads, a welcome legacy of British 19th-century administration, makes a car a real asset for touring the island.

Cephalonia suffered terrible destruction from the 1953 earthquake, and its two main towns, Argostoli, the capital, and Lixouri, were not rebuilt with great taste. But the pretty fishing harbour of **Fiskardo**, port of entry from Lefkas, escaped unscathed and makes a pleasant base for your excursions. It is named after Norman crusader Robert Guiscard, who died here in 1085. He apparently stayed long enough to provide work for his own architects, as the ruined church north-east of town has twin towers of distinctly Norman allure.

Beautifully situated on the west coast of Fiskardo's peninsula, **Assos** is as charming a port as you will find anywhere in the Ionian Islands. In the shadow of an imposing ruined Venetian castle, the pretty vine-covered cottages are proof enough that post-earthquake reconstruction can be attractive. Immediately to the south, surrounded by soaring cliffs, is **Myrtos Bay**, finest beach on the island, with surf waves worthy of Hawaii. Don't let the children wade too far out.

Zakynthos

14 A1

One of the reasons the new-old official Greek name Zakynthos is slow to catch on is the popularity of the Venetian slogan: *Zante, Zante, fior di Levante* ("flower of the Levant"). Only on rare rainy days can shameless Englishmen be heard singing: *Zakynthos, Zakynthos, where's my mackintosh?*

This pretty island, really a long way from the Levant, is indeed blessed with beautiful gardens and wild flowers, a special joy in spring. The heady wines from its vineyards justify a trip the rest of the year. It has suffered frequent earthquakes, three in the 19th century as well as the big one of 1953, but rebuilding has been intelligent and tasteful.

Zakynthos Town

The capital has retained something of its old Italian atmosphere, with the quayside *campanile* an unmistakable homage to the lengthy Venetian colonization. Behind the port, churches have been rebuilt in their original Italian Renaissance or Baroque style. On St Mark's Square, Greek heritage is emphasized by the **Dionysios Solomos museum** honouring the Zakynthos-born poet who in the 19th century championed modern popular (Demotic) Greek as the nation's literary language. Art treasures salvaged from earthquake-torn churches are housed in the **Museum of Byzantine Art** on Solomos Square. The **Venetian citadel** affords a fine view down to the Peloponnese.

Beaches

Most peaceful and pleasant of the beach resorts is **Alikes**, a small fishing village up on the north-east coast. The most popular—and crowded—is **Laganas**, with a sandy beach 6½ km. (4 mi.) long. Along with **Geraki** further east, it provides protection for some remarkably stoical turtles. At the island's south-east corner, the fishing port of **Vassilikos** has a good sandy beach.

Epirus

Literally "the mainland", Epirus is split between Greece and Albania, with the Pindus mountains to the east separating it from Thessaly. This mountainous land of sheep pastures and dense forests has always been remote from the rest of the country. It is worth a few days' explora-

The Lion Loses His Head

For most of its history, Epirus was little more than a backwater, until 1787 when the Turks appointed as governor the grandiose Albanian brigand, Ali Pasha. The Lion of Ioannina, as he styled himself, fought for and against his Turkish masters, supported and betrayed Napoleon, the British, Russians, Greeks and anyone else who served his purposes. By 1807, he was undisputed ruler of Epirus and most of Albania, too. With 500 women in his harem and scores of assassins at his beck and call, his life was an astounding mixture of sensuality, sadistic cruelty—he murdered his son's mistress and 16 of her girl friends—and an enlightened taste for the arts. He fascinated Lord Byron. After years of quiet amusement at his troublemaking, the Turks decided to crush Ali, who was penning down Turkish troops badly needed to deal with the Greek independence movement. In 1822, after their siege of Ioannina had failed, the Turks invited Ali to negotiate at an island monastery in the middle of Ioannina's lake. There, he was ambushed by Turkish troops and finally executed. His body was buried in Ioannina but, with the kind of nice touch Ali himself would have appreciated, the head was put on show for the citizens and then taken to Constantinople.

tion, to shop for jewellery in the Ioannina bazaar, pay homage to Zeus at Dodona and picnic out in the mountains.

Igoumenitsa   *10 A2*

For those arriving by ferry from Italy, this bustling transit town makes a most unromantic first view of Greece. On the waterfront, refresh yourself at one of the cafés, settle your business at the shipping agencies (return bookings, ferry-routes, currency exchange) and head out of town as soon as possible. Roads run down to Prevesa and the southern Ionian Islands or east over the mountains to Ioannina.

Ioannina   *10 B1*

A two-hour drive from Igoumenitsa brings you to the Epirote capital on Lake Ioannina, known in antiquity as Pamvotis. Facing Mount Mitsikéli, it is built on a rocky promontory at a refreshing

The Pindus mountain range between Ioannina and the port of Igoumenitsa were once a formidable barrier protecting the brilliant, brutal Albanian despot, Ali Pasha, from his nominal Turkish overlords. This herd is likely to provide the spicy lamb tripe sausages (kokorétsi) *served in the Epirus capital.*

altitude of 520 m. (1,706 ft.). Much of the old town was burned down by Ali Pasha during the Turkish siege of 1820, but the **bazaar** retains its colourful atmosphere among shops selling gold, silver, copper, brass and embroidery. Centre of town is around bustling Platía Pírrou and Kentrikí.

The Muslim past survives in the maze of streets crowded into the **citadel** where Turks and Jews lived side by side. In the north-east corner, the 17th-century **Aslan Mosque** with its slender minaret now

Ágios Pandeleímon monastery, where Ali Pasha made his last stand—note the Turkish bullet holes in his bedroom floor. The 11th-century **Ágios Nikólaos Dílios** has some good frescoes of *Judas* and the *Last Judgment*. Not the least of the island's attractions are the restaurants serving lake trout, crayfish, eels and frogs' legs with the good local wine.

Perama Caves

Just five minutes' drive north of town is a bewitching wonderland of stalactites and stalagmites stretching in galleries and caverns over 2 km. undergound. Discovered in World War II by families seeking refuge from bombardment, they have now been subtly illuminated and can be comfortably visited on a guided tour. Among the traces found of previous inhabitants were the teeth and bones of a family of bears hibernating here 600,000 years ago.

Dodona   *10 B1*

Some 20 km. (12½ mi.) down the Arta road, south-west of Ioannina, Greece's most ancient oracle stands in an appropriately lovely natural setting for Mother Earth to have been worshipped as far back as 1900 B.C. Beyond the sanctuary's remains, green meadows dotted with oaks and an occasional silver olive stretch away to the slopes of Mount Tómaros rising gently in the violet distance to the south.

By 800 B.C., the Greeks had taken over the sanctuary to consult the oracle of Zeus. Priests and priestesses interpreted his words from the rustling of leaves in a sacred oak tree and sounds from the rhythmic beating of a copper vessel. In A.D. 390, when the Christian Emperor Theodosius ordered all pagan sanctuaries closed, the sacred oak was destroyed.

The most impressive remaining monument is the great **theatre** (3rd century B.C.), beautifully restored to stage a classical drama festival each summer. Bigger even than the great Epidaurus

houses a **Folk Museum** exhibiting fierce weaponry and colourful Epirote costumes. Behind it is the old **Synagogue**—Ioannina had 6,000 Jews in the 19th century. Facing the south-west, the **tomb of Ali Pasha** occupies the site of his palace beside the **Fethi Mosque**.

The **Archaeological Museum** has some well-displayed finds from the Dodona sanctuary, notably terracotta figurines and inscribed lead oracle tablets.

Take a boat tour out to the **lake island** (*Nissí Ioanína*) and the 16th-century theatre (see p. 225), it was used by the Romans as an arena for gladiators. To the north, a long wall with a gate and towers enclosed the acropolis. The **sanctuary** lies on a terrace east of the theatre. First of the buildings, of which only foundations remain, is an assembly hall for the shrine elders, a small rectangular Temple of Aphrodite and beyond that, the Shrine of Zeus which enclosed the sacred oak, sheltered by a temple built in the 3rd century B.C.

Metsovo   *10 B1*

This delightful village 915 m. (3,000 ft.) up in the Pindus mountains makes a bracing excursion 50 km. (31 mi.) east of Ioannina. The sinuous road affords splendid views over the mountains and thick forests clinging to the ravines. Metsovo was a refuge for wealthy Christians fleeing the Turkish capture of Constantinople. Built on terraces up the mountainside on both sides of a ravine (linked by a bridge), the handsome **patrician mansions** of massive stone with wooden balconies are their imposing legacy. Grandest of them is the house of the Tossitsa family, converted into a **Folk Art Museum** displaying fine local embroidery, woollen textiles and rugs. Sample the tangy hard Metsovo cheese.

Parga   *10 B2*

Back on the coast 48 km. (30 mi.) south of Igoumenitsa, this resort is prettily situated but often overcrowded. From its **Norman castle** (the Venetian Lion of St Mark is a later addition), look down on the harbour, quite picturesque with its little islets in the bay, surrounded by groves of orange and olive trees. Swimmers head for **Khristogiali beach**.

Arta   *10 B2*

Travelers heading for the Gulf of Corinth stop by this lively commercial town to admire its elegant 17th-century humpbacked **Turkish bridge** over the Arachthos river. According to a popular song, the master builder reinforced the struc-

ture by walling his wife up in the foundations. If you have business in town, visit the six-domed church, **Panagía Parigorítissa**, built in the 13th century. In the sombre but imposing interior, notice the Italian style of the sculpture derived from Byzantine Epirus's links with Naples. The iconostasis has a 15th-century *Virgin the Comforter* and a later *Virgin and Child*.

Missolonghi   *10 C3*

Once a thriving fishing port, this unprepossessing town in the province of Etolia, south of Epirus, is a pilgrimage strictly for Byron fans. It was here in 1824 that the romantic poet, rallying to the cause of Greece's freedom fighters, died of fever, probably malaria. The mosquitoes have gone, but Lord George Noel Gordon Byron's heart is buried beneath his statue in the **Heroes' Garden**, beside the tomb of Markos Botsaris, commander of the local forces who saw the city razed by the Turks two years after Byron's death. In the centre of town, the **Museum of the Revolution** (Platía Bótsaris) displays Byronic memorabilia along with a graphic account of the horrors to which the town was subjected.

Bitter Last Words

Let Byron's epitaph not be an umpteenth misty tribute to Greece but, from his *Childe Harold's Pilgrimage*, a clear-eyed elegy about his mother country's archaeological bandits:

Cold is the heart, fair Greece, that looks on Thee,
Nor feels as Lovers o'er the dust they loved;
Dull is the eye that will not weep to see
Thy walls defaced, thy mouldering shrines removed
By British hands, which it had best behoved
To guard those relics ne'er to be restored.
Curst be the hour when from their isle they roved,
And once again thy hapless bosome gored,
And snatched thy shrinking Gods to Northern climes abhorred!

ROGUES AND HEROES

Outside the church, the Greeks have never had much time for saintly men. The legendary heroes were magnificently, even hilariously flawed. If Achilles and Odysseus were admired for their strength and courage, it was the former's pouting sulks and the latter's sneaky duplicity that made them more humanly endearing. The cultural and political glory of the Byzantine Empire was achieved by a bloodthirsty thug who fully earned his title of Basil the Bulgar-Slayer.

It is no accident that the most popular heroes in Greece's fight for independence from the Turks were klephts and merchant seamen who divided their energies between trade and piracy. The seamen's descendants have moved their techniques into corporate offices and are now known as shipping magnates. If Georgios and Andreas Papandreou are acclaimed by their countrymen as champions of democracy, their methods were often as tough as that of their opponents.

Let's take a closer look at just a few of these heroic rogues and roguish heroes.

Theodoros Kolokotronis (1770–1843)
He was born, say all the Greek textbooks, under a tree in the Peloponnese. For generations, the Kolokotronis clan had led a band of klephts preying mainly on rich Greek landowners known contemptuously as Turkish Christians for their collaboration with the Ottoman authorities. With the hindsight of his prowess in the War of Independence, Kolokotronis was endowed with the aura of a Robin Hood, but there is no evidence that he ever distributed his booty to the poor. Heroic paintings of him show the great bandit in traditional flowing pantaloons over slippers and gold-bound leggings. On his gold-braided tunic he wore lion-head epaulettes to match his great white mane of hair, fierce moustache and predatory stare.

Inspired by the French Revolution which, he said, "opened the eyes of the world", he concentrated his attacks on the Turks, who drove him to seek refuge in the Ionian islands. His hero had been the greatest klepht of them all, Napoleon, but on Zante (Zakynthos) he joined the British army of Sir Richard Church.

Back in the Peloponnese after the Napoleonic Wars, he resumed the fight against the Turks. In 1822, he captured the Turkish garrison in Nafplio. But still more bandit than committed patriot, he refused to let the Greek government hold its national assembly there and kidnapped four of its members to block retaliatory measures against him. Now virtual master of the Peloponnese, he furthered the national cause again with a famous victory over the Turks at Dervenaki Pass (near Argos). He used the 13th-century Crusader castle of Karitaina as his stronghold against the Ottoman armies of Ibrahim Pasha. Proving he could match the enemy in brutality, his capture of the key town of Tripolis in 1824 resulted in the wholesale massacre of its Turkish civil population.

He finally did hand Nafplio over to the Greek government in 1824, in exchange for half the support funds that Lord Byron had brought from London. He rebelled again and was thrown in jail. In 1832 he broke up the National Assembly in an abortive attempt to impose his choice of the Russian Admiral Ricord in place of King Otto. His valour is celebrated with equestrian statues in Nafplio and Athens.

Konstantinos Kanaris (1790–1877)
The great Aegean seaman also began life as an outlaw but settled down with age into a more statesmanlike posture. He was born on the heroic island of Psara, west of Chios and perpetual thorn in Turkey's side until a massacre wiped out nine-tenths of its population. Before the independence struggle began in earnest, Kanaris plied the Mediterranean in a merchant freighter but made most of his money from smuggling and piracy. He looked like every schoolboy's image of a pirate, kerchief tied around his brow, bristling moustache, dagger at the ready in his cummerbund.

With the outbreak of war—Psara was, with Spetses and Hydra, the first of the islands to revolt—Kanaris wrought havoc among the Ottoman fleet. His most famous victory came in November, 1822, when his fireship destroyed the Turkish admiral's flagship off the island of Tenedos (Turkish Bozca). This action stopped an advance to relieve Nafplio and drove the Ottoman fleet

Admiral Kanaris

Ari Onassis

back to its harbours in the Dardanelles. Kanaris became an admiral.

During the equally turbulent years of peace, Kanaris stowed away his dagger and supported the moderate Ioannis Kapodistrias. He was one of the few Greek leaders to obey the new Constitution. As prime minister in the 1860s, he championed democratic reforms but was not averse to employing the old strongarm tactics when the king resisted. Returning from a tour, Otto was stopped from landing at Piraeus, and Kanaris promoted the enthronement of the more amenable Danish King George I.

Ari Onassis (1906–1975)

The shipping magnate's full name was Aristotle Socrates Onassis. More appropriate for this not very philosophical fellow would have been Odysseus for his opportunistic cunning and Croesus for his fabled opulence. He was born in Smyrna, Turkey (now Izmir), from which his family of prosperous tobacco merchants fled after the defeat of the Greek fleet in 1922. Ari became a telephone operator in Buenos Aires. By the age of 19, he had revived the family tobacco business, importing Turkish tobacco. With dual Greek and Argentinian citizenship, he became Greek consul-general.

He had made his first million dollars by 1931. A year later, convinced that the Great Depression was a great business opportunity, he bought his first ships, six Canadian freighters, for $120,000—five years earlier they would have cost 2 million *each*. In 1939, he made the same diagnosis for World

War II, buying his first oil tanker. He put his merchant fleet at the disposal of America and its allies and in return—"Never give nothing for nothing" was the Onassis motto—he acquired 23 Liberty ships (wartime cargo vessels) for a bouzouki song.

Back in Greece in 1946, he married Athina (Tina), the daughter of fellow shipping magnate Stavros Livanos. With Stavros Niarchos as his brother-in-law (married to Tina's sister Eugenie), Onassis belonged to the most powerful shipping clan in the world. But family ties were never as strong as business rivalry and personal vanity. If Onassis acquired an island, Skorpios (off Lefkas), then Niarchos must have one, too, Spetsopoula (off Spetses). The toys they fought for were yachts and women. Niarchos divorced to steal away Tina, and Onassis retaliated with his biggest coup of all, his marriage to Jackie, the widow of President Kennedy.

Business was not neglected. The money he lost from a fleet of whalers he more than recouped by turning from blubber to petroleum. Again anticipating crisis, Onassis built the world's first supertanker in 1953. Three years later, he made a cool $115 million out of the diversion of oil shipments when Egypt blocked the Suez Canal. In 1957 he founded Olympic Airways (nationalized in 1975). For many years, he was principal stockholder in the company owning the Monte Carlo casino.

He did not like giving money to charities or cultural foundations, but did much to make bouzouki music fashionable by having it played on his yacht and in smart nightclubs. In Greek politics, he played all sides. He kept in with the colonels' dictatorship of 1967 by agreeing to invest $600 million, then reneged on the deal in time to win the favour of the democrats who overthrew the colonels in 1974. By the time of his death in the Paris suburb of Neuilly a year later, Onassis's billions were countless, but he left a few more tangible figures: 6 supertankers with a total capacity of 2 million tons, 56 merchant ships totalling 5,586,000 tons; 87 companies in 12 countries; 217 bank accounts.

Georgios and Andreas Papandreou

As prime minister at 20 years' interval, father and son were both fierce libertarians. Steeled by years of ruthless treatment at the hands of their enemies, these staunch champions of democracy proved equally ruthless in its defence. It was a national tradition that went back to Pericles himself.

Georgios Papandreou (1888–1968) founded the Social Democratic party in 1935. With brilliant oratory, this charismatic demagogue in the purest ancient sense of the word soon posed a threat to the dictatorship of Ioannis Metaxas. His best men were jailed and tortured and he himself was driven into exile in 1938. During World War II he formed in Cairo a government-in-exile which he brought back to liberated Athens in October 1944. His efforts to disarm resistance fighters ended in confrontation between left-wing partisans and the British army, forcing him to resign.

Back in power in 1963, he was in perpetual conflict with King Constantine II who as commander-in-chief resisted his purge of right-wing extremists in the army. Exploiting Papandreou's anti-monarchist rallies as part of what they claimed was a Communist threat to the state, army colonels staged a coup in 1967. Georgios Papandreou was jailed, released in failing health and died the following year. His funeral, the biggest in modern Greek history, turned into a massive demonstration for democracy against a dictatorship that was to last another six years.

His activist son, Andreas Papandreou (1919–89) followed him to prison on treason charges, but not for the first time. In 1939, he had been jailed by dictator Metaxas before going into exile to study in the United States. In the 40s and 50s, he taught economics at Harvard, Minnesota, Northwestern (Illinois) and Berkeley.

Andreas resumed his political career in Greece in 1964 as minister in his father's government. Under the colonels, he was exiled again, but this time to Sweden and Canada since the United States was the Greek regime's discreet but firm ally.

Andreas returned in 1974 with scores to settle. Electoral campaigns for his socialist PASOK party branded his father's old conservative enemies as nothing less than traitors for having handed the country over to the colonels. On similar grounds, he was equally hostile to the U.S. With fiery rhetoric reminiscent of his father's but an ideology much further to the left, he became prime minister in 1981 on the simple campaign slogan of *Allagi*—Change. He pushed through sweeping social reforms in welfare, education and health. But party cronies lived too well off the fat of the land and financial scandals marred the Papandreou crusading image. This was what cost him victory and his health, too, in his 1989 election battle. The fact that he had jilted his 65-year-old American wife Margaret for the sexy 34-year-old air hostess Dimitra upset only a prim and proper minority. Outside the church, the Greeks have never had much time for saintly men.

Andreas Papandreou

PELOPONNESE

Peninsula of Kings and Heroes, Home of the Olympic Ideal

The Peloponnese has ever been a land of courage and exaltation: Mycenae, awesome citadel of King Agamemnon's destiny; Epidaurus, grandiose theatre for the royal tragedies; Olympia, shrine of sacred Games that interrupted wars; the Taygetos mountains, training ground for dauntless Spartans and, centuries later, bastion of Byzantine culture's last flourish at Mistra. It was not inappropriate that the march towards Greek independence in 1821 began with a proclamation in the Peloponnese.

To the visitor curious to penetrate the Greek spirit, the mainland's predominantly mountainous southern peninsula presents a vigorous but always rewarding challenge. The secret to handling the great sites of antiquity, here as elsewhere, is to have a comfortable and pleasant base in the vicinity. But this is particularly true in the Peloponnese where so many of the archaeological sites are perched on hilltops. Even with places like Olympia situated in the plain, there is plenty of ground to cover, so take it easy. To enjoy them all, you should be well rested, make an early start and have a chance to relax or take a swim afterwards. So we always propose some strategically located resorts like Nafplio for the north-east (the Argolid's Epidaurus and Mycenae), Githio for the south

Leonidio's cemetery nestles against the Parnon mountains separating Sparta from the Aegean.

(Mistra and the castles of Mani), Killini for the west (Olympia and Bassae).

In any case, unless you love sweltering in the sun of high summer, the Peloponnese is best visited in spring and autumn. Nearly all the archaeological sites are located well inland and do not enjoy the sea breezes you get out in the islands. Which brings us to the peninsula's little bonus—the nearby islands. We describe here the Saronic islands of Aegina, Poros, Hydra and Spetses, which could each serve as a refreshing base for the Argolid if you do come in the summer. And off the west coast, the Ionian islands of Zakynthos, Cephalonia and Ithaca (see p. 210) all have ferry services to Killini or Patra.

To the ancients, the Peloponnese itself, despite the narrow isthmus joining it to Attica, was an island. Its name means the "island of Pelops", a legendary king who dominated the region by winning a chariot race against his rival. Today, the island is at least a technical reality with the Corinth canal cutting through the isthmus. That is where we start our tour.

Corinth
15 D1

What is left of the ancient centre of luxury and sin that St Paul used as his missionary base in Greece? No discernible luxury, and the only important sin is the dreary modern construction of **New Corinth** since successive earthquakes of 1858 and 1928. Its only reasonable cafés are on the waterfront, and the closest beach is a 10-minute drive west to **Lechaion,** site of its ancient port.

Corinth's strategic position commanding traffic from the Adriatic through the Gulf of Corinth to the Aegean has lost commercial importance now that most freighters are too wide for the canal. But Peloponnese-bound drivers from Athens make a natural fuel and refreshment stop here. So take a closer look at the canal, visit the site of ancient Corinth, its museum and, if it is not too hot, the hilltop citadel.

Corinth Canal
15 D1

The waterway makes a neat slice through the narrow neck of land linking Athens to the peninsula's north coast. The canal is almost 6½ km. (4 mi.) long but only 25 m. (82 ft.) wide and 8 m. (26 ft.) deep. The modern construction, begun by the French in 1882, completed by the Greeks in 1893, is the accomplishment of an ancient dream. Periander, enlightened Tyrant of Corinth, made an abortive attempt to chop through the isthmus at the end of the 7th century B.C. Roman Emperor Nero made a more determined effort in A.D. 67, breaking ground himself with a golden shovel before 6,000 Jewish slaves from Palestine continued the work—interrupted by insurrection in Gaul. Meanwhile, merchants were content to have their ships hauled on trolleys across the narrow neck of land rather than negotiate the more dangerous sea route around the peninsula. Traces of their slipway, the *diolkos,* can still be seen cutting diagonally across the western end of the canal.

Ancient Corinth
15 D1

South-west of the modern city, the archaeological site occupies a plateau overlooking the Gulf of Corinth at the foot of what was once an almost impregnable citadel, Acrocorinth. It was, until the rise of Athens, the most prosperous and populous of Greek cities. It led colonization with settlements in Sicilian Syracuse and the island of Corfu. The city's ceramics industry, textiles and fine bronzeware made its fortune throughout the Mediterranean and beyond. First to turn out the three-tiered trireme, its shipbuilding won orders from all over the Aegean. Even after Athens' ceramics and other fancy goods captured overseas markets, Corinth remained a synonym for luxury, elegance and sin—sailors sang the praises of its exceptional brothels. The town's most celebrated contribution to Greek art was appropriately the decorative Corinthian column, adding gracefully carved acanthus leaves to the capital. The Romans plundered and destroyed the city in 146 B.C. But when Paul arrived 200 years later, after Julius Caesar had rebuilt the town, the apostle still found it necessary to rail against the "filthiness of flesh and spirit" he found there.

Just outside the archaeological site proper are the ruins of a small **Roman theatre** and a larger **arena** for gladiators or, when filled with water, for mock sea battles. Inside the enclosure, see in the **museum** the fine Corinthian ceramics, earlier Geometric and the pottery of its heyday (7th century B.C.) gaily decorated with warriors, cockerels and swans. Other exhibits come from the town's Roman era, mosaics and statuary of the 2nd century A.D.

Step down to the **Temple of Apollo** (6th century B.C.) of which seven monolithic limestone columns remain, Doric not Corinthian. The rest of the site is mostly Roman. Below the temple, the vast **Agora** (marketplace) has a long portico closing off the south side. The double colonnade originally had 71 Doric columns along the façade and 34 Ionic in the interior. At the rear, archaeologists identified 33 taverns and nightclubs. Night quarters were upstairs. Across the Agora's centre is another row of shops with, in the middle, remains of a **Bema**, or judge's tribune, where the Roman proconsul acquitted Paul of improper preaching in A.D. 51.

The paved **Lechaion Road** running north of the Agora led to the old port. Down a stairway off to the right is the **Peirene Fountain**, a Roman structure of colonnades and arched chambers surrounding a sunken rectangular basin. Its waters were sprung from the ground by a hoof-kick of winged Pegasus.

Acrocorinth

South of town, the citadel atop a solid limestone crag 575 m. (1,886 ft.) high was practically impregnable by invaders and continues to resist all but the hardiest tourists. They find the view from the top repays their effort. Many feel this must have been the hill up which Corinth's first king, Sisyphus, was condemned to push a huge rock only to see it roll back down before he got to the top. The natural fortress served a succession of Greeks, Romans, Crusaders, Byzantines and Turks. Of three massive fortified gates on your way to the top, the first is Turkish, the second Franco-Venetian, while the innermost with two square towers is part Byzantine, part ancient Greek, dating back to the 4th century B.C. Beyond the third gate, pick your way among ruined mosques, Turkish houses, cisterns and Byzantine chapels. A **keep** dominates a 13th-century stronghold built by Guillaume de Villehardouin. A path to the right leads to the **Upper Peirene Fountain**. The water is still here, clean and fresh, but not drinkable. Double back to climb to the summit where a column marks the site of a Temple of Aphrodite famous for its religious harlots. From here there's a magnificent view over to Mount Parnassus and south across the mountains of the Peloponnese.

Argolid 15 D1

In this north-east corner of the Peloponnese, the charming town of Nafplio makes a perfect base to visit the great archaeological sites of Mycenae, Epidaurus and Tiryns. Dominated by the city of Argos in classical times, the region was a constant political and military rival to Sparta.

Nafplio 15 D1

Nauplia, Nafplio, to the Venetians Napoli, this cheerful low-key flower-bedecked resort was for a moment capital of newly independent Greece. The presidency of Ioannis Kapodistrias and the brief stay of King Otto before he moved to Athens in 1834 left a legacy of elegant neoclassical houses to add to the prevalent Venetian style. The city stands on a rocky promontory overlooking a large bay, with the formidable 18th-century Venetian **Fort Palamidi** looming to the south. Drive up there before the heat of the day for the view from its ramparts.

The waterfront is lively, with the best quayside seafood restaurants along Bouboulína Street. Out in the bay is the fortified islet of **Bourdzi**, built by the Venetians in 1471 and serving later as a prison and hangman's home.

In the centre of the old town, Syntagma Square is an amalgam of the city's history: a stone Venetian lion, behind it a Turkish mosque used for modern Greece's first parliament, now a meeting-hall and cinema; a Venetian arsenal converted into an **Archaeological Museum** exhibiting a splendid suit of Mycenaean armour, sculpted gravestones and ancient jewellery.

But perhaps the town's most attractive museum is the **Peloponnesian Folklore Foundation** in a handsome neoclassical house in Ipsilántou Street between Syntagma and the port. It displays regional jewellery, costumes, fabrics and looms in action.

At the little Venetian church of **Ágios Spirídon**, the wall beside the portal is

scarred by bullet holes. It was here, in 1831, that Kapodistrias (see p. 205) was assassinated on his way to worship. His killers were members of the Mavromikhalis family, feudal lords of the Mani in the southern Peloponnese (see p. 234). By their bloody code of honour, they were avenging Kapodistrias's arrest of their patriarch, Petrobey. The President's **statue** stands on Platía Dikastérion near the bus station.

Epidaurus
15 D1

Hard to believe that what might justly be claimed as the most beautiful theatre in the world was in its day just a sideshow. Nestling between two hills in the tranquil pine-scented Argolid plain, 30 km. (19 mi.) east of Nafplio, Epidaurus *(Arhéa Epídavros)* was ancient Greece's most prestigious sanctuary of Asclepius, god of healing. It was half health spa, half Lourdes.

*R*esiding in the 19th century in Bourdzi island's
Venetian fortress of Castel Pasqualigo, Nafplio's municipal hangman
was kept at a safe distance from the local populace. In the War of
Independence, political prisoners were given a more salubrious
location up in Fort Palamidi.

*S*cholars consider Epidaurus to be the ancient world's greatest achievement in theatrical architecture. *Polyclitus applied intricate mathematical formulas to develop an auditorium in which ideal sight-lines could be combined with the almost perfect acoustics. For these purposes, the curve of the terraced seating flattens out slightly and is not completely concentric with the circular stage.*

surviving foundations of the stone *skene* (scene), forerunner of the modern backdrop. The auditorium had 34 rows and added 21 more with artificial earth-fill in the 2nd century B.C. to bring the capacity to 12,000. Dignitaries were—and still are for the Annual Festival of Greek Drama (see p. 256)—seated in front-row reddish stone thrones. From the gods at the top, you *can* hear a pin drop down on the orchestra altar. But more than the proverbial acoustics, it is the theatre's grandiose natural setting between Mount Velanidhía to the north and Mount Kharáni to the south that finally drive the most intrepid writer to utter the word "breathtaking".

The little **museum** is worth a visit on the way out for its model reconstructing the original sanctuary and sculpture from the temples. Most remarkable are the floral sculpture and rosettes from the

National Health Service

Sick pilgrims from all over Greece came to worship at Epidaurus and seek cures from the doctor-priests of Asclepios. Regions from Messenia in the south to Thessaly in the north all went after the lucrative trade involved in having the god of healing born on their territory. But Epidaurus won out with the claim that the centaur Chiron had galloped down from Mount Pilion to teach Apollo's son Asclepios all he needed to know about medicinal herbs. Asclepios' symbolic serpent entwined around his staff became the emblem of doctors worldwide. Epidaurus got its great boost after 430 B.C. when plague-hounded Athenians arrived in droves.

While it may not have cured the plague, a visit to Epidaurus could be beneficial. The medicinal herbs, ritual baths and the intensity of the sanctuary's whole ceremonial process had an accumulative impact, particularly on nervous disorders and psychological complaints. Like the bandstand and casino at Baden-Baden, Vichy or Montecatini, the theatre was intended to provide a little therapeutic entertainment. There was also a stadium for remedial athletics. At the peak of its popularity in the 4th century B.C., Epidaurus financed its temples and the theatre in large part with donations from the hopeful sick and grateful healed.

Roman and Visigoth plunderers have reduced the sanctuary, north-west of the museum, to barely discernible ruins. But the **theatre** is one of the country's best preserved monuments, generally attributed to Polyclitus the Younger in the 4th century B.C. Entrance to stage and auditorium is through one of two reconstructed *parodoi*, double-columned stone door frames. The circular orchestra, where the chorus sang and danced, is 20 m. (66 ft.) in diameter with the base of an altar at its centre. Behind it are the coffered ceiling of a Tholos rotunda and the superbly carved Corinthian capital of one of its columns.

If you need to cool off, take a dip at the nearby beach of **Palea Epidavros**.

Mycenae   *15 D1*

If Aeschylus, Sophocles and Euripides had been film makers hunting appropriate locations for their tragedies about the house of Atreus, they might have chosen Mycenae anyway. Even today, long after the dust has settled on scholarly arguments and lab tests proving or disproving that this or that group of stones was Queen Clytemnestra's bathroom or King Agamemnon's tomb, you *know* that something terrible and magnificent happened here. In Greece, legend and reality are inseparable. Nowhere is this truer than at Mycenae, citadel of the kings that dominated the Peloponnese from 1400 to 1200 B.C. (see p. 16). The sky bears down on a grim fortress atop its windswept crag surrounded by rolling hills of olive groves. Of course, Agamemnon marched from here to lead the Greek armada against Troy. And the dark ramparts enclosing the royal tombs and palace are the obvious setting for the acts of passion, betrayal, murder and revenge following his return.

Thirty minutes' drive north of Naflio, the visit begins mundanely in the site's vast car park just beyond the little town of Mykines. Pocketing your flashlight for the site's darker corners, ignore for the moment the excavations bordering the approach road and head for the **citadel** at the top of the hill. Built between 1350 and 1200 B.C., the ramparts of massive untrimmed blocks were known to classical Greeks 800 years later as "Cyclopean walls". They could not imagine anyone but the gods' one-eyed giant labourers being able to haul these boulders into place. (As with Athenian democracy, the employment of mere mortal slaves was conveniently ignored.) The entrance at the north-west corner

All in the Family

The House of Atreus was not a nice house. With brother Thyestes' Mycenaean throne as the stakes, Atreus bet he could make the sun turn back in its tracks. He invited his brother to dinner and served up two of his sons as the main course. The sun was so horrified that it turned back in its tracks. But a bastard son, Aegisthus, survived and murdered Uncle Atreus to put his father back on the throne.

The Spartans, never sentimental, forced Thyestes to abdicate in favour of Atreus' eldest son, Agamemnon. Chip off the old block, Agamemnon killed a fellow Peloponnesian king and married his widow, Clytemnestra. Meanwhile, her sister Helen, married to Agamemnon's brother, went off to Troy with her lover Paris (see p. 233), reason enough for half of Greece to take to its ships to get her back.

While Agamemnon was away starring in the *Iliad*, that bastard Aegisthus reappeared in Mycenae to seduce Clytemnestra. Not that we should start feeling sorry for Agamemnon. Crossing the Aegean, he had sacrificed his daughter Iphigenia to appease the spiteful goddess Artemis. Now he was on his way home with the Trojan king's daughter Cassandra as his mistress. With her knack of foreseeing disasters that nobody wanted to know about, she was coming to the right place.

Warned of Agamemnon's arrival by a chain of mountaintop beacons lit all across the Aegean, Aegisthus went out to welcome the conquering hero with a no-hard-feelings embrace. Back home, Clytemnestra prepared a banquet and hot bath for her travel-weary husband. Cassandra, as usual, said she smelt trouble and stayed outside the palace. As Agamemnon stepped out of the tub, Clytemnestra threw a net over him, making him an easy target for the sword of Aegisthus. Clytemnestra chopped his head off and then ran out to do the same to Cassandra.

But Orestes, the son Clytemnestra had by Agamemnon, went into hiding until he was old enough for revenge. He came back disguised as a peasant and slew both Aegisthus and Clytemnestra. He chopped off his mother's head and brandished aloft for all to see the still bloodstained net in which she had trapped his father.

of the hill is through the splendid **Lion Gate,** Europe's earliest known monumental sculpture. Above a colossal limestone lintel, two now headless beasts stand with their front paws on small al-

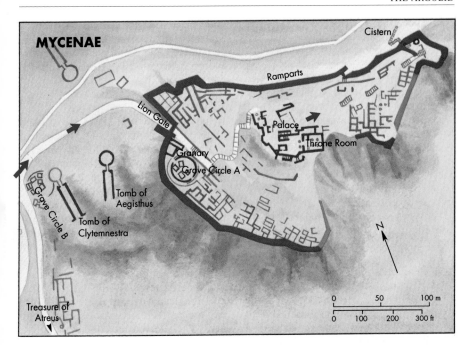

Turning Myth Into Reality

After locating the city of Troy in Asia Minor, German businessman-turned-archaeologist Heinrich Schliemann tracked down the man who had commanded its destruction. He began digging at Mycenae in 1874 and found the tombs, skeletons and treasures that convinced him this was Agamemnon's palace. Other scholars deny the famous golden death mask is of Agamemnon, but agree that Schliemann's excavations had indeed uncovered the home of the Mycenaean kings. They accept that Agamemnon was in all likelihood one of them. Those who believe that "truth" is too important to be left to the scientists will prefer the crazy German who gave up wholesaling groceries to the Russians to find the stone fabric of the poets' vision.

tars on either side of a palace column, the whole forming a coat-of-arms proclaiming Mycenaean power.

Just inside the gate to the right is a **granary** in which earthenware storage-jars were found containing grains of carbonized wheat. Beyond it is the **Grave Circle A.** The circular stone parapet enclosed six royal shaft graves—large rectangular family mausoleums—and several smaller graves for commoners. Schliemann found 19 skeletons—eight men, nine women and two children—along with treasures buried with them (now in Athens' National Museum).

A stairway and cobbled ramp lead up to the **Palace.** Cross the courtyard between the remains of a two-columned porch into the **Throne Room** *(megaron).* Notice the bases of four pillars that surrounded a central hearth. The room was decorated with frescoes exhibited now in Athens. Romantics identify an area off to the left as part of the bathroom where Agamemnon was murdered—traces of red plaster found on the floor have not been subjected to forensic study.

In Hellenistic times a small shrine to Athena was built on the upper terrace and private houses east of the main palace. Beyond them, at the far end of the fortress, the adventurous can explore the pitch-black depths of the palace **cistern**, 99 slippery steps down.

Outside the fortress, coming back downhill from the Lion Gate, visit the two monumental **tombs of Clytemnestra** and **Aegisthus**. Scientifically proposed dates of 1250 and 1500 B.C. respectively make it unlikely that the queen and her lover were both buried here, but these "beehive" constructions were typical of Mycenaean royal mausoleums. Tall, vaulted burial chambers stand at the end of long stone passageways dug into the hillside. The entrance's weight-relieving triangular lintel was originally covered by a sculpted frieze.

Closer to the car park, excavations are continuing on **Grave Circle B**, grouping 14 royal shaft graves and 12 commoners' graves.

Driving back, just down the road on the right, stop off at the greatest of the Mycenaean beehive tombs, known as the **Treasury of Atreus**. The main burial vault of this monumental mausoleum is 13.4 m. (44 ft.) high and 14.6 m. (48 ft.) in diameter. Off to the right is a smaller chamber that housed the treasury or the remains of the king.

Argos   15 D1
Visible from afar, on a high rock, Argos was once the region's dominant city (Homer spoke of Argives as a synonym for Greeks). The modern town has little interest beyond its open-air market as a

good place to stock up for your picnics. The **museum** has some good Mycenaean and Geometric pottery and impressive bronze helmet and breastplate from the 7th century B.C.

Tiryns
Rising proudly from the Argolid plain 5 km. (3 mi.) from Nafplio, this ancient citadel served as a satellite fortress for the Mycenaeans in the 13th century B.C. Said to be born here, Hercules may have been needed to help build the massive **Cyclopean walls** that make Tiryns' fortifications even more imposing than those of Mycenae. Some of the huge boulders weigh as much as 20 tons, forming ramparts up to 11 m. (36 ft.) thick. At the top of a chariot ramp, you pass through inner and outer gateways. Built into the eastern fortifications are huge "Gothic" vaulted galleries incorporating six chambers. They served as artillery positions and for storage.

Only the foundations remain of the **Royal Palace** and its entrance hall, the Propylaea. The western bastion protects a well-preserved staircase leading out of the fortress, a terrible trap for invaders. If all is clear, turn right at the bottom and skirt the outer wall to underground galleries leading to two cisterns. Double back and cross through the lower citadel to exit at the chariot ramp.

For anyone unaware of the exploits of the mighty house of Atreus, the Lion Gate leading to the Palace of Mycenae bears eloquent testimony to the family's power. Most massive of the gateway's gigantic ashlar masonry is the monolithic lintel supporting the carved lions, 16 ft. across, 8 ft. deep and 3½ ft. thick in the middle. Notice between the two lions the pillar tapering downwards, like those of Crete's Palace of Knossos.

The South

The coast road down from the Argolid takes you into the heartland of the Peloponnese. The austerely beautiful lunar landscapes of the interior alternate rugged mountains and the plains of Spartan Laconia and Messinia. The peninsula culminates in three prongs with the off-beat resort of Monemvasia to the east, Venetian Methoni to the west and the dramatic Mani country in the middle.

Arcadian Coast   *15 D2*
The winding corniche mountain road gives you splendid views out over the southern Aegean with occasional cut-offs descending to shingle or sandy coves for a refreshing bathe. Buy some peaches at the market town of **Astros**, for instance, and eat them down on the beach at nearby **Paralion Astros**. Perched on the mountainside among terraced olive groves, **Tyros** is a pleasant little village overlooking the resort of **Paralia Tyrou**. An old watchtower stands guard over the beach of **Sambatiki**, with its harbourside tavernas.

As the road turns inland, stop off in **Leonidio** to stroll among its old balconied houses and wood-panelled cafés with marble tables. The locally baked bread is excellent. From here a rough road climbs up past the Elona monastery into the magnificent scenery of **Mount Parnon**. The cool hill town of **Kosmas** makes a refreshing stop for a coffee on the tree-shaded square.

On the other side of the mountain, **Geraki** has a 13th-century fortress built by a dynasty of French Crusaders with several Byzantine churches inside its fortifications. In **Ágios Geórgios**, there are some noteworthy frescoes; the English might like to light a candle for the icon of their patron, Saint George.

Sparta   *15 C2*
Even if it were not a convenient stop on the way to the marvels of Mistra, a pilgrimage to this characterless modern town would provide a useful, if melancholy, lesson in history. Once an omnipotent city-state, founded only on military might and disdaining the culture of "soft" Athenians and other rivals, Sparta has not a single monument to show for its past greatness. Thucydides, great historian of the Peloponnesian Wars, wrote: "If some day Sparta were devastated, leaving only its sanctuaries and the foundations of public buildings, the posterity of a distant future would find it hard to believe that its power was equal to its renown."

Today, scarcely a stone or two remain of its sanctuaries and public buildings. The town slumbers in the Evrotas valley with, to the west, the brooding Taygetos mountains where Spartan soldiers hardened their bodies and discarded their weaklings in the ravines. Maybe for old time's sake, the Greek army has installed a garrison on the southern edge of town. But those who fail basic training are sent home alive.

In the **museum**, east of the town's central square, Spartan soldiers are depicted on Archaic vases. A bas-relief (6th century B.C.) shows those two unhappy couples, Helen and Menelaus, and Clytemnestra and Agamemnon. A powerful marble torso is said to be of Leonidas, hero of Thermopylae. Sadly, the "Tomb of Leonidas" in the nearby ruins is in fact a little Hellenistic temple. Similarly, all that is to be seen of "Ancient Sparta" are the remains of a theatre (2nd century B.C.), a temple (1st century A.D.) and a 10th-century Byzantine monastery standing among pine trees and eucalyptus.

The Spiral of Defeat
Sparta lost its supremacy in the 4th century B.C. to Epaminondas of Thebes and his Peloponnesian allies. The Macedonians reduced it to a vassal-state. In A.D. 396 the Visigoths razed the city, and in the 9th century, a Slav invasion drove the last Spartan landowners and peasants to flee to the Mani peninsula. It was not until 1834 that a new town was built, by King Otto.

MISTRA

Kastro

UPPER MISTRA

Agia Sofia

Palataki

Palace of the Despots

Pantanassa Convent

Mansion of Frangopoulos

Perivleptos Monastery

Odegetria Afentiko

Vrontikhion Monastery

LOWER MISTRA

Lascaris Mansion

Evangelistria Church

Agii Theodori

Turkish Fountain

Metropolis

Mistra   15 C2

The glories of this great medieval Byzantine city will be best enjoyed if you take them in easy stages. A short drive west into the Taygetos mountains from Sparta, the town grew out of a 13th-century fortress built by French leftovers from the Crusades on a hillside that can be tough to tackle in hot weather. The splendid tile-domed monasteries are well restored, but even the ruined mansions and palace, in their enchanting wilderness, provide a vivid insight into Mistra's golden era.

Nearby, the pleasant little new town of **Nea Mistra** has several restaurants and hotels. With car parks located near the top and bottom of Mistra's hill, you can divide your visit into two halves: the monasteries and museum of Lower Mistra, and the palace, Agía Sofia church and fortress of Upper Mistra.

Lower Mistra

Entering through a gatehouse in the fortifications, turn right (north) to the **Metrópolis**, 13th-century church of St Demetrios. The main church's paintings of scenes from Christ's life have been "beheaded" by structural transformations, but in the narthex are some good frescoes of the *Last Judgment* and the *Second Coming*. In the courtyard, the upstairs **museum** has among its icons and frescoes a striking 15th-century portrait on gilded metal of *Christ Enthroned*. Its piercing expression suggests the new humanist influence of Mistra's philosopher Gemistus.

Continue north past the 14th-century cruciform **Evangelístria Church**, a little gem of finely cut masonry and tile-framed windows. Just beyond is the **Vrontochión Monastery**, Mistra's wealthiest. Of its two churches, the smaller **Ágii**

Theódori was built in 1290 and restored in the 20th century with a multiple-windowed lantern dome. The **Odigítria** (1310), also known as Afentikó, is Mistra's finest architectural achievement. The harmonious blend of rose-tiled domes, vaults, side chapels and belfry fits magnificently into the hillside setting of vines, wild olives and cypresses. Climb up behind the church to see its roofs overlooking the sprawling Laconian plain to the east. Odigítria artfully combines a lower three-aisled basilica with a five-domed cruciform upper church. Among the frescoes are an exquisite *Procession of the Martyrs* in the chapel to the right of the entrance and *Christ's Miracles* in the narthex.

Take the long climb slowly southwards to the 15th-century **Pantánassa**

Byzantium's Peloponnesian Flame

Captured from Guillaume de Villehardouin in 1262, Mistra was the shining centre of Byzantine culture until its surrender to the Turks in 1460. Constantinople was a beleaguered capital, and architects, painters and thinkers sought refuge at the court of the Despot of Mistra, usually a son of the emperor. (Despot in Greek means lord, not necessarily tyrannical.)

A Greek cultural renewal, reviving classical learning, was led by neo-Platonist Georgios Gemistus Plethon (1355–1452). He had considerable influence on Renaissance philosophy in Italy after travelling to Florence in 1438, carrying with him many ancient Greek texts that Italians discovered for the first time. At Mistra itself, Gemistus's humanism had a strong impact on the last phase of Byzantine painting. Frescoes and icons in the monasteries showed more personal touches of psychological subtlety in their hitherto rigidly formal religious subjects.

After 1460, the pashas moved into the despots' palace and the churches became mosques. But a flourishing silk industry helped the city prosper well into the 17th century. In 1769, the Russians fostered an short-lived Greek attempt to recapture Mistra. The Turks sent in an Albanian army which crushed the rebellion and set Mistra on fire. It was sacked again in 1825 and the few remaining citizens moved out when Sparta was rebuilt nine years later.

Convent, last to be built here and the only one still active. Nuns tend the flowers and offer embroidery for sale. The church is notable for frescoes filled with the new life, joy and deep spirituality that characterized Mistra's late Byzantine art. Most impressive are the *Entry into Jerusalem* west of the apse and the dramatic *Raising of Lazarus*.

Wind your way down past the impressive shell of the balconied **mansion of Frangopoulos**, founder of Pantánassa. Beyond, through a stone gateway, is the 14th-century **Perívleptos Monastery**. Clinging to the rocky hillside, its church has up on its vaults the best preserved frescoes in Mistra—lively, intimate scenes from the New Testament.

On your way back towards the entrance-gatehouse, take a look to the left at the **Laskares mansion**, a typical Byzantine house of the 14th century with ground-floor stable and large upper-storey windows and terrace. Beyond is a Turkish fountain.

Upper Mistra

The major reward for the precipitous climb to the hilltop **kástro**, Villehardouin's 13th-century castle fortified with a second rampart, are the views over the whole town and the Laconian plain. From the towers at either end of the ramparts, gaze into the formidable Taygetos ravines.

Downhill, the 14th-century palace church of **Agía Sofía** has an elegant bell tower. Its only notable surviving frescoes are a *Christ Enthroned* in the apse and a *Birth of the Virgin* in one of the chapels to the right.

Continue down past the fortress-like mansion known as Palataki (Little Palace) to the ruins of the **Palace of the Despots**. The right wing may have been built by Villehardouin and turned by his Byzantine successors into a guard house when they built the larger wing to the left. The upstairs gallery and throne room are distinguished by their eight massive Gothic bays.

The Truth About Helen
Mycenaean and Spartan propaganda encouraged the idea that Helen had been taken against her will from her husband, King Menelaus of Sparta, Agamemnon's brother. Heavily wooed and seduced, perhaps, but not unwilling.

Back home in Troy, Paris had revealed he was not a common herdsman (see p. 86) but King Priam's long-lost son. Visiting the Trojan court, Menelaus invited Paris to stay in Sparta, where he wined and dined him for nine days. Paris, obsessed by Aphrodite's promise that fair Helen would be his, heaped gifts on Menelaus' wife. He stared at her dewy-eyed, heaved great sighs, and generally flirted outrageously. He used corny tricks like ostentatiously drinking from her goblet at the very spot touched by her lips, even writing "I love you, Helen" in wine on the table top. Helen was bowled over but terrified that Menelaus would notice. The king remained oblivious, even leaving them alone together when he went off to Crete for his grandfather's funeral. Helen promptly eloped with Paris to spend their first night of love on Cranaë before setting sail from Githio to Troy.

Githio   15 D2
With pretty beaches in town and nearby, this delightful fishing village, ancient Sparta's port, makes an ideal base for visiting both Mistra and the Mani. Behind the harbour, explore the charming wooden and wrought-iron balconied fishermen's cottages hugging the lower slopes of Mount Koúmaros. A short causeway crosses to the pine-clad islet of **Marathonisi**, known in antiquity as Cranaë. It was here that Helen and Paris spent their first night after the elopement.

Monemvasia   15 D2
Accessible from the mainland by causeway and bridge—its name means "single entrance"—this medieval town on a craggy promontory has the relaxed charm and atmosphere of an Aegean island. The quickest direct route is by boat from Piraeus, but if you are driving through the Peloponnese, the road from Githio passes through some dramatic, if rather arid countryside.

Like the Mani, Monemvasia's remote fortified rock on the south-east coast was a refuge for Greeks fleeing the 9th-century invasion of the Slavs. The Venetians fortified the top of the promontory and the Turks added mosques and a bath house. In 1821, Monemvasia was the first bastion to fall to the Greeks, but the surrendering Turkish garrison perpetrated a terrible massacre before leaving.

The town was progressively abandoned in the 20th century, but elegant little buff stone terraced houses are being tastefully renovated as restaurants, hotels and holiday apartments. Daytime visitors find accommodation across the causeway at the small mainland resort of **Gefira**. (Like the Aegean islands, the exposed promontory is buffeted by the meltemi in July and August.)

Park outside the gate of Monemvasia's fortifications—one of the town's joys is the absence of traffic—and walk up the narrow stone-paved main street to the village square, **Platía Dzamíou**. The Venetian bell tower here is the convenient landmark to guide all your walks. The main church, **Elkómenos Christós** (Christ in Chains), was rebuilt by the Venetians in the 17th century, retaining a Byzantine bas-relief of peacocks over the porch. Opposite is a Turkish mosque (*Paléo Dzamí*) being converted for the town museum.

The promontory is dotted with churches and chapels with very mammary domes, but only a few are still in use. Take a look at the charming 16th-century Venetian **Panagía Chrisafítissa** down by the seafront ramparts. As you

Sweet Death
Except for Richard III's enemy Clarence, who was drowned in a barrel of it, the English had quite a taste for "Malmsey" wine. This sweet dessert wine made now in Tinos, Cyprus or even Spain came originally from Monemvasia grapes. Nobody here today seems to have heard of it.

wander among the handsome Byzantine and Venetian houses, look out for traces of ancient marble blocks, columns and pediment fragments filched long ago from temple ruins at nearby Epidaurus Limera. Due south of the village square, a gateway through the fortifications leads out to a rocky beach for swimming.

Walk up to the clifftop **kástro** where the old upper town lies in romantic ruin among a wilderness of flowers, shrubs, olives and fig trees. The 12th-century church of **Agía Sofía** has a handsome brick and stone exterior and a 16-sided drum supporting its dome. Some fine fresco fragments include a *Christ Pantocrator* (Christ Omnipotent). Climbing west of the church to the promontory's highest point, the **citadel**, you get a view on proverbial clear days extending, it is said, to Crete.

Kythira   *14 A3*

Campers and hikers fleeing the crowds can take a boat from Monemvasia, Neapoli or Githio. The sweetest thing about this rather arid island is its delicious honey. There is a beach on the north-east coast at **Agia Pelagia**. The capital, **Chora**, on the south coast, has some Venetian houses and a fortress out on the promontory. The prettiest village, with an old water mill, is over to the west at **Mylopotamos**.

Mani   *15 C2–3*

Castles, ghost towns and wild, unspoiled landscapes characterize this windswept peninsula. The Maniotes have maintained a reputation for being highly independent-minded, though the blood vendettas appear to belong to their past.

They can claim to be the last remnant of the ancient Spartans, having fled from the Laconian plain in the wake of the Slav invasions. The earliest settlers clung to paganism until the 9th century. Many became pirates and adventurers who moved on to Corsica, taking their ferocious code of honour with them. The rest stayed to build formidable forts and tower houses in the mountains or on cliffs overlooking the sea. The toughest became village chieftains commanding a feudal allegiance that lasted till modern times. Petrobey Mavromikhalis, the most famous of them, was prominent in the fight for Greek independence, but less for national freedom than to ensure the Maniote landlords' time-honoured rights.

From Githio, a Mani circuit tour, about 160 km. (100 mi.), can be managed comfortably in a day. Heading across the neck of the peninsula towards the west coast, you pass the restored 13th-century **Passavá castle** of Jean de Neuilly, Marshal of the Morea (as the Peloponnese was then known). A turnoff 12 km. (7½ mi.) further on takes you north to the remains of **Kelefá castle**, a sprawling Turkish fort of the 17th century.

In **Areopoli**, the small local capital, you will see good examples of the region's characteristic sturdy tower houses. In keeping with the Mani's belligerent history, notice the soldier saints as the preferred motif of stone reliefs in the 18th-century **Taxiárchi church**. The town is known for its good bread.

From the cliffs of **Pirgos Dirou** drive down to the cave entrance of a fascinating **underground lake**. Take the half-hour tour by flatboat among artfully

*A*ll walks around the enchanting town of Monemvasia seem to start or end with the Venetian bell tower at the entrance to Dzamíou Square.

*V*athia is little more than a ghost town now, but its tower-houses are typical of the sturdy defences erected by the Maniotes to protect their independence, not just from the Turks but from the rest of Greece, too. The view extends south to Cape Matapan (Tenaro), whose coves have for centuries provided havens for pirates. In one of them is the cave from which Hercules pulled the three-headed dog Cerberus from the gates of hell.

ing village built at the end of the 19th century. Along the coast, **Vathia** is the best of the tower-house ghost towns.

It is an hour's brisk walk from Porto Kagio to the lighthouse at **Cape Matapan**, southernmost point of the Greek mainland (but there's nothing special to see). The British won a naval battle here against the Italians in 1941.

If you do not want to double back past Gerolimin, the wild, deserted eastern route is on the sunless side of the hills in late afternoon. But the views are still rewarding, especially from **Kokkala**, with its pretty little creek for a quiet swim, and **Kotrona**, further north.

Those heading west via Kalamata pass through the splendid rugged landscapes of **Outer Mani** *(Exo Máni)*—ravines, craggy green or brown hills with flashing views of the sea below. Make a stop at the 13th-century church of Ágios Dimítrios in a lovely setting of greenery overlooking the Gulf of Messinia, outside **Kardamili**, a pretty fishing village. Its old mansions are being turned into guest houses, and there's another fine church, the 18th-century Ágios Spirídon.

Kalamata   15 C2
Capital of Messinia, this industrial town was badly hit by earthquake in 1986. The old **Turkish quarter** remains the best part of town to visit, and the **market**, although modernized, is still colourful. Kalamata draws pride from being the first city to revolt in the 1821 uprising.

Messene   15 C2
The archaeological site of this ancient city lies in a magnificent pastoral setting at the foot of Mount Ithómi, 25 km. (16 mi.) north of modern Messini. Messene was a victorious ally of Epaminondas in ending Spartan hegemony in the Peloponnese in 371 B.C. The fortified city rebuilt by the Theban general is concentric with the little country village of **Mavromati**. Ancient ruins poke out of gardens and orchards among the houses, but the best preserved **fortifications** for

illuminated limestone stalagmites and stalactites that have been growing drip by drip for up to 400 million years. A few steps from the grotto, you can swim at the small white-rock beach.

The road south passes through increasingly rugged countryside where the villages thin out, many lying in ghostly ruin. The view from the fortified village of **Nomia** is splendid. Take a look at the deserted tower houses in **Koeta**.

Nestling in a bay under soaring rocky cliffs, **Gerolimin** is an attractive little fishing village built at the end of the 19th which the town was celebrated lie to the north of Mavromati. The grand **Arcadia Gate** is protected by a system of towers around its double entrance. Notice the chariot-wheel ruts in the paved road leading to the gate. The walls extended 9 km. (5½ mi.) around the city to enclose farmland, too. Vestiges of a semicircular temple and a small theatre remain from the city's **Sanctuary of Asclepius**, which offered modest competition to the centre of healing at Epidaurus (see p. 222).

Pylos
14 B2

Messinia's major west-coast seaport is a lively town on the south shore of the magnificent natural harbour of **Navarino**, 6 km. (4 mi.) long. It was here that Greek freedom was at last guaranteed when an allied force of British, French and Russians annihilated the Turkish fleet in 1827. The town's quayside **Platía Trión Navárkhon** (Three Admirals Square) honours the victors with a refreshing tree-shaded place from which to watch the yachts sail in and the citizens stroll by on their evening *vólta*. Walk up to the restored Turkish fortress of **Neókastro** for a view over the bay from the outer bastion.

But for a close-up, we recommend a harbour cruise. Out in the centre of the harbour on Tortoise Rock *(Chelonáki)* is a **British Memorial** to the great battle. On Sfaktiria island, closing off the bay to the west, are French and Greek monuments. The boat also visits **Paleokastro**, a rocky promontory (inaccessible by road) where a 30-minute walk brings you to the ruined battlements and towers of a castle dating back to the 13th century. Beyond it to the north is the **Grotto of Nestor**, a cave with strange animal-shaped stalagmites which encouraged the legend that the old sage, King Nestor, sheltered his cows here.

Methoni
14 B2

Just 20 minutes' drive south of Pylos, the great attraction of this old Venetian stronghold is the arc of its golden sandy beach. The view out over a group of small green islands is one of the prettiest seaside vistas in the Peloponnese. There is good fishing to be had from the islands of **Sapiendza** and **Schiza.**

Methoni was a vital position from which the Venetians controlled the passage of ships heading for the Adriatic. The Turks made repeated efforts to capture it and finally succeeded in the 18th century. Dominating the town's promontory is the Venetians' great **citadel** with monumental gateways and two large bastions used as arsenals. At the southern end of the fortress over a wooden bridge is the hexagonal **Bourdzi Tower**, a handsome backdrop for scenic photographs.

Nestor's Palace

This intriguing archaeological site on **Englianos Hill**, 14 km. (9 mi.) north of Pylos, is avoided by the package tours because its "picturesque" quality is marred by a corrugated iron shelter. It is still well worth a visit. King of ancient Pylos, old Nestor, garrulous but dignified, was Agamemnon's most trusted advisor on the Trojan campaign. His contingent of 90 ships was second only to Agamemnon's in the Greek fleet. His palace, built in 1300 B.C., is as big as contemporaneous Mycenae, and traces of frescoes suggest it was just as richly decorated. But it suffered greater damage in a conflagration in 1200 B.C. Luckily, the fire baked solid the palace accountants' tablets which a Cambridge scholar deciphered as Linear B, momentous first evidence that the Peloponnesians of the Mycenaean era spoke a form of Greek (see p. 16). In the palace's **royal apartments**, you can see the throne room with a round clay hearth surrounded by four columns, similar to the arrangement at Mycenae. In the **queen's chambers** is a bathroom with a terracotta tub still intact, along with jars and pitchers for pouring in the hot water. Clearly, as in the case of the Linear B tablets, the fire was good for anything earthenware.

Olympia and the West

The western region provides contrasting landscapes for its two great classical shrines. The sanctuary of Olympia lies in the luxuriant green Alfios valley, while Bassae's temple to Apollo stands in the bleak grandeur of Mount Lycaeon's peaks haunted of old by werewolves. The seaside resort of Killini offers some more cheerful relaxation.

Olympia   14 B1

The short drive east of Pyrgos should convince you that Hercules was not just a muscle-bound brute. It was he, the ancients said, who chose this magnificent setting, at once serene and grandiose, for the sacred games that for a brief moment every four years united the belligerent Greek world. At the foot of Mount Kronos near the confluence of the Alfios and Kladeos rivers, he hedged in a sacred grove *(altis)* of planes, wild olives, poplars, oaks and pines. With votive offerings hanging from their branches, the trees remained as important as the altars and temples built subsequently.

From the 10th century B.C., altars were erected to Hera and then Zeus. The temples and treasury shrines that followed were toppled by a shattering earthquake in the 6th century A.D. But the ruins, taking on a golden glow in the late afternoon sun, still offer eloquent testimony to the sanctuary's grandeur.

Sanctuary and Precincts

The main path from the entrance leads through the **Gymnasium** (3rd century B.C.) providing a long practice area for the discus, javelin and runners. There are column bases of porticoes along the east and south sides. Beyond it is the **Palaestra**, training school for wrestling and boxing. The practice ring was in the central courtyard, surrounded by changing rooms, baths and rooms for oil massage—notice the lipped receptacles.

Make your way south through the debris of later Roman houses and brick walls of a Byzantine church to the stone rectangle of **Phidias's Workshop**. It was here, after his ostracism from Athens (see p. 76), that the great sculptor worked on his statue of Zeus to be enthroned in the god's temple. The artist's tools, clay moulds and a cup inscribed with his name are displayed in the site's museum.

Further south is the **Leonidaion** (330 B.C.), a hostelry for officials with rooms facing inward to a square peristyle court.

Take the **Processional Road** east, passing on the right the **Bouleuterion** hall for games officials, where judges and athletes both took an oath of fair dealing.

Turn left into the sanctuary proper where a ramp leads to the **Temple of Zeus**. Built from 470 to 456 B.C., it lies in total ruin but the tumbled capitals and drums of Doric columns are an impressive sight. It was 64 m. (210 ft.) long, 28 m. (90 ft.) wide, close to the dimensions of the Parthenon. Above the columns at either end were sculpted pediments of King Pelops' chariot race and Lapith hunters fighting with Centaurs, displayed in the museum.

Skirt the temple and head left (west) to the half-concealed remains of the **Philippeion**, a rotunda built by Philip of Macedonia (and completed by son Alexander) to commemorate himself and his family. Beside it is the long and narrow **Temple of Hera**, built around 600 B.C. Some of its Doric columns have been

---

Big God, Big Emperor
Inside the temple, only privileged dignitaries could see Phidias's colossal Zeus. The god's statue was clad in ivory and gold and seated on an ebony and ivory throne, in one hand an eagle-crested sceptre, in the other a winged victory. Regarded by the ancients as one of the Seven Wonders of the World, it was over 12 m. (40 ft.) high and would have knocked the roof off had it come to life and stood up. In the 1st century A.D., Augustus's general Agrippa decided to please his boss by erecting a similarly gigantic effigy of the emperor, but outside the temple for everyone to see.

resurrected. The head from Hera's statue is now in the museum. The goddess was originally Olympia's principal deity, carrying on a pre-Hellenic cult of Mother Earth. But the Greeks put an end to such matriarchal leanings by putting in a statue of Zeus to accompany his wife, along with Praxiteles' superb sculpture of Hermes (in the museum).

Continue east past the semi-circular **Nympheion of Herod Atticus**. This monumental fountain was built by the rich Athenian patron of the arts in A.D. 160

The Olympic Games

The games began as a one-day contest of footracing, a purely local affair for the Olympian region of Elis. The valley was great horse-breeding country and the games soon added horse-racing and chariot races. (One of the myths of the games' foundation is the chariot-race in which Pelops defeated the Elians' rival, Oinomaus.)

Gradually, boxing, wrestling, discus, javelin and jumping were also included, attracting athletes from further afield. In 776 B.C., the games were formally inaugurated as a Panhellenic event and by the second half of the 7th century athletes were travelling from all over the Greek world, including the colonies in Italy and Asia Minor. As might have been expected, Sparta dominated the early competitions, but they were overtaken by the Sicilians and other Italians. From 472 B.C., the games became a five-day event. The first day was given over to sacrifices, general festivities in the sanctuary. The athletes and judges took an oath of fair-dealing. The games began on the second day with chariot races and the pentathlon. In the latter event, the champion was the winner of a wrestling play-off among finalists of running, jumping, discus and javelin. The third day was boys' day. The sporting climax came on the fourth day with running, naked and in full armour, jumping, wrestling, boxing and pankration. Pankration? This combination of boxing and wrestling was a splendid demonstration of the Olympic spirit. Strangling, kicking in the stomach, twisting the opponent's foot out of its socket and breaking his fingers were all allowed. But biting and gouging were for some reason forbidden.

On the fifth day, the victors celebrated with sacrifices and a banquet. Their prize was a wreath of wild olive.

to capture springwater from Mount Kronos. Beyond, on the way to the Stadium, is a terrace of 12 **Treasury Shrines** erected by cities and colonies for votive offerings to the gods. Below the terrace is a row of bases from bronze statues of Zeus financed by athletes' fines for cheating.

Stadium

This is in fact the third Olympic stadium. The other two were located within the sanctuary, but the last was placed outside in the late 5th century B.C. as the games lost their religious significance. Just as in the modern era, professionalism and political prestige gained the upper hand.

The main entrance is through a stone passageway covered now by a Roman arch. The finishing line for the runners is clearly marked at the entrance end, 192 m. (210 yd., one *stadium*) from the other end. Only a few dignitaries and judges had stone seats. Otherwise, the capacity crowd of 40,000—men only, as athletes performed naked—sat on the ground or wooden benches. The Hippodrome for horse and chariot races was situated south of the stadium, but all trace has been washed away by river flooding.

Museum

Take a look in the entrance hall at the model of the whole sanctuary. The central exhibit is the **Pediments Gallery**, displaying the carved friezes from the Temple of Zeus. The East Pediment presents the legendary chariot race by which King Pelops from Lydia in Asia Minor won from King Oinomaus control of the peninsula that was to bear his name. Zeus (headless) stands in the centre. On his right are Pelops and his bride-to-be, Hippodameia. On Zeus's left are Oinomaus and his wife. Beside the kings are soothsayers and servants, kneeling by horses and chariots (missing). The reclining figures are symbols of Olympia's rivers, Alfios and Kladeos. The West Pediment presents the livelier Centaurs Fight-

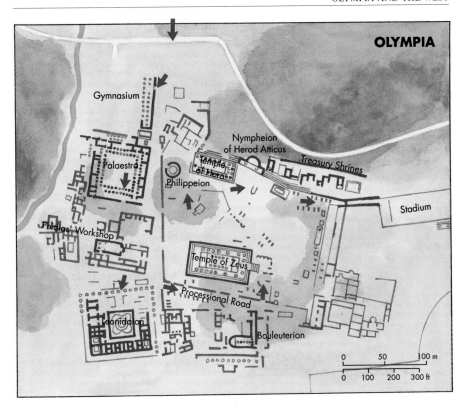

OLYMPIA

Gymnasium

Nympheion
of Herod Atticus

Treasury Shrines

Palaestra

Temple
of Hera

Philippeion

Stadium

Phidias' Workshop

Temple of Zeus

Processional Road

Leonidaion

Bouleuterion

0   50   100 m

0   100   200   300 ft

ing with Lapiths, with Apollo standing between them. The monstrous, lustful sensuality of the Centaurs contrasts with the physical beauty of the Lapiths (Thessalian hunters). The scene was a frequently used theme of the Hellenic ideal (epitomized at Olympia) triumphing over barbarity. Fragments of the Labours of Hercules from the temple's metope friezes show the hero conquering a lion and shovelling away in the Augean Stables.

Beyond the central hall, in **Gallery 4**, is a fine terracotta statue of Zeus and Ganymede (470 B.C.), showing the god adamantly satisfied with his pretty prey, who for his part seems blithely oblivious to his privileged destiny. Be sure to see nearby the tools of Phidias, found in the sculptor's workshop, including a bronze goldsmith's hammer, clay moulds and his wine cup with the words "I belong to Phidias" embossed on the base. Off to the right, in **Gallery 6**, is Praxiteles' exquisite statue of Hermes (340 B.C.) from the Temple of Hera. The head of Hera (6th century B.C.) from her colossal statue is in Gallery 2 to the left of the entrance.

Bassae *(Vassé)*
Before undertaking the 2-hour drive south-east from Olympia, check whether the protective scaffolding has been removed from this magnificent but fragile temple. The closest town is **Andritsena**, a mountain community of ramshackle gabled wooden houses, where carpenters, weavers and ironsmiths share the streets with the farmers' pigs and goats.

The road continues 14 km. (9 mi.) south past some formidable ravines to a site of splendid rocky desolation 1,132 m. (3,714 ft.) up on Mount Kotílion. The

241

Temple of Apollo was built by Ictinus from 450 to 425 B.C. while he was commuting to Athens to work on the Parthenon. The grey limestone edifice has several particularities: it departs from the golden length-width proportions of 9:4 to an exceptionally narrow 15 columns long and only 6 wide; its orientation is north-south rather than east-west; it combines all three architectural orders for its construction—Doric on the outside, Ionic and Corinthian within. One of the Corinthian columns is still standing on the south side. Its marble metope friezes are in the British Museum.

Killini   *14 B1*

Over on the north-west coast, hillsides silver and green with olive and fruit trees sweep clear down to the sea. But the real attraction for the weary traveller is the long stretch of golden sand in this lazy beach resort. You don't have to stray far from the sunbathers to see shepherds and their flocks in the greenery just above. The resort makes a good base for excursions around the Peloponnese. Down the coast at **Loutra Killinis** are some mineral springs built over old Roman baths, but again it is the beach that counts.

North Coast

The ferry service at Patras makes it for many a necessary stop, but the only other reason to dally on this overcrowded coast is the delightful little detour up Bouraikos valley to Kalavryta and beyond to the historic Agía Lávra monastery.

Patras   *14 B1*

Largest city of the Peloponnese with a population of 160,000, Patras is the main Greek port on the Ionian Sea. It has some pleasant green squares around the waterfront. West of the seaport, the large modern neo-Byzantine church of **Ágios Andréas** is said to be built on the spot where the Scots' patron, Saint Andrew, was crucified on an X-shaped cross (reproduced on the Scottish flag). The church's prize relic is the saint's silver-mounted skull, recently retrieved from the Vatican.

Kalavryta   *15 C1*

To get to this breezy town in the Aroania mountains, take a hair-raising but exhilarating 90-minute train ride along the Bouraikos river. Start out from the coastal town of **Diakofto**, surrounded by orchards and producing delicious honey. The **narrow-gauge railway** built in the late 19th century labours up beautiful gorges, in and out of tunnels and across striated escarpments. After one stop at Mega Spileo, you reach cheerful Kalavryta with its central square full of refreshing greenery and lively cafés.

It has recovered from the reprisal raid of December 13, 1943, when German troops killed 1,436 males and burned down the town. The hands of the metropolitan clock have been halted at 2.34, the hour of the massacre.

From here, you can hire a taxi to **Agía Lávra monastery**, celebrated as the site where the proclamation of Archbishop Germanos of Patras launched nationwide revolt against the Turks on March 25, 1821.

*M*onasteries in the Peloponnese were frequently high-risk centres of rebel military activity. The monastery of Mega Spileo has now been rebuilt after being blown up in 1934 by a store of gunpowder left over from the War of Independence.

Saronic Islands

Apart from Aegina, which inevitably bears the boisterous mark of its proximity to Athens, the islands' easy-going simplicity makes for a pleasant day trip—or longer if you have contracted "mainland fever". They are all within easy reach of the ports of Ermioni, Galatas and Methana.

Aegina   15 E1
Too close for comfort to Athens, the island's capital, **Aegina Town**, certainly has a zing to its quayside scene, more Athenian than "tourist", but not exactly laid-back-islander. The crowded beach at **Agia Marina** is best avoided, but the well-preserved **Temple of Aphaia**, 5th century B.C., is in the neighbourhood.

Poros   15 E1
Galatas' 5-minute ferry crossing to the island is just a 2-hour drive from Nafplio. Poros is a favourite holiday spot for the Greeks themselves. Behind its pretty little port, the town's blue-shuttered white houses cling to hills topped with pine trees. Visit the ruined **Temple of Poseidon** where Athenian orator Demosthenes took poison in 322 B.C. rather than submit to his Macedonian enemies. Of the beaches, **Askeli** gets a little crowded, but **Neori** is fine, especially at sunset.

Hydra   15 E2
The island is little more than 18 kilometres of rock, but enormously popular with artists. **Hydra Town** has a spectacular harbour, some good seafood restaurants and handsome sea-captains' houses for painters to paint. Overlooking the port, one of the finest, **Tombazi mansion**, is the island's branch of the Athenian School of Fine Arts. **Mandraki beach** is the most popular, but **Kamini** and **Vlichos** are quieter.

Spetses   15 D2
The charm of this island's Aleppo pines, cypresses and oleander has attracted a

mixture of Athens' smart set (whooshing in by hydrofoil) and Britain's package tours. Liveliest spot in **Spetses Town** is the café-lined square overlooking the harbour. In the courtyards and little squares of the town's back streets, notice the grey, white and black pebble mosaics of marine and mythological scenes. The beaches of **Agii Anargiri** and **Agia Paraskevi** are fine, but if you want something quieter, take a boat over to the pebble beaches on the island's northwest coast.

*O*nly an Impressionist's palette could do full justice
to this overgrown garden on Hydra. Small wonder that painters have
been flocking here for years to capture the island's subtle plays of
light and colour.

245

What Happens When You Don't Rent a Beach Umbrella?

One of the chief wonders of ancient Greek civilization is how they found the time and energy to *do* all that. It was just as hot in those days, and there is no evidence that they did all their building, sculpting, thinking and writing in the winter time. So we have no excuse. Just remember: siestas are even more enjoyable if you actually do something in between. Without suggesting anything too much like work, here are a few ideas.

Activities we look at here have an uncanny knack of capturing the spirit of Greece both ancient and modern. The real bargains in shopping are the products of the country's authentic folk arts. The best jewellery renews ancient designs. If most of the sports are resolutely modern—difficult to imagine Achilles water-skiing—sailing in the Aegean can evoke a miniature Odyssey. Entertainment is not only an over-amplified bouzouki cassette, it can also be Orestes avenging his father under a full moon at Epidaurus. And the year-round town and village festivals maintain a link between the ancient customs of pagan carnivals and the more solemn religious processions of the Orthodox Church.

*B*rass and copper pots and pans make a glowing centrepiece in Athens' Monastiraki flea market.

Shopping

Walk into the bazaar with your eyes wide open and you will soon sift the wheat from the chaff. Rugs, pottery, lace and embroidery, furs, gold and silver jewellery, moderate or expensive, these are the bargains to look for. But let's deal first with the chaff.

Souvenir Junk

Some of it is so marvellously awful as to demand your immediate attention. To be fair, the shopkeepers go out of their way to warn you by putting up a sign. You cannot miss it. "Greek Art," it says, hoping to enhance the wares with that ancient seal of aesthetic quality evoked by the word "Greek". Kitschmongery here knows no limits. Miniature white Corinthian columns are now bottles of ouzo. The Parthenon is a basket for nuts and raisins, the Phaistos Disk a cocktail mat, key ring or earring, the Charioteer of Delphi a bedside lamp, the Athens Poseidon a garden dwarf. Truly provocative kitsch-collectors buy a statue of an over-endowed satyr just to be able to declare it at customs.

When the Ship Comes In

Opening hours are a haphazard business, varying from region to region. Almost all shops close for the sacred siesta (from about 2.30 to 5 p.m.), many reopening (until about 8.30 p.m.) only on Tuesdays and Fridays. One thing you can rely on: in the resorts visited by big-spending cruisers, the boutiques will stay open until the last passenger has regained the ship.

Folk Art

No, the craftwork is not all mass produced in factories. Hand-made creations of traditional artisans maintain a high standard and a remarkably low price. Styles in wood carving, fabrics, lace and embroidery obviously differ considerably from north to south and from the islands to mountain villages on the mainland. The major cities have craftwork from all over the country. It is a good idea to look at the range—and price—of goods there to compare with what you might find in villages like Kritsa or Anogia in Crete (lace and embroidery) or Metsovo in Epirus (wood carving).

In any case, the first stop before you go out to buy anything should be the **folk art museums** where you can see, unhustled by shopkeepers, the best of regional production. Most of the museums also have excellent shops with knowledgeable assistants to advise you, though the range of goods may not be as wide as you will find in bazaars and specialist shops. Among the most important: Athens, the Benaki and the Greek Folk Art; Iraklion, Historical Museum; Thessaloniki, Macedonian Folklore; Skyros, Faltaitz Museum; Nafplio, Peloponnesian Folklore Foundation; Ioannina, Epirus Folk Museum.

Rugs

The celebrated shaggy flokati rugs have not changed much since they draped the walls and floors of Mycenaean palaces or served as winter bedcovers for Helen and Paris. They are priced by the kilo (a square metre weighs about 2.5 kilos).

You should soon be able to tell the difference between the machine-made variety and the much tighter-packed hand-made rugs. Pure sheep's wool shag is spun from fibres into yarn and then looped on a loom to create a rug that is straggly on the surface and matted underneath. To give them a finish that is both fluffy and compact, the rugs are soaked for a few days under running water. The industry has flourished in northern Greece where the villages like Metsovo have fast mountain streams. The rugs may be dyed bright red, a more subdued blue or brown, or left creamy "natural". The village of Arachova, near Delphi, has given its name to a vividly patterned version that is popular as a wall-hanging.

Tagári, rug-like shoulder bags, big with Sixties hippies, are making a comeback with the ecological generation.

Pottery

The ancient art is not dead. It is worth making a trip out to the Maroussi suburb of Athens to see the variety of local and regional production. The pottery of the Dodecanese and Rhodes in particular is admired for its vivid versions of Turkish design. The famous Lindos pottery with tulips and roses on a dark green background is made now in the town of Rhodes. Visit factories like the Ikaros to see the patterns being hand-painted.

In Crete, most of the major north coast towns produce attractive replicas of Minoan and Geometric-patterned vases. Unglazed pottery from the village of Margaritis is considered the finest handwork produced in the Aegean.

Ceramics in the Peloponnese have a distinctive green glaze with pale green and yellow designs. Nafplio has a good selection, and Corinth has revived its ancient tradition. Be a little more wary in the shops around the great archaeological sites of Mycenae, Epidaurus and Olympia.

The highly decorative Epirote pottery you will find at Ioannina and Metsovo goes for bright reds, blues and greens.

On the trade routes to Bulgaria and Turkey, Kavala is the most Oriental of Greek towns. Wares of its bazaar stand out against a background of the 16th-century Turkish aqueduct.

Jewellery

The styling of gold and silver jewellery is dictated more by ancient history than any more recent regional tradition. Designers have moved beyond the time-honoured lacy fine silver filigree to draw inspiration from the great museum collections. Difficult to improve on the necklaces, bracelets, rings and earrings of King Minos's jewellers in Crete, Queen Clytemnestra's at Mycenae or those of Philip and Alexander in Macedonia. Just as timeless are the ancient designs for plates, bowls and chalices. But you will also find modern designs executed with admirable workmanship.

Gold and silver are sold by weight, with a relatively tiny fraction of the cost added for workmanship and creativity. The bazaars at Rhodes and Ioannina remain the most enjoyable places to hunt for treasure. Athens' best jewellery shops are in the Voukourestíou and Panepistimíou area; in Iraklion near the museum. Elsewhere you can be sure there will be good jewellery shops in major resorts like Agios Nikolaos in Crete or Nafplio in the Peloponnese, and wherever the cruise ships regularly stop—Mykonos, Santorini, Corfu, and so on.

Antiques

Lord Elgin would not stand a chance today. Anything that predates Greek independence in 1821 is considered an antique and must have an export permit,

Nibbling As You Go

When you go walking through town, even if it is only to window-shop, take along a bag. As you pass a market or corner grocer, how can you resist the olives, pickles, dried meat and fish, cracked wheat and every other imaginable grain? Or the nuts, beans, dried fruit (figs, raisins and apricots), spices and chocolate, ouzo-drenched fig cake wrapped in vine leaves? Or honey for a cup of yoghurt? Here is a short shopping list:

Almonds–*amígdala*
Apricots–*veríkoka*
Capers–*kapári*
Cracked wheat–*pligoúri*
Dates–*chourmás*
Figs–*síka*
Honey–*méli*
Olives–*eliés*
Peaches–*rodákina*
Peanuts–*fistíkia arápika*
Pistachios–*fistíkia egínis*
Raisins–*stafída sultanína*
Walnuts–*karídia*

practically impossible for anything truly ancient. Customs officials have a keen eye open for the big pieces, while little smugglable items like coins and terracotta or bronze figurines are probably fake anyway. If you are in the market for Byzantine icons (easily faked, too), you will find reputable dealers on Athens' Amalías Avenue, Voukourestíou or around the Monastiráki district. Those content with good replicas or modern icons in the traditional style will find the best bargains in the museum-shops and monasteries, too, notably at Mistra and Mount Athos.

Furs

Not the kind of thing you readily think of buying on a Greek summer holiday. But there are real bargains to be had in mink, chinchilla, red fox, squirrel, stone marten and Persian lamb. Hats, coats, stoles, capes and patchwork bed-quilts are made up from imported pelts hand-sewn in northern Greek towns like Kastoria. Take a look at the range in Athens (around Syntagma) or Thessaloniki (along Odós Egnatía) before making the trip. Kastoria prices are unbeatable, especially in summer.

Clothes and Leatherware

The folk look looks much better on Greek folk. At best, a fisherman's sweater, a pair of sandals or handmade boots (especially from Archangelos on Rhodes). But the mediocre workmanship on the leather luggage does not justify the vast displays it commands at every resort.

*R*ethymnon's shops are good places to examine
Crete's reputation for hand-woven fabrics. If you fall in love with
the richly textured material but prefer to have the clothes made up
back home, buy it by the bolt. Most shops will ship it for you.
Even with mailing costs, it remains a bargain.

251

Sports

Ancient Olympic champions returning to see what's going on in Greece these days might be puzzled by all that swimming. In their day, swimming was something you did to escape a shipwreck, not a sport. Today, on the other hand, not many people will be doing much running, jumping, boxing or wrestling—except, perhaps, in the odd hooligan bar in Corfu or Kos. And those frisbees are rather sissy compared with a discus.

Still, the Aegean and Ionian seas are magnificent playgrounds, and we have a couple of suggestions for some more "Spartan" activity inland.

Water Sports

The seas around the islands and mainland coasts are warm enough for swimming from May to mid-October. The Aegean is a few degrees warmer than the Ionian Sea in May, but, probably due to the meltemi wind, the Aegean cools off faster in October. For sports where you will want to rent equipment, obviously the major resorts are the places to go. But in even the tiniest, secluded fishing harbour you should be able to find a little caïque to hire.

Swimming

Choosing the right beach from the hundreds available is not so obvious. The ideal beach is not always the one with the finest sand. On the Aegean islands, locate a few pebble beaches for the days when the meltemi is blowing. Rock ledge beaches have the considerable advantage of being uncrowded, but you should keep plastic sandals handy if you are going to paddle around on the rocks.

For children, make sure you have some really safe shallow bathing available—lifeguards are rare to non-existent.

Nudist bathing is officially forbidden, but in practice, you will find several beaches where people take it all off. The criterion seems to be relatively secluded

places not frequented by families or by the Greeks themselves.

As for pollution, the obvious beaches to avoid are those close to major ports—Piraeus, Patras, Igoumenitsa, Thessaloniki and Iraklion. The European Commission's Blue Flag for top-rated cleanliness has recently been awarded to seven beaches: Vrontados (Chios), Faliraki, Kallithea and Reni (Rhodes), Vaï and Elounda (Crete) and Loutraki (near Corinth). The Green Flag for clean waters went to Nisaki, Gouvia and Benitses

252

(Corfu), Sani, Kalithea and Porto Carras (Chalkidiki), Tigaki (Kos) and Cher-
sonisos (Crete). There are no doubt
many more, but Greece submitted for
inspection only 100 beaches—from
24,000 km. (15,000 mi.) of coastline.

Snorkelling and Scuba Diving
The joy of underwater swimming around
the Greek coasts is not just for the marine fauna and flora you will see, but the
vestiges of ancient ports and cities. On
Crete's Mirabello Bay, for instance, you

*On the island of Rhodes,
even the laziest beach bums
occasionally get out from under
their parasols to swim or cool off
on a windsurf board. But not too
often.*

can swim out from Elounda to see the submerged ruins of Olous, a Greco-Roman settlement. Across the bay, part of the Minoan ruins of Mochlos are also underwater.

But for the most part, you will have to content yourself with glimpses snatched by snorkelling. Like underwater photography, scuba diving is restricted to government-designated places where you cannot disturb ancient shipwrecks and archaeological sites. They include Corfu's Paleokastritsa, which has a good diving school, and Chalkidiki in the north.

Windsurfing and Water Skiing

Equipment can be hired at all the major resorts. Schools for water skiing are available at Porto Carras and Gerakini in Chalkidiki and on the islands of Corfu, Chios, Lesbos and Skiathos. But adepts of both sports are being increasingly shunted away from popular family beaches.

Opportunities for straight surfing are limited. Nothing on the Hawaiian or Australian scale, but Mykonos' Ormos Bay attracts serious *aficionados* and Cephalonia's Myrtos has possibilities.

Sailing

Even just chugging around in a caïque fitted with an outboard motor, you can face the open sea and imagine yourself Jason with or without his Argonauts. If you fancy yourself a full-blown Odysseus, the National Tourist Office can help you charter a yacht at Piraeus. Renting smaller sailing vessels is possible at any fair-sized port in the islands. You can take sailing lessons at the Kalamaria Naval Club in Thessaloniki. For landlubbers who lub boats just enough to watch them, Thessaloniki has a regatta in Navy Week at the end of June.

Fishing

Shore or boat fishing can catch you some seabass, swordfish, dentex and a host of eastern Mediterranean fish that have no English names. No special licence is needed, though underwater spear fishing is restricted. Enquire at the local tourist office. It is sometimes possible to "hitch a ride" with a friendly professional fisherman going out at night to fish with flare lanterns. Another useful friend is the local taverna chef to cook your catch.

Try freshwater fishing on the lakes at Ioannina and Kastoria.

Tennis and Golf

Most big resort hotels have hard courts, and there are public courts in the large towns—in Athens, the Agios Kosmas Sports Centre, in Iraklion behind the Archaeological Museum. Thessaloniki Sports Club accepts non-members.

Golf is more limited—on Rhodes at Afandou, at Porto Carras on Chalkidiki, and at Athens' Glifada Golf Club, if you do not mind the jumbo jets landing and taking off just beyond the bunker.

Mountain Climbing and Skiing

Enquire at the Greek Alpine Club in Athens for information about guides, equipment and which mountains may be off-limits for reasons of military security. In winter on Mount Parnassus, the villages of Arachova and Delphi turn into winter sports resorts. On Mount Pilion in Thessaly, you will find good skiing facilities at Hania.

In the Peloponnese, skiers head for the slopes of Ostrakina and Vrissopoulos, both near Olympia.

Horse Riding

The Macedonians keep up their ancient horse riding traditions at the Northern Greece Riding Club in Thessaloniki. There are also facilities on Chalkidiki at Porto Carras, Sani and Palini Beach, and at Thermi on the island of Samothrace.

Cricket

Cricket? Yes, the great English game is played on the green(ish) field of Corfu Town's Esplanade.

254

Entertainment

The entertainment the Greeks themselves most enjoy is their own conversation. The *vólta* (evening stroll, a veritable parade) along the harbour promenade or around the main town square, and then an hour or two at a café under the plane trees, this is their daily theatre. The curtain rises with a fulsome greeting or, drama, a cold snub. Who is wooing whom? *That* is her new fiancé? Will his rich uncle from America buy the supermarket? What about the politician's mistress? The building promoter's "heart attack"? The pleasure is contagious and infects the hitherto most introverted visitor from cooler climes. To execute an authentic *vólta*, you should dress with a certain decorum, let's say casual elegance. No camera, no shopping bag. Arm in arm rather than hand in hand, and you're set to join the gossiping throng.

And after the *vólta*, you still have time to take in some more formal musical or theatrical entertainment. Sound and light spectacles, with English-language commentaries, start around 9 p.m. In Athens, the Acropolis show takes place on Pnyx hill. On Rhodes, in the capital's municipal gardens, they recount the siege of Suleiman the Magnificent. Corfu's history is narrated in the Old Fort.

Music and Dance

Greek music is more than the ubiquitous twangy movie themes from *Never on Sunday* and *Zorba the Greek*, but the power of modern sound-amplifying systems insists that we start there.

Some purists claim that the long-necked mandolin-like bouzouki instrument, which has given its name to the music and the night clubs where it is performed, is not even Greek, but Turkish. The *syrtáki* dance popularized by Anthony Quinn's Zorba is in fact a combination, invented for the film, of several distinct traditional dances. The *zeybéki-ko*, coming originally from Asia Minor, is an introspective dance of meditation with the man swaying slowly, arms outstretched, eyes half-closed, leaning backwards, bending his knees, occasionally taking long steps sideways or forwards like a drugged flamingo and making a sudden sharp twist or leap before retrieving his more deliberate rhythm. This blossoms into the *khassápikos* or butcher's dance, in which two or three men join arms and find a community of spirit by swaying, dipping and stepping together, the sudden changes signalled by a shout or squeeze of the shoulder from the lead dancer carrying a handkerchief. These dances are in turn linked to the slow, majestic *tsamíko* performed by the mountain klephts; the dragging round-dances, *syrtós*, of the islands; the faster *kalamationós* of the southern Peloponnese and *soústa*, the hop-dance of Crete.

The hybrid *syrtáki* is performed at hosts of resort tavernas and nightclubs in Piraeus, Athens and Thessaloniki. This is where the dancers smash plates or toss gardenias, according to their temperament (both are added to the bill). You can, of course, join in. Your best chance of seeing the more traditional dances is at country weddings, festivals or, in a more formal setting but certainly authentic, the Dora Stratou Theatre on Athens' Mousion hill.

The alternately harsh and plaintive popular music that inspired composer Mikis Theodorakis was the *rembétika*. This was created by the militant urban youth of the tempestuous 1920s after the mass exchange of Turkish and Greek populations.

Symphonic and choral music are performed at Athens' ancient Odeon of Herodes Atticus from mid-June to late September, along with foreign opera and ballet companies. The concerts and recitals are part of the Athens Festival which highlights classical Greek drama (see p. 256). Tickets can be hard to come by unless you book well in advance, but the bigger hotels can sometimes help, at slightly higher prices.

Theatre

Even if you do not understand a word, an evening of classical Greek drama can be a magical experience. In Athens, the tragedies of Aeschylus, Sophocles and Euripides or the comedies of Aristophanes are performed on the slopes of the Acropolis as part of the capital's summer festival. The open-air Odeon of Herodes Atticus (see p. 75–76), with the Parthenon illuminated behind you, recaptures the ancient atmosphere. (Most of the dramas received their premières at the nearby Theatre of Dionysus, no longer in use.)

The acoustics are good, but take binoculars if you have to sit at the top of the amphitheatre. You will have a plastic seat on the marble terraces, but you'll be more comfortable if you supplement that with some padding of your own. The plays are performed in modern rather than ancient Greek, which most of today's Athenians would have a hard time following. To get the maximum enjoyment, as you might for an opera, try to read the text in English or at least a synopsis of the plot before you go. Tickets are not as difficult to get as for the festival's concerts and operas, but you still need to make advance bookings.

For many, the spectacle in the magnificent mountain setting of Epidaurus in the Peloponnese (see p. 225) is even more impressive. Performances are at weekends from mid-June to early September; obtaining tickets is usually easier than in Athens. The productions are nearly all of classical drama performed, as in Athens, by the National Theatre of Greece, but with Europe's cultural frontiers breaking down, you may also see works by Shakespeare, Racine or Goethe.

In the north, classical drama is performed at the ancient amphitheatres of Philippi and Thasos. In October, Thessaloniki holds a flourishing arts festival, the Demetriada, with good theatre and symphony music.

A more recent tradition, from the last years of the Ottoman Empire, is the shadow puppet theatre, adored by children and adults alike. As with so many authentic folk arts, its death is regularly reported, only to be resuscitated by a new troupe of cultural conservationists, mostly in Patras and Athens, but also in small towns in Epirus or the Peloponnese. It is known to the Greeks as *Kharaghiozis*, after its principal character, "Black Eyes", an indomitable down-and-out, once the great symbol of Greek resistance. Barba Yorgos is his uncle, a well-meaning but simple-minded fellow from the mountains; Hadjiavatis is the friendly Turk, Morphonios a silly dandy and Stavrakas a city layabout. Again, if you cannot follow the intricacies of the plot, you will soon be caught up in the boisterous atmosphere. It helps to go with children, they usually catch on much faster.

Cinema

In the summer, films are always shown in the open air. Cinephiles must bow to the custom of a sudden 20-minute break in the middle for refreshment. But since the Greeks do not dub their foreign films, everything is presented in its original version with Greek subtitles. This has the strange effect of the Greeks in the audience often laughing before you do, because the subtitles translate the jokes much faster than they are spoken. But you can get your own back, since they apparently do not always translate *all* the jokes.

It is the accordion rather than the bouzouki that produces the most soulful Greek music—here in a Monastiráki tavern in Athens.

256

FESTIVALS

Despite the country's rapid modernization, the Greeks still seem strongly attached to their old traditions, cultural, religious and pagan. Some of the festivals are nationwide, some celebrated only regionally.

January 1: New Year's Day or *Protochroniá*—St Basil's Day, in whose name you may be offered a sprig of basil, symbol of hospitality. For good luck, gamblers see the New Year in around the card-table. Corfiote drivers drop off presents for policemen directing traffic at intersections—a gesture of generosity, they say, not to buy off traffic fines. In the Peloponnese, they serve a Cake of Kings *(vasilópitta)* concealing a good-luck coin as in the English Christmas pudding.

January 6: for Epiphany, a cross is thrown into the harbour, river or lake and young men dive into the ice-cold water to retrieve it. The one who recovers it receives a special blessing and a crucifix.

January 8: the women of Monoklisia and Nea Petra in Macedonia and Strimni in Thrace continue a tradition of ancient Dionysian fertility rites. They lock their men up to do the chores while they go off to carouse in the streets and taverns.

February: Carnival is celebrated most boisterously in Patras in the Peloponnese, Iraklion and Rethymnon in Crete. There are costumed parties on Rhodes, and bonfires in the hills of Macedonia.

Clean Monday: first day of Orthodox Lent, general house cleaning, laundry and kite-flying; frugal meals of *lagána* (unleavened bread) and *taramá* (salty fish-eggs), olives without oil and *halvá* (sesame paste). In Athens, thousands gather to eat beans and fish soup and dance on Pnyx hill.

Orthodox Easter: festivities are observed with particular fervour in Macedonia and Thrace and in the southern Peloponnese. Candlelit funeral processions follow a flower-bedecked sculpted bier on Good Friday. On Holy Saturday at midnight, the priest hands down the sacred flame from candle to candle for each household to light an oil lamp in front of its icon. On Sunday, besides eggs, dyed red,

258

Dance group of the Dora Stratou Theatre

thousands of lambs are sacrificed for roasting, exactly as in ancient Greece at the approach of spring. On Tuesday, Megara in Attica has a festival of songs, dances and athletics, again like ancient Greece.

May 21: the Allies' courageous 1941 Battle of Crete is commemorated at Chania with three days of music and dancing. On the same date at the other end of the country, in Lagadas, Macedonia, a fire-walking ceremony celebrates the feast of St Constantine and St Helen. But the ecstatic ordeal is, once again, more reminiscent of Dionysian than Christian rituals. The Orthodox Church disapproves.

June: Athens and Epidaurus begin their summer arts festivals (see p. 256). For John the Baptist, on June 24, bonfires flare across the country, with boys jumping over the embers. Navy Week in Thessaloniki and in ports around the Peloponnese.

July: wine festivals in Rethymnon (Crete) and Alexandroupolis (Thrace). July 29–30, St Soulas Day donkey races at Soroni (Rhodes).

August: classical drama festivals at Philippi and Thasos. Dance festivals on Rhodes at Maritsa, Embonas and Kallithea. August 15, Assumption, celebrated with dancing and processions in Kremasti and Trianda (Rhodes), fireworks, craftwork fair and dancing at Mochlos (Crete).

September 8–9: regatta at the island of Spetses to celebrate 1822 victory over the Ottoman fleet's superior numbers.

October: Thessaloniki's arts festival reviving a Byzantine tradition.

November 7–9: Crete's "national holiday" celebrates the 1866 explosion at the Monastery of Arkadi (see p. 131). Festivities both at the monastery and Rethymnon.

November 30: St Andrew's Day celebrated in Patras with a big procession.

December: Christmas Eve and New Year's Eve celebrated with carols in the streets.

259

The Good, Simple Things of a Mediterranean Feast

The basic ingredients of a Greek meal have not really changed since Plato's Banquet. Lamb, goat and veal are charcoal-grilled much as they were by Agamemnon's soldiers at the gates of Troy. Red mullet and octopus, beans and lentils, the olives, oil and lemon, basil and oregano, figs and almonds, even the resinous taste of the wine all form a gastronomic link between Greece ancient and modern. The honey with your yoghurt was in the nectar of the gods.

After the pleasant fatigue of a day at the beach or a challenging pilgrimage to an ancient sanctuary, the Greek dinner table offers a time of total relaxation. Ambience is more important here than *haute cuisine*. Greek cooking makes no pretence of emulating the sophistication of the French or the infinite variety of the Chinese. Yet the people's natural zest for life can always conjure the savoury ingredients of a Mediterranean market into something wholesome, satisfying and not without its own subtlety.

Where
You will never discover the little adventure of Greek cooking if you stick to your hotel dining room. Playing it safe to palates intimidated by anything "strange", hotel cooking remains bland and unadventurous. Even when a "local

This old café sign is a decorative tribute to the true centre of Greek town life.

speciality" is offered, like the yoghurt and cucumber appetizer known as *dzadziki,* the essential garlic is almost imperceptible, on the assumption that it would upset north European or American guests. The problem posed by hotel restaurants may also be true of many tavernas situated in the very centre of the tourist traffic. Many find it more profitable to cater to a fairly low common denominator. Try, whenever possible, to go where the Greeks go. In port towns, for instance, the Greeks often keep away from the crowded harbourside establishments. In the backstreet taverna, among people who tolerate much but nothing bland, you will enjoy the real zing of a garlicky *dzadziki*, often rendered even more refreshing with a touch of mint.

Look out for three varieties of snack bar. For yoghurt or cheese snacks, try the *galaktopolio* (dairy counter). The *psistariá* (grill) serves different kinds of meat kebab. For a better selection of desserts than is usually served in restaurants, go to the *zacharoplastío* (pastry shop).

261

Greek or Turkish?

Nothing makes the Greeks more angry than to hear they have no cuisine of their own. Detractors dismiss it as a mishmash of their numerous conquerors, the last in date being the Turks, establishing, for example, a proprietary claim to the thick coffee and honey-drenched pastry. But even these, the Greeks insist, are Greek in origin.

We taught the Western world how to cook, they protest. When the Romans conquered Greece, the first things they wanted to take home were our philosophers and our cooks. Our chefs were always held in such high esteem that we had laws protecting their recipes with patents that they could sell at the *agora*. They took a two-year course at culinary schools in Athens.

Classical Greek cooking had much in common with French *nouvelle cuisine*: finesse in simplicity, authentic tastes, roast and grilled rather than stewed in rich sauces, using just herbs and a very few basic ingredients. In Plato's *Republic*, frugal Socrates proposes an ideal diet that would serve very well for your midday holiday meal: bread, olives, cheese, vegetables and fruit. Epicurus, who held that the highest good is pleasure but not necessarily self-indulgence, declared: "Simple dishes are as satisfying as sumptuous banquets." Archestrate, the first gastronomy critic (4th century B.C.), travelled from his native Gela in Sicily throughout the Mediterranean world and composed an epic poem on his findings, named *Hedypathia* (Voluptuousness). Among the few fragments that survive of his work are descriptions of dog's or sow's belly cooked in olive oil and powdered with cumin; eel in Chinese cabbage; and an enthusiastic endorsement of Rhodes sturgeon.

For a short while, it became the fashion to disguise the food and have the guests guess what they were eating. At one banquet, they argued about whether they had eaten chicken, fish or veal and it turned out to be basically vegetable marrow. Some of the more respectable ancient Greek legacies to world cuisine: fried scampi, turbot with herbs, blood sausage (black pudding), thrush in honey and grilled frogs' legs.

So Roman cuisine was indeed essentially Greek. That is what Constantine and company brought with them when the Eastern Empire was established in Byzantium. What the Venetians and Genoese brought in also came from the Greco-Roman tradition. And, the Greeks argue, the Turks took over the Byzantine tradition, richer and sweeter, but still fundamentally Greek.

You will also come across the traditional Greek *kafenion* (café), particularly in the provinces. But this is more of a men's club than a public café, popular for political debate, backgammon and very strong coffee. Strangers are not refused admission, but the place is considered, if not off limits, then at least a haven for Greeks among themselves, understandably in such a tourist-saturated country.

When

If you decide to "go Greek" and accept wholeheartedly the institution of the afternoon siesta, you may want to modify your meal times. The Greeks themselves get in a prolonged morning's work and have lunch around 2 p.m., siesta until 5, maybe work some more until 8.30 and then dine late around 9.30. The restaurants will serve you earlier, from midday and early evening, but you will miss the more authentic Greek scene if you just keep "tourist hours".

The strenuous effects of climate and sightseeing may persuade you, contrary to local custom, to stick to a light lunch and keep the substantial meal for the evening.

The Menu

The tantalizing thing about the many tasty Greek specialities we will describe here is that only a fraction of them are available at any one time. The menu printed in English often contains them all, but only those items with a price against them are being served that day. Rather than submit to this frustration, do what the Greeks do and go back to the kitchen to see what is being cooked. The cold appetizers are arrayed in glass display-cases. Cuts of meat and the fish catch of the day are lying ready in glass-windowed refrigerators. Hot dishes are simmering on the stove in casseroles— the cook will take off the lid for you to peek in and sniff. The management is more than happy for you to point out your choices here and avoid later misun-

*G*reek salad, the most refreshing of dishes for a hot day, quickly becomes the symbol of a whole holiday.

derstandings. Remember fish and meat are usually priced by weight, so that the size you choose there in the kitchen becomes your responsibility when the bill arrives.

Appetizers
It is the Greek custom to eat appetizers *(mezédes)* with an apéritif of ouzo and cold water, separately from the main meal. For convenience, they are usually served at resort tavernas as part of the dinner. But the essence of the *mezé* remains its leisurely enjoyment, something not just to gulp down while you are waiting for the main dish, but to savour for itself.

Besides that garlicky yoghurt-and-cucumber *dzadzíki*, the range is impressive: *taramá*, a creamy paste of cod's roe mixed with breadcrumbs, egg yolk, lemon juice, salt, pepper and olive oil; *dol-*

mádes, little parcels of vine leaves, filled with rice, and sometimes pine kernels and minced mutton, braised in olive oil and lemon and served cold; aubergine salad *(melitzanosaláta)* puréed with onion and garlic; the ubiquitous Greek salad *(saláta choriátiki*, literally "village salad"), a refreshing mixture of tomato, cucumber, feta goat cheese and black olives; small pieces of fried squid *(kalamarákia tiganitá)* or cold marinated octopus salad *(chtapódi)*; cheese pies *(tirópitakia)*, small pastry triangles of goat and ewe cheese; marinated mushrooms and white beans; a spicy trio of *pastoúrma*: thin peppery, garlicky slices of dried mutton, beef or goat; *loukánika*, spicy sausage, and mussels *(míthia)*; and, of course, dishes of olives, green, black, brown or silvery, the best wrinkled from Thrace, the best smooth from the southern Peloponnese.

263

Soups

Resort tavernas often do not like serving soups, because of the temptation to treat these filling dishes as a complete meal. But the best known is light enough to appear as an accompaniment—*avgolémono*, egg and lemon with chicken broth, thickened with rice. At Easter, join the Orthodox Greeks who break the Lenten fast with the traditional *magirítsa*, lamb tripe soup, spiced and cooked with lettuce, egg and lemon. In Thessaloniki's finer restaurants—and this merchant's city has many—look out for the *patsás* tripe soup, all year round. Santorini is particular reputed for its bean soup *(fassouláta)*, while connoisseurs swear by the Sifnos-style chick pea soup *(revíthia soúpa)* with onions, olive and lemon. The best seafood restaurants keep a cauldron of fish soup going and occasionally a spicy squid and tomato *(kalamariáki)*.

Fish

The surest pleasure of the Greek table is its seafood. Go down to the harbour to see what has been caught that day. When you see someone buying the best, find out where his restaurant is. Now, for your personal choice of fish, the trip back to the kitchen really becomes important. Simplest is often best: have the fish grilled—red mullet *(barboúnia)*, swordfish *(xifías)*, often served on the skewer, sole *(glóssa)*, and bream *(lithríni)* are among the most popular, served with garlicky mashed potatoes. In Chios, you can try flying fish *(chelidonópsaro)*. The sardines *(sardéles)* are good baked and little whitebait *(marídes)* and mussels are served fried. You may come across a host of other Greek fish which have no unanimously accepted English equivalents.

If you like your seafood stewed, try the octopus with white wine, tomatoes and potatoes; or prawns *(garídes)* in white wine and feta cheese. Skyros is particularly reputed for its shellfish, notably giant crab *(kaniás)*. Corfu boasts a delicious but sometimes exorbitant *astakós*, a clawless crustacean properly known as crayfish, spiny or rock lobster, but not just "lobster", as some tourist menus suggest.

Meat

Your first encounter with Greek meat specialities is likely to be at the *psistariá*, snack bar serving *souvlákia*, garlic-marinated lamb kebabs with onions, and *gíros*, slices of meat from spit-roasted cones of pork, veal or lamb (also known as *donér kebáb*). This latter often comes with bread and salad. The taverna may also serve *souvlákia* along with *keftédes*, spicy lamb meat balls, a real feast when minced with mint, onion, eggs and bacon. *Kokorétsi*, lamb tripe sausages, demand a robust stomach. Roast leg of lamb *(arní yiouvetsi)*, served with pasta, is the grand Easter dish. In summer, you are more likely to find lamb chops. Crete is celebrated for its braised beef with onions *(stiffádo)*, while Corfu does a fine stewed steak *(sofríto)*. A grilled steak *(brizóles)* will generally come well done unless you specify otherwise, and is not usually tender enough to risk less than medium.

Two famous casserole dishes are the test of a restaurant's quality. *Moussaká* has as many variations as there are regions and islands, but basically, it alternates layers of sliced aubergine with chopped lamb, onions, aubergine pulp and béchamel sauce, topped with a layer of aubergine skins. The more Italianate *pastítsio* uses lamb, mutton or goat in alternating layers with macaroni, mixed variously with seasoned tomatoes, eggs and cheese, topped with a sprinkling of breadcrumbs.

The best of wild game is to be found up in Macedonia in September. Try the rabbit *(kounéli)*, sautéed with a lemon sauce. Braised hare in walnuts *(lagós me sáltsa karithiá)* is a dish for the gods, but mere mortals will also appreciate the partridge *(pérdikes)* sautéed and served with pasta.

Cheeses

They are made out of ewe's or goat's milk. Feta is the best known of the soft cheeses, popping up in almost every "Greek salad". *Kaséri* is best eaten fresh. On Crete, *anthótyro* and *manoúri* are relatively bland, *graviéra* is harder and sharper. Other hard cheeses are the *agrafáou* and the salty *kefalotíri*. A rare blue cheese to look out for is *kopanistí*.

Desserts

The Greeks eat their after-dinner dessert at the pastry shop *(zacharoplastío)* on the way home. Tavernas rarely have a full selection. Among the most popular, all, you will notice, with honey: *baklavá*, a honey-drenched flaky pastry with walnuts and almonds; *loukoúm*, a doughnut-like honey fritter; *kataífi*, a sort of shredded wheat filled with honey or syrup and chopped almonds; *pítta me méli*, honey cake. *Galaktoboúriko* is a refreshing custard pie. And remember at the dairy shop *(galaktopolío)* the perfect sour-sweet mixture of fresh yoghurt and honey. The best of the fruit are the pomegranates, peaches, apricots, grapes and melon.

Bread

One of the sweetest-smelling places in a Greek village is the bakery. If you are shopping for a picnic, get here early for the freshest *kouloúria* rings of white bread sprinkled with sesame seeds. *Choriátiko* is country bread, flat, off-white and very tasty. And take along a few *moustalevriá,* wine-flavoured sesame biscuits. At the end of the day, the ovens are made available for neighbours' family roasts. If you have rented a house, make friends with the baker and he will do your leg of lamb, too.

Coffee

Unless you prefer bland instant (known imaginatively here as *nes*), make the little effort to get the thick black Levantine brew that they do *not* call Turkish coffee. *Ellinikó* is what you say for the tradi-tional coffee served, grounds and all, from a long-handled copper or aluminium pot. But to be sure of getting it freshly brewed to your liking, correctly served with an accompanying glass of iced water, mention *éna varí glikó* (heavy and sweet), *glikí vastró* (sweet but boiled thinner), *éna métrio* (medium), or *éna skéto* (without sugar).

Wines

Greek wine had a much better reputation in the ancient world than it does now. Fermented alcoholic drinks had preceded Greek civilization, but it was the Greeks who turned the growing of vines into an agricultural practice. They were the first to understand the importance of pruning the plants and exploiting dry, stony ground.

Retsína, the unique resinous white wine, was a favourite of the ancient Greeks. Today, pine resin is still added in fermentation to permit longer conservation in a hot climate. It takes four, at most five minutes to acquire the taste and discover how well it goes with both seafood and lamb. The best, produced in the villages of Messoghia north-east of Athens, comes straight from the barrel—you can specify *varéli*. The strongest seems to be the home-brewed stuff in the monasteries.

Non-resinous whites refined enough for special celebrations are **Robóla** of Cephalonia, **Pallíni** from Attica, and **Château Carras** from Chalkidiki. The Peloponnese produces the best non-resinous whites for everyday consumption: **Deméstica** and **Lac des Roches**.

Go easier on the red wines, notoriously full bodied and rich in alcohol. Among the best are the **Náousa** from Macedonia, Santorini's volcanic **Kaldéra** and the well-known **Mavrodáfni** from Patras.

Samos is still famous for its **Sámena** muscatel dessert wine.

If you develop a taste for aniseed-flavoured ouzo, neat or with ice and water, one of the finest is **Plomári** from Lesbos.

HOTELS AND RESTAURANTS

The Right Place at the Right Price

KEY

⊨ Hotel   ⇒ Restaurant

Hotels *(for a double room with bath, in drachmas)*

⫙⫙⫙ Higher-priced: above 10,000
⫙⫙ Medium-priced: 6,000–10,000
⫙ Lower-priced: below 6,000

Restaurants *(for a full meal—a couple of starters, a main course and dessert—in drachmas)*

⫙⫙⫙ Higher-priced: above 2,250
⫙⫙ Medium-priced: 1,500–2,250
⫙ Lower-priced: below 1,500

Many Greek hotels are family-run concerns, with more charm than comfort. But charm is what people go to Greece for—so the occasional leaky shower or creaking bed should be taken with a pinch of philosophy. Things are rapidly changing, however, and Greece does have some outstanding establishments.

Restaurants tend to be very informal, changing hands and names frequently. Stars for gastronomic excellence do not really apply in Greece, where all depends on the chef's whim, the fish catch that day and the mood of the waiter. You can eat extremely pleasantly—on the smallest islands, too—in modest little tavernas that don't even have a name. Ask the locals; they will direct you to Geor-

gio's or Eleni's—where the fish is fresh and the *dzadzíki* as tangy as it should be.

Below is a cross-section of hotels and restaurants in the biggest cities and islands of Greece, set in alphabetical order by town. All were recommended by experienced travellers.

ATHENS AND ENVIRONS

Adrian   ⊨⫙⫙
Adrianou 74
105 56 **Athens**
Tel. (01) 325 0454, 325 0461
22 rooms. Roof garden.

Apostolis   ⇒⫙⫙
Gortinias 11
Athens
Tel. (01) 801 1989
Taverna in the Kifissia district.

Aristides   ⊨⫙
Sokratous 50
104 31 **Athens**
Tel. (01) 522 3881; tlx. 21-9355
90 rooms.

Astir Palace   ⊨⇒⫙⫙⫙
Vas. Sofias/Panepistimiou
106 71 **Athens**
Tel. (01) 364 3112; tlx. 22-2380
69 rooms. Luxury hotel with excellent restaurant and coffee shop.

Athenaeum   ⊨⇒⫙⫙
Inter-Continental
Singrou 89-93
117 45 **Athens**
Tel. (01) 902 3666; tlx. 22-1554
560 rooms. Luxury hotel. Four restaurants. Swimming pool. Fitness centre.

Athens Chandris   ⊨⇒⫙⫙⫙
Hotel
Singrou 385
175 64 **Paleo Faliro**
Tel. (01) 941 4824; tlx. 21-8112
350 rooms. Two restaurants. Swimming pool. In a coastal suburb. Free shuttle service to Syntagma.

Athens Hilton   ⊨⇒⫙⫙⫙
Vas. Sofias 46
106 76 **Athens**
Tel. (01) 722 0201; tlx. 21-5808
472 rooms. Luxury hotel with view of the Acropolis. Four restaurants. Swimming pool, health club. Night club.

Athinais   ⊨⇒⫙⫙
Vas. Sofias 99
115 21 **Athens**
Tel. (01) 643 1133; tlx. 21-9336
84 rooms. Roof garden. Snack bar.

Attalos   ⊨⫙
Athinas 29
105 54 **Athens**
Tel. (01) 321 2801/3; tlx. 21-8829
80 rooms. Roof-garden bar with view of the Acropolis.

Bakaliarakia   ⇒⫙
Kidathineon 41
Athens
Tel. (01) 322 5048
Basement taverna in Plaka.

Balthazar ⇌ ▥
Tsocha 27
Athens
Tel. (01) 644 1215
Restaurant with attractive bar,
in renovated mansion near
the US Embassy.

Banghion ⌇ ▯
Pl. Omonias 16
104 31 Athens
Tel. (01) 324 2309
54 rooms.

Belle Helene ⇌ ▯▯▯
Pl. Politias
Athens
Tel. (01) 807 7994
Attractive setting in a park
in the Kifissia district.

Blue Pine ⇌ ▯▯▯
Tsaldari 27
Athens
Tel. (01) 807 7745
In the Kifissia district.
Closed Sun.

Bokaris ⇌ ▯▯
Sokratous 17
Athens
Tel. (01) 801 2589

Brutus ⇌ ▯▯
Voulgaroktonou 67
Athens
Tel. (01) 363 6700
Quiet, pleasant taverna in
the Kolonaki district.

Candia ⌇⇌ ▯▯
Deligianni 40
104 38 Athens
Tel. (01) 524 6112/6;
tlx. 22-6687
123 rooms.
Swimming pool, roof garden.

Carlton ⌇ ▯
Pl. Omonias 7
104 31 Athens
Tel. (01) 522 3201
33 rooms.

The Cellar ⇌ ▯▯
Kidathineon
Athens
Basement taverna. Popular among
the Athenians.

Corfu ⇌ ▥
Kriezotou 6
Athens
Tel. (01) 361 3011
Traditional Greek cuisine. Centrally
situated.

Delphi ⌇ ▯
Ag. Konstantinou 21
104 37 Athens
Tel. (01) 522 2751
22 rooms.

Delphi ⇌ ▥
Nikis 13
Athens
Tel. (01) 323 4869
Centrally situated, popular lunchtime
rendezvous.

Dionysos ⇌ ▥
Rob. Gali 43
Athens
Tel. (01) 923 3182, 923 1936
Restaurant with patisserie.
Spectacular view of the Acropolis.
Outdoor dining.

Dioskouri ⇌ ▯▯▯
Dimitriou Vas. 16
Athens
Tel. (01) 671 3997
Seafood and grilled dishes. Outdoor
dining. In the Neo Psichico district.

Divani-Zafolia
Alexandras ⌇⇌ ▯▯▯
Alexandras 87-89
105 62 Athens
Tel. (01) 644 9012; tlx. 21-4468
180 rooms. Roof garden, pool.

Ekali Grill ⇌ ▯▯▯
Lofou 15
Athens
Tel. (01) 813 2685
Elegant restaurant with piano music.
Salad bar. In the Ekali district.

Electra Palace ⌇⇌ ▯▯▯
Nikodimou 18
105 57 Athens
Tel. (01) 324 1401/7; tlx. 21-6896
120 rooms. Swimming pool.

Fatsios ⇌ ▯▯
Efroniou 5
Athens
Tel. (01) 721 7421
Greek and Oriental specialities.
Near the US Embassy.

Filippos ⌇ ▯
Mitseon 27
117 42 Athens
Tel. (01) 922 3611/5
48 rooms.

Gekas ⌇⇌ ▯▯
Okeanidon 21
117 45 Athens
Tel. (01) 932 1594; tlx. 21-0708
35 rooms. Parking.

Gerofinikas ⇌ ▯▯▯
Pindarou 10
Athens
Tel. (01) 362 2719
Greek cuisine and cosmopolitan
atmosphere in the Kolonaki district.

Grand Chalet ⇌ ▯▯▯
Kokkinara 38
Athens
Tel. (01) 808 4837
International cuisine with Greek
specialities. Piano music.
In the Kifissia district.

Grande Bretagne ⌇⇌ ▯▯▯
Syntagma
105 63 Athens
Tel. (01) 323 0251/9; tlx. 21-9615,
21-5346
450 rooms. Traditional luxury hotel.
Three restaurants.

Hatzakou ⇌ ▯▯▯
Pl. Plakas 1
Athens
Tel. (01) 801 3461
Taverna in the Kifissia district.

Hermes ⌇ ▯
Apollonos 19
105 57 Athens
Tel. (01) 323 5514/6
45 rooms.

Ideal ⇌ ▯▯
Panepistimiou 46
Athens
Tel. (01) 361 4001
Pleasant, tastefully decorated
restaurant. Late dining possible.

Ilisia ⌇⇌ ▯▯
Michalakopoulou 25
115 28 Athens
Tel. (01) 724 4051/6; tlx. 21-4924
69 rooms. Snack bar.

Imperial ⌇ ▯
Mitropoleos 46
104 32 Athens
Tel. (01) 322- 617/8
21 rooms.

Je reviens ⇌ ▯▯▯
Xenokratous 49
Athens
Tel. (01) 721 0535, 721 1174
French and Greek cuisine. Garden.
In the Kolonaki district.

Kanaris ⇌ ▯▯
Mikrolimano
Tel. (01) 412 2533, 417 5190
Piraeus
The best seafood in Piraeus.

Karavitis ⚑ ▯
Arktinou 35
Athens
Tel. (01) 721 5155
Traditional taverna. Wine from the
barrel. In the Pangrati district.

Kentriko ⚑ ▯▯
Kolokotroni
Tel. (01) 323 5623
Athens
Popular restaurant. Terrace.

King Minos ◨⚑ ▯▯▯
Pireos 1
105 52 **Athens**
Tel. (01) 523 1111/8; tlx. 21-5339
178 rooms.

Kostoyanis ⚑ ▯▯
Zaïmi 37
Athens
Tel. (01) 822 0624
Taverna.

Leto ◨ ▯
Missaraliotou 15
117 42 **Athens**
Tel. (01) 923 2697
20 rooms.

Lycabette ◨ ▯▯
Valaoritou 6
106 71 **Athens**
Tel. (01) 363 3514/8; tlx. 22-1147
39 rooms.

Marathon ◨⚑ ▯▯
Karolou 23
104 37 **Athens**
Tel. (01) 523 1865
92 rooms. View of the Acropolis and
Lycabettus. Roof garden, disco.
Garage.

Mayemenos Avlos ⚑ ▯▯
Aminda/Zalevkou
Athens
Tel. (01) 722 3195
Popular after-theatre restaurant and
patisserie. In the Pangrati district.

Moustakas ⚑ ▯▯
Harilaou Trikoupi/Kritis
Athens
Tel. (01) 801 4584
Taverna in the Kifissia district.

Myrtia ⚑ ▯▯▯
Markou Mousourou 35
Athens
Tel. (01) 701 2276
Taverna with Greek cuisine. Large
choice of starters. Garden, bouzouki
music. In the Pangrati district.
Closed Sun.

Niki ◨ ▯
Nikis 27
105 57 **Athens**
Tel. (01) 322 0913/5

Novotel Mirayia ◨⚑ ▯▯▯
Athenes
Michail Voda 4-6
104 39 **Athens**
Tel. (01) 862 7133, 862 7053;
tlx. 22-6264
195 rooms. Roof garden with swim-
ming pool. Underground parking.

O Morias ⚑ ▯
Vas. Konstantinou 108/ Peloponissou
Athens
Tel. (01) 659 9409
Family taverna in
the Ag. Paraskevi district.
Wine from the barrel.

Piccolo Mondo ⚑ ▯▯▯
Kifissias 217
Athens
Tel. (01) 802 0437
French cuisine. Piano music. Reser-
vation essential. In the Kifissia
district. Closed Sun.

Pini-Lini ⚑ ▯
Agnanton 1
Athens
Tel. (01) 921 6347
Greek specialities.

Plaka ◨⚑ ▯▯
Kapnikareas 7
105 56 **Athens**
Tel. (01) 322 2096/8; tlx. 22-1020
67 rooms.

Plaza ◨⚑ ▯▯
Acharnon 78/Katrivanou
104 34 **Athens**
Tel. (01) 822 5111; tlx. 21-4686
126 rooms. Roof garden.

President ◨⚑ ▯▯▯
Kifissias 43
115 23 **Athens**
Tel. (01) 692 4600; tlx. 21-8585
513 rooms. Roof garden.
Swimming pool, disco. Cafeteria.
Taverna.

Psaropoulos ⚑ ▯▯
Kalanion 2
Paralia Glifada
Tel. (01) 894 5677
Waterside fish taverna.

Rodia ⚑ ▯▯
Aristipou 44
Athens
Tel. (01) 722 9883

Roumba ⚑ ▯▯▯
Damareos 130
Athens
Tel. (01) 701 4910
Closed Tues. In the Pangrati district.

St. George ◨⚑ ▯▯▯
Lycabettus
Kleomenous 2
106 75 **Athens**
Tel. (01) 729 0711/9; tlx. 21-4253
149 rooms.
Swimming pool, roof garden.
Grill room with panoramic view of
the Acropolis.

Socrates' Prison ⚑ ▯
Mitseon 20
Athens
Tel. (01) 922 3434
Taverna.

Strofi ⚑ ▯▯
Rob. Gali 25
Athens
Tel. (01) 921 4130
Outdoor dining. Spectacular view of
the Acropolis.

Themistokles ⚑ ▯
Vas. Georgiou B 31
Athens
Tel. (01) 721 9553
Taverna in the Pangrati district.

Thespis ⚑ ▯▯
Thespidos
Athens
Taverna with outside dining,
roof garden.

Titania ◨⚑ ▯▯
Panepistimiou 52
106 78 **Athens**
Tel. (01) 360 9611/9; tlx. 21-4673
375 rooms.
Piano bar. Snack bar.
Garage.

Vladimir ⚑ ▯▯▯
Aristodimou 12
Athens
Tel. (01) 721 7407
In the Kolonaki district.

Xinos ⚑ ▯▯
Angelou Geronta 4
Tel. (01) 322 1065
Greek cuisine.
Taverna in Plaka.

Zonar's ⚑ ▯
Panepistimiou
Athens
Tel. (01) 323 0336
Patisserie.

CORFU

Kerkira Golf Hotel ⌨️ ═ ▯▯▯
Alikes
Tel. (0661) 31785
240 rooms. Swimming pool, private beach. Musical entertainment.

Arion Hotel ⌨️ ═ ▯▯
Fiakon 6
491 00 **Corfu Town**
Tel. (0661) 37950
102 rooms. Family-run hotel. Swimming pool, garden.

Hotel Bella Vanezia ⌨️ ▯
Nap. Zambelli
491 00 **Corfu Town**
Tel. (0661) 46500, 44290
32 rooms.View of Corfu Town. Patio.

Bretagne Hotel ⌨️ ▯
Kapa Georgaki 27
Garitsa
491 00 **Corfu Town**
Tel. (0661) 30724
44 rooms. Near the airport.

Calypso Hotel ⌨️ ▯
Vraila 4
491 00 **Corfu Town**
Tel. (0661) 30723
27 rooms. Central location.

Corfu Palace Hotel ⌨️ ═ ▯▯▯
Demokratias
491 00 **Corfu Town**
Tel. (0661) 39485/6
220 rooms. Overlooking Garitsa Bay. Outdoor and indoor swimming pools, subtropical garden. Live music.

Mandarin Palace ═ ▯▯▯
Restaurant
Paleokastritsa Road
Corfu Town
(near Kontokali)
Tel. (0661) 38596/40022
Cantonese cuisine. Outdoor dining. Dinner only.

Marina Hotel ⌨️ ═ ▯▯
Anemomilos
491 00 **Corfu Town**
Tel. (0661) 32783/5
102 rooms. Waterside situation. Swimming pool, terrace.

Mr. Pizza Ristorante ═ ▯
Prosalendou 41
Corfu Town
Tel. (0661) 34321
In the Old Port area. Pizza restaurant with some Greek food. Lunch only.

Orestes Restaurant ═ ▯▯
Xenofondos 78
Corfu Town
Tel. (0661) 35664
In the New Port area. Traditional Greek cuisine. Seafood specialities. Outdoor dining. Lunch only.

Ragnatela Restaurant/ ═ ▯
Pizzeria
George Aspioti 3
Corfu Town
Tel. (0661) 40640
Italian cuisine. Outdoor dining, garden. Dinner only.

Thomas Taverna ═ ▯
Main road to Dasia
Corfu Town
(after Kommeno Bay)
Tel. (0661) 91245
Popular local taverna. Traditional Greek cuisine. Lunch only.

Chandris Dasia ⌨️ ═ ▯▯▯
Complex
490 83 **Dasia Bay**
Tel. (0661) 33871/5
527 rooms. Bungalows and villas in landscaped garden. View of sea and mountains. Swimming pool, tennis, private beach.

Grand Glifada Hotel ⌨️ ═ ▯▯▯
Glifada Beach
491 00 **Glifada**
Tel. (0661) 45110
242 rooms. Overlooking glorious sandy beach and open sea. Swimming pool, colourful garden. Dancing most nights.

Bacchus Taverna ═ ▯
Nafsicas 25
Kanoni
Tel. (0661) 24096
Greek/international cuisine. Outdoor dining.

Corfu Hilton Hotel ⌨️ ═ ▯▯▯
Nafsicas
491 00 **Kanoni**
Tel. (0661) 36540
255 rooms. Panoramic view of the sea and hills. Outside and indoor swimming pools, garden, tennis, private beach, bowling.

Nausicaa Restaurant/ ═ ▯▯▯
Bistro
Nafsicas
Kanoni
Tel. (0661) 44354
Greek/international cuisine. Outdoor dining. Music two to three times per week. Dinner only.

Gloupos Taverna ═ ▯▯▯
Milia
Kinopiastes
Tel. (0661) 56283
Popular taverna. Outdoor dining. Greek dancing.

Tripa Taverna ═ ▯▯▯
Kinopiastes
Tel. (0661) 56333
Popular local taverna. Traditional Greek cuisine. Outdoor dining. Dinner only. Greek dancing often.

Chez George Taverna ═ ▯▯
Paleokastritsa
Tel. (0663) 41233
Beachside taverna. Lunch only.

CRETE

Minos Beach ⌨️ ═ ▯▯▯
721 00 **Agios Nikolaos**
Tel. (0841) 22345/9
132 rooms. Luxury hotel. Good cuisine.

La Jetée ═ ▯▯▯
Kato Galatas
Chania
Tel. (0821) 31626
Small, intimate French bistro with excellent French cuisine.

Porto Veneziano ⌨️ ▯▯
Enetikos Limin
731 32 **Chania**
Tel. (0821) 29311/3
63 rooms. Situated in Chania Old Town, near the Venetian harbour.

Retro ═ ▯▯▯
Mavrogenidon 1
Chania
Tel. (0821) 58386, 43688
Situated in beautiful old Turkish house with garden. Good cuisine.

Elounda Beach ⌨️ ═ ▯▯▯
720 53 **Elounda**
Tel. (0841) 41412/3
301 rooms. Luxury hotel in traditional Cretan style.

Elounda Mare ⌨️ ═ ▯▯▯
720 53 **Elounda**
Tel. (0841) 41102/3, 41398
90 rooms. Luxury hotel.

Creta Maris 🛏🍴▯▯▯
Limin Chersonisou
700 14 **Iraklion**
Tel. (0897) 22115, 22127
745 rooms. Luxury hotel.

Cretan Village 🛏🍴▯▯▯
Limin Chersonisou
700 14 **Iraklion**
Tel. (0897) 22996/7
288 rooms.
Built in traditional style of
an old Cretan village.

Dore 🍴▯▯▯
5th Floor, Dore Building
Pl. Eleftherias
Iraklion
Tel. (081) 225212
European cuisine.
Panoramic view of
city and sea.
Piano music most nights.

Galaxy 🛏🍴▯▯▯
Dimokratias 67
713 06 **Iraklion**
Tel. (081) 238812
140 rooms. In residential area.

Galera 🍴▯▯▯
Knossou 185
Iraklion
Tel. (081) 210491
Seafood specialities.
Closed Mon.

Grecotel Creta Sun 🛏🍴▯▯▯
Gouves
P.O. Box 106
Iraklion
Tel. (0897) 41103
350 rooms.
Large swimming pool.

Idi 🛏▯
Zaros
700 02 **Iraklion**
Tel. (0894) 31301/2
35 rooms.
In the foothills of Psiloreitis.
Swimming pool.

Knossos 🍴▯▯
Pl. Elef. Venizelou
Iraklion
Tel. (081) 282848
Central location. Popular local
restaurant.

Kyriakos 🍴▯▯
Dimokratias 53
Iraklion
Tel. (081) 224649
Popular restaurant. Good cuisine.
Closed Wed.

Minos 🍴▯▯
Dedalou 10
Iraklion
Tel. (081) 281263
Greek taverna-style food.

La Parisienne 🍴▯▯
Ag. Titou 7
Iraklion
Small, intimate restaurant. French
cuisine.

Pizza Napoli 🍴▯
Pl. Eleftherias
Iraklion
Tel. (081) 223023, 226434
Popular, centrally-situated pizzeria/
restaurant. Open all year.

Silva Maris 🛏🍴▯▯
Limin Chersonisou
700 14 **Iraklion**
Tel. (0897) 22850/7, 22205
249 rooms.

Vardia 🍴▯
The Harbour
Iraklion
Tel. (081) 223736
Good choice of mezé.

Andamosi 🍴▯
Myrtios
Tel. (0832) 31408
Exceptional view. Simple, taverna-
style food.

New Alianthos Beach 🛏▯
Plakias
740 60 **Myrtios**
Tel. (0832) 31227
124 rooms. South coast, family-run
hotel. Magnificent scenery.

Grecotel Creta 🛏🍴▯▯▯
Palace
Adelianos Kambos
741 00 **Rethymnon**
Tel. (0831) 22381
336 rooms. Beautiful luxury complex
built in village style.
Three swimming pools.

Grecotel Rithymna 🛏🍴▯▯
Beach
Adelianos Kambos
741 00 **Rethymnon**
Tel. (0831) 29491, 71002
569 rooms. Luxury mini-resort on a
long, sandy beach. Excellent facilities
for children.

Ta Kakavia 🍴▯▯
The Harbour
Rethymnon
Fish taverna. Picturesque location.

Fereniki 🛏▯
Georgioupolis
730 08 **Vamos**
Tel. (0825) 61345, 61297
30 rooms. Quiet situation in a small
resort with magnificent beach.

RHODES

Faliraki Beach Hotel 🛏🍴▯▯▯
851 00 **Faliraki**
Tel. (0241) 22741/85403;
tlx. 292219/292604
300 rooms. Restaurants, bars,
sea-water swimming pools, tennis.
Open Apr. to Oct.

Mandis Cyprus Taverna 🍴▯
Ixia
Tel. 325/4
Cypriot specialities.

Rodos Bay Hotel 🛏🍴▯▯▯
Trianton
851 00 **Ixia**
Tel. (0241) 23661/5; tlx. 292150
330 rooms. Rooftop swimming pool.
Open Apr. to Oct.

Rodos Palace Hotel 🛏🍴▯▯▯
Trianton
851 00 **Ixia**
Tel. (0241) 25222/26222;
tlx. 292212/3
610 rooms. Luxury hotel. Bungalows.
Private beach. Restaurants, bars,
disco/night club, outdoor and indoor
swimming pools, tennis, health
centre. Open Apr. to Oct.

La Rotisserie 🍴▯▯▯
Rodos Palace Hotel
Ixia
Tel. (0241) 25222/26222

Tzaki Taverna 🍴▯
Ixia
Tel. (0241) 26604
Classic Greek taverna with live
bouzouki music.

Captain's House 🍴▯▯▯
A. Zorvou 5
Psaropoule
Tel. (0241) 26836
Steak house. French cuisine. Seafood
dishes also available.

Alexis Taverna 🍴▯▯
Sokratous 18
Rhodes Town
Fish restaurant. Good cuisine.

Anixis Taverna ⇌ ▯
Rhodes Town
Tel. (0241) 91666
Greek taverna food. Rustic setting.
Opposite Rhodes airport.

Argo Taverna ⇌ ▯▯▯
Pl. Ippocratous 23-24
Rhodes Town
Tel. (0241) 34232
Fish restaurant. Charming location
in Old Town.

Cleo's Ristorante ⇌ ▯▯▯
Ag. Fanouriou 17
Rhodes Town
Tel. (0241) 28415
Elegant, sophisticated restaurant in
Old Town. Italian and French
cuisine.

Constantin Hotel ⊨ ⇌ ▯▯
Amerikis 65
851 00 Rhodes Town
Tel. (0241) 22971/24758; tlx. 29217
139 rooms.
Close to the beach.
All rooms with balcony.

Dodecanese Taverna ⇌ ▯▯
Pl. M. Evreon
Rhodes Town
Fish taverna in Old Town.

Ellinikon Restaurant ⇌ ▯▯▯
A. Diakou 29
Rhodes Town
Tel. (0241) 28111

Grand Hotel ⊨ ⇌ ▯▯▯
Astir Palace
G. Papanikolaou
851 00 Rhodes Town
Tel. (0241) 26284; tlx. 292121
390 rooms. Luxury hotel. Outdoor
and indoor swimming pools,
piano bar, health centre, tennis,
night club. Two restaurants.
Cafeteria.

Leon d'Oro ⇌ ▯▯
Canada/Virones
Rhodes Town
Tel. (0241) 21495
Italian cuisine.

Loukoulos ⇌ ▯▯▯
Amerikis 13
Rhodes Town
Good Greek cuisine.

Macnemara's Bistro ⇌ ▯▯
A. Rodiou 52
Rhodes Town
Tel. (0241) 25492
British cuisine.

Mollye's ⇌ ▯
I. Dragoumi 25
Rhodes Town
Varied cuisine. Vegetarian dishes
available.

Pacific Restaurant ⇌ ▯▯
Akti Kanari 33
Rhodes Town
Tel. (0241) 23857

Pithagoras Taverna ⇌ ▯▯▯
Pithagoras 22
Rhodes Town
Tel. (0241) 23711
In Old Town. Seafood restaurant
with French atmosphere.

Queen's Garden ⇌ ▯▯
Valaoritou 1
Rhodes Town
Tel. (0241) 35360
Chinese cuisine.

Roumelli ⇌ ▯▯
New Market
Rhodes Town
Good roast meat.

Spartalis Hotel ⊨ ▯▯
N. Plastira 2
851 00 Rhodes Town
Tel. (0241) 24371
79 rooms. Close to Mandraki.

Pension Stella ⊨ ▯
Dilberaki 58
851 00 Rhodes Town
Tel. (0241) 24935
20 rooms. Many rooms with balcony.
Family-run guesthouse in heart of
New Town. Five minutes walk from
best beach. Open Apr. to Oct.

Tay's Restaurant ⇌ ▯▯▯
Ippodamou 280
Rhodes Town
Tel. (0241) 36931
In Old Town. Garden setting.
Italian cuisine.

THESSALONIKI AND ENVIRONS

ABC ⊨ ▯▯
Angelaki 41
546 21 Thessaloniki
Tel. (031) 26 5421/5
103 rooms. Cafeteria. Breakfast room
with fireplace.

Anthimos ⇌ ▯▯
(6 km from Thessaloniki Thermi)
Tel. (031) 41 4882
Fish taverna.

Aproopto ⇌ ▯▯
Lori Margariti 11
Thessaloniki
Tel. (031) 28 3245
Ouzeria.

Archipelagos ⇌ ▯▯
Kanari
Nea Krini
Tel. (031) 43 5800
Fish taverna.

Astoria ⊨ ⇌ ▯▯
Tsimiski 20/Salaminos
546 24 Thessaloniki
Tel. (031) 52 7121/5
88 rooms. Soundproofed. American
breakfast.

Capitol ⊨ ⇌ ▯▯
Monastiriou 8
546 29 Thessaloniki
Tel. (031) 51 6221
194 rooms.

Capsis ⊨ ⇌ ▯▯
Monastiriou 18
546 30 Thessaloniki
Tel. (031) 52 1321/9
430 rooms. Swimming pool, sauna.

City ⊨ ▯▯
Komninon 11
546 24 Thessaloniki
Tel. (031) 26 9421/8
104 rooms. Some rooms with
veranda. Cafeteria.

Electra Palace ⊨ ⇌ ▯▯▯
Pl. Aristotelous 5A
546 24 Thessaloniki
Tel. (031) 23 2221
131 rooms. Two restaurants, coffee
shop. Shopping arcade.

Fletsios ⇌ ▯▯
Thermis/Panoramatos
Thessaloniki
Tel. (031) 46 1913

Gallery ⇌ ▯▯▯
Them. Sofouli 89
Thessaloniki
Tel. (031) 41 4795
International cuisine. Violin music.

El Greco ⊨ ⇌ ▯▯
Egnatia 23
546 30 Thessaloniki
Tel. (031) 52 0620/9
90 rooms.

Klimataria ⟺▯▯
Pavlou Mela 34
Thessaloniki
Tel. (031) 27 7854
Grill.

Krikelas ⟺▯▯
Ethnikis Antistasseos 32
Thessaloniki
Tel. (031) 41 1289
Wonderful hors d' oeuvres (mezé),
delicious roast lamb.

Makedonia Palace 🛏⟺▯▯▯
Megalou Alexandrou
546 40 **Thessaloniki**
Tel. (031) 83 7520/9
294 rooms. Waterside luxury hotel.
Swimming pool.

Makedoniki ⟺▯
Kedrinos Lofos
Thessaloniki
Tel. (031) 21 1873
Taverna.

Nefeli 🛏⟺▯▯
Komninon 1
552 36 **Panorama**
Tel. (031) 94 2002
66 rooms. Roof garden. Night club.

O Geros Tou Moria ⟺▯▯
Filippou 10
Thessaloniki
Tel. (031) 22 4418

Oi Lykoi Woolves ⟺▯
Vas. Georgiou 41
Thessaloniki
Tel. (031) 21 6921
Grill.

Olympia 🛏⟺▯▯
Olimpou 65
Thessaloniki
Tel. (031) 23 5421
110 rooms.

Olympos ⟺▯
Koritsas 24
Thessaloniki
Tel. (031) 21 6921
Grill.

Olympos ⟺▯▯
Leof. Nikis 5
Tel. (031) 27 5715
Good Greek cuisine,

Panorama 🛏⟺▯▯
Analipseos 26
552 36 **Panorama**
Tel. (031) 94 1123
50 rooms. Good Greek cuisine.

Porto Marina ⟺▯▯
Nik. Plastira 57
Nea Krimi
Tel. (031) 41 2781
Fish taverna.

Pyrgos ⟺▯
Eleftheriou Venizelou/Poli 13
Thessaloniki
Tel. (031) 20 7769
Taverna.

Queen Olga 🛏⟺▯▯
Vas. Olgas 44
546 41 **Thessaloniki**
Tel. (031) 82 4621/9
150 rooms.
Lounge with view of the sea.
Garage.

Ragias ⟺▯▯
Nikis 13
Thessaloniki
Tel. (031) 22 7468

Retro ⟺▯▯
Nik. Plastira at Aretsou 25
Thessaloniki
Tel. (031) 41 7064
Piano bar.

Sokaki ⟺▯▯
Kalapothaki 4
Thessaloniki
Tel. (031) 22 9184
Live music.

Stratis ⟺▯▯
Nikis 19
Thessaloniki
Tel. (031) 23 4782, 27 9353
Waterside taverna.

Sun Beach 🛏▯▯
540 07 **Agia Triada**
Tel. (0392) 51 221
123 rooms.

Ta Nissia ⟺▯▯
Proxenou Koromila 13
Thessaloniki
Tel. (031) 28 5991

Vergina 🛏▯
Monastiriou 19
Thessaloniki
Tel. (031) 52 7400
133 rooms.

Votsalo ⟺▯▯
Proxenou Koromila 17
Thessaloniki

BERLITZ INFO

All the Nuts and Bolts
For a Successful Journey

CONTENTS

ACCOMMODATION

Hotels *(xenodochio)* are divided into six categories: L luxury, A (expensive), B (moderate), C (inexpensive), D (cheap) and E (a real bargain—and a real surprise at times, for better or worse!). Room prices are government controlled, but regulations are not always strictly upheld, and rates may vary unpredictably. The base rate must be displayed in each room, along with any extra charges depending on various factors such as the facilities provided (air-conditioning, hot water, telephone, etc.), your length of stay, and of course, seasonal variations. Some places may insist you take full or half board during high season. A government tax is added to the bill. Reductions can usually be made for children.

274

If you plan to visit Greece in July or August, you should book in advance. Most travel agents and the NTOG (National Tourist Organization of Greece) list hotels and rates in a comprehensive index (see under TOURIST INFORMATION OFFICES for the addresses of the NTOG). Reservations can also be made through:

Hellenic Chamber of Hotels
Stadíou 24, PC 105 64, Athens
Tel. 3233.501 or 3236.641

If you're in Athens, you can make on-the-spot reservations with the Hotel Chamber at:

Karagiórgi Servías 2, Athens
Tel. 3237.193

Private accommodation. It's very easy to rent rooms *(domátia)* in private homes. Islanders meet the boats with offers of "Rooms"—usually in English—and in every town and village you will see signs proclaiming "Rooms for rent". Prices are generally negotiable (though with increasing difficulty as high season approaches). In some places, the rooms are run by the local Tourist Police, who have to ensure that the hotels are all filled up first. So in low season, many of the private rooms are closed down to favour hotel business.

If you have difficulty finding somewhere to stay, contact the NTOG or the local Tourist Police, who will almost always manage to find something for you. When demand is high, certain "informal" arrangements can be made, but you will probably have to pay much higher than usual. Some of the inexpensive hotels, as well as the island tavernas, offer "roof-space", which is exactly that—a space on the roof where they will usually provide a mattress. For the more adventurous travellers with sleeping bags, spending the night out under the stars might not be such a bad solution.

Villas. Ranging from small, simple cottages to quite lavish summer houses, villas can be let for monthly and sometimes weekly rates. When booking, check the facilities—which normally, but not always, include refrigerator, hot water and electricity. In low season you can try asking the Tourist Police or local inhabitants for any possibilities. Otherwise your travel agent or the NTOG will give you names and addresses.

Youth hostels. There aren't very many hostels *(xenón neótitos)* in Greece, but they are simple, clean and relaxed, and you might even be let in without a membership card, if there's room. The doors close at around 10 or 11 p.m., and the maximum stay is usually five days. There are three hostels in Athens, one in Piraeus, Delphi, Litochoro, Mycenae, Nafplio, Olympia, Patras, Thessaloniki, two on Corfu, one on Santorini, and seven on Crete. The Greek Youth Hostel Headquarters is at:

Dragatsaníou 4, off Platía Klafthmónos

You can also stay at the **Y.M.C.A.**:

Omírou 28, Athens
Tel. 3626.970

or the **Y.W.C.A.**:

Amerikis 11, Athens
Tel. 3624.294

See also AGROTOURISM and CAMPING.

I'd like a single/ double room.	**Tha íthela éna monó/ dipló domátio.**
with bath/shower	**me bánio/dous**
What's the rate per night?	**Piá íne i timí giá mía níkta?**

AGROTOURISM

The Greek General Secretariat for the Equality of the Two Sexes has set up a series of rural-based womens' cooperatives dedicated to preserving traditional handicrafts. "Agrotourists" of either sex are welcome to stay in the villagers' homes and help with the daily tasks. Write to the NTOG for a brochure giving details of each cooperative and information on how to reserve rooms.

Ambelakia, 32 km. from Larissa: cotton dyeing.

Petra, Lesbos: weaving, pottery

Chios: four mastic-producing villages in the south of the island.

Arachova, at the foot of Mount Parnassus: agriculture, weaving.

Agios Germanos, in Northern Greece near the Prespa lakes: agriculture.

Maronia, 3 km. south-east of Komotini, Thrace: agriculture.

AIRPORTS
(ΑΕΡΟΔΡΟΜΙΟ—*aerodrómio*)

The international airport serving **Athens** (tel. 9699.111.) is 10 km. from the city centre. It has two separate terminals reached by different buses: the West Terminal handling only the foreign and domestic flights of Olympic Airways (Greece's national airline), and the East Terminal which receives all other international flights. There's a free shuttle service between the two terminals from 8 a.m. to 8 p.m.

You will find in both terminals the National Tourist Organization (EOT), a currency exchange office, hotel-reservation counters, news-stands, car-hire agencies, refreshment facilities and a duty-free shop. Porters are plentiful.

A taxi ride to town takes about 25 minutes; there's also direct bus service with coaches leaving every 20 minutes or so.

Thessaloniki has a modern international airport at Mikra, 15 km. from the centre of town, with links to Athens, Limnos, Lesbos, Crete, Rhodes and, in summer, Skiathos. An Olympic Airways bus meets all Olympic flights and drops passengers off at the city terminal, but most passengers choose to take a taxi from the stand outside the terminal. The ride takes 20 to 30 minutes.

There are international airports on **Rhodes, Crete** and **Corfu**, and some of the following island airports are also starting to handle traffic from abroad: Chios, Kos, Limnos, Lesbos, Mykonos, Paros, Samos, Santorini, Skiathos, Skyros and Thasos.

All airports have bus services (cheaper than taxis) to the major towns. Travellers on package tours will normally be met at the airport and transferred by special coach to their hotel.

See also GETTING TO GREECE, ISLAND-HOPPING and TRANSPORT.

Porter!	Achthofóre!
Taxi!	Taxí!
Where's the bus for...?	Pou íne to leoforío giá?

ALPHABET

The exotic letters of the Greek alphabet needn't be a mystery to you. The table below lists the Greek letters in their capital and lower case forms, followed by the letters they correspond to in English. See also LANGUAGE, USEFUL EXPRESSIONS and VOCABULARY section.

Α	α	a	as in bar
Β	β	v	
Γ	γ	g	as in go*
Δ	δ	d	like th in this
Ε	ε	e	as in get
Ζ	ζ	z	
Η	η	i	like ee in meet
Θ	θ	th	as in thin
Ι	ι	i	like ee in meet
Κ	κ	k	
Λ	λ	l	
Μ	μ	m	
Ν	ν	n	
Ξ	ξ	x	like ks in thanks
Ο	ο	o	as in bone
Π	π	p	
Ρ	ρ	r	
Σ	σ, ς	s	as in kiss
Τ	τ	t	
Υ	υ	i	like ee in meet
Φ	φ	f	
Χ	χ	ch	as in Scottish loch
Ψ	ψ	ps	as in tipsy
Ω	ω	o	as in bone
ΟΥ	ου	ou	as in soup

---

*except before **i**- and **e**-sounds, when it's pronounced like **y** in yes

ANIMAL WELFARE

Call the following numbers for on-the-spot help if ever you come across any animals in distress.

Hellenic Animal Welfare Society, Athens Tel: 6435.391/6444.473

Union of Animal Friends: Animal Shelter, Pallini Tel: 666.7669

Where there is no animal welfare representative, please contact the local Ministry vet. or the Tourist Police. If they can't help, get in touch with the Athens number above.

ANTIQUITIES

If you find an antiquity *(archéa)*, you must report it to the Greek Archaeological Service which may permit you to export it upon payment of a fee. Before you buy an antiquity, make sure that the dealer obtains an export permit for it. Travellers caught trying to smuggle antiquities are subject to prosecution.

Many underwater archaeological sites have been declared off-limits to amateur divers (but not snorkellers), with penalties decreed for anyone even touching an antiquity at such places.

Greek Archaeological Service
Polignótou 13, Athens

Gen. Dir. of Antiquities and Restorations
Aristídou 14, Athens
Tel. 3243.015

BICYCLE AND MOTORSCOOTER HIRE
(enikiásis podiláton/motopodiláton)

In all the major tourist centres there are firms that hire out bicycles, motorscooters and mopeds. Rates vary widely, so shopping around may be wise. Bicycling is not very widespread, and the cycles for rent are not in the best condition. But scooters and mopeds are ideal for getting around—they're economical and fun, you can go just about anywhere and you can usually take them along on the trains or boats. Check them carefully before setting off because you're likely to be charged for any repairs needed. Most agents charge a non-negotiable insurance fee for all motorized two-wheelers. Remember that it is illegal to run motorbikes during siesta hours (2 p.m. to 6 p.m.) and after 11 p.m. And be careful! Don't end up in a Greek hospital like a surprising number of unwary tourists.

What's the rental charge for one day?	**Póso kostízi giá mía iméra?**

CAMPING
(ΚΑΜΠΙΝΓΚ—*"camping"*)

Officially, camping is permitted only at authorized sites set up by the NTOG and several private companies, varying from casual to very organized. In practice, however, camping is tolerated in most places, provided you use some discretion, ask permission from the landowner and don't leave a mess. On the islands especially, the accommodation shortage has caused police to turn a blind eye to visitors camping or sleeping on the beaches and other unauthorized spots. Some island towns have public facilities where campers can pay to have a hot shower. Keep in mind that if you stay in the official campgrounds, you'll have fresh water and other facilities and will often find shade, beach access and a certain measure of security. Considering the climate, cost and safety factor, it can be a great way to visit Greece. If you do decide to camp, bring your own equipment since the few supplies available tend to be expensive and it's rare to find them for rent.

Most private sites are open from April to October. For a full list of campgrounds and camping information, contact the NTOG office in your country. In Greece, call at the EOT office or local Tourist Police, or telephone 9410.580 for general information. See under TOURIST INFORMATION for NTOG addresses.

Is there a campsite nearby?	**Ipárchi éna méros giá camping edó kondá?**
May we camp here?	**Boroúme na kataskinósoume edó?**
We have a tent/ caravan.	**Échoume mía skiní/ trochóspito.**

CAR HIRE
(ΕΝΟΙΚΙΑΣΕΙΣ ΑΥΤΟΚΙΝΗΤΩΝ *enikiásis aftokiníton)*

See also DRIVING IN GREECE. Officially, an International Driving Permit is compulsory for all foreigners hiring a car in Greece, although firms accept virtually any national licence, stipulating that it must have been held for at least one year. To be safe, you should obtain the International Permit from your car association before leaving. Some firms won't rent to drivers under 21 or even 25 years old.

Many agencies ask for a deposit equivalent to the estimated total cost of your rental, though this requirement is waived for major credit card holders. Third-party liability insurance is often included in the rate, and complete coverage is available for a small extra charge. All rates are subject to stamp duty and local taxes. Off season, you can expect a reduction. Greece is one of the most expensive countries for car hire; it's more economical to book the car in advance and pay in your home country.

You can find major car hire agencies all over Greece with most types of cars, including a few air-conditioned models. There are also local companies with more negotiable rates, especially on the islands. Since island roads are usually unsurfaced, the rental cars get a lot of rough wear, so don't expect them to be in new condition. Prefer a four-wheel-drive vehicle for getting off the beaten track.

For renting a motor home or camper, contact:

Motor Caravan Club, Athinón 251, Athens Tel. 5812.103

CHILDREN

It's no exaggeration to say that the Greeks adore children and seem to have found a happy middle road between freedom and discipline. Young children often go out with their parents in the evening and are accepted almost everywhere. If your child strays, inform anyone around who speaks your language and go to the nearest policeman. It's most unlikely that any harm will come to him or her.

If you need a baby-sitter, enquire at the hotel reception desk and arrangements will be made, as long as you give enough notice. In private accommodation, your hosts will gladly find a solution.

A service that might come in handy in Athens:

Panathenaíki Union Domestic Service Tel. 3640.816/3635.748

They provide not only babysitters but cleaners, nurses and other domestic help as well.

Can you get us a baby-sitter for tonight?	**Boríte na mas vríte mía baby-sitter giapópse?**

CIGARETTES, CIGARS, TOBACCO
(tsigára, poúra, kapnós)

The sign to look for is ΚΑΠΝΟΠΩ-ΛΕΙΟ—*kapnopolío* (tobacconist). Greek tobacco, most of which comes from Macedonia, is world famous. Most leading foreign cigarettes are available but are at least two to three times the price of local brands.

A packet of cigarettes/ box of matches, please.	**Éna pakéto tsigára/ spírta, parakaló**
filter-tipped	**me fíltro**
without filter	**chorís fíltro**

CLIMATE

On the whole, apart from the northern regions and the interior mountainous areas, Greece enjoys a truly Mediterranean climate, though there's more variation than is usually imagined. As a general rule, the blossom season is from March to June, the dry season from July to October, and the cool, rainy season from November to March.

In summer it can get stiflingly hot, though along the coasts and on the islands this heat is tempered by fresh breezes. In

°Fahrenheit		Jan	Feb	Mar	Apr	May	Jun	Jul	Aug	Sep	Oct	Nov	Dec
Athens	max.	55	57	60	68	77	86	92	92	84	75	66	58
	min.	44	44	46	52	61	68	73	73	67	60	53	47
Naxos	max.	58	59	61	67	73	78	81	82	78	75	68	62
	min.	50	49	51	56	61	68	72	72	69	64	58	53
Thessaloniki	max.	49	53	58	67	77	85	90	90	82	71	61	53
	min.	35	37	41	49	58	65	70	69	63	55	47	39
°Celsuis		Jan	Feb	Mar	Apr	May	Jun	Jul	Aug	Sep	Oct	Nov	Dec
Athens	max.	13	14	16	20	25	30	33	33	29	24	19	14
	min.	7	7	8	11	16	20	23	23	19	16	12	8
Naxos	max.	14	15	16	19	23	26	27	28	26	24	20	17
	min.	10	9	11	13	16	20	22	22	21	18	14	12
Thessaloniki	max.	9	12	14	19	25	29	32	32	28	22	16	12
	min.	2	3	5	9	14	18	21	21	17	13	8	4

Minimum temperatures measured just before sunrise, maximum in the afternoon.

winter, it's very unpredictable, usually quite humid and chilly. In the north and in the mountains you'll find freezing temperatures along with snow—you can always go skiing! In other parts of the mainland and on the islands, the temperature rarely falls below the low 40s (approx. 6°C). The most temperate climate is found on the islands, including Corfu and Crete.

With all this in mind, it's easy to see why everyone recommends Greece in the spring or autumn. In April and especially May, you will be treated to a colourful display of wild flowers and refreshing greenery sadly lacking at the height of the dry season. In May, June, September and October, temperatures, crowds and prices are pleasantly lower than during the high season in July and August. You can usually go swimming everywhere from May to October, and in the mild southern waters, the sea should be warm even in April and November.

CLOTHING

Because of its Mediterranean climate, Greece tends to be informal. But in the large cities, people dress appropriately for the occasion, and during business hours you'll see just as many suits, shirts, ties and city dresses as you would in more temperate climes. On the islands, dress is decidedly relaxed.

From May to September you won't need an extensive wardrobe—light-weight drip-dry clothing is the most practical (cotton is preferable to synthetics in hot weather). Bring a sweater or jacket for the evening. On the beach, toplessness is acceptable in most places, except near small villages where local people will object. However, when you're walking to and from bathing areas, slip on a shirt or cover-up. A good pair of sunglasses and a wide-brimmed hat will come in handy, as well as a sturdy pair of shoes for hiking or exploring ruins.

During the rest of the year it can get chilly and wet so you'll need a warm jacket or coat and perhaps a raincoat.

COMMUNICATIONS

Post Office (ΤΑΧΥΔΡΟΜΕΙΟ—*tachidromío*). The post offices handle letters, stamps, parcels, cheque cashing, money orders and exchange but not telegrams or phone calls. Hours are usually from 7.30 a.m. to 2.30 p.m. Monday to Friday (2 p.m. for money orders and parcels); the offices at Omónia, Syntagma and Eólu in Athens close at 8 p.m. Registered letters and parcels are checked in front of you at the post office, so don't seal them beforehand.

You can also buy stamps at news-stands and in souvenir shops, but at a 10% surcharge. Letter boxes are yellow.

Mail. If you want to receive mail in Greece but don't have a fixed address, have your letters sent to you c/o:

Poste Restante
(town name, e.g. Athens), Greece

You can have your mail sent to most fair-sized cities (on the islands, have it addressed to the main town). In Athens it will be kept for you at the main post office, Eólou 100, and in Thessaloniki at Tsimiski 43–45. Mail takes much longer to reach the islands—especially those without airports. Take along your passport when you go to claim your mail.

From Greece, air-mail letters generally take 5 to 8 days to reach Europe and 8 to 10 days for the U.S.A. (Postcards take a bit longer.) For details on express mail service, phone (01) 3214.609.

Telegrams and telephone (*tilegráfima; tiléfono*). You will need to locate the Greek Telecommunications Organization Office (OTE) in your vicinity. There is at least one branch office on every island and in all the principal towns on the mainland. This is where you can send cables and telexes and make local and international phone calls. The telephone system is very advanced, but at peak hours the international lines can get busy and you may have to wait. You can dial direct to most parts of the world and make reverse-charge (collect) calls.

Calling from a public phone booth costs very little for a local call. Blue booths are for domestic calls only and yellow ones, with instructions in English, are linked to the international dialling system. To call Athens from outside the city, dial first the area code, 01.

The OTE in Athens, at Patisíon 85, provides 24-hour service. The main OTE office in Thessaloniki is at Ermoú 48.

For international calls, dial first the country's number, then the area code and the subscriber's number. Some country codes:

Australia	0061
Austria	0043
Belgium	0032
Canada	001
Denmark	0045
Eire	00353
Finland	00358
India	0091
Japan	0081
Netherlands	0031
New Zealand	0064
Norway	0047
Singapore	0065
South Africa	0027
Sweden	0046
Switzerland	0041
United Kingdom	0044
United States	001
West Germany	0049

Other services:

Directory information	131
OTE general information	134
International telegrams	165
Operator (domestic)	151
Operator (international)	162
Instructions for international calls	169
Information for international calls	161

Where's the nearest post office?	**Pou íne to kodinótero tachidromío?**
A stamp for this letter/postcard, please.	**Éna grammatósimo giaftó to grámma/ kart postál, parakaló.**
express	**exprés**
airmail	**aeroporikós**
registered	**sistiméno**
I want to send a telegram to...	**Thélo na stílo éna tilegráfima sto...**
Can you get me this number in...?	**Boríte na mou párete aftó ton arithmó...?**
person-to-person	**prosopikí klísi**
Have you any mail for...?	**Échete grámmata giá..?**

COMPLAINTS *(parápono)*

Your hotel manager, the owner of the establishment in question or your travel agency representative should be your first recourse for complaints. If you aren't satisfied, the local Tourist Police will be very interested to hear of any problems—or phone 3223.111, a service for tourist complaints. Most times, just mentioning the name Tourist Police should get results. If you do need to make a complaint on the premises, try to do so with a smile and avoid losing your temper. There's no point getting angry about mysterious cancellations or postponements of bus, boat or even flight departures on the islands— schedules are largely theoretical.

CONSULATES *(proxenío)*

Contact the consulate of your home country if things go *seriously* wrong—for example, if you lose your passport, get in trouble with the police, or have an accident. The Consul can issue emergency passports, give advice on obtaining money from home, provide a list of lawyers, interpreters and doctors. He cannot pay your bills, lend you money, find you a job or obtain a work permit for you.

Australia. Dimitríou Soútsou 37, Athens; tel. (01)644.303

Canada. Gennadíou 4/Ipsilántou, Athens; tel. (01)7239.511

Denmark. Filikís Eterías 15, Athens; tel. (01)7249.315-7

Eire. Vass. Konstantínou 7, Athens; tel. (01)7232.771

Finland. Eratosthénous 1/Vass. Konstantínou, Athens; tel. (01)7519.795/7011.775

India. Meleágrou 4, Athens; tel. (01) 7216.227/7216.481

Japan. Messoghíon 2–4, Athens; tel. (01) 7758.101-3

Netherlands. Vass. Konstantínou 5–7, Athens; tel. (01)7239.701-4/7235.159

New Zealand: An. Tsócha 15–17, Ambelokípi; tel. (01)6410.311

Norway: Vass. Konstantínou 7, Athens; tel. (01)7246.173-4

South Africa: Kifisías 124, Athens; tel. (01) 6922.236/6922.125

Sweden. Vass. Konstantínou 7, Athens; tel. (01)7224.504-5

U.K. Ploutárchou 1/Ipsilántou, Athens; tel. (01)7236.211

Vódzi 2, Patras; tel. (061)277.329

Venizélou 8, Thessaloniki; tel. (031)278.006

Thessaloníkis 45, Kavala; tel. (051)223.704

Alexándras 10, Corfu Town; tel. (0661) 30.055/emergency 39.211

25 Martíou 23, Rhodes Town; tel. (0241) 272.47/219.54

U.S.A.: Vass. Sofías 91, Athens; tel. (01) 7212.951

COURTESIES

The simple courtesies mean a lot in Greece and not only win friends but smooth your way. Greek hospitality is sincere and generous—at times it can even be overwhelming. Whatever you do, don't refuse it. When a taxi driver offers a cigarette, it's polite to accept, unless, of course, you're a nonsmoker. He's not looking for a tip, it's just his way of extending a welcome. Don't turn down an offer of coffee and the inevitable glass of water unless it's obvious somebody is trying to sell you something.

Should you find yourself in a Greek home, particularly in a village, expect to be lavishly plied with both food and drink—and don't feel embarrassed if you are the only person served while your hostess looks on, it's a traditional expression of hospitality.

Greeks, in common with most continental Europeans, wish each other "bon appétit" before starting a meal. In Greek, the expression is *kalí órexi!* A common toast when drinking is *stin igía sas!* meaning "Cheers!". A reply to any toast, *epísis!* means "the same to you".

Staring isn't considered rude in Greece. On the contrary, it's a way of passing a compliment or satisfying curiosity (a common Greek trait), and it means no harm at all. Don't be surprised if you're asked personal questions about the size of your family or how much you earn—it's simply the Greeks' genuine interest at work.

Photography can be a joy; Greeks love to have their picture taken, but don't forget to ask permission first.

A major "don't": avoid showing or waving your hand with the palm out. Greeks call this gesture *moúntsa,* and it is considered offensive.

Like the Spanish *mañana,* the Greek *ávrio* does not necessarily mean tomorrow but, rather, soon. Learn to take your time and smile. You won't improve matters by rushing or getting upset.

CRIME AND THEFT *(églima; klopí)*

See also EMERGENCY and POLICE. You'll be glad to know that crime is very rare in Greece. If you've left something in a shop or restaurant, the proprietor is sure to do his best to find it. Honesty is a matter of pride among the Greeks. Yet it's only common sense to lock up your valuables and watch your handbag in crowds—not necessarily because of the local people, but perhaps because of your fellow-tourists...

I want to report a theft.	**Thélo na katangílo mía klopí.**

CUSTOMS AND ENTRY REGULATIONS

Visitors from EEC countries only need an identity card to enter Greece. Citizens of other countries must be in possession of a valid passport. A stay of up to three months is permitted to all citizens of English-speaking countries. To extend your stay you must apply to the police two weeks before your time runs out. Though European and North American residents are not subject to any health requirements,

	Cigarettes		Cigars		Tobacco		Spirits			Wine	Perfume	Eau de Cologne	Coffee	Tea
1)	300	or	75	or	400 g.		1½ l.	and	5 l.	75 g.	⅜ l.	1,000 g.	200 g.
2)	200	or	50	or	250 g.		1 l.	or	2 l.	50 g.	¼ l.	500 g.	100 g.
3)	400	or	100	or	500 g.								

1) Residents of a European country with VAT-paid items bought inside the EEC.
2) Residents of a European country with items bought outside the EEC, or duty-free goods bought inside the EEC.
3) Residents of a country outside Europe. For other allowances, see 1) or 2), whichever applies.

visitors from other places may need a smallpox vaccination. Check with your travel agent before departure.

If you need more information concerning permission to stay in Greece, ask your local Greek consulate or contact the following service:

Athens Alien's Bureau,
Alexándras 173, Athens
Tel. 7705.711

The chart at the bottom of page 281 shows the major customs allowances for Greece. For what you can bring back home, ask before your departure for the customs form setting out allowances.

Certain prescription drugs, including tranquillizers and headache preparations, cannot be carried into the country without a prescription or official medical document. Fines, and even jail sentences, have been imposed.

In addition to personal clothing, you may take into Greece a camera and a reasonable amount of film, a pair of binoculars, a typewriter, a radio, a tape recorder, musical instrument and sports equipment, including a surfboard which should be declared when you enter the country.

Currency restrictions: Foreign visitors to Greece can bring up to 100,000 drachmas into the country and leave with no more than 20,000 drs, in denominations of up to 5,000 drs. There is no limit on foreign currency or traveller's cheques you may import or export as a tourist, though amounts in excess of $1,000 should be declared.

I've nothing to declare.	**Den écho na dilóso típota.**
It's for my personal use.	**Íne giá prosopikí chrísi.**

DRIVING IN GREECE

To bring your car into Greece you'll need car registration papers, nationality plate or sticker, International Driving Permit (not required for British motorists) and insurance coverage (the Green Card is no longer compulsory within the EEC but comprehensive coverage is advisable). The Motor Insurance Bureau can give you details concerning the Greek representatives of foreign insurance companies and other information for coverage in Greece. It's located at:

Xenofóndos 10, Athens
Tel. 3236.733

When you enter Greece with your car it will be noted in your passport, and you won't be able to leave the country without your vehicle unless you go through a lengthy procedure to get a special paper withdrawing it from circulation. So selling your car in Greece is not an option, and leaving it there, for whatever reason, will involve some paperwork.

The standard European red warning triangle is required in Greece for emergencies. Seat belts are obligatory. Motorcycle drivers and their passengers must wear helmets.

Drive on the right and pass on the left. The Greeks have a bad habit of not always returning to the near-side lane, and of passing on the right or left without warning.

The motorways (expressways) are good. Tolls are charged according to distance. But on secondary roads, you can expect anything—poor banking, wandering livestock (donkeys, goats and flocks of sheep), bumps, potholes, falling rocks, surprise curves and, naturally, Greek drivers, who range from reasonable to totally unpredictable. Don't hesitate to use your horn when rounding blind corners—the Greeks blast away and expect you to do the same. The island roads are often unsurfaced, and like the other narrow, winding roads found throughout all of Greece, demand special caution and attention.

In Athens, the government has introduced restrictions on driving in an effort to cut down on pollution in the city centre. These apply to local vehicles, including rental cars. On odd-numbered days, cars with odd-numbered license plates can circulate, while even-numbered days are reserved for cars with even-numbered licence plates. These restrictions are in force between 6 a.m. and 8 p.m. weekdays.

Breakdowns. The **Automobile Association of Greece (ELPA)** offers tourist information and breakdown assistance, which is free for minor repairs. The patrol network covers all the major highways of the mainland. Their vehicles bear the sign: "OVELPA"/"Assistance Routière ATCC"/ "Road Assistance". If you have a rental car, get in touch with the company which hired you the car.

Tourist information:	tel. 174
24-hour road assistance:	tel. 104

Fuel and Oil. While service stations are generally plentiful, the supply of petrol (gasoline) may be less than adequate. Fill up wherever possible, even if the tank is already half-full. Most petrol stations close at 7 p.m. or earlier (especially on weekends); only a few stay open in turns after that hour.

You can get normal petrol (84–86 octane), super (92–95), lead-free *(amólivdos)* and diesel.

Road signs. Most road signs are the standard pictographs used throughout Europe. However, you may encounter the following written signs in Greece:

No through road	ΑΔΙΕΞΟΔΟΣ
Stop	ΑΛΤ
Bad road surface	ΑΝΩΜΑΛΙΑ ΟΔΟΣΤΡΩΜΑΤΟΣ
No waiting	ΑΠΑΓΟΡΕΥΕΤΑΙ Η ΑΝΑΜΟΝΗ
No entry	ΑΠΑΓΟΡΕΥΕΤΑΙ Η ΕΙΣΟΔΟΣ
No parking	ΑΠΑΓΟΡΕΥΕΤΑΙ Η ΣΤΑΘΜΕΥΣΙΣ
Pedestrian crossing	ΔΙΑΒΑΣΙΣ ΠΕΖΩΝ
Reduce speed	ΕΛΑΤΤΩΣΑΤΕ ΤΑΧΥΤΗΤΑΝ
Dangerous incline	ΕΠΙΚΙΝΔΥΝΟΣ ΚΑΤΩΦΕΡΕΙΑ
Roadworks in progress	ΕΡΓΑ ΕΠΙ ΤΗΣ ΟΔΟΥ
Caution	ΚΙΝΔΥΝΟΣ
One-way traffic	ΜΟΝΟΔΡΟΜΟΣ
Diversion (Detour)	ΠΑΡΑΚΑΜΠΤΗΡΙΟΣ
Cyclists	ΠΟΔΗΛΑΤΑΙ
Keep right	ΠΟΡΕΙΑ ΥΠΟΧΡΕΩΤΙΚΗ ΔΕΞΙΑ
Bus stop	ΣΤΑΣΙΣ ΛΕΩΦΟΡΕΙΟΥ

The following phrases may be useful:

(International) Driving Licence	**(diethnís) ádia odigíseos**
car registration	**adía kikloforías**
Green Card	**asfáli aftokinítu**
Are we on the right road for...?	**Ímaste sto sostó drómo giá?**

Full tank, please.	**Na to gemísete me venzíni.**
normal/super	**aplí/soúper**
Check the oil/tyres/battery.	**Na elénxete ta ládia/ta lásticha/ ti bataría.**
My car has broken down.	**Épatha mía vlávi.**
There's been an accident.	**Égine éna dstíchima.**

ELECTRIC CURRENT

The general rule is 220-volt, 50-cycle A.C. current. Sockets are either two- or three-pin. If you bring your own electrical appliances, you'd better bring an international adaptor, which are hard to find in island shops (though major hotels may occasionally provide them).

EMERGENCIES

Except in out-of-the-way places, you'll usually find someone who speaks English who will be able to help you. But if you're by yourself and near a phone, here are some important numbers to remember:

All over Greece:

Police/Emergencies	100
Fire	199
Road assistance	104
Tourist Police	171

Depending on the nature of the emergency, see also CONSULATES and POLICE. And here are a few words we hope you'll never need to use:

Careful!	**Prosochí!**
Fire!	**Fotiá!**
Help!	**Voíthia!**
Stop!	**Stamatíste!**

GETTING TO GREECE

Because of the complexity and incredible variety of choices and fares, you should ask the advice of an informed travel agent well before your departure. For communi-cations between the islands, see ISLAND-HOPPING.

By Air
Scheduled flights. Athens is served by in-tercontinental routes from the entire world. Although there are also services to the ma-jor islands and other regions of Greece from most European airports, most flights are routed via Athens.

By asking around a bit, you'll find nu-merous ways to get a lower price than the standard airfare, such as APEX, stand-by, etc. This is especially true for British and Australian travellers. Coming from North America you may not find many bargain flights directly to Athens unless you are flying from New York City or perhaps Montreal. It's worth getting a cheap flight to a major European city and going on to Greece from there.

Charters and package tours. There are liter-ally hundreds of package tours available, with flight/hotel arrangements often com-bining mainland Greece with one or more of the islands. Consider different types of package or "theme" tours such as the "Wanderer" holiday for the traveller plan-ning a walking tour, using vouchers for accommodation in inexpensive lodgings.

Charter flights can be the least expensive way to fly into Greece, but these tickets must meet many different conditions, so you should check them carefully. From North America, in addition to the econom-ical charter flights arranged by clubs or associations, low-cost air travel is now available to the public at large. The least expensive is the Advance Booking Charter (ABC), which must be reserved and paid for a number of weeks in advance.

By Road
At fares only slightly lower than some air tickets, express coach service operates be-tween London and Athens, a long, hard trip taking about three days, compared to three hours by plane.

For most motorists, the preferred itiner-ary from northern Europe is via Brussels, Munich, Belgrade and Niš to Thessaloniki in northern Greece, about 3,250 kilometres (over 2,000 miles). You can reduce time by loading yourself onto an auto-train for part of the journey (expensive), or by driv-ing through France and Italy and taking one of the Italy–Greece ferries for the final stage of the trip. Car ferries operate fre-quently in summer. The most popular routes are Brindisi–Patras and Venice–Pa-tras. A service is also available from Tou-lon, France to Patras.

By Rail
There are two main routes from Paris (al-though a number of variations are pos-sible). The cheaper route is via the Simplon Pass in Switzerland, Venice, Ljubljana, Bel-grade and Thessaloniki. The other route, which is more interesting, goes via Bolog-na, Brindisi and Patras, with the ferry crossing included in the fare. Both trips take about 2 or 3 days with few stops along the way.

Young people under 26 can buy an *Inter-Rail Card* which allows one month of un-limited 2nd-class travel on all participating European railways. Senior citizens can ob-tain a *Rail Europ Senior* card which allows a 50% reduction. Anyone living outside Europe and North Africa can purchase a *Eurailpass* before leaving home; it permits unlimited 1st-class rail travel in 16 Europe-an countries, including Greece. People in-tending to undertake a lot of rail travel once in Greece (not particularly recom-mended since the trains are rather slow) might want to buy a *Greek Tourist Card* which is available for unlimited 2nd-class travel on the Greek railways.

By Sea
Most travellers use the ferries which link Greece to Italy. The usual points of cross-ing are from Brindisi in the south of Italy to Patras (16 hours) for those heading to Athens or the Peloponnese; Igoumenitsa (11 hours), destination central or western Greece; or Corfu (9 hours). Less regular but also feasible are ferries from Ancona, Bari, and Venice as well as from Zadar or Rijeka in Yugoslavia.

From North America, cargo/passenger services are available to Piraeus in Greece. Departures are approximately three to four times per month with dates and ports of call subject to cargo requirements. Booking should be made well in advance. You might also consider taking one of the Mediterra-nean cruises with Greek ports included in their itinerary.

There are cargo/passenger services from Southampton to Piraeus, the journey last-ing about 10 days.

GUIDES AND INTERPRETERS
(xenagós; dierminéas)

Guides from the tour agencies accompany groups to various sites. If you want a personal guide you should enquire at the tourist office or in an agency. In Athens, bilingual, licensed guides to all the museums and sites are available through the guides' association:

Somateion Xenagón, Apolónos 9a
Tel. 3229.705

We'd like an English-speaking guide.	**Tha thélame éna xenagó na milá i angliká.**

HAIRDRESSERS AND BARBERS

The hairdressers (ΚΟΜΜΩΤΗΡΙΟ—*kommotírio*) and barbers (ΚΟΥΡΕΙΟ—*kourío*) in Greece are amiable, but don't expect them to be fast. Tip 10–15 %.

I'd like a...	**Thélo...**
shampoo and set	**loúsimo ke miz-en-pli**
haircut	**koúrema**
blow-dry	**chténisma me to pistoláki**
permanent wave	**permanád**
colour rinse	**mía dekolorasión**
manicure	**manikioúr**
Don't cut it too short.	**Mi ta kópsete kondá.**
A little more off here.	**Lígo pió kondá edó.**

HEALTH AND MEDICAL CARE

It is sensible to take out health insurance covering the risk of illness or accident while you're on holiday. Your insurance representative or travel agent at home will be able to advise you best. On the spot, you can turn to a Greek insurance company for coverage corresponding to your requirements and length of stay. Emergency treatment is free, but the system can be complicated, and in any case, if you have an insurance you'll get better medical care. British citizens are entitled to the same health cover as the Greeks, but they should apply to the Department of Health and Social Security for a special form before leaving the U.K.

The two main health hazards are sunburn and minor stomach upsets. Work on your suntan gradually, using a strong sunfilter cream and avoiding the midday sun. Wear a hat and sunglasses. Moderation in eating and drinking should help ease you into the change of diet; any serious problems lasting more than a day or so require a doctor's attention.

If mosquitoes are a nuisance, buy an inflammable coil called *Katól*, which will keep them out of your bedroom. If you should step on a sea urchin, apply lemon juice or olive oil. A jellyfish sting can be relieved by ammonia, but see a doctor if there's severe swelling.

Bring a reasonable supply of your personal medications and favourite remedies in case they aren't available here (see under CUSTOMS for regulations concerning prescription drugs).

Pharmacies (ΦΑΡΜΑΚΕΙΟ—*farmakío*). These are easily recognized by the sign—a red cross on a white background. Outside normal hours, pharmacists take turns offering a 24-hour service. (The address of the pharmacist on duty is posted on all pharmacy doors.) They can generally give advice on minor problems such as cuts, sunburn, blisters, throat infections and gastric disorders.
See also EMERGENCY and POLICE.

Where's the nearest (all-night) pharmacy?	**Pou íne to kodinótero (dianikterévon) farmakío?**
I need a/an...	**Chriázome éna...**
doctor	**giatró**
dentist	**odontogiatró**
ambulance	**asthenofóro**
hospital	**nosokomío**
Sunstroke	**Ilíasi**
Fever	**Piretós**
Upset stomach	**Varistomachiá**

HITCH-HIKING (oto-stop)

In a country where human contact is valued, it is considered perfectly normal to give someone a lift. You can rest assured that it's generally safe, even for women, so unless you're pressed for time it can be a fine way to see the country. Rides are short but frequent, and hitch-hiking often ends up being faster than other means of transport.

Can you give me/us a lift to...?	Boríte na me/mas páte méchri to...?

ISLAND-HOPPING

A guideline to help you get to all the islands mentioned in this book (but remember these details are subject to change). The list is not exhaustive. The number of flight departures decreases in winter—consult the Olympic Airways timetable for details. See also TRANSPORT, and page 39.

Aegina: frequent ferries from Piraeus (15 daily in summer).

Alonnisos: regular boat service from Agios Konstantinos and Volos on the mainland via Skiathos and Skopelos. Direct service to Kymi on Euboea.

Amorgos: ferries from Naxos via Iraklion, Schinussa, Kufonision and Keros, or via Donussa. Direct link with Astypalaea.

Andros: ferries from Rafina and Tinos.

Antipaxi: see Paxi

Astypalaea: regular links with Amorgos and Kalymnos.

Cephalonia: ferries from Corfu via Paxi and Ithaca; from Igoumenitsa, Patras, or Piraeus through Corinth Canal. Weekly ferry to Paxi.

Direct flights to and from Athens, Corfu and Zakynthos.

Chalki: ferries stop twice a week—one on the way to Rhodes, one to Karpathos, Kasos and Crete.

Chios: ferries from Piraeus, Samos, Lesbos; boats to Turkey.

Direct flights to and from Athens, Mykonos, Lesbos and Samos.

Corfu: overnight car-ferry service from Brindisi, Italy. Ferries to Patras, Igoumenitsa, Piraeus (22 hours), Paxi, Ithaca, Cephalonia.

Direct flights to and from Athens, Cephalonia, Zakynthos.

Crete: several ferries daily from Piraeus. Daily car ferry from Piraeus to Iraklion, and from Piraeus to Chania. Boats to Santorini, Patmos and Rhodes.

Direct flights from Athens to Iraklion and Chania. Flights from Iraklion to Athens, Mykonos, Paros, Rhodes, Thessaloni-

ki and Santorini, and from Chania to Athens and Thessaloniki.

Delos: motor launch from Mykonos, when the sea isn't too choppy. In summer, excursions from Tinos, Naxos and Paros, several times weekly.

Hydra: four ferries daily from Piraeus via Aegina, Methana and Poros (going on to Spetses).

Ios: ferries from Piraeus to Santorini and Crete stop in Ios. Frequent connections to Naxos, Santorini and Paros. One or two boats daily to Mykonos and Tinos. Several boats weekly to Sifnos, Serifos, Sikinos and Folegandros.

Ithaca: ferry from Vasiliki on Lefkas to Frikes via Fiscardo on Cephalonia, or from Astakos on mainland to Vathi, continuing to Agia Efimia on Cephalonia.

Kalymnos: frequent motor launch connection with Kos. The weekly north–south Dodecanese ferry stops at Kalymnos.

Karpathos: ferries from Piraeus via Crete twice weekly. Three ferries per week from Rhodes. Weekly ferry to Kasos, Crete, Santorini and Piraeus.

Flights to and from Rhodes and Kasos.

Kos: daily ferries to Rhodes and Piraeus; daily except Mondays to Kalymnos, Leros and Patmos. Excursion boats make day trips to Kalymnos, Pserimos, Patmos, Astypalaea and Nisyros.

Flights to and from Athens, Leros, Rhodes, Samos, Thessaloniki.

Kythira: ferries from Neapolis. Daily flights to and from Athens.

Lefkas: ferries from Nidri and Vasiliki to Frikes on Ithaca and Fiskardo and Sami on Cephalonia.

Lesbos: ferry connections with Piraeus, Limnos and Chios, as well as the Turkish mainland.

Direct flights to and from Athens, Iraklion, Thessaloniki, Limnos, Chios, Samos and Rhodes.

Limnos: ferry connections with Kavala (direct or via Samothrace), Kymi on Euboea, Agios Konstantinos, and with Piraeus via Chios and Leros.

Flights to and from Athens, Thessaloniki and Lesbos.

Mykonos: passenger ferries operate from Piraeus and Rafina. Connections with Naxos and Santorini. Practically every Aegean cruise ship calls for several hours.

Small plane and helicopter charter from Athens. Flights to and from Athens, Santorini, Iraklion, Lesbos, Samos, Chios and Rhodes.

Naxos: ferries from Piraeus and Rafina. Day trips in summer to Paros, Mykonos, Delos, Tinos, Ios, Santorini.

Paros: ferries from Piraeus and Rafina via Syros, with onward connections to Naxos, Ios, Santorini, Crete. Excursions to Delos and Mykonos. Day trips to Naxos.

Flights to and from Athens, Iraklion and Rhodes.

Patmos: ferry connections with Piraeus, Samos, Lipsos, Leros, Kalymnos, Kos, Rhodes. Weekly north–south Dodecanese ferry. Hydrofoil service to Rhodes and Leros. Excursions to Ikaria, Samos and Lipsos.

Paxi: ferries from Corfu and Parga on the mainland. Links with Cephalonia and Lefkas. Excursions from Corfu to Paxi and Antipaxi.

Poros: several ferries and hydrofoils from Piraeus daily. One boat daily for Hydra and Spetses.

Rhodes: ferries from Piraeus and Iraklion. Daily ferries from Rhodes to Kos, Leros, Kalymnos and Patmos; twice weekly to Symi, Tilos and Nisiros. One ferry per week to Santorini; two to Paros.

Flights to and from Athens, Iraklion, Karpathos, Kasos, Kos, Mykonos, Lesbos, Paros, Thessaloniki, Santorini.

Samos: passenger ferries from Piraeus via the Cyclades, plus boats to Chios, Patmos and Ikaria. Hydrofoils to Rhodes and Kos. Regular ferry service to Kusadasi, Turkey.

Flights to and from Athens, Chios, Kos, Mykonos, Lesbos, Thessaloniki.

Samothrace: ferries from Alexandroupoli on the mainland, plus some boats from Kavala on routes including stops in the Sporades, Agios Konstantinos and Kymi.

Nearest airport is at Alexandroupoli, linked by scheduled flight to Athens.

Santorini: passenger ferries from Piraeus, some continuing on to Crete. Excursions by boat in season to Anafi, Folegandros, Ios, Amorgos, Iraklion and Rethymnon.

Flights to and from Athens, Iraklion, Rhodes and Mykonos.

Sifnos: ferry service from Piraeus, plus connections to Paros, Kimolos, Milos and Serifos. Occasional boats to Kithnos and Syros.

Skiathos: regular passenger ferries from Volos, Agios Konstantinos and Kymi link Skiathos with the other Sporades. Also ferries to Skyros. Seasonal motor launch excursions to Skopelos and Alonnisos.

Flights to and from Athens and Thessaloniki.

Skopelos: daily boat service to and from Skiathos and Alonnisos as part of regular Sporades runs from the mainland and Euboea. Daily hydrofoil service from Volos and Agios Konstantinos.

Skyros: regular boat service from Kymi on Euboea with bus connections from and to Athens.

Flights to and from Athens (max. 16-seater plane).

Spetses: ferry from Piraeus every day except Sunday, via Aegina, Methana, Poros, Hydra and Ermioni.

Symi: two ferries weekly from Rhodes.

Thasos: frequent passenger ferries from Kavala and Keramoti.

Tinos: passenger ferries connect Tinos with Piraeus, Rafina and Mykonos. Day trips by motor launch to Mykonos, Delos, Naxos and Paros.

Zakynthos: ferries from Killini—seven per day in summer, five per day off-season.

Flights to and from Athens, Cephalonia, Corfu.

LANGUAGE

Many Greeks have relatives abroad or have worked in Germany, Australia or the U.S.A., so they often speak English or German, and some know French as well. Still, you will certainly meet Greeks who speak only their own language. To help you communicate, you might find the Berlitz phrase book *Greek for Travellers* useful; it covers most of the situations you'll encounter.

The Greeks themselves actually have two languages—classical *katharévousa,* until recently the language of the courts and parliament and still used by a few conservative newspapers, and *dimotikí,* the spoken language and now also the official one. This is what you'll hear in Greece today.

There are a number of different ways of transliterating Greek into English; in this book, for the names of towns and islands, we have used the English spellings that seemed the most familiar—Athens, Piraeus, Mykonos, Lesbos, and so on—with an occasional Greek transcription when the Greek name differs considerably from the English. Corfu, for example, is known to the Greeks as *Kerkíra*. The stress mark on Greek words indicates the syllable that should be emphasized.

Try to learn the Greek alphabet before you leave home—you'll find it invaluable for deciphering signposts (always written in capital letters). See the sections ALPHABET, USEFUL EXPRESSIONS and VOCABULARY.

MAPS *(chártis)*

The EOT provides free, simple maps of various parts of the country. These are also available at hotel reception desks and in many kiosks and shops. Sometimes those found in the kiosks tend to exaggerate the quality of the roads and the number of beaches. The road maps in this book were prepared by Hallwag, Bern.

I'd like a street map of...	Tha íthela éna odikó chárti tou...
a road map of the region	éna chárti aftís tis periochís

MONEY MATTERS

Currency. Greece's monetary unit is the drachma (*drachmi,* abbreviated drs.—in Greek, Δρχ).

Coins: 1, 2, 5, 10, 20, 50 drs.

Banknotes: 50, 100, 500, 1,000, 5,000 drs.

For currency restrictions, see CUSTOMS AND ENTRY REGULATIONS.

Banks (ΤΡΑΠΕΖΑ—*trapéza*). Hours vary slightly, but in general banks are open from 8.30 a.m. to 2 p.m., Monday to Thursday, and until 1.30 p.m. on Fridays. In Athens, the Syntagma branch of the National Bank of Greece is open from 8 a.m. to 9 p.m. Monday to Friday, and from 8 a.m. to 8 p.m. on Saturdays, Sunday and public holidays. You can change foreign currency in most major hotels, but the banks give the best exchange rates. Always take your passport when you want to change money.

Credit cards and travellers cheques *(pistotikí karta; "traveller's cheque")*. Internationally known credit cards are honoured in most shops (indicated by a sign in the window) and by all banks, car hire firms and leading hotels. Traveller's cheques, widely accepted, are best cashed at a bank (remember to take your passport). Cash cards don't work—instead of paying out money, the machines have a nasty tendency to swallow up the cards fed into them.

You might be able to pay for goods in some places with foreign currency, but it's less hassle for everybody if you pay in drachmas.

I want to change some pounds/dollars.	Thélo na alláxo merikés líres/dollária.
Do you accept credit cards/traveller's cheques?	Pérnete pistotikí kárta/traveller's cheques?

NEWSPAPERS and MAGAZINES *(efimerída; periodikó)*

Most foreign dailies—including the principal British newspapers and the Paris-based *International Herald Tribune*—appear on news-stands the day following publication. There is a good selection of foreign magazines from most European countries. On the islands, supply is tailored to demand, and in summer on the more frequented islands, you'll find a good pick of European periodicals and the major American weekly news magazines. Off-season there are few if any non-Greek publications on sale around the islands.

There is an English-language daily newspaper, the *Athens News*, and a monthly magazine in English, *The Athenian*, which has a comprehensive listing of restaurants, nightclubs, cinemas and theatres in the capital, and a directory of useful phone numbers. The NTOG issues *The Week in Athens* free of charge.

Have you any English-language newspapers?	Échete anglikés efimerídes?

PHOTOGRAPHY

A photo shop is advertised by the sign ΦΩΤΟΓΡΑΦΕΙΟ *(fotografío)*. Major brands of colour and black-and-white film are widely available but are not a bargain, so it's best to bring film with you and take it home for processing. Polaroid film is difficult to find. Don't leave film in your car—it will be ruined by the heat.

Hand-held cameras may be used in some museums and at archaeological sites for a slight charge. For security reasons, it is illegal to use a telephoto lens aboard an aircraft flying over Greece.

I'd like some film for this camera.	**Tha íthila éna film giaftí ti michaní.**
black-and-white film	**asprómavro film**
colour film	**énchromo film**
colour slides	**énchromo film giá sláids**
35-mm film	**éna film triánda pénde milimétr**
super-8	**soúper-októ**
May I take a picture?	**Boró na páro mía fotografía?**

POLICE *(astinomía)*

Policemen wear blue uniforms. The tourist police *(touristikí astinomía)* is a special branch whose job it is to help foreign visitors personally and to inspect hotels and restaurants to ensure that proper standards and prices are maintained. The flags sewn on their jackets indicate which foreign languages they speak.

The tourist police in Athens is on duty 24 hours a day (phone **171**). Other numbers are listed below (an asterisk refers to the regular police):

Aegina	22-391
Alonnisos*	65-205
Chania	24-477
Chios	22-581
Corfu	30-265
Corinth	23-282
Delphi	82-200
Iraklion	283-190
Hydra	52-205
Igoumenitsa	22-302
Ioannina	25-673
Kalymnos*	28-302
Kastoria	22-696
Kavala	222-905
Kos	28-227

Larissa	227-900
Lefkas	92-389
Lesbos	22-776
Limnos	22-200
Missolonghi	22-555
Mykonos	22-482
Nafplio	27-776
Naxos*	22-100
Paros	21-673
Patmos*	31-303
Patras	220-902
Piraeus	4523-670
Poros	22-462
Rethymnon	28-156
Rhodes	27-423
Samos	27-980
Santorini*	22-649
Sifnos*	31-210
Skiathos	22-005
Skopelos*	22-235
Skyros	81-274
Sparta	28-701
Spetses	73-100
Thasos	22-500
Thessaloniki	522-589
Tinos	22-255
Volos	27-094
Vouliagmeni	8946-555
Zakynthos	22-550

Where's the nearest police station?	**Pou íne kodinótero astinomikó tmíma?**

PUBLIC HOLIDAYS *(argíes)*

Banks, offices and shops are closed on the following national holidays:

January 1	*Protochroniá*	New Year's Day
January 6	*ton Theofanion*	Epiphany
March 25	*Ikostí Pémti Martíou*	Greek Independence Day
May 1	*Protomagiá*	May Day

August 15	*Dekapendávgoustos (tis Panagías)*	Assumption Day
October 28	*Ikostí Ogdóï Oktovríou*	"No" Day
December 25	*Christoúgenna*	Christmas Day
December 26	*Défteri iméra ton Christoúgennon*	St. Stephen's Day
Movable dates:	*Katharí Deftéra*	First day of Lent: Clean Monday
	Megáli Paraskeví	Good Friday
	Deftéra tou Páscha	Easter Monday

In addition to these nationwide holidays, Athens celebrates its patron saint's day—*tou Agíou Dionisíou* (St. Dionysios the Areopagite) on October 3—as a legal holiday.

Note: The dates on which the movable holy days are celebrated often differ from those in Catholic and Protestant countries.

Are you open tomorrow?	**Échete aniktá ávrio?**

RADIO and TV *(rádio; tileórasi)*

The Greek National Radio (ERT) broadcasts the news and weather in English in the morning, afternoon and evening.

On short-wave bands, reception of the World Service of the BBC is extremely clear. Voice of America's English programmes are also easily picked up.

Most hotels, and some bars and restaurants have TV lounges. Many of the programmes are well-known series in English with Greek subtitles.

RELIGIOUS SERVICES

The national church is the Greek Orthodox. Visitors of certain other faiths will be able to attend services (in Greek, unless otherwise mentioned) at the following places:

Catholic
St. Denis, Venizélou 24, Athens. Mass in Latin.
Ágios Iákovos, Platía Dimarchíou, Corfu Town.

Catholic churches of Iraklion, Patros Antoniou, Chania, Chalidon, Rethmnon and Agios Nikolaos, Crete.
St. Mary's, Kathopoúli, Rhodes. Mass in Latin and English.
Frángon 39, Thessaloniki.

Protestant
St. Paul's, Filellínon 29, Athens. Services in English.
St. Andrew's, Sína 66, Athens. Services in English.
Holy Trinity Church, Mavíli 21, Corfu Town. Services in English.
Konst. Paleológou 6, Thessaloniki.

Jewish
Beth Shalom Synagogue, Melikóni 5, Athens. Services in English.
Synagogue, Odós Paleológou, Corfu Town.
Sholom Synagogue, Dosiádou, near Platía Evréon Martíron, Rhodes.
The Jewish Club, Tsimiskí 24, Thessaloniki.

Some of the smaller islands also have Catholic churches.

RESTAURANTS

See also page 261. Dining in Greece is often outdoors and is a simple, honest affair without frills or pretension unless you're in one of the fancier establishments.

Eateries are divided into four categories (Deluxe, A, B, C), and the prices are government-controlled except in the deluxe restaurants. Most widespread are the tavernas where you'll find basic Greek food, grilled and roasted favourites, though not always a menu. It's quite acceptable to go straight to the kitchen to see what's cooking and decide then and there what you'd like. *Olígo*, meaning "just a little", will get you a half portion. It's best to fix on prices at this time, especially if there's no menu.

In restaurants *(éstiatório)*, service and food may be a bit more formal than the tavernas, with more choice of the grilled and baked specialities of Greece. But again, don't expect elegant, sophisticated dining except in the deluxe establishments. In the tourist centres, the menus often have quaint English translations.

Hours for eating follow the dictates of the sun, so expect to dine later than usual.

For lunch the restaurants and tavernas are open as early as noon but don't get crowded until about 2 p.m. A long siesta follows. Dinner is usually eaten at around 9 p.m. or so, though it's possible to be served from 7.30 p.m. on. And don't be surprised to see diners lingering long after midnight, as most places stay open until 2 a.m.

Breakfast, which for most Greeks is a basic affair of coffee, sometimes with bread and butter, might be more fun if you head for a *zacharoplastío,* a pastry shop with a wonderful pick of pastries and cakes.

To help you order...	
Could we have a table?	**Tha boroúsamena échoume éna trapézi?**
I'd like a/an/some...	**Tha íthela...**
beer	**mía bíra**
coffee	**éna kafé**
milk	**gála**
tea	**éna tsáï**
(ice) water	**(pagoméno) neró**
mineral water	**metallikó neró**
wine	**krasí**
meat	**kréas**
fish	**psári**
potatoes	**patátes**
rice	**rízi**
salad	**mía saláta**
soup	**mía soúpa**
dessert	**éna glikó**
bread	**psomí**
sugar	**záchari**
cutlery	**macheropírouna**
a glass	**éna potíri**

SIESTA

From approximately 2.00 to 5.00 p.m., most activity ceases as the Greeks honour the sensible and venerable Mediterranean tradition of the siesta. In the heat of the afternoon, tourists will find this a pleasant habit to adopt. Most shops and businesses close, so apart from napping or sunning on the beach, there's not much else to do.

SIGHTSEEING TOURS

Agencies on the mainland as well as on the islands organize tours ranging from half-day trips to one-week tours. It's best to ask your local travel agent or the NTOG for suggestions of typical circuits. You can also contact the Association of Greek Tour Operators (AGTO):

Stadíou 5, 105 62 Athens
Tel. 3229.121

SPORTS

With its climate, Greek gives you a wide choice of sports, most of which are geared naturally enough to water activities. Keep in mind the sun however, and don't overdo it.

Sailing. You can generally find sailboats to rent, and some schools as well, in various places. Ask the Greek Tourist Office for their brochure mapping out all the marinas, or contact the Sailing Club Federation:

Xenofóntos 15 (near Syntagma)
Tel. 323.5560/323.6813

Snorkelling and Diving. For detailed information, write to the Greek Federation of Underwater Activities:

Ágios Kosmás, Ellinikón, Athens
Tel. 981.9961

Strict rules regulate the use of scuba apparatus, but it is permitted—from sunrise to sunset, and for viewing fish only—in certain places. Ask at the local tourist office or your hotel if equipment is available. Snorkelling is great fun, and the equipment isn't expensive to buy or rent. There are countless good spots for snorkelling but some are only accessible by boat.

Fishing. Tackle, bait and boats or good shore perches are no problem to find in this land of fishermen. Licences are not required for amateur angling, and one of the taverna chefs will usually cook up your catch. Try to arrange to go out with the local boatmen. Underwater fishing is not permitted everywhere—check first. The Amateur Anglers and Maritime Sports Club will have current information:

Aktí Moutsópoulos, Piraeus
Tel. 451.5731

Windsurfing. You'll find boards for rent in many places in Greece, as this popular sport has been catching on these past years. Contact the Hellenic Windsurfing Association for more information:

Filellínon 7, Athens
Tel. 323.0068

Hiking and Skiing. Climbers and hikers will be delighted to know that Greece has beautiful wild mountains and virgin forests, with a number of national parks and an extensive trail system including mountain huts ranging from simple to very organized. There are numerous possibilities for skiing in Greece, from December to March.

Some convenient addresses in Athens for skiers and hikers:

Greek Alpine Club, Eólou 68–70
Tel. 321.2429

Hellenic Alpine Federation, Karagiórgi 7
Tel. 323.4555

Greek Touring Club, Polytechníou 12
Tel. 524.8601

Hellenic Federation of Excursion Clubs, Dragatsaníou 4
Tel. 323.4107

Other popular sports include **water-skiing, tennis, golf** (18-hole courses at Glifada, Athens; Ropa Valley, Corfu; Porto Carras, Chalkidiki; Afandou, Rhodes), **hunting, flying, horse riding,** and **caving.** Some useful addresses:

Water-skiing Federation, Stournára 32, Athens
Tel. 523.1875

National Airclub of Greece, Akadimías 27, Athens
Tel. 361.7242

Hellenic Riding Club, Paradíssou 18, Maroússi
Tel. 681.2506

TIME DIFFERENCES

The chart below shows the time difference between Greece and various cities in winter. In summer, Greek clocks are put forward one hour; the time differences remain the same if your country has summer time too.

Los Angeles	2 a.m.
New York	5 a.m.
London	10 a.m.
Greece	**noon**
Johannesburg	noon
Sydney	9 p.m.
Auckland	11 p.m.

What time is it?　　**Ti óra íne?**

TIPPING

By law, service charges are included in the bill at hotels, restaurants and tavernas. Whether you leave a tip or not is up to you to decide.

Hairdresser/Barber	10%
Hotel porter, per bag	30–50 drs.
Lavatory attendant	20 drs.
Maid, per day	100 drs.
Taxi driver	10% (optional)
Tour guide (½ day)	100–200 drs. (optional)
Waiter	5% (optional)

TOILETS (ΤΟΥΑΛΕΤΤΕΣ—*toualéttes*)

Public toilets are usually located in parks and squares throughout the city centres. If there's someone in attendance, you should leave a small tip. In cafés, if you drop in specifically to use the facilities, it's customary to have a drink before leaving. Keep in mind that you won't always find modern, efficient plumbing, so be careful about what you put in the toilets and remember the lack of water on dry islands in the summer. Except in modest establishments, there are generally two doors, marked ΓΥΝΑΙΚΩΝ (ladies) and ΑΝΔΡΩΝ (men).

TOURIST INFORMATION OFFICES
(grafío pliroforión tourismoú)

Outside Greece you can contact the following National Tourist Organization of Greece (NTOG) offices, which will supply you with a wide range of colourful and informative brochures and maps in English. They'll also let you consult the master directory of hotels in Greece, listing all facilities and prices.

Australia and New Zealand. 51-57 Pitt St., Sydney, NSW 2000; tel. 241 1663/4

Canada. 80 Bloor St. West, Suite 1403, Toronto, Ont. M5S 2V1; tel. (416) 968 2220 1233 rue de la Montagne, Montreal, Que. H3G 1Z2; tel. (514) 871 1535

Denmark. Vester Farimagsgade 3, DK 1606 Copenhagen; tel. 31 32 53 32

Finland. Iso Robertinkatu 3–5 C 38, 00120 Helsinki; tel. (0) 607 552

Japan. 11 Mori Building, 2-6-4 Toranomon, Minato-Ku, Tokyo 105; tel. 503-5001/2

Netherlands. Leidsestraat 13, NS Amsterdam; tel. (020)254-212/3

Norway. Øvre Slottsgaten 15B, 0157 Oslo 1; tel. (02) 42 65 01

Sweden. Grev Turegatan 2, P.O. Box 5298, 102 46 Stockholm; tel. (08) 23 05 80

U.K. 195-7 Regent St, London W1R 8DL; tel. (01) 734 5997

U.S.A. 645 5th Ave, New York, N.Y. 10022; tel. (212) 421 5777

611 W. 6th St, Los Angeles, CA 90017; tel. (213) 626 6696

168 N. Michigan Ave, Chicago, IL 60601; tel. (312) 782 1084

In Greece itself, the NTOG *(Ellinikós Organismós Tourismoú, EOT)* has offices in all the major centres.

Athens. Central headquarters: Amerikís 2, 105 84 Athens; tel: 3223.111/9

Main information office: Karagiórgi Servías 2 (just off Syntagma); tel: 322.2545, 325.2267 and 322.8547. Hours: Monday to Friday 8 a.m. to 2 p.m. and 2.30 to 8 p.m.; Saturday 8 a.m. to 2 p.m.

Festivals: Voukourestíou 1; tel. 323.4467

Airport office: tel. 9799.500

Corfu Town. Diikitírion; tel. 30.298/30.360

Crete. Agios Nikolaos: on the bridge over the lake in the port police building. **Chania:** in the Mosque of the Janissaries on the harbour; tel. 26.426. **Iraklion:** opposite the Archaeological Museum; tel. 228.203/ 228.225. **Rethymnon:** on the seafront promenade; tel. 29.148/24.143. All offices keep

the same hours: 7.30 a.m. to 7.30 p.m.; Sundays and holidays until 2.30 p.m.

Kavala. Filellínon 2; tel. 228.762

Rhodes Town. Platía Rímini; 8 a.m. to 8 p.m. Sunday 9 a.m. to noon.

Thessaloniki. Platía Aristotélou 8; tel. 222.935/271.888

Airport office: tel. 473.212, ext. 215

Patra. Iróon Politechníou, Glifáda; tel. 420.305

Piraeus. Marina Zeas, EOT building; tel. 413.5716

TRANSPORT

See also ISLAND-HOPPING.

Planes. The domestic air routes are served by Olympic Airways. Although the fares are relatively cheap compared to domestic lines in other countries, they are naturally more expensive than buses or trains. There are daily flights from Athens to the major islands and all the other big cities on the mainland, but in the summer you should definitely book your tickets as much in advance as possible. This can be done through your travel agent or any Olympic office. Check at the NTOG office in your area for fare information and timetables. For reservations and information, contact the Olympic Airways Office:

Singroú 96, Athens
Tel. 9292.251

For flight information, call 981.1201 or 981.1202.

Boats. This is the most popular way to get around, especially for island-hopping. The most reliable information will be with the local port authorities. It is forever changing, depending on the weather, occasional strikes and other whimsical turns of fate. Individual agents handle only one or two shipping lines and cannot be relied on to tell you their competitors' schedules. Nor should you depend on the information you get on one island about boats sailing from another island: in more ways than one, the outlook is insular. Between neighbouring islands there's often impromptu boat traffic—wander along the waterfront with your baggage and you might chance on a caïque going to the next island. There is really a great choice, the length of the trip and the routes varying with the boat. Greek boats being what they are, you are just as likely to fall upon a sleek, modern ship as an old sea-worn tub, which nevertheless manages to get you there, no matter the weather.

Although the boats are privately owned, the prices are government controlled. But depending on the facilities, speed, and other factors, the same trip will cost differently from one ship to the next, so it's worth looking around if you have the time to do so. There may be as many as four fare classes, but for daytime trips most will find the cheapest perfectly adequate. Passsenger fares in Greek waters are, in fact, among the lowest in the world. You might load up on drinks and snacks beforehand, however, as these are quite expensive on board.

Piraeus Port Authorities: tel. 417.2657/ 451.1311

If you intend to cruise in Greek waters with a **yacht**, you should contact your local NTOG office, the port authorities in Greece or the Yacht Brokers and Experts Association:

Alkionídes 36, Athens
Tel. 981.6582/982.7107

You'll find port customs, health and passport control, anchorage and general facilities at more than 50 ports. A great way to see Greece...

Buses. In most places the bus service is reliable, punctual and fairly frequent. The fares are reasonable and even remote villages can be reached. However, you won't find high comfort, and though some of the main routes are served by air-conditioned buses, most vehicles usually get unbearably hot and crowded in the summer.

The State Railway Service (OSE) has a few buses leaving from the train stations. But most buses are run by KTEL, a private company which usually has several terminuses in the larger towns for different towns of departure.

On the main islands there are efficient inter-regional buses, but the smaller islands depend on rural market buses which can be a real experience, to say the least. Whether you get treated to blaring bouzouki music or singing passengers, squashed between the children, chickens, lambs, fish, baskets and wash-tubs you'll certainly enjoy the scenery and appreciate the efficacy of the driver's religious medallions as you tear around the heart-stopping bends.

Always confirm the departure times and the possibilities for same-day return trips— but bear in mind that some of these buses don't leave until full. Keep your ticket until the end of the trip. Bus stop signs read ΣΤΑΣΙΣ *(stásis)*.

The two main terminals in Athens for bus service through mainland Greece are at:

Kifissou 100 (take bus 051 near Platía Omónia)

Liossíon 260 (bus 024 at the entrance to the National Garden near Syntagma).

Taxis remain relatively cheap throughout mainland Greece, on Corfu, Crete and Rhodes. On the other islands though, rides can cost up to ten times the bus fare. Drivers are generally honest and helpful, but you may find exceptions to this in the big cities, along with claims to "broken" meters. You should insist on established prices, and make sure the meter is set to "1" ("2" is the double fare for night hours, 1–5 a.m.). If there's no meter, agree on a fare before setting off.

There can be charges for luggage, late-night service, waiting and special holidays. In rush hour taxis can be difficult to find, and sometimes you'll find yourself having to share.

The city taxi is written ΤΑΞΙ. The rural *agoréon* operates outside city limits.

Trains. Inexpensive and in places very scenic, the Greek railways are not extensive, and rather slow. All the major cities are linked by rail, and narrow-gauge lines cover the northern and western coasts and the central part of the Peloponnese. In Athens, trains leave from Stathmós Larísis on Odós Delighiánni for northern Greece, and from the station across the tracks for the Peloponnese. Information can be found at the OSE, the State Railways Organization.

Underground/Subway. Athens has a 20-stop underground system, but most of it actually runs above ground level. It connects the centre of Athens with Piraeus in the south and Kifisiá, a residential suburb, to the north. It's a good, fast, economical way to go, providing you avoid the rush hours. Cancel your ticket as you go to the platform by placing it with the arrows pointing into the machine which operates the turnstile. Keep it until the end of your journey because you'll be asked for it at the exit.

USEFUL EXPRESSIONS and VOCABULARY

yes/no	**ne/ókhi**
please/thank you	**parakaló/efkharistó**
excuse me/you're welcome	**me sinchoríte/típota**
all right	**ev táxi**
It doesn't matter	**Den pirázi**
How are you?	**Ti kánete?**
Good morning	**Kaliméra**
Good evening	**Kalispéra**
Good night	**Kali níkta**
Hello	**Yásou**
Goodbye	**Yásou/andio/hérete**
what/why/who	**ti/yiatí/piós** (male) **piá** (female)
where/when/how	**pou/póte/pos**
how long/how far	**póso keró/póso makriá**
yesterday/today/ tomorrow	**chtes/símera/ ávrio**
day/week/month/year	**iméra/evdomáda/ mínas/chrónos**
now/later	**tóra/metá**
left/right	**aristerá/dexiá**
up/down	**epáno/káto**
good/bad	**kalós/kakós**
big/small	**megálos/mikrós**
cheap/expensive	**ftinós/akrivós**
hot/cold	**zestós/kríos**
old/new	**paliós/néos**
open/closed	**aniktós/klistós**
near/far	**kondá/makriá**
here/there	**edhó/ekí**
north/south	**vória/nótia**
east/west	**anatoliká/thitiká**
danger	**kínthinos**
entrance/exit	**ísothos/éxothos**
Keep out	**Apagorévete ee ísothos**
I am/We are...	**Íme/Ímaste...**
lost	**échasa to thrómo**
hungry	**pinó**
thirsty	**thipsó**
tired	**kourasménos**
ill	**árostos**
I'd like...	**Tha íthela...**
I want	**Thélo**
I have	**Ého**
Can I...?	**Bóro na...?**
Have you...?	**Éhete...?**
Is there...?	**Éhi...?**
ship/port	**plíon, karávi/limáni**
car/motorbike	**aftokínito/mechanáki**
petrol(gas)/garage	**venzíni/garáz**
map/ticket	**chárti/isitírio**
church/museum	**eklisía/mouséo**
village/ruins	**chorió/arhéa**
food/bakery/market	**fayíto/fournos/agorá**
beach/sea	**paralía/thálassa**
kiosk/post office	**períptero/tachidromío**
bank/money	**trápeza/leftá**
pharmacy/hospital	**farmakío/nosokomío**
policeman/police station	**astílaka/astinomía**
Does anyone here speak English?	**Milá kanís angliká?**
I don't understand.	**Den katalavéno.**
Please write it down.	**Parakaló grápste to.**
What does this mean?	**Ti siméni aftó?**
How much is that?	**Póso káni aftó?**
Where are the toilets?	**Pou íne toualéttes?**
Waiter, please!	**Parakaló!**
Can you help me?	**Voïthíste me?**
Call a doctor— quickly!	**Kaléste éna giatró— grígora!**
What do you want?	**Ti thélete?**
Just a minute.	**Éna leptó.**
Go away!	**Fígete!**

Days of the week

Sunday	**Kiriakí**
Monday	**Deftéra**
Tuesday	**Tríti**
Wednesday	**Tetárti**
Thursday	**Pémti**
Friday	**Paraskeví**
Saturday	**Sávvato**

Months

January	**Ianouários**
February	**Fevrouários**
March	**Mártios**
April	**Aprílios**
May	**Máios**
June	**Ioúnios**
July	**Ioúlios**
August	**Ávgoustos**
September	**Septémvrios**
October	**Októvrios**
November	**Noémvrios**
December	**Dekémvrios**

Numbers

1	éna	16	dekaéxi
2	dío	17	dekaeptá
3	tría	18	dekaoktó
4	téssara	19	dekaenniá
5	pénde	20	íkosi
6	éxi	21	íkosi éna
7	eptá	30	triánda
8	októ	40	saránda
9	enniá	50	penínda
10	déka	60	exínda
11	éndeka	70	evdomínda
12	dódeka	80	ogdónda
13	dekatría	90	enenínda
14	dekatéssera	100	ekató
15	dekapénde	1000	chília

WATER *(neró)*

Tap water is safe to drink in Greece (though if it comes unfiltered from a water tank you may prefer to buy bottled water). On the islands, not only is the water safe, but village connoisseurs debate the special qualities and taste of waters from different springs. In the dry season, most islands turn the supply off for a few hours every day—find out when in advance. Water shortage is a real problem at such times, so keep your usage to a minimum. You may notice water-supply trucks coming around daily to fill up the tanks.

A bottle of mineral water	**éna boukáli metallikó neró**
fizzy (carbonated)	**me anthrakikó**
still (non-carbonated)	**chorís anthrakikó**
Is this drinking water?	**Íne pósimo aftó to neró?**

WEIGHTS AND MEASURES

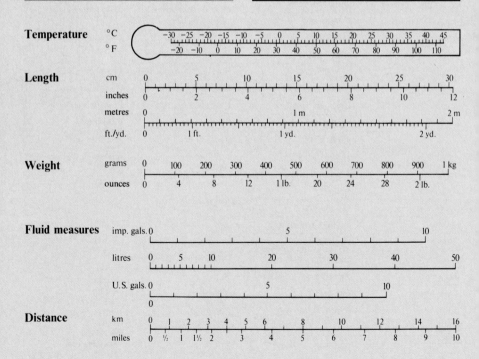

Temperature °C −30 −25 −20 −15 −10 −5 0 5 10 15 20 25 30 35 40 45
°F −20 −10 0 10 20 30 40 50 60 70 80 90 100 110

Length
cm 0 5 10 15 20 25 30
inches 0 2 4 6 8 10 12
metres 0 1 m 2 m
ft./yd. 0 1 ft. 1 yd. 2 yd.

Weight
grams 0 100 200 300 400 500 600 700 800 900 1 kg
ounces 0 4 8 12 1 lb. 20 24 28 2 lb.

Fluid measures
imp. gals. 0 5 10
litres 0 5 10 20 30 40 50
U.S. gals. 0 5 10
0

Distance
km 0 1 2 3 4 5 6 8 10 12 14 16
miles 0 ½ 1 1½ 2 3 4 5 6 7 8 9 10

Road Atlas

GRIECHENLAND   ΕΛΛΑΣ   GREECE   GRECE

Autobahn mit Anschlussstelle
Ἐθνική ὁδός πού συνδέεται μέ κυρίους
δρόμους
— Motorway with interchange
Autoroute avec échangeur

Autobahn im Bau mit Eröffnungsdatum
Ἐθνική ὁδός ὑπό κατασκευήν μέ ἡμερομηνία
ἐνάρξεως
①1989 ①1989
I - VI VII - XII
— Motorway under construction with opening date
Autoroute en construction avec date de mise en service

Autostrasse (international, regional)
Αὐτοκινητόδρομος (Διευθνής, Ἀστικός)
— Dual carriageway (international, regional)
Route rapide à chaussées séparées (internationale, régionale)

Grosse internationale Durchgangsstrasse
Μεγάλης Διεθνής ὁδός
— Major international throughroute
Route de grand transit internationale

Sonstige internationale Fernverkehrsstrasse
Ὑπόλοιποι Διεθνής ὑπεραστικοί ὁδοί
— Other international troughroute
Autre route de transit internationale

Überregionale Fernverkehrsstrasse
Ὑπεραστική ἐθνική ὁδός
— Interregional throughroute
Route de transit interrégionale

Regionale Verbindungsstrasse
Ἀστικός ἐνδιάμεσος δρόμος
— Regional connecting road
Route de liaison régionale

Lokale Verbindungsstrasse
Πάροδος ἐνδιαμέσον δρόμον
— Local road
Route de liaison locale

Strassen im Bau
Ὀδοί ὑπό κατασκευήν
— Roads under construction
Routes en construction

Gesperrte Strasse
Ἀπαγορεύεται ἡ Διέλευσις
— Closed road
Route interdite

Entfernungen in km
Ἀπόστασις σέ χιλιόμετρα
10
5 3 3 4 2 5
7 2 3
10
— Distances in km
Distances en km

Strassennummern: Europastrasse, Autobahn, Nationalstrasse
Ἀριθμημένοι ὁδοί: Εὐρωπαϊκός δρόμος, ἐθνική ὁδός
E 7 A 9 60
— Road classification: European road, motorway, national road
Numéros des routes: route européenne, autoroute, route nationale

Pass, Berg, Ort mit Höhenangabe (m)
Πέρασμα δρόμου σέ βουνό, βουνό, Περιοχή μέ
γραμμένο ὑψόμετρο (m)
1472 1158 Varda
○ΒΑΡΔΑ
966
— Pass, summit, locality with altitude (m)
Col, sommet, localité avec altitude (m)

Eisenbahn, Berg-/Luftseilbahn
Σιδηρόδρομος, Τελεφερίκ
— Railway, mountain/cable railway
Voie ferrée, téléphérique/funiculaire

Autoverlad: per Fähre
Μετακίνησις: Φέρρυ-μπόουτ
2h
— Car transport: by ferry
Transport des autos: par bac

Internationaler Flughafen, Flugplatz
Διεθνές Ἀεροδιάδρομος, Ἀεροδρόμιο
✈ ✈
— International airport, airfield
Aéroport international, aérodrome

Bemerkenswerter Ort, Antike Stätte
Ἀξιοθέατες περιοχές, Παλαιά Μνημεία
★ ﬩
— Place of interest, site of antiquity
Localité intéressante, vestige antique

Schloss/Burg, Kirche/Kloster, Ruine
Πύργος/Κάστρο, Ἐκκλησία/Μοναστήρι,
Ἐρείπιον
⚑ ⚑ ∟
— Castle, church/monastery, ruin
Château/fort, église/couvent, ruine

Campingplatz, Höhle, Leuchtturm
Τόπος κατασκηνώσεως, Σπηλιά, Φάρος
▲ ∩ ⚑
— Camping site, cave, lighthouse
Camping, grotte, phare

Einzelstehendes Haus
Μοναδικό σπίτι
▬
— Country house
Maison isolée

Osteuropa: Grenzübergang
Ἀνατολική Εὐρώπη: Διέλευσις Συνόρων
⊖
— Eastern Europe: border crossing
Europe de l'Est: passage de la frontière

Staatsgrenze
Κρατικά σύνορα
— National boundary
Frontière d'État

1: 1 000 000

0   10   20   40   60   80 km

0   10   20   30   40   50 miles

Hallwag

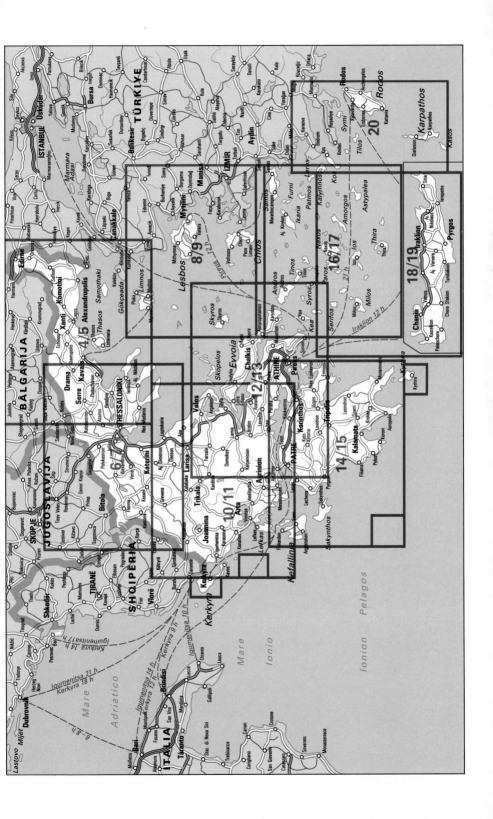

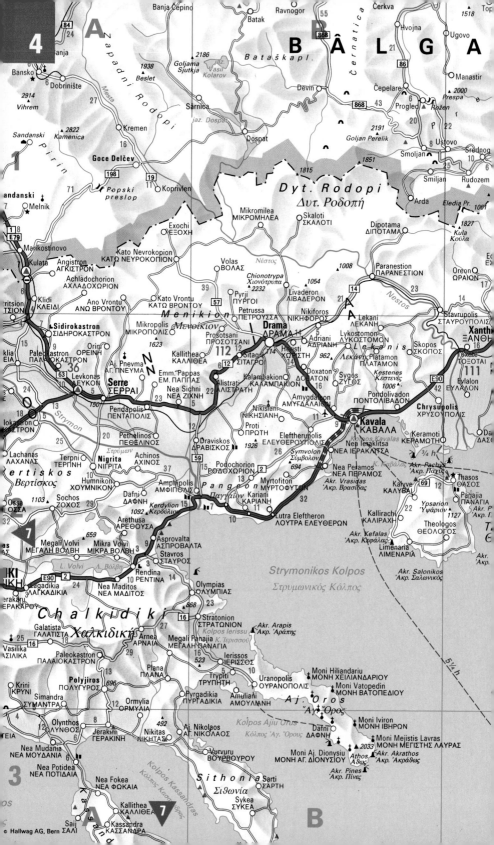

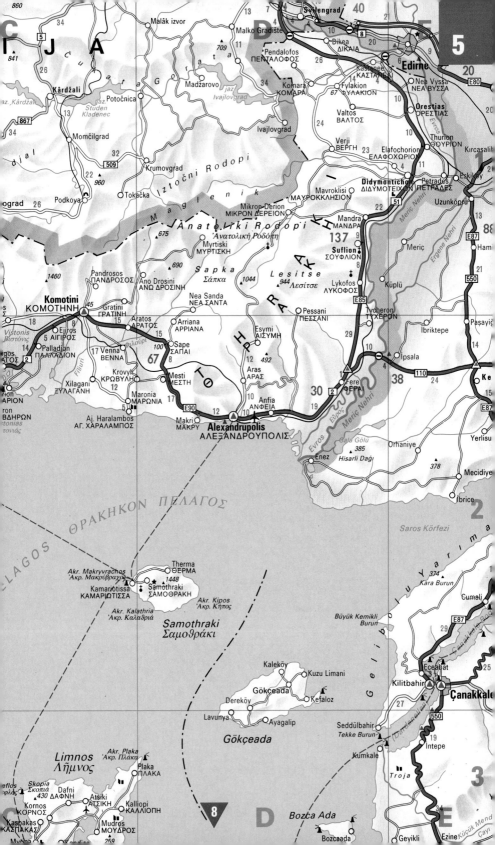

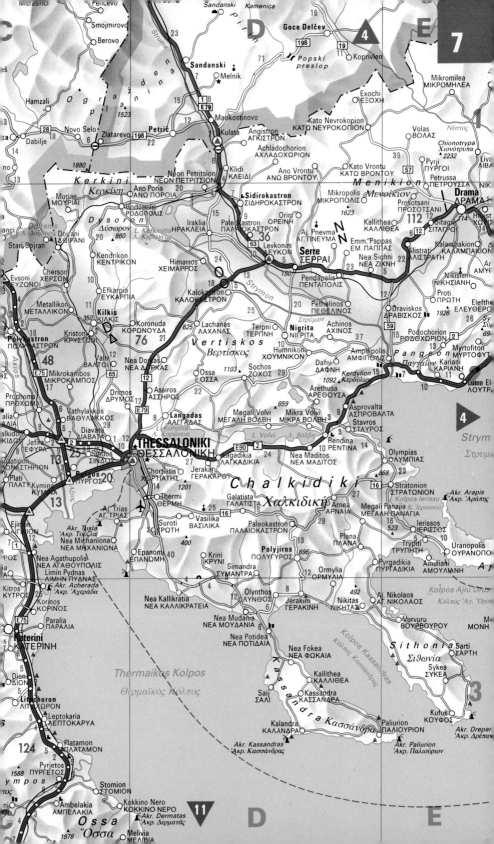

A

B 5

C

Gökçeada

1

Limnos
Λῆμνος

Akr. Plaka
Άκρ. Πλάκα

Plaka
ΠΛΑΚΑ

Akr. Murtseflos
Άκρ. Μουρτζεφλός

Skopia
Σκοπιά

Dafni
ΔΑΦΝΗ
430

Atsiki
ΑΤΣΙΚΗ

Kalliopi
ΚΑΛΛΙΟΠΗ

Kornos
ΚΟΡΝΟΣ

Kaspakas
ΚΑΣΠΑΚΑΣ

Mudros
ΜΟΥΔΡΟΣ
259

Myrina
ΜΥΡΙΝΑ

Kondias
ΚΟΝΤΙΑΣ

Akr. Tigani
Άκρ. Τηγάνι

264

Akr. Aj. Irinis
Άκρ. Άγ. Ειρήνης

Bozca A

B

Akr. Kalamaki
Άκρ. Καλαμάκι

Aj. Efstratios
ΑΓ. ΕΥΣΤΡΑΤΙΟΣ

303

Aj. Efstratios
Άγ. Εὐστράτιος

Akr. Trypiti
Άκρ. Τρυπητή

Akr. Fu
Άκρ. Φο

A

Sigrion
ΣΥΓΡΙΟΝ
1

Akk. Sigrion
Άκρ. Σύγριον

Eres
ΕΡΕΣ

Skala E
ΣΚΑΛΑ ΕΝ

Piperion
Πιπέριον

E
G
E
O
N

P
E
L
A
G
O
S

rii S p o r a d e s
ειοι Σ π ο ρ ά δ ε ς

Akr. Kartsino
Άκρ. Κάρτσινο

Skyros
Σκύρος

2

403

Skyros
ΣΚΥΡΟΣ

Linaria
ΛΙΝΑΡΙΑ

792

opula
πούλα

13

Kochylas
Κοχύλας

Valaxa
Βάλαξα

Akr. Lithari
Άκρ. Λιθάρι

Antipsara
Αντίψαρα

Psara
ΨΑΡΑ

Akr. Melani
Άκρ. Μελάνι

Kymis
Κύμης

Psara
Ψαρά

Akr. Ochthonia
Άκρ. Όχθονιά

chthonia
ΧΘΩΝΙΑ

arion
ΝΑΡΙΟΝ

a
ΥΡΑ

20

Pireus – Istanbul (Kranverladung)

Venedig – Izmir 65½ h

Split – Izmir 54½ h

Volos – Tartous (Syrien) 40 h

A
A

2

Almyropotamos
ΑΛΜΥΡΟΠΟΤΑΜΟΣ

© Hallwag AG, Bern

B 16

C

Pireus

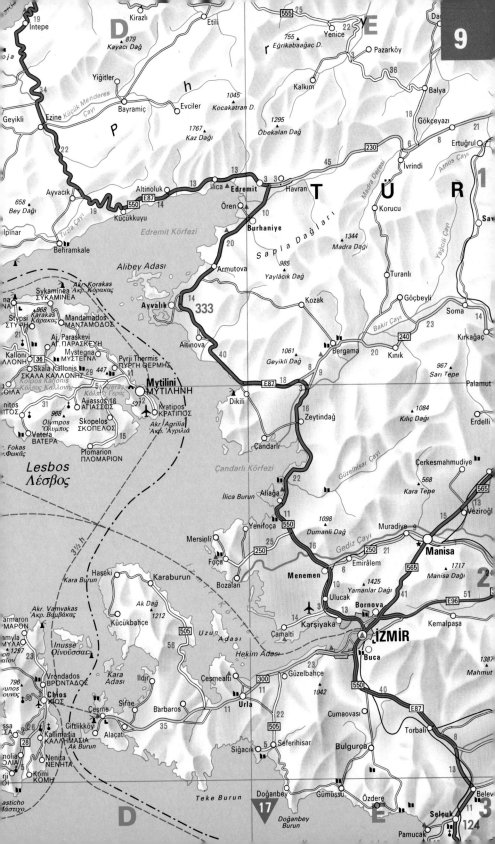

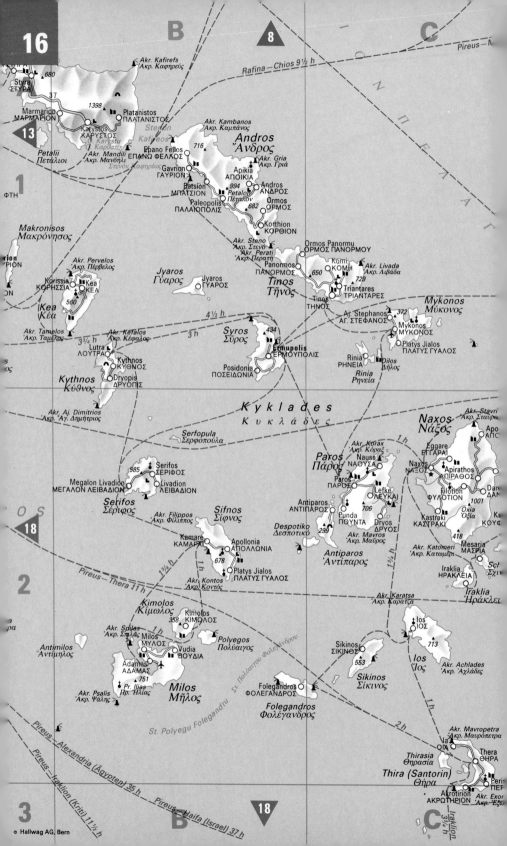

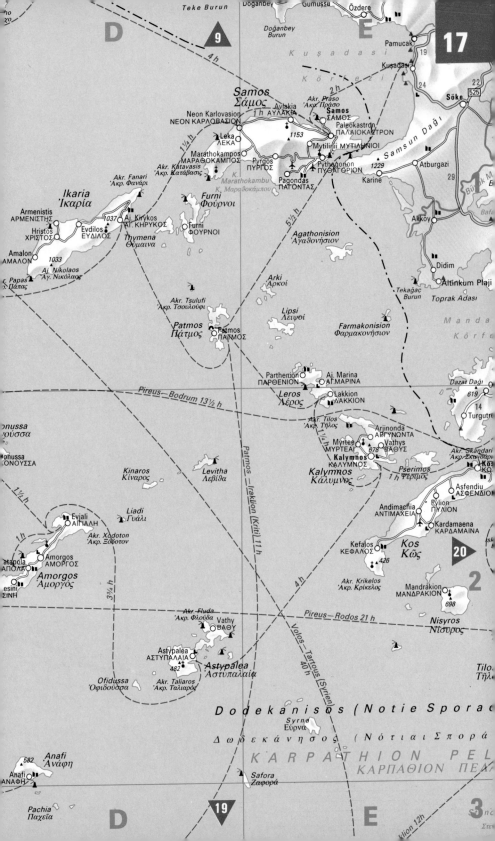

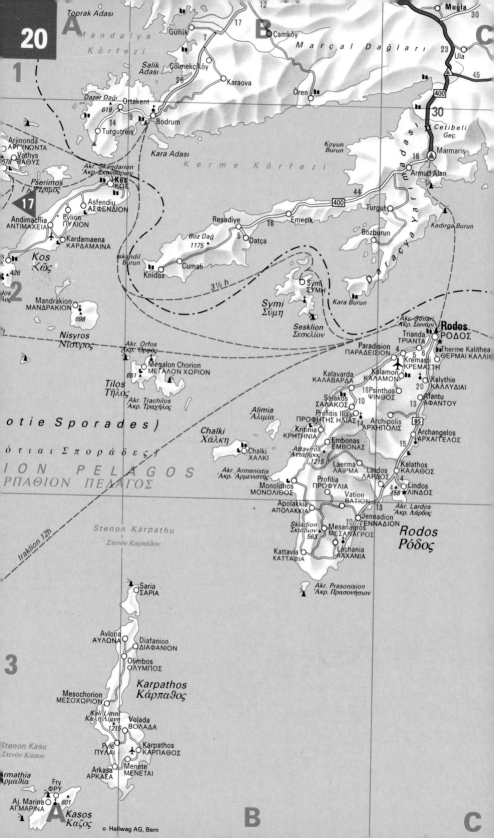

INDEX

For easy reference, names of large towns and all islands have been set in **bold face**. Page numbers in **bold face** refer to the main entry, and those in *italics* to the hotel and restaurant selection. An asterisk indicates a map.